DEVOTIONAL POETICS
AND
THE INDIAN SUBLIME

DEVOTIONAL POETICS AND THE INDIAN SUBLIME

Vijay Mishra

D.K.Printworld(P)Ltd.
NEW DELHI - 110 015

Cataloging in Publication Data — DK

Mishra, Vijay.
Devotional poetics and the Indian sublime.
Includes bibliographical references.
Includes index.

1. Hinduism — Prayer-books and devotions — History and Ciriticism. 2. Sublime, The. 3. Devotional poetry, Indic — History and criticism. I. Title.

First Indian Edition: 2000
ISBN 81-246-0156-9

The publication of this book in India is made possible by permission of the State University of New York Press. This edition is for sale in India, Nepal and Bhutan only.

Printed and Published by:
D.K. Printworld (P) Ltd.
An Intercontinental Publishing Enterprise
Regd. office : '*Sri Kunj*', F-52, Bali Nagar
New Delhi - 110 015
Phones : (011) 545-3975, 546-6019; *Fax* : (011) 546-5926
E-mail: dkprint@4mis.com

CONTENTS

For my son Rohan

God is a concept by which we measure our pain.

JOHN LENNON

What's amazing is that such an idea

—the idea of the necessity of God—

could enter the head of man.

DOSTOYEVSKY

PREFACE

In his breathtaking survey of Western readings of India Ronald Inden (*Imagining India*) warns us against a number of things that, against his advice, I undertake in this book. I speak of the Hindu mind; I collapse Indian thought with Hinduism; I equate classical or high Hinduism with "monist pantheism" and I use discourses obviously supplied by European psychology, heirs to what Inden calls the "degenerative psychohistory masterminded by Hegel" (129), to advance my argument. I also look upon the work of the poststructuralists much more favorably and find Madeleine Biardeau's and David Shulman's studies particularly useful. I find in their works readings that deconstruct two dominant visions of India—the despotic and the quasifeudal—through the concept of the "decenteredness" of Indian culture. I can see an initial unease on the part of someone like Inden toward this book. This reader would say that my book removes agents out of Indian history and underplays local, contingent moments in favor of what Inden has called the mystique of "the Grecian urn of archetypes." The criticism would, however, be only partly true. For what my book tries to do is examine the connection between the contingent—the moment when the self recognizes its being in history—and the metanarratives through which the culture defines the contingent. The argument here is that in Indian culture, metanarratives continue to have meaning even as the subject enters the social or the "real." In the various texts of Hinduism that I examine—from the canonical Sanskrit texts to the vernacular compositions of itinerant singers—human agents affirm the value of tradition even as they question its ideology.

Surely to examine the ways in which Hinduism is systemic is not to dehistoricize the religion but to demonstrate how movements and ideas are historically reworked within parameters that remain largely unchanged in culture, and how the Hindu desire to "push an idea to its logical extreme" leads to the creation of absolutist categories (such as the Law of Dharma) with their own "historical depth and enduring features" that produce an intentional chasm between the self and the social order, between the renouncer and the man-in-the-world. There is no better proof text of such absolutist categories in Hindu life than Indian popular cinema where a film such as *Aisī Bhī Kyā Jaldī Haī* ("What's the Rush?" 1996) cannot finally accept that a daughter brought up by her father may want to return to her father on her wedding night. Popular cinema, rather than art cinema (where the narrative of implied incest may be permissible) carries the grand metanarratives of Hinduism and shows the complex ways in which Indian agents function within (and not against) prior metanarratives. In the context of this larger design, what the book attempts to do is bring to Indian culture a hermeneutic pluralism. However, in redressing idealist or romantic or even racist European readings of India I do not want to affirm another kind of essentialism, the kind that believes that comparative theory cannot be applied to different cultures and the kind that gives an unproblematic primacy to the native informant. The native informant is read with sensitivity in this book but never prioritized in an unproblematic manner. And comparative literary theory is strategically applied throughout.

The literary archives that form the basis of this study are well known and hence there is little in this book that would not be familiar to people who are interested in Indian languages and culture. The book, however, does attempt to make aspects of the Hindu world available to the interdisciplinary student of English and Comparative Literature, and Cultural Studies. In my translations, especially, I have kept this wider reader in mind. The translations from Sanskrit and from Old and Middle Hindi, in particular, are meant to be user-friendly and attempts have been made not so much for literal sincerity as for artistic correspondence. By the latter I mean translations that capture the aesthetic design and feeling of the original rather than their prosaic meanings even if this results in what George Steiner has called "upward betrayal." A great poet like Tulsidas is simply unreadable in literal translations. What is worse, the non-Hindi reader gets no sense of the real strengths of this remarkable epic poet from these translations. The Tulsidas translator has to acknowledge—as all translators must—that a translator is a traitor (*traduttore traditore*) and he/she may have to distort literal meaning to convey emotional and aesthetic feeling. As George Steiner observed in *After Babel*: "The translator invades, extracts, and brings home" (298).

While the final product, I hope, has been written with clarity and the argument is relatively straightforward, I must admit that the book has not been easy to write. This is largely due to the many stages the book has had to go through over its very long gestation period. The book began as a relatively straightforward literary history of North Indian bhakti (or devotional) literature. It then became an author study, then a philosophical study of the medieval Indian saint Kabir, and finally a study of the nexus between the emotional and the religious. It was the last of these that led to my reconceptualizing the various drafts through an understanding of the *sublime*. The "topicality" of the term aside, what struck me was the absence of the term in critical engagements with Indian culture. I felt that if any religion was truly sublime that religion was Hinduism and if any culture was "unpresentable" (because of its sheer complexity) that culture had to be Indian culture. And so I began to connect aesthetics with belief and began to rethink the contribution of the category of the sublime to our theorization of devotional aesthetics. It was only after I had read with great interest the theorization of the sublime from Longinus to Kant that it dawned on me that Indian devotional poetics may be theorized through the category of the sublime. The question that struck me immediately was: What indeed is the sublime object of devotion in a literary genre trying to come to grips with its object as something so vast that it is unpresentable to the imagination and to consciousness? It is this question of representation—and in particular of sublime (non) representation—and its lack that took me back to my earlier drafts and I began to rewrite my book very quickly by asking two fundamental questions: What is the nature of the Indian sublime? Is there something about the problematic of (non)representation in medieval Indian authors to which we can relate even now? The first of these is discussed at length, the second exists only as an anxiety in the margins of the text. Whether the argument finally works is for the reader to decide.

Many friends, and many libraries have helped me along in this long and arduous journey and I would like to thank them here. The research for this book was undertaken in the Bodleian, Oxford, the Menzies Library of the Australian National University, the Murdoch University Library, the University of Allahabad Library, the University of Delhi Library, the Sāhitya Sammelan, Allahabad, and the Nāgrīpracāriṇī Sabhā, Varanasi. I would like to thank the relevant staff of these libraries for their patience and help. When I began my research in India many years ago it was my good fortune to meet people like Agam Capoor and his family, who made an Indian from the diaspora feel so totally at home. During the long writing period of this book I became indebted, in both scholarly and human sense, to many people. Among them the following have been especially helpful: S. T. Arasu, Richard Barz, the late A. L. Basham, Wimal Dissanayake, John Frodsham, John Frow, David George, Peter Jeffery, W. H. McLeod, Meenakshi Mukherjee, Sujit Mukherjee, Michael O'-Toole, the late S. A. A. Rizvi, Horst Ruthrof, Krishna Somers, Parasnath Tiwari, Harish Trivedi, and Rob Wilson. Peter Reeves, an indefatigable supporter of Indian Studies in Australia, encouraged me to complete the book and has taken a keen interest in its development. Stella Baker and Cynthia Baker typed early drafts of this book while Diana Clegg, sometime secretary of the English and Comparative Literature Program at Murdoch University, transferred the text onto a word processor. My ideas were sharpened through discussions with my friends Greg Bailey and Bob Hodge, who are responsible for whatever is of enduring value in the ensuing pages and who would have written a much better book. Anonymous readers of the manuscript have made a number of suggestions and recommendations and I thank them for saving me from many pitfalls. Murdoch University has not only been the enlightened venue for my teaching and research for these past twenty years but has also awarded me travel grants to India, Great Britain, and the United States to undertake research. The award of a Large Grant by the Australia Research Council (albeit for a different project) meant that I had time enough during 1995–96 to edit this book. My many Indian friends in Perth (far too many to be named individually) have made discussions about Indian aesthetics such an exciting subject at their characteristically extravagant parties. I thank them all. My children Rohan and Paras and my wife Nalini have been and continue to be so thoroughly supportive of my research. It is not their fault that the book did not appear sooner or that it has not reached their standards of excellence.

A NOTE ON TRANSLITERATION

Diacritics have been used for all non-English words where necessary with the following exceptions: (1) words that are now readily recognizable as "Indian" words by the reader or words that have been absorbed into the English language (e.g., Krishna, Shiva, Vishnu, Upanishads, Brahmin, Sufi, moksha, karma, dharma, kshatriya, shudra, samsara), (2) names of Indian writers both ancient and modern and of philosophical systems (e.g., Kabir, Tulsidas, Shankara, Shandilya, Narada, Kalidasa, Valmiki, Hazariprasad Dvivedi, Sankhya) as well as names of characters in fiction (e.g., Yudhishthira, Drona, Dhritarashtra, Sanjaya). In respect of (2) it must be noted that both palatal and cerebral spirants have been transliterated as *sh*, both voiceless palatal consonants (aspirate and nonaspirate) as *ch*, and the cerebral vowel as *ri*. Again where necessary the *anusvāra* is indicated in the standard fashion and the *anunāsika* or nasal resonance by a tilde over the vowel. Where it was necessary to highlight key words, sandhi rules have not been applied. Titles of texts as well as publication details have been given as in the original with the proviso that place names bear their "official" spellings. In some cases citations from texts written in English and other European languages have been silently modified in line with the general principles of transliteration outlined above. On the matter of sexist language, to avoid the excessive use of the slash (him/her) masculine pronouns have been used only when it is obvious that the speaker is male.

CHAPTER ONE

The Sublime Object of Devotion

The study of aesthetics privileges the imagination. Since the source texts of this study belong, by and large, to the Indian literary and philosophical imagination, it would make our task easier if we flag an Indian "imperative" at the outset: "In India aesthetic and epistemological categories cease to be distinct since the culture accepts the ontological dependency of philosophy on figuration." Paul de Man, whose words lie behind the definition of the "Indian imperative" just given, raises this view to the level of a universal principle when he writes: "All philosophy is condemned, to the extent that it is dependent on figuration, to be literary and, as the depository of this very problem, all literature is to some extent philosophical."[1] De Man, however, also recognizes that this claim can be made because neither literature nor philosophy has definable limits, and because both are "sites" for ideological thinking or analysis. In other words, aesthetics is as much a space from which critical thinking can take place as ideology, and a critical theory that ignores the role and function of aesthetics has profound limitations. Systematic critical thinking about the nexus between art and ideology and between art and philosophy is then advanced as a way of integrating the domains of philosophy, aesthetics and ideology. If, however, claims have been made on behalf of Western aesthetic ideology, notably by de Man and Derrida, that the domain of aesthetics is not neutral, that it invades other discourses and that it offers critiques of society as such, similar claims have not been made on behalf of Indian aesthetics nor indeed on behalf of Indian culture.

To begin to entertain even the possibility of engaging with Indian aesthetics from a comparative perspective we have to put to rest a few ghostly specters that continue to haunt us. Among them are some quite perverse Orientalist positions of the kind taken by classicists like S. H. Butcher, who said that what India had was in fact a feminine imagination that because it ran "riot in its own prodigal wealth"[2] could never produce art of the quality of Greek and Roman antiquity. The centrality of figurality and aesthetics in philosphical thought was hence immediately nipped in the bud through claims that "India [was] a land dominated by imagination rather than reason."[3] In these endlessly reprised criticisms, imagination (the domain of aesthetics, of figuration) was simply presented as an antiphilosophical faculty (not as an essential part of it), which in turn produced a "civilization" totally lacking in practical politics or ethics. And even when Western discourses of "empirical realism," positivism, or scientific linguistics were deployed to examine Indian culture so as to give it some kind of objective legitimacy, the results were the same: the culture, it was felt, simply didn't possess the necessary apparatuses for ideological self-critique. The doubts raised here were endorsed by Husserl too who remained skeptical of Indian philosophy on the grounds that it did not raise genuinely critical questions of "validity, grounding, and evidence."[4] And finally—a point made by Ronald Inden repeatedly—the idea of human agency ("the realized capacity of people to act effectively upon their world"[5]) was never introduced as an historical factor in discussions about India, one suspects largely because it was felt that a nation lured to sleep by its sense of fatalism had no place for the individual as agent.

So much then by way of claiming a space for the importance of the interdependency of philosophy and figuration. To move on with our argument, how then do we go about giving legitimacy to Indian ways of thinking, how do we reinscribe the imagination back into philosophy (and vice versa) and respect Indian culture as an object of knowledge in terms of its own intrinsic ways of thinking? To begin with, what we must avoid are two established Orientalist practices: the empirical and the romantic. But we should also be careful of the "easy" postmodern alternative that, in the name of the contingent and the primacy of the human agent, sets out to underplay the extent to which individual, group or local histories and agents frame their discourses of empowerment in preexistent metanarratives and are in turn framed by them. Ronald Inden (who makes a very strong case for the contingent and for the local) himself qualifies the demand for the "local" by saying that a cultural dominant like the renouncer-ideal has been put to productive use in India. Although Inden explains the success of Gandhi's nonviolence rhetoric in terms of a prior, Orientalist construction of the Hindu character, the fact remains that alongside the rhetoric there was also a body, a corporeality, Winston Churchill's dismissive "naked fakir," that confirmed the *paraṃparā* or the metanarrative of the saint as the renouncer who acquired power through *tapas* or excessive austerity.

The question we return to—the question of legitimacy already foreshadowed and the power of figuration in Indian thought generally—must not be discussed in isolation and principally in terms of an oppositional discourse in which on one side of the divide is theosophy, archetypal symbology, and romanticism and on the other is empirical history, quantitative sociology, pragmatic literary history, and the primacy of the human self as agent of change. If we were to adopt an oppositional logic, we would have to accept that Orientalist and Enlightenment discourses made no contribution to our understanding of Indian culture. Nothing can be further from the truth.[6] Even totally mistaken readings are readings nevertheless and when such (mis)readings come from William Jones or Hegel we do have to take them seriously and not dismiss them outright. If, as well, we would want to argue that Indian thought itself has to be examined in terms of the hermeneutics of literary and philosophical interconnections and not exclusiveness, then again we need to critically examine everything that has been written about the culture. Unlike far too many Western apologists, in a postcolonial world Indians themselves are no longer testy or anxiety-prone about how history or the colonizer may have read them.[7] Indeed, the entire Indian commentarial tradition (itself highly fractious and unstable on questions of truth) is one of openness and debate and not one of exclusivism. It is for this reason that we need to debate Indian culture from comparative and interdisciplinary, from ideological as well as transcendental perspectives. Misreadings, after all, can be much more exciting than readings that have room for no alternative entry points, readings so defensive or derisive that one cannot engage with them productively, let alone critically.

Ever since the publication of Edward Said's singularly influential *Orientalism*,[8] we have witnessed an interest in the "Orient" distinguished by an awareness of what James Clifford has called "discrepant readings" and engagement with native informants.[9] These novel critical readings and engagements have, however, been characterized as well by discussions on the extent to which the Western "I" itself was constructed through erstwhile Orientalist discourses. In the studies of both Inden and Kate Teltscher[10] this is readily evident. Yet it could be argued, and persuasively one suspects, that in the margins of Hegel, William Jones, and Schlegel (let alone Jung, Eliade, Zimmer, and Joseph Campbell) some such awareness of the subject being contaminated by the objects of analysis was always present. If we take a leaf out of current postcolonial theory this knowledge is not as extraordinary as it sounds because any engagement with the Other affects both the source culture and the receptor culture. Note, for example, the position of the subject as Schlegel praises a Hindu race for whom no conception in the "department of metaphysics [was] unknown":

> But this absorption of all thought and all consciousness in God—this solitary enduring feeling of internal and external union with the Deity, they [the Hindus] have carried to a

> pitch and extreme that may almost be called a moral and intellectual self-annihilation. This is the same philosophy, though in a different form, which in the history of European intellect and science, has received the denomination of *mysticism*.[11]

The speaking subject here learns as he finds in classical Hinduism a definition of mysticism missing from Western texts. It is clear—as in Schopenhauer as well—that such definitions would have a significant impact on European understanding of mysticism. By itself, the degree to which the European self gets "contaminated" is not particularly interesting. What is interesting especially in Schlegel's remarkably representative passage is the use of a discourse that is not unlike the discourse of high Sanskrit critical commentary. German idealism read India romantically for sure, but it rarely read it as an "enigma" in the way in which British empiricism so often did.[12] To ignore that tradition of discursive representations of India helps no one at all, and certainly not those of us who wish to give India a presence within contemporary critical and cultural theory. In a strange sort of a way that heritage is part of the history of Hinduism itself, especially when that Hinduism is being written about in English and for a largely non-Indian audience.

To get on with the task of examining questions of Indian aesthetics more fully I would want to look at an aesthetic order that has rarely been applied to Indian culture. This aesthetic order is the sublime. The proof texts that I will be using for the Indian sublime belong to the religion of the "emotional laity," the essential feature of which is "devotional theism."[13] Since devotional theism is the central tenet of Hinduism itself (any working definition of Hinduism must emphasize worship or puja, and devotion or bhakti), its discussion, and its development, would provide us with important texts and ideas with which to examine questions about Indian aesthetics as such. Devotional poetry, after all, is *the* dominant genre of Indian literature in much the same way as Sankhya philosophy is *the* dominant philosophy of India. A good many texts that were not composed with devotion in mind were gradually brought into the fold of devotion either through interpolations or through reading practices that transformed them into allegories of the sacred. In Indian literary history there are in fact two major continuous literary genres to around the end of the sixteenth century at least: devotional verse and epic narrative. The third important genre, drama, gave Indian literature its theory (and especially the theory of rasa) and hence occupies a kind of "arche-generic" place in the tradition. Dramatic modes of narration are used extensively in the epic as can be seen in the explicit use of the device "he said" (Sanjaya *uvāca*, "said," Arjuna *uvāca*, etc.) throughout. However, the push to recode epic (and dramatic) narratives through the devotional was so strong that in time composers of these narratives certainly but characters too (albeit selectively) were given Godlike status.

The transformation of the pan-Indian epics (the *Rāmāyaṇa* and *Mahābhārata*) into a religious mode is too obvious to be repeated here. However, as a relatively autonomous genre not necessarily linked to drama and the epic (Tulsidas's sixteenth-century epic the *Rāmacaritamānasa* is an exception here) devotional verse's great moment comes somewhat late and is historically connected to the advent of the so-called bhakti (devotional) movement which reached its glorious period in the first half of the second millennium C.E. It has been argued that in India devotional poetry signals a decisive break in Hinduism that occurred when a predominantly intellectual and ritualistic religion shifted its religious practices to incorporate the concept of loving communion/union with a personal God. In the intellectual version of Hinduism as presented in the canonical texts or, more accurately, valorized through Orientalist readings of classical Indian high culture by Indians and non-Indians alike, the emotional dimensions of life were seen very much as an aberration unworthy of any systematic philosophical reflection, and largely rejected out of hand as a means of understanding the intricacies of religion. Clearly a principle of exclusion was at work here that, in the hands of the clerisy, led to the delegitimation of the emotional and the glorification of matters intellectual in religion. Matters of feeling, when seen through this principle of austere intellectualism, were a function of art and not of belief, and emotion, the dimension that underpins judgement, had no place in the religious encounter. The exact moment of this demarcation and distinction is, however, not at all clear-cut since even in the great text of Hinduism, the *Bhagavadgītā*, karmic certainty is tempered by the need for a degree of emotional engagement: "my devotee is my beloved," says Krishna at one point in the text. The search for the original moment is always difficult, but specially so when "an ontology of plurality-with-unity,"[14] to borrow Inden's very rich idea, is the defining characteristic of the culture in question. Inden himself, however, denies, it seems, any possibility of the transcendental by generalizing the "factical character of the world."[15] Transcendental investigations can be critical investigations in that they take us to conditions, like the sublime, that need to be addressed in ontological terms.

Sublime Aesthetics

"Whereas the beautiful is a metaphysical and ideological principle," writes Paul de Man, "the sublime aspires to being a transcendental one."[16] De Man is referring to Kant's well-known distinction between the sublime and the beautiful where Kant speaks of the beautiful as a thing that achieves the ends (the teleology) of freedom by means of nature (what Lyotard calls the "principle of a teleology of nature for freedom"[17]) and the sublime as a thing that informs us about "the teleology of our own faculties . . . about the relationship between imagination and reason."[18] For the beautiful nature is a frame, a reference; for the sublime nature resists totalizing and hence cannot be linked to a prior order, history or teleology. Shot through with contradictions, and emphatically connected to the limits of our own faculties, the sublime is "a purely inward experience of consciousness"[19] and is not, as Kant himself observes, "to be looked for in the things of nature, but only in our own ideas."[20] Attractive as well as repulsive, pleasurable (in the nirvanic sense) but also painful (in the physical sense), beyond the "parergon" and yet meaningful because, finally, it has to be contained within the law of reason, it is never an objective fact as such although it is signified by natural elements that are impossibly vast, or so "absolutely great" that they are beyond any kind of "adequation."

> Endowed with a determinable end and a definite size, they [the things of nature] cannot produce the feeling of the sublime, or let us say the *superelevated. Erhaben*, the sublime, is not only high, elevated, nor even very elevated. Very high, absolutely high, higher than comparable height, more than comparative, a size not measurable in height, the sublime is *superelevation* beyond itself.[21]

In this very astute reading of Derrida the beautiful may be found in art because art can be framed or bound (there is a "parergon of the beautiful"[22]). The sublime on the other hand is to be discovered, as Kant himself had noted, not in nature as artist, the creator of forms, but in nature as raw and formless: "bold, overhanging, and as it were, threatening rocks, thunderclouds piled up the vault of heaven . . . volcanoes in all their violence of destruction"[23] are its correlates. The beautiful is easy enough to grasp because it presents the indeterminate concept of understanding (the feeling of the beautiful results from a form); the sublime, on the other hand, presents the indeterminate concept of reason because it can be "provided by the without-form," and is therefore the function of a "higher faculty" in us.[24] This being so, it follows, that the desire to totalize the sublime will remain supreme because this is how the law of reason operates. We sense an underlying tension here. Reason must totalize (this is a transcendental fact) but the sublime makes the act of totalizing difficult. To begin with, the sublime resists being articulated in language for the simple reason that the unpresentable cannot be signified; it creates "a breach . . . in the examination of the aesthetic faculty of judgement,"[25] as "the relation of thinking to the object presented breaks down."[26] There is thus on the one had a failure of articulation and on the other the demand by reason that questions of totality be addressed because the sublime is the point at which the relationship between reason and imagination becomes most acute. It is a question about "the teleology of our own faculties" as the sublime signifies the primacy of reason because it is reason that alone can permit imagination, the faculty of presentation *and* the sublime, to come into being "at the expense of the totalizing power of the mind."[27] The point is made by Lyotard in the following unusually accessible passage:

> Seen in critical terms, [Kant's] Analytic of the Sublime finds its "legitimacy" in a principle that is expounded by critical thought and that motivates it: a principle of thinking's getting carried away. As it is expounded and deduced in its thematic, sublime feeling is analyzed as a double defiance. Imagination at the limits of *what* it can present does violence to itself in order to present *that* it can no longer present. Reason, for its part, seeks, unreasonably, to violate the interdict it imposes on itself and which is strictly critical, the interdict that prohibits it from finding objects corresponding to its concepts in sensible intuition. In these two aspects, thinking defies its own finitude, as if fascinated by its own excessiveness. It is this desire for limitlessness that it feels in the sublime "state": happiness and unhappiness.[28]

Here the imagination is elevated "from a metaphysical (and hence, ideological) to a transcendental (and, hence, critical) principle."[29] This is Paul de Man's insightful observation that the sublime is ultimately a matter of transcendental principles, about beings, matters that are always already there. In other words, the difference between the beautiful and the sublime is itself transcendental. In this reading the sublime, an absolute principle of negation, is either present or not present depending upon whether a civilization, finally, has made the necessary linguistic investment in the project. Since the sublime is really a discourse of reflection (how we read a particular object, its substantialization) and not of the object itself (its empirical existence) it follows that certain intrinsic conditions of judgment and certain rhetorical devices are essential for the sublime to exist as a category in any given civilization. This mode of theorizing is a far cry from the theories of an early reader of the subject, Edmund Burke, for whom the beautiful and the sublime were primarily sensationist principles of pleasure and pain.[30] As we shall see, part of the difficulty with British Orientalist readings of India relates to the extent to which these readings of Indian culture had Burke's definitions of the sublime in mind. The fact that there is such a thing as pleasurable alienation began to emerge as a useful idea with which to explain the seeming antinomies of Hinduism. Pleasurable alienation or the sublime's lack of (re)presentation in the mind is precisely what the idea of God is to the believer. In both instances—in sublime and religious apprehension—the sense of awe, a mental violence to the imagination, takes us to the dimension of experiencing what Lyotard has called the "pleasure in the Real."[31] Kant quotes approvingly "thou shalt not make unto thee any graven image" as the exemplary discourse of the sublime moment because in this command of the Judaic God lies the essence of the absolute unpresentability of the sublime.

The beautiful is about forms and teleology; it is a reflective judgment singularly immediate; it is only in thought without an object in the strict sense of the word. But it is also a distinctly Enlightenment concept and has about it that special ordering of nature that formed the basis of colonization itself. On the other hand, the sublime, being antiform, "is a sudden blazing, and without future"[32] and as a consequence is not a form of any special value to Enlightenment instrumentality. Sublime emotion as negation, as lack (of a teleology), as surplus and excess meant that the word was more often used for Indian thought (Hegel's review of Wilhelm von Humboldt's lectures on the *Bhagavadgītā* is a case in point) than the term beautiful or the related term "taste." Pleasure in the beautiful was predicated upon the idea of ratio or proportion in the objects of nature in terms of quality (and this was seen as a very European "principle") whereas in the sublime one began "with the quantity of judgement rather than its quality."[33] The magnitude of the sublime—as mathematical (quality) or dynamical (quantity)—being immeasurable defies comparison and creates a chasm between the reflective mind (the signified) and the sublime object (the signifier), which is how many of the early discourses of Orientalism were framed. The same magnitude, the same lack of grounding in linguistic referents is reflected further in the sense of contrariness that seems to be internal to sublime reflections: pleasure and pain, attraction and repulsion, and so on. These contradictory sensations disallow a determinate judgment such as the idea of the absolute because to admit as much would mean that sublime judgment is not an indeterminate "concept of reason."[34] We pause to ask the obvious. Are we not in fact pushing toward the realm of incommensurability and of irreconcilable heterogeneities? Is this not what Lyotard has called an instance of the "differend" because it is subjectively final without a concept of teleology or form?[35] The Kantian sublime, as one reading of it has it, erases the differend through the idea of slippage or leakage, and indeed through the idea of reason placing a lid on sublime excess moments after imagination has been given the freedom to enter into sublime abyss. But is this so? Or is it that the experience of the sublime introduces a transcendental principle (transcendental because the object remains unknown) that is almost supersensory or, to use Schlegel's description of the Hindu imagination, "mystical" and hence incapable of being contained? Can the subject ever return to the law of reason after experiencing the sublime?[36]

It is clear that aesthetically and politically the category of the sublime may be put to very productive uses. Its capacities of doing "violence" to the order of nature and its freedom have great comparative possibilities especially when it comes to reading disjunctive aesthetic moments in non-Western cultures. It is, as I have already suggested, an idea that is more likely to bypass the restrictions of imperialist discourses than the beautiful, which is confined by a rather rigid Enlightenment outlook. To repeat a point I have already made, the number of times "Oriental" art has been referred to (explicitly or implicitly) as *sublime* in Orientalist and colonial discourses probably exceeds the number of times the term *beautiful* has been used. The point is that whereas the beautiful is about the West and history, about principles of order, the sublime is a threat to the imagination, a subversive impulse with the sole aim of disturbing or doing violence to the intellect.

In a very real sense the idea of systems of thought doing violence to the intellect generally is at the center of one of the best-known philosophical engagements with the Orient. I have in mind the works of G. W. F. Hegel, the "philosopher par excellence [who represented] like few others the glory and greatness as well as the futility and arrogance of philosophy."[37] In spite of his dismissal of Hindu culture as a product of a fantastic, feminine imagination we need to return to the "Orientalist" Hegel because it is Hegel who allows us to rethink the sublime with reference to India. There is a positive side to this if we recall that "in a truly dialectical system such as Hegel's, what appears to be inferior and enslaved (*untergeordnet*) may well turn out to be the master."[38] After all, Hegel did concede, albeit dismissively, that there may be something sublime in Oriental cultures too. But there is yet another reason why we turn to Hegel in matters of theories of symbolic form: whether we like it or not on the question of art belonging to the order of the symbolic, we are all Hegelians.[39] Hegel's purely pragmatic fascination with the Hindu world (insofar as Hindu India was a useful example to him of a nation with a totally nonexistent historical spirit that reinforced his understanding of the "fixity of species"[40]) may be used here to suggest ways in which one version of the Indian sublime had already been foreshadowed, negatively as it so happened, in Hegelian aesthetics. There are three key Hegelian ideas that must be noted very quickly at this point. These ideas are: first, Hebraic poetry alone is sublime since it rejects the idea of divine representationalism; second, the sublime itself is the absolutely beautiful; third, there is a schism between the order of language and the order of the sacred. On the second point, one feels that Hegel is remarkably close to Longinus's sublime (*hupsous*) to the extent that in Hegel's reading too there is something about an elevated style that exerts on the reader an "irresistible force and mastery."[41] On the third point both Hegel and Kant are in accord. For both "the loss of the symbolic, the loss of adequation of sign to meaning, is a necessary negative moment."[42] Politically, however, we are entering very dangerous territory here. Much of what Hegel says comes close to a racist reading of non-Western cultures. He uses the category of the sublime in effect to damn Hindu culture and to make a radical distinction between races with and without history (the Nazis used the same argument to defend their genocide of the Romany gypsies). Nevertheless, if we can set aside Hegel's racism, his reading of Indian culture as an instance of an undertheorized sublime that does violence to history and to the imagination demands serious consideration. Space does not allow us to examine Hegel's readings of India in great detail and so we will have to limit ourselves to only those aspects of his argument that have a bearing on this book.

For Hegel Hindu India is an object as well as a source text of a fantastic imagination that is marked by a collective dreaming about the Absolute Spirit. Working from German and English translations of Sanskrit texts (especially those of William Jones, Henry Thomas Colebrooke, Franz Bopp, and Friedrich von Schlegel) as well as studies of India by J. A. Dubois, James Mill, and W. von Humboldt (notably the latter's lectures on the *Bhagavadgītā*), Hegel read the "sign" of the Hindu Brahman (the Absolute Spirit) as a confirmation of the total mergence of Self and Other in a (Hindu) semantic universe from which the principle of understanding and morality had been removed. By "understanding" Hegel of course meant the faculty that makes the self both aware of its own individuality and conscious of its grounding in the external world.[43] As for the austere idea or the impossible ideal of the Absolute Spirit this noble concept, Hegel argued, gets troped, for the Hindu, through a pantheistic doctrine that transforms the Absolute (as pure thought) into a sensuous object. Hegel's real objection is to the way in which an avataric or reincarnation principle leads to the Absolute Spirit being "degraded to vulgarity and senselessness." The sensory world is not the world of the sublime, which is always a matter for the Spirit. It is here that Hegel senses something quite special in Hindu culture but he holds himself back because he is enslaved by his own refusal (which for Hegel is a matter of teleological necessity) to grant Indian history any legitimacy whatsoever. Whether Hegel misreads or misunderstands Indian culture is not the real issue, although the collapsing of two different concepts of the Absolute Spirit (Brahman neuter, the impersonal Parabrahman) and God-the-creator (Brahman masculine, the personal *īśvara*) into a single figure creates serious problems. These problems are, however, not peculiar to Hegel because the Indian imagination too has periodically confused the two categories. Nevertheless, the confusion or mix-up is capable of producing some startling observations. As a race that constructed its sublime object in terms of an Absolute Spirit, the Hindu becomes European, but as a race that confused (as Hegel seems to understand it) "the idea" with its manifold avataric manifestations (where the sublime object becomes presentable) the Hindu demonstrates all the weaknesses of a fanciful child. It is the latter reading that leads Hegel to make the jump from metaphysics to Hindu history, which is then read as a grand mythic narrative that cannot chronicle the growth of human consciousness in its interaction with historical events. Indian history is seen, to borrow Hayden White's Hegelian taxonomy, as only one act in a "Tragic Drama of four acts," which is how complete histories are always written.[44] History for the Hindu (because the category of the sublime is missing from the culture) is therefore altogether nonexistent.

> It is because the Hindoos have no History in the form of annals (historia) that they have no History in the form of transactions (res gestae); that is, no growth expanding into a veritable political condition.[45]

The past and the present, annals and transactions, in this Hindu rendition of "history" are never integrated into a dynamic whole where a given moment captures, crystallizes, and transcends a nation's long history. This moment requires that the subject remain grounded in the "concrete particularity of the world"[46] and is capable of critically engaging with events. In Hegel's *Aesthetics* (*The Philosophy of Fine Art*) the same argument is repeated as a severe and, dare one say, racist reprimand:

> The Hindoo race has consequently proved itself unable to comprehend either persons or events as part of continuous history.[47]

The reference to a lack in the symbolic order of the Hindu arises out of Hegel's understanding of the pseudosublime orientation of Hindu thinking. In the *Aesthetics* the (false) Indian sublime is treated negatively as an instance of the trope of "Fantastic Symbolism" in which each object is referred back to the Divine in a pantheistic economy that fails to distinguish between a monotheistic principle (that produces a "single field of unified knowledge"[48] and hence prefigures the true sublime) and a polytheistic principle of divine immanence in the totality of nature. In the Hindu pantheistic economy the objects are not representations of the Divine but are its very being: the symbol becomes the thing represented, "it has no differentiation either within or outside of itself."[49] In this version of Hinduism the finite intermingles with the infinite or the Absolute. Since the subject, defined as the Atman, wishes to identify itself with the infinite Brahman, what is true of the external world becomes true of the self as well: the distinction between consciousness and self-consciousness totally disappears as we now "live and move amongst *simulacra*" (51). Against "Fantastic Symbolism" Hegel positions the trope of true symbolism, which is marked by a sense of difference between the sign and what it signifies and which lays the linguistic foundation of the sublime. Yet precisely because of the manner in which Hindu symbols are referred back to the Absolute, they are presented to the mind as if they were sublime representations. For the moment we sense that the return of multiplicity to oneness—Atman into Brahman—is indeed sublime. In an important passage Hegel seems to be saying as much:

> In this melting down of all clear definition . . . we may rather seek for features analogous to the type of the *sublime* than

> see any illustration of real symbolism. . . . For in the Sublime . . . the finite phenomenon only expresses the Absolute, which it would previsage for conscious sense to the extent that in so doing it escapes from the world of appearance, which fails to comprehend its content. (55)

The avataric melting down of difference, the complete unity of the idea and its representation, leads to the construction of sublime objects (of religion). In short, Hindu representations of "gods," as Hegel comments a few sentences later, strike "the opening notes of 'the Sublime' symphony." However, even as Hegel makes this concession—that what we have here is an instance of sublime aesthetics—he undercuts this possibility through a critique that would suggest that since for the Hindu the Absolute is made presentable, instead of signifying the impossibility of the object to be a stand-in for the initial signifier (the Absolute), this very act designates that the impossible idea can in fact be presented. It is at this point that Hegel effectively uses the discourse of critical judgment on the sublime to "outwit" the Hindu position as he sees it. The difficulty here is in Hegel's own prose (as translated), which I would like to quote in full:

> The main difference, however, between it [the Indian Sublime] and the true Sublimity consists in this, that the Hindoo imagination does not in the wild exuberance of its images bring about the essential nothingness of the phenomena which it makes use of, but rather through just this very measurelessness and unlimited range of its visions believes that it has annihilated and made to vanish all difference and opposition between the Absolute and its mode of configuration. In this extreme type of exaggeration, then, there is ultimately little of real kinship with either true symbolism or Sublimity: it is equally remote from the true sphere of beauty. (56)

So here we have it, neither sublime nor beautiful; something almost pre-Symbolic (in the narrowly Lacanian sense) because far too sensuous, which in fact is what Hegel's grounds for objection are. At the same time—and this point is often overlooked by recent post-Orientalist commentators—Hegel is deeply conscious of the quite extraordinary imaginative powers of the Hindu. In no other major civilization is there such breadth; nowhere else do we find a riot of divinities (from animal gods to human reincarnations) incongruously, but to the Hindu self-evidently, linked to an abstract principle of the Absolute. While the Absolute remains abstract, its avataric substantializations through a "rampant chaos of mythological and iconographic details"[50] contradict and cancel out its sublime possibilities.

We ask a number of questions at this stage. Why has the category of the sublime been withdrawn from the Hindu? Why is it that the supreme sense of inadequation found in the negative representations of Brahman has not led to a commentarial tradition based on the category of the sublime by Orientalists and by Indians themselves? And why is it that Hegel in fact uses the contradictory rhetoric of the sublime itself (attraction and repulsion; the sublime as an indeterminate as well as a "rationalizing" contemplation) to mount this critique? The simple answer, from Hegel's point of view, is that Hindus "contort the sensuous phenomenon into a plurality of Divinities" even as they construct the spiritual abstraction of God in terms of a protosublime aesthetics in which Brahman cannot be presented to consciousness. In short, the difficulty arises because of a cultural desire to offer manifestations of the divine in nature (the idea behind Hindu polytheism that allows the divine to be sensuously apprehended) even though in the process the purity of the concept itself is tainted. Of course, the confusion is both Hegel's and the Hindus': Hegel demands a concrete individual identity that is not simply part of an indeterminate "being-in-itself" (such as the Hindu Brahman); the Hindus opt for a sublime where the nature of the "being-in-itself" is always a "fusion" of Atman and Brahman. This distinction, and especially Hegel's continued insistence on the concrete particularity of the self, means that in his reconceptualization of the Kantian sublime as the impossible idea (the Absolute) without any representation in the Real ("itself essentially without form and out of the reach of concrete external existence" [86]) still requires a separation of the Absolute from the subject. The Absolute must still be contained within system and history.

For Hegel, then, to arrive at the sublime there must be an "express separation of the essential substance from the sensuous present, that is from the empirical facts of external appearance" (85). This being the case, the sublime object cannot be compromised by its possible symbolic equivalents: no matter what images or icons we construct the two, the idea and its symbolic referent, are never identical. For the Hindu it is not a matter of never denying this proposition but of continually attempting to trope the infinite by grounding it in the phenomenal even as the canonical texts stress the impossibility of such a grounding. And this procedure does violence to the concept itself as it introduces a discontinuity between the two ways in which the Absolute is conceptualized. From a Hegelian point of view, sublime empowerment (for the Hindu subject) is therefore trivialized through a constant transformation of the Absolute into objects of sensuality. The Hindu procedure of objectifying the Absolute through a fantastic symbolization has the effect of grounding it in sensuous objects, in a subjective content known to the self. As we have noticed this procedure is unthinkable to Hegel since for him the sublime object is pure thought, "unaffected by every expression of the finite categories," and "only present to thought in its purity" (87). The stage is then set for Hegel to redefine the Kantian sublime, in both its positive and negative aspects, through a rethinking of this "one absolute substance." For Kant the sublime was a moment of radical empowerment of a particular faculty of the mind under the interdiction of reason. During this fleeting moment there is a letting-go of the law of reason as the subject, "an epistemological entrepreneur" to use Terry Eagleton's telling phrase,[51] is engaged with ideas too large for comprehension. At the same time Kant links these absolutely great ideas to the formless and to "the loss of adequation of sign and meaning."[52] On this point—on the essential negativity of the sublime moment—Kant and Hegel are in agreement. However, when it comes to the one substance or the Absolute, the issue becomes somewhat more complex since for Hegel the one substance must always be "posited above the particular appearance" or substance "in which it is assumed to have found a representation." At the same time this very representation has to be conceived as possessing no real validity because the ultimate essence is "out of reach of concrete external existence." Yet the very fact that the one essence is represented as the positive sublime effectively destroys true sublimity, which Kant too had realized was always an absence or a negation. The negative representation of the absolute is to be found in Hebrew poetry where the "positive immanence of the Absolute is done away with." And if the Divine is represented (as it has to be) this is done on the explicit understanding that the symbol is no substitute for the thing-in-itself because the Absolute can never be troped (through incarnations, for instance). Metaphorical language must disappear if the divine essence is to be grasped.

As we have already suggested, the subtext here is Hegel's prioritization of Western history, the only history where the tragic drama of life in four acts is fully played out. It is this understanding of a teleology of history, intrinsic in a sense to Western historical consciousness alone, that leads him to discover true sublimity only in the figure of the Hebrew God who, after all, is at the heart of Hegel's system and history. Where the Hindu God is measured either mathematically (as the supposedly sixty-four million gods) or quantitatively (as a grotesque reincarnation in the form of a man-lion), the Hebrew God stridently proclaims that there can be no image-substitute for him. His glory may be seen in the world around us but he cannot be symbolized. In spite of this, Hegel remains fascinated by the Hindu "God" as Brahman Absolute (in the neuter). The constant return to Hindu symbolism and Hindu pantheism in his aesthetic theory underlines both his fascination with and unease about the status granted to Hindu speculative thought. For the fact is, if Hegelian aesthetics is removed, for the moment, from its grand European narrative of history, and from the imperative of the detached concrete subject, Hegel's negative sublimity finds its highest form not in the Hebrew God, whom he embraces as the exemplary instance of the sublime, but in Brahman. Hegel's argument is based on the observation that the Hebrew God has no signifieds to which he can be linked. Yet this is clearly not so because the Hebrew tradition has always engaged in a kind of surreptitious semantic overcoding: the Hebrew God has been represented as the just, the wrathful, the avenger, and so on. This God is also a lawgiver and prone to speaking to his subjects, or intervening in their histories. Against this, although one version of the Hindu God—as the masculinized Brahman—has acquired all the features of fantastic symbolization attributed to him by Hegel, in its pure abstract form as Brahman (neuter) it never speaks, is never spoken to, is without quality, and cannot be represented in any form whatsoever. As the *Bhagavadgītā* reminds us: "It is by a rare chance that a man sees him" (2.29). About this unmanifest being the tradition remains remarkably consistent. Whenever the Absolute is presented or given visual form in Hindu thought, the reference is to Brahma the Creator (a personalized *īśvara*) and not to Brahma(n) the Absolute (a non-relational Parabrahman), although admittedly the Krishna of the *Bhagavadgītā* does have a tendency to confuse the two. Nevertheless, the fact that the Hebrew God is capable of being spoken of as the just, the wrathful, the avenger and so on is certainly one way of linking him to the positive sublime. Against this, Brahman has no "descriptive semantics" at all; nor can it be represented to consciousness in anything other than in a negative fashion. It is clear, therefore, that for Hegel only those civilizations capable of grasping the world historical Spirit can in fact disengage the Absolute from its sensuous representation. The sublime then becomes for Hegel a term of value linked to a particular version of telos and not simply a mode of radical empowerment in the face of the interdiction of reason. History empowers some people with the capacity for the true sublime; those who lack history only have its lower form, pantheistic art, available to them. Hegel is absolutely correct in connecting Hindu art with the Hindu's (self-conscious) misreading of the historical process. However, to understand the Indian sublime one has to disengage Hegel's absolute identification of the true sublime with the Enlightenment conception of history. It is only when we can disengage the two—the sublime and history—and begin to rethink the Absolute as incapable of being the source of history, that we can understand how the two Brahmans function in Hindu culture. In the Indian sublime, then, two principles are at work: the first is the principle of nondifferentiation and absolute nonrepresentation; the second is its very opposite, of excessive representation and differentiation. The latter principle makes its way into the myriad of reincarnations that invade the Hindu religious universe; the former into what is vulgarly referred to as the mystical tradition in which the relationship between the one and the many is kept intact through an essentially mystical logic. At the same time, for an austere Vedantin like Shankara, the purity of the idea of Brahman as the Absolute would sit quite comfortably with Hegel's own rendition of the sublime.

The argument sketched thus far forces us to rethink the Indian sublime critically and creatively so that what to Hegel was an aberration can now be transformed into a statement about a sublime that would eschew the kind of value judgments that led Hegel to conceive of a Hindu dreaming race whose reading of the Absolute led to the perfect deadening of consciousness. The religious imaginary of the Hindu, in the Hegelian argument, is one that is troped through metaphors that reinforce animistic identifications and prevent the ego from entering into the symbolic order of difference. But where Hegel would interpret this state of affairs as a sign of the false sublime or of pantheistic/fantastic symbolism, the Indian would read the same category through metaphors of unpresentability. In this Hindu reading the Indian sublime is boundless; the human mind aspires toward the infinite as it defies the parergon, the frame, and confronts that which cannot be presented in all its totality to the imagination. Sublime thought reaches its grand point in the civilization's engagement with Brahman.

In theorizing the Indian sublime we must, therefore, renegotiate Hegel's fantastic or pantheistic symbolism by considering the perennial Hindu engagement with questions of multiplicity (the ontology of plurality-with-unity already referred to) as a structural principle at the heart of Indian culture itself. How is it that the one (Brahman) and the many (Brahma) have maintained a peaceful coexistence over all these years? One way of addressing this question is to consider it purely as a philosophical problem and examine the innumerable commentaries written on texts that deal with the problematic of the one and the many. Attractive—and relatively straightforward—as this procedure is, examination of commentaries will not lead us to the thought processes of the culture itself. For an understanding of these in all their complexity, one of the richest archives is obviously the literary corpus of the culture. I would therefore want to shift the focus, as already foreshadowed, to the literary texts of the culture without in any way establishing an absolute demarcation between the aesthetic and the religious. Indeed, it could be argued that the religious, for the Hindu, is by and large a matter of aesthetics.

The literary genre in which the aesthetic and the religious intertwine in ways that make it impossible to disentangle the two is the poetry of devotion. This genre presents us with a powerful archive about questions relating to the representation of the Absolute. In devotional or bhakti poetry the sublime object of devotion is obviously Brahman in both its neuter and masculine forms. In a clear departure from Hegel, I would want to claim that bhakti or devotional poetry is superimposed upon a sublime narrative where the subject searches for an impossible ideal that is symbolized through a plethora of Gods and Goddesses. Although this impossible ideal is represented through the image or the icon, the Absolute Brahman as the ideal, however, remains the sublime object that, ultimately, defies all representation in time and space. The manner in which the one and the many (plurality-with-unity) gets articulated needs to be thought through the concept of an absent center in Hindu culture that is symbolized by the sign of Brahman as pure negation. To grasp the Indian sublime it is necessary, for the moment, to engage with the relationship between center and periphery in Indian culture. Without this narrative of (cultural) deferral, the special nature of the Indian sublime would continue to elude us.

THE CENTER CANNOT HOLD

Recent research on Hinduism undertaken by a group of largely post-structuralist Indologists has shifted our focus from the traditional Indological paradigms of comparative philology and self-contained pragmatic literary histories to a reading and analysis of the dynamics or "logic" of the culture itself. A key scholar in this regard is the French Sanskritist Madeleine Biardeau whose works show a particularly astute analysis of Indian culture. In her book on Hinduism, she explains the seemingly endless contradictions of Hinduism by examining the structural imperatives of the renouncer and the socialized individual through the way in which desire or *kāma* operates in the culture.[53] Since the narrative of desire is based on a wish to own or possess something else (though this something else may be introjected if the cultural ego has not advanced beyond the *imaginary*) and implies a lack (of something), the aim of life may be seen as a search for unity with an absent body that would lead to some form of self-empowerment or personal happiness. There is nothing specifically Indian about this definition of the object of desire. Indian informants, however, may point out that the Indian subject is motivated by a grand desire (a sublime desire in fact) aimed at union with Brahman. From what we have said so far the qualification that we need to make at this juncture is that the object of desire, Brahman, cannot be presented to consciousness as an "idea." This success-in-failure, which Hegel saw as the basis of symbolic art (and which he felt was missing from Hindu fantastic art), can be seen as a theory of the Indian's own primal narrative of desire in which desire has for its object the impossible ideal of Brahman. We can now see the entire history of Hindu speculative thought, reformulated in a markedly Kantian language, as an aesthetic of self-surrender through the momentary (because always under the interdiction of the law of reason) ascendancy of the imagination. What is the duration of this self-surrender? Can it be given a spatiotemporal permanence or must it be constantly deferred because reason will always impose a lid on it—the sublime, to invoke Freud, will get sublimated? Or is it that the momentary freedom granted by reason also signals reason's own abdication of power? In the state of Brahmanhood, can the law of reason come into play anyway?

In the context of the foregoing general remarks, the place of devotional literature in Indian culture (and perhaps in all cultures) is in need of some very serious critical rethinking. In the immediate context of Indian devotional literature, the core of my argument may be formulated as follows: devotional poetry is a figurative means by which the subject's search in the phenomenal world of a transcendental personalization of Atman and Brahman gets articulated. In this transcendental personalization the identity of the self with the cosmic principle of creation itself is symbolically established. The self participates in an essentially apocalyptic act of dissolution (Schopenhauer's oceanic sublime) that leads to the self's absorption in a larger principle of being. The structure in which this works is, however, not stable since, as David Shulman has boldly observed, the culture itself is characterized by a tendency toward deferral and decenteredness. In terms of such a characterization of the culture Brahman alone becomes the idea that could give meaning to a world that presents itself as one that is decentered and continually displaces meaning.[54] It must be said displacement or deferral is not related to either a Hindu dreaming "race" or a Hindu nation without a sense of history—both propositions that have had their day with the Orientalists—rather it is a consequence of a pervasive brahminical ideology that "elevated linguistic, social, political, moral, and religious conventions to the level of absolute realities, permanent and eternal."[55] We can think through all this in a slightly different, and I suspect much more original, fashion if we consider the process of decentering of meaning and deferral of self as signs of a very mature culture's awareness of the impossibility of any referential certainties in language. The desire toward Brahmanhood can only be deflected because Brahman cannot, finally, be represented. Brahman is not Logos or the Word, but its negation, which is then transformed into an ontology of "neither this nor that." Like the Lacanian Real, Brahman as the sublime is an "embodiment of pure negativity, emptiness."[56] The logic of devotional poetry, as we shall see later, arises out of this: at the heart of devotional poetry is a black hole, an all-pervasive emptiness, as language searches for signifiers that would reflect the extinction of Self and Other in Brahman. Devotional poetry resists closure because Brahman cannot be signified except as a hole, a gap, a void, an emptiness around which revolves the Hindu symbolic order. Everything else that we might say about Hindu devotional texts is a variation on this fundamentally sublime theme of the construction of meaning around a void, an emptiness.

If the referent is missing because emptiness displaces itself, silence begets silence, then in Hindu culture symbolic systems and overarching structural invariants are especially important. The center of a text—because the center is missing—must be found elsewhere, in ritual (as acts) or in those transindividual and absolute frames of references or "limit situations" (as metaphysics) such as karma and dharma that function as Hindu metatexts. This point is clear in Madeleine Biardeau's definition of dharma as "the socio-cosmic order which organizes the empirical world."[57] But dharma as well as karma are also one with Brahman in their sublimity. They are not the fantastic symbolism of a juvenile race (Hegel's reading), but Real in the strict Lacanian sense—"that is, it is impossible to occupy [their] position . . . one cannot attain [them], but one cannot escape [them]." The qualification is Žižek's, who goes on to write, "This is why the only way to avoid the Real is to produce an utterance of pure metalanguage which, by its patent absurdity, materializes its own impossibility."[58] So many definitions of Brahman in the canon are utterances of pure metalanguage.

It is not surprising that the culture's dominant hermeneutic of reading is also metalinguistic based as it is on an abstract precognitive reading practice that collapses both hermeneutics and poetics. Behind this reading practice stands an audience "that did not think of itself as an audience but as a community of believers."[59] The culture calls this reading practice "rasa," which may be read as an early version of the Rezeptionsästhetik of the Konstanz School.[60] But where European reception theory begins with the idea of individual acts of consciousness and the constructed worlds through these acts, rasa theory is a formal pattern of possible aesthetic moments superimposed upon a grid based on a taxonomy of emotional states. Rasa has little of the intersubjective dynamism of European reception theory and does not, on the whole, take into account those shifting horizons of expectations that could lead to a more socially complex and ideologically self-aware literary response. The agent of this response is an ideal spectator who is "a *sahṛdaya*, a man 'whose heart is at one with the author's.'"[61] Nevertheless rasa theoreticians do seek to find a way out of the crude domain of subjective responses by developing sets of aesthetic categories of taste understood by the "sahṛdaya or connoisseur"[62] that would correspond to the eight or nine known basic emotions of the subject. In its emphasis on emotional response, rasa theory predates Edmund Burke's sensationist readings of the sublime and the beautiful, which too were based on identifying through psychosomatic categories emotions such as pain and pleasure. One final question remains: How does rasa theory relate to theories of absence we have outlined above?

Since the coherence of the Hindu imaginative world arises out of transcendental Hindu laws which, for the Hindu, are grounded in a self-evident ontology, a given literary text is viewed not in terms of its inner dynamism (of design, of character, etc.) but as a carrier of a multiplicity of rasas where response, the starting point of the aesthetic process, takes priority over structure. Read through rasa theory such well-known texts as Kalidasa's *Śakuntalā*, a thoroughly dramatic work, and Jayadeva's *Gītagovinda*, a "stilled drama" or *citrakāvya*, are unified aesthetic objects because both are dominated by the erotic rasa *śṛṅgāra*. It is this rasa—*śṛṅgāra*—that gives these texts their coherence, even though this rasa, which exists only as an abstraction, has little to do with the real, lived experience of the audience. The theory in fact closes the literary text off from those principles that lead to actual, historical identifications. Rasa theory thus reinforces *imaginary* identifications by insinuating in effect a radical incommensurability between emotion and text. The implied distantiation between noncontingent stable emotions and their abstraction (between *bhāva* and rasa) is linked to the general theory of Sanskrit poetics. We have to be clear on one point though. It doesn't follow that Indian texts are therefore incoherent and lack, as suggested by S. H. Butcher, "unity . . . spiritual freedom."[63] Rasa in fact imposes both a "reading coherence" and psychological variety as well as individual introspection in spite of van Buitenen's contrary views on the subject.[64]

The way in which we should address rasa theory is not in terms of objective harmonies in the texts themselves but rather in terms of a number of cultural imperatives as such. At the level of generality, rasa is the state of *ānanda*, a word that carries with it the senses of both blissful joy and union with Brahman[65] as well as "orgasmic rapture."[66] At the more specific level, individual rasas may reflect other tendencies in the culture. One especially productive rasa is *śṛṅgāra* or the erotic, a rasa that indicates rather well the element of deferral that is at the heart of the culture itself. It is not unusual for poets to represent the narrative of lovers through two interdependent aspects of *śṛṅgāra* rasa: love in union (*sambhoga*) and love in separation (*vipralambha*). What Friedhelm Hardy calls "bridal mysticism"[67]—or the poetics of *viraha*—breaks the formal limits of the abstract category of *śṛṅgāra* by destabilizing that aesthetic response through an uncanny narrative in which love becomes both union and separation. Love has to be displaced or deferred, its unity destabilized: desire becomes its own lack. We get here echoes of the perennial metaphysics of the negative way in Hinduism: "*neti*, *neti*, not thus, not thus," exclaim the gurus of the Upanishads when attempting to represent in words the ineffable mystery of Brahman. Thus in Jayadeva's treatment of the theme of Radha-Krishna eroticism in the *Gītagovinda* and indeed in many other bhakti appropriations of precisely this theme, what is emphasized is the flux itself, the alternation between union and separation, between desire and its fulfilment, between attraction and rejection, between bliss and despondency. The subject situated between *sambhoga* and *vipralambha*, union and its absence, experiences moments of uncertainty that cannot be grounded in any single reality. Yet far from signifying a cultural uncertainty, a lack of spiritual unity or freedom, the move here is totally structural and part of a system that is linked to our conception of an absent center in Indian culture. The insistence upon flux, upon alternation, is also summed up in other key (metaphysical) dualities such as *pravṛtti*/*nivṛtti* (activity and repose) and *surati*/*nirati* (enjoyment and salvation) where a congealed desire toward instability is situated in the space of the slash that divides the two terms. The alternation that I speak of here is not to be explained away as a matter of a failure to think through the domains of reason, ethics and aesthetics. Rather the stress on flux, on negation, on difference and otherness arise out of theories of language and culture that predate de Saussure and Durkheim by a couple of millennia.

The Self and the Oceanic Sublime

We began at the difficult end of the Self-Other nexus by examining Brahman as the misunderstood sublime object of Hegel. We must now look at the cultural economy of the "Self" itself in classical Hindu thought.[68] It goes without saying that no comparable civilization has argued over definitions of selfhood as intensely as the Indian. Throughout its long and august history almost every branch of knowledge (philosophy, literature, religion, linguistics) has grappled with this extremely elusive concept. There is, however, one point on which all departments of knowledge are in agreement: the self is other than what our faculties persuade us it is. In other words, the construction of the self through social processes (which would require a social Other and a rigorous engagement with questions of agency) has to be read against a self that comes already formed and constructed with reference to a Self-Brahman structure. In an essentialist distinction between the true (ideal, spiritual) and not true (social) selves, the true self comes into being only when it can become identical with an abstraction beyond its own self as social agent. Once such a "double conception" is advanced as the ground for the definition of the self, a culture must then give this principle a frame of reference. The brahminical orthodoxy who were traditional arbiters on questions of knowledge put a mechanism in place which stipulated that the self came into being already karmically formed (an earlier life explained the present human condition) and self-representation or self-definition could not be removed from both an earlier life-experience and future life-stages. These life-stages themselves were predicated upon "caste mentalities" in which those "caste-selves" that were particularly privileged could dream of union with Brahman as the goal of the final stage of their life. There is, then, a prior system that acts as a template, as a sanctioned pattern, for the realization of the [privileged] self and this prior system has "historical depth and enduring features."[69] The power of this sanctioned pattern and its structural endurance may be seen in the metaphysical uses of the two crucial words for the self in Sanskrit, *ātman* and *aham*. Compounds such as *ātma-vidyā* or *ātma-brahman*, "knowledge of the soul or the supreme spirit," *ahaṃ-kāra*, "conception of one's individuality, self-consciousness" (with its technical meanings in Sankhya philosophy) and sentences such as *so [a]ham*, "I myself," and *aham brahma asmi*, "I am Brahman," indicate an uncompromisingly abstract conception of the self in the domain of philosophy and aesthetics. At the social level, this sublime otherness of the self means that the ideal the self aspired to was the condition of the renouncer, a fact that would have fitted in perfectly with the designs of the Hindu priestly caste. Shankara, that fiercely nondualistic eighth–ninth-century thinker and defender of high intellectualism, never failed to remind us that the world was unreal, Brahman alone was real and the self was none other than Brahman: *brahma satyaṃ jagan mithyā jivo brahmaiva nāparaḥ*. The growth of the self in this cryptic formulation is toward a supreme undivided (*akhaṇḍa*) reality into which the self finally dissolves. But like all other aspirations toward such a transcendent, "unpresentable" being, the implied state of bliss remains a goal, a desired end rather than an experiential state. The difficulties posed by this very desire for union become evident when we examine Krishna's own attempts at defining three key concepts that underlie Hindu definitions of the self: *brahman*, *(adhy)ātman* and *karman* (*Bhagavadgītā* 8.1–5). In defining the *adhyātman*, Krishna introduces another term *svabhāva*, and describes the *adhyātman* in terms of this *svabhāva: svabhāvo [a]dhyātmam ucyate* ("the *adhyātman* is the inherent nature of the individual self"). Literally translated as self-being (or the state of being that defines one's own self) the *svabhāva* (the prefix *sva* implies ownership as in *svadharma*) introduces a term through which the *adhyātman* (which is also Brahman) is given expression in the world we inhabit. In this section of the *Bhagavadgītā*, Krishna's unease with the *adhyātman* (Arjuna's question in fact begins with: *kim tad brahma kim adhyātmam*) is obvious as he continues to make further distinctions by introducing the perishable part of being (*adhibhūta*), the divine agent (*puruṣa*), and perhaps even a God lower than Brahman to whom sacrifices are offered (*adhiyajña*). The use of a technical Sankhya (dualistic) terminology to make precise distinctions between the various states of the self demonstrates both an unease with narrow definitions of the concept of the self as well as its irrelevance in the greater cosmic design in which the ideal of nondifferentiation is the overriding imperative. Our argument, of course, is that both at the level of Brahman and at the level of the self what we get here is again the semantics of unpresentability that we have equated with the sublime.

The experience of oneness is captured in one of Hinduism's most open-ended words, moksha. The difficulties posed by the term "moksha" (and the experience of it) should not deter us from investigating its meaning further. The term clearly defies description (it is a void, a semantic absence, antiteleological in the Hegelian system), which means that realist readings of it are not going to be particularly helpful. The Indian psychoanalyst Sudhir Kakar suggests that moksha could be discussed through structural or metaphorical analogies.[70] One such analogy suggested by Kakar comes straight out of the handbook of devotionalism and is called *samādhi*, a trancelike state that is referred to in *nirguṇa* bhakti (monistic devotionalism) as the *sahaja* or "easy" state of the enlightened individual engrossed in total contemplation. The self in such a state is pure consciousness, that is, Brahman. In a significant way, though, this identification is again a version of the oceanic sublime, the goal of desire unchecked by the reality principle. Of course, Hindu culture does not interpret the condition of *samādhi* in quite this fashion. It would claim that before the self ceases to be it has been in play constantly and to its fullest capacity through a process of socialization based upon the four stages of Hindu life. In other words, the self experiences the material conditions of being—sexual life, work, play, and so on—before arriving at the state of moksha (or its analogue in *samādhi*). We know, however, that these stages cannot be segmented unproblematically and in that order. Lived experience (which is always linked to specific social conditions) would contradict the implied teleology of the four stages of life: final renunciation (the fourth stage) need not lead to moksha because the ritual of living through the four stages of Hindu life is no guarantee of flight from eternal recurrence. Against the real, lived conditions of Indian life, what the metanarrative endorses is the dogma of the "essentialist" self presented as a canonical literal truth, and not its construction through social processes. The self as presented here is not a product of the processes of change; it is somehow contained within the system and moves unproblematically through history. The nature of individual life in any one of the stages is subordinated to the overall structure which in itself is bonded to the transcendental laws of dharma and karma. There is no better example of this "bondage" to transcendental laws than in India's grandest text, the *Mahābhārata*. Soon after Krishna had spoken to Arjuna on the field of battle the great teacher Drona tells Yudhishthira: "And I swear to you, I shall put down my weapons only when I have heard most grievous tidings from a man whose word I trust."[71] Drona's reply to Yudhishthira's less than heroic request as to how his teacher could be killed in battle is clearly framed in the absolutist discourse of dharma. He, Drona, will lay down his arms when dharma itself iies in tatters. In this great moment of dramatic irony in the epic, it is Yudhishthira, the dharma-raja but forever the flawed epic hero, who will be instrumental in the destruction of dharma.

Moksha, for sure, is the grand "unpresentable" idea, the goal of life. But it is dharma that tells us what life itself is all about. Dharma, of course, is hard to disentangle from the related concept karma, both of which are really about actual social practices, and about the moral order through which "the individual, the society, and the cosmos,"[72] become meaningful. Even so, canonical Hindu culture tends to shift the orientation of dharma and karma from the social to the sublime. Indeed, such is the significance of dharma in Hindu thought that, as van Buitenen has mapped out so brilliantly, the entry of God into the Hindu worldview led not to the establishment of the Law (because dharma was already given) or a new code of justice—either of which function in the domain of the social—but to the final positing of a category of being who in its self-sufficiency knows "the bliss of wanting nothing."[73] Although in the real world of actual social relations the type of dharma that a person follows is based upon a number of things, including the period in which one lives, the caste to which one belongs and, more importantly, the immediate responsibilities that one has to one's family, this dharma (a self-dharma or a *svadharma*) is meaningful only insofar as it reinforces in the public sphere the force of its own eternal and ungraspable laws. In the words of Sudhir Kakar:

> Hindus share the belief that the legitimacy of social institutions lies in the dharma they incorporate rather than in utilitarian contractual agreements and obligations. . . . Moreover, it is generally believed that social conflict, oppression and unrest do not stem from the organization of social relations, but originate in the *adharma* (not dharma) of those in positions of power.[74]

"Generally believed" is the decisive phrase here because there is no evidence that dharma actually manifests itself in society as a set of interdependent social relations. An adharmic course of action can be explained in purely pragmatic terms while at the same time the mere invocation of the principle of dharma in an everyday discussion may lift an act—a crime for instance—to the level of an offence to the ethico-cosmic order. Thus Vishnu reincarnates himself whenever dharma is challenged not because perversion of power ultimately corrupts but because a much larger metaphysical issue is at stake here. To understand Hindu time, destiny and history one needs to return to dharma's twin, the crucial category of karma.

The Hindu worldview sees present life as a moment in a much longer and, in the end, cyclical journey. Time gets locked into this circularity and history gets quickly transformed into an immemorial tradition. "Indian time, in the immensity of its ages and its cyclical form, functioned as the sign of the essentially Indian," writes Thomas R. Trautmann.[75] In this immensity of time where the experience of time has to be "more psychological than historical . . . dreamlike,"[76] the category of karma emerges as a means of establishing some connection between lived experience (as action) and historical time however vague and ill-defined. The idea of karma implies that although acts arise out of real material conditions, they produce consequences well beyond the confines of one's life in this world. It is, of course, easy to trivialize karma as fatalism—which is what a brand of Orientalism did—but this is to totally misunderstand the concept. Indeed, there is something rather special about karma: of the three crucial determinants of the Hindu collective self (moksha, dharma, and karma), karma is perhaps the only one that has some room for individual growth through action for which, finally, the subject is responsible. In fact, correct or proper action—Krishna spoke about his own karma, his own action that kept the universe going, and had insisted upon the selflessness of the karmic act—redefined leads to the idea of social action and perhaps even to an "Indian" individualism that is intricately connected to the primary Law of Dharma. It is for this reason that the *Bhagavadgītā* is of such central importance to Indian thought. Not surprisingly the latter concept—the relationship between action and the proper dharma—is argued at length in the *Bhagavadgītā*. In this invaluable source text of karmic theory Krishna as the *karmayogin*, the doer of karma, emphasizes the importance of disinterested action against the ideological distinctions between the renouncer and the man-in-the-world. In Krishna's argument, "he is both the renouncer (*sa saṃnyāsī*) and the doer (*ca yogī*) who performs the task set for him (*karma karoti yaḥ*) without interest in its consequences or fruits (*anāśritaḥ karmaphalaṃ*)" provided that "consequences" are in harmony with the dictates of the Law of Dharma at any given time.[77] Earlier in the *Bhagavadgītā* Krishna had redefined karma by pointing out that there is no necessary and self-evident connection between karma and action, since there can be karma in inaction too. That these discussions have taken place for so long reflect the importance of the metanarratives of dharma and karma in Indian attempts to come to terms with ideas of self and agency. One speaks of "agency" because Krishna is quite explicit on the question of "work": selves are never immune from the idea of work and the ultimate symbol of "nonwork"—the life of the renouncer—is itself a form of action. Yet even as Krishna connects karma to forms of protosocial action and to questions of ethics (or right acts), the metatextual status of the key terms in the *Bhagavadgītā* (moksha, dharma, and karma) remain more or less intact. We return thus to our initial remarks about the presentation in discourse of these metarealities. How does one represent the ultimate goal of life, fetishized in the ideal of renunciation, that would lead to unity with Brahman? It is here that Hindu metaphysics intersects with theories of the sublime and indeed presents us with one of the most fully developed of all sublimes.

Moksha, dharma, and karma as preexistent (meta)narratives explains why the "sense of rationality as *social*"[78] is largely missing from Indian culture. The phrase just quoted is from Richard Rorty's criticism of Hegel's philosophy but has relevance here. In spite of Krishna's own very clear directive in the *Bhagavadgītā*, the "texts" of moksha, dharma, and karma tend to transform the social being into a metaphysical essence. As we have seen, one consequence of this tendency—the construction of individuals as "incumbents of positions which survive them"[79]—is that when it comes to questions of selfhood, the "I" is aestheticized (not socialized) through the metaphorics of the sublime. In other words, the "I" becomes unpresentable to thought and is not linked primarily to the corporeality of the body. The corporeal "I" (as the socially lived being) is pushed to the margins of the text and surfaces in a text such as the *Bhagavadgītā* only when Krishna refers to Arjuna's left-handedness (or his ambidexterity), his eunuchlike cowardice, and so on. The return of the self to the body (for instance, through a Tantric metaphorics of the body) is one of the great interventions of bhakti ideology. The metaphorical urge to "think the unthinkable, to grasp the unconditioned"[80] would gradually lead to the problematizing of the sublime narrative of noncorporeal beings—Atman and Brahman. Although in the four stages of human life, the terms *brahmacarya, gṛhastha, vānaprastha,* and *saṃnyāsa* make very clear references to the physical self and imply actual, lived experiences, until we encounter the body in the later bhakti texts, we continue to find selves framed in the narratives of metatexts that claim quite unproblematically that the world (and hence the body) is in fact unreal (*asat*) because it cannot participate in the only true reality (*sat*), which is Brahman the sublime.

To keep our use of the word "sublime" in focus let us return to the most creative theorist of the sublime, Immanuel Kant, for whom the sublime is unpresentable to the mind because it is "an outrage to the imagination."[81] Where the beautiful is signified by the trope of order and organic form as the imagination creates harmonies and unities, the sublime is marked, in the mind, by a continuing tension, a tussle to grasp and transform, to represent and contain, the essentially formless. This feature of a dissonance between phenomenon (the object) and the subject (the mind) is what defines the threat of the sublime as it creates worlds too large, too vast for the mind to handle. The sublime, therefore, confronts us with the urgency of representation (which is what the mind must always do under the dictate of reason) and its corresponding lack, our desire for fulfilment and the denial of it, because the interdiction of reason under which the mind works (and which supports the aesthetic of the beautiful), would reject the sublime outright. In Kant's theory of the mind, the law of reason would initially seek to condemn the mind's fraternization with the sublime because it always wishes to totalize and explain. But in the presence of the sublime—an inalienable *a priori* capacity of the mind—reason momentarily gives way and allows the mind to confront its apocalyptic, *pralaya*-orientated (the destruction of the world at the end of an aeon) capacities. Confrontation is one thing though, but representation is another. Without the totalizing capacity of reason how can one represent that which is beyond representation? For Kant the experience of the sublime is a momentary lapse in which reason gives in to the powers of the imagination. If the giving in were not momentary, the encounter with the sublime would make life impossible because reason would no longer be in total control. For Kant judgment is the emotional third element in a larger theory of the mind in which reason and ethics are politically more conspicuous. For our argument, however, the sublime needs to be connected somewhat more directly with the idea of God itself. While Kant certainly acknowledges the sublimity of the Biblical phrase in which God cannot be "imaged" in any way, we need to get back to Hegel for a definition of a sublime more suited to the task at hand here: "[the sublime is marked by an attempt] to express the infinite, without being able to find an object in the realm of the phenomenal existence such as is clearly fitted for its representation," wrote Hegel.[82] Thus Krishna's attempt at self-representation in the *Bhagavadgītā* is doomed to failure: *ahaṃ kṛtsnasya prabhāvaḥ pralayas tathā* ("I am the creation and the dissolution of the world"). As the paradigmatic text of the immanence of the divine in the external world, and the consequent self-surrender of the individual in the face of this immanent presence, the *Bhagavadgītā* is a wonderful source text about the aesthetics of the sublime in Hindu culture. The failure of representation implicit in Krishna's definition of his own self says something quite crucial about the whole concept of how the infinite may be imaged. And yet even as Krishna appropriates, momentarily, the discourse of the positive sublime, the words that he uses—"the creation and the dissolution"—powerfully underline a countertendency toward self-extinction in the Indian sublime although the statement itself wishes to identify and represent the infinite. A countertendency toward dissolution implicit in any literary representation of that desire demonstrates that the moment it is imaged, it has to be immediately recast, deferred, reformulated. "I am the sacrifice, I am the worship, I am the spices . . . I am the fire, and I am the victim . . . the mystic figure *Oṃ*" (9.16–17), proclaims Krishna, in a language that opens out into a series of almost endless metaphors.

What we detect here is a tendency that takes us back to "the oceanic sublime," to the nirvana principle. In psychoanalytic parlance, moksha is the principle of death, the feeling-state designated by the term "oceanic sublime" (*ozeanisches Gefühl*) used by Freud in *Civilization and Its Discontents* (1930). The sometime Sanskritist and now the *enfant terrible* of psychoanalysis, J. Moussaieff Masson, has traced the origin of the "oceanic sublime" (which Freud borrowed from Romain Rolland) to an uncompromisingly *advaita* (nondualistic) text called *Aṣṭāvakrasaṃhitā*. Masson claims that this text "denies the reality of all phenomena of the outer and inner world in favour of the one reality that is Brahman, and which is also the same as the innermost self, the Atman."[83] "You are an infinite ocean" (*tvayy anantamahambodhau*), begins one of the relevant verses from this text. In examining this text further, Masson discovers recurring themes of disquiet and unease with the world's transience punctuated by the desire for a long, trancelike sleep. The point being made here, of course, is that if the world is indeed Maya, an illusion, a construction of Vishnu's power, then the return of the self to the undifferentiated moment of the oceanic sublime in moksha is the only way to effectively destroy the illusory nature of the world in the first place. Arthur Schopenhauer, whom Freud quotes approvingly, had recognized, after the Hindus, the separation of the phenomenon (representation or idea) from the thing-in-itself (the will). He wrote:

> The world that appears to the senses has no true being, but only a ceaseless becoming; it is, and it is not; and its comprehension is not so much a knowledge as an illusion.[84]

To grasp the world as "ceaseless becoming" one must confront that which is most unimaginable, like Arjuna's encounter with Krishna's transfiguration. Here the sublime arises from a confrontation with a power superior to the subject which threatens Arjuna with extinction. Where Kant had invoked the law of reason and situated the sublime in the ambiguous interstices of desire and control, Schopenhauer goes straight to the Vedantic concept of oneness and annihilation. What we don't get in Schopenhauer or in the Vedanta is a theory of the mind (which, some would argue, is lacking in Hindu philosophy generally); instead the sublime, in this definition, lifts will to the state of pure, universal knowing so that the subject can claim, with the Upanishads, *tat tvam asi* ("that art thou"). In Schopenhauer's appropriation of Hindu and Buddhist texts the sublime gets directly connected to the threatening concept of self-extinction or death. Death as the cause and moment of terror and therefore of the sublime (Edmund Burke) now becomes a process of dissolution and dispersal through which difference and individuality disappear. Self-extinction rather than momentary suspension of the law of reason becomes the cornerstone of the sublime in both Schopenhauer and in Krishna.

Orientalism and the Indian Sublime

"Orientalism" is a word that one critiques, not endorses. Yet its quite proper interrogation and deconstruction, especially in light of Edward Said's magnificent work, should not mean that its value as a scholarly enterprise should be collapsed into the politics of representation, power, and imperialism. I think that Thomas R. Trautmann's useful strategic distinction between Orientalism^1 and Orientalism^2 (the former a matter of scholarly analysis and disputation, the latter one of ethnographic classification and racism) can be used productively to rethink the legacy of Orientalism.[85] In the hands of key British and German Orientalists, Orientalism^1, I would suggest, grasped the nature of the Indian sublime in ways not unlike the project of this book. Space doesn't permit me to examine their research extensively—and, at any rate, Trautmann covers the general field admirably in his book—but some reference to the work of these Orientalists is crucial to what I have to say. In 1785, for instance, Charles Wilkins published his epoch-making translation of the *Bhagavadgītā*, to which Warren Hastings, the first governor-general of Bengal, added a letter of support.[86] Dated 4 October 1784, this letter acts as a preface to the translation itself. There is much here that is of great value and requires unpacking, both as a document about the nature of "business or mercantile support" for "Orientalist research" and as an exemplary discourse about the new field of knowledge. Of special interest to us, in the latter context, is Hastings's use of the word "sublime."[87] The words "sublime" and "sublimity" occur thrice in the introduction: "a thousand sublime descriptions," "elevated to a track of sublimity," and "of a sublimity of conception." The context in which the second of these phrases occurs is particularly interesting:

> Many passages will be found obscure, many will seem redundant; others will be found cloathed with ornaments of fancy unsuited to our taste, and some elevated to a track of sublimity into which our habits of judgment will find it difficult to pursue them. (7)

The use of the term "sublimity" is meant to suggest not only an elevated aesthetic moment but also the presence in the source text of a form of representation that had gained immense currency through the many reprints of, and commentaries on, Boileau's French translation of Longinus's essay on the sublime

(*Peri Hupsous*).[88] More specifically, Hastings use of "the sublime" with reference to Hindu texts relies on Edmund Burke's immensely influential essay on the beautiful and the sublime published in 1757. However, unlike Burke, later a Member of Parliament and leading advocate of the impeachment proceedings against Hastings, who read the British imperial encounter with India as a sublime process of colonization,[89] Hastings does not pursue historical and cultural difference and, overawed by the object of his reading, simply conflates the Indian and the English/European sublimes. What is clear from the passage cited above is the concept of an "alternative" sublime, a sublime not quite in tune with the discourses of the Enlightenment, which would have preferred not texts of fancy but of the imagination.[90]

When we return to Wilkins's translation we find that the word *sublime* is used twice: once in lecture IX and again in lecture XIV. In both these instances the person speaking is Krishna himself who, as the Hindu God, would arouse in the Hindu spectator the necessary feelings of the sublime. An examination of Wilkins's use of *sublime* is therefore mandatory at this stage of our exposition.

In the first usage the translated phrase reads "sublime and immaculate" (78). The Sanskrit original is *pavitram idam uttamam.* The two key substantives are in the neuter gender and in the nominative and accusative case respectively. The deictic *idam* ("this") is also declined in the accusative. Literally these words may be rendered as "purifier this supreme." Wilkins, however, has translated *pavitram* ("purifier") as "immaculate" and *uttamam* as "sublime." No other major translator since has translated *uttamam* as "sublime" though Barbara Stoler Miller gives the ninth chapter the subheading "The Sublime Mystery." A quick glance at nine translations confirms this observation: "supreme Purifier, this" (Annie Besant), "it is the best means of sanctification" (T. Telang), "a supreme purifier in this" (Edgerton), "supreme sanctity" (Radhakrishnan), "distilling the purest essence" (Zaehner), "it is the supreme purifier" (Kees Bolle), "the highest purifier" (Herman), "a supreme purifier, this" (Sergeant), "the ultimate purification" (van Buitenen). At this stage of his discourse Krishna is concerned with the "most mysterious secret," the mysteries of creation, with his own "terrible" self as part of it. Wilkins's use of the word *sublime*, it seems, is meant to prepare the reader for the divine manifestation of Krishna's self and the very real issues surrounding the means by which this "truth" can be represented. What Krishna offers is a series of metaphors with the use of the copula to indicate oneness of being: "I am the sacrifice; I am the worship; I am the spices . . .":

> ahaṃ kratur ahaṃ yajñaḥ
> svadhā 'ham aham auṣadham . . .
> aham agnir ahaṃ hutam . . .
> vedyaṃ pavitram oṃkāra . . . (9. 16–17).

The second usage of the sublime occurs as Krishna continues to expand on Sankhya theory in lecture XIV: "I will now reveal unto thee a most sublime knowledge":

> param bhūyah pravakṣyāmi
> jñānānāṃ jñānam uttamam

The phrase translated by Wilkins into "sublime knowledge" is *jñānam uttamam*. Again the Sanskrit word that is translated as "sublime" is *uttamam*, a superlative normally translated as highest, supreme, most excellent, best, and so on by other translators. Indeed Sanskrit has no separate word for "sublime" as such that cannot be subsumed under a whole host of superlatives, although the adjective *ucca/atyucca* (high or lofty) with the intensive use of the prefix *ati* to mean "exceedingly" or "transcending" may be used for the sublime experience. In some ways *atyucca* could be read as "exceedingly great," which is not unlike Derrida's own definition of Kant's use of the term: the colossal, the absolutely large, and so on.[91] Wilkins, therefore, stands apart with his translation of the superlative as "sublime," which is probably as much a reflection of the fellow Orientalist William Jones's own sense of the Oriental sublime as it is a response to the highly nuanced nature of the Sanskrit original. In fact, what I am foreshadowing is the leap made by early Orientalists such as Wilkins into the Indian sublime through the then fashionable interest in the sublime in England and Europe. Since the category of the sublime had not undergone the kind of rigorous analysis we find in Kant, its use by English translators and administrators reflect uses more commonly associated with Burke, Dennis, and Boileau's "Longinus."[92] Nevertheless, under Burke's powerful influence the sublime had already become a category associated with intense aesthetic experiences that the mind found impossible to bring to fullness through any adequate representation. However, as we have seen, Burke had adopted an essentially sensationist theory of the sublime when he referred to terror as the most intense of its sources: "Whatever is fitted in any sort to excite the ideas of pain, and danger, that is to say, whatever is in any sort terrible, or is conversant about terrible objects, or operates in a manner analogous to terror, is the source of the *sublime*; that is, it is productive of the strongest emotion which the mind is capable of feeling," wrote Burke.[93] Though Burke and Longinus (the latter through Boileau, Addison, and Dennis) are the precursor theoreticians of the sublime here, its application to an alien culture suggests precisely the connection between the sublime and the unimaginable that underlined its usage back in eighteenth-century England. Yet it remained a totally undertheorized and in political terms a highly imperial position. What is missing is indeed Hegel's ideal of the nonrepresentation of the Absolute Spirit in its pure negativity, the gap around which the symbolic order is structured. This is the ideal to which the oral poets of the *Bhagavadgītā* too were attempting to aspire.

Something of this correlate or search for an object is seen in the writings of John Zephaniah Holwell, who in 1767 (ten years after Burke's seminal essay but eighteen years before Wilkins's translation of the *Bhagavadgītā*) had written a book that dealt with the social, religious, and political history of the "Empire of Hindostan" entitled *Interesting Historical Events Relative to the Provinces of Bengal and the Empire of Hindostan.*[94] Holwell, however, was "one of the earliest exponents of British enthusiasm for the Hindu religion"[95] and must be used with both caution and detachment. In spite of this what strikes me immediately is that even as Holwell glorifies Hinduism and emphasizes its monotheism, he shows considerable familiarity with eighteenth-century discussions of the sublime. And in fact Holwell's use of the sublime is much more varied than Wilkins's and Hastings's both better intellects and deeper thinkers. Examining one of the Hindu *śāstras* where the creator and his creation are defined, Holwell begins, "The foregoing simple and sublime descriptions of the Supreme Being"(66). Since the section referred to deals with the indefinable characteristics of the creator, the use of the sublime to designate the creator is not unlike Kant's own classic example from the Bible in which believers are warned that they should not "make graven images" because the object of these graven images is not given to iconic representations. According to Holwell, that prohibition from the Book of Exodus is varied in the *śāstras* to "Thou shalt not make enquiry into the essence and nature of the existence of the Eternal One, by what law he governs" (66). Other examples drawn from a much wider use of the word sublime may be cited here: "How much more rational and sublime the text of Bramah" (70); "We have seen that the original divine institutes of Bramah are simple and sublime, comprehending the whole compass of all that is" (76–77); "his fourth sublime book" (97); and "[i]n the same sublime allegorical manner, hath Bramah described the creation of Surjee" (101).

Although Holwell and other early British Orientalists such as Alexander Dow and Nathaniel Brassey Halhed were keen to discover connections between Hinduism and Christianity, sometimes with excessive zeal ("Hinduism, in Holwell, reads like Milton with transmigration," writes Thomas R. Trautmann[96]), their accounts nevertheless show how the late eighteenth century grasped the essential problematic of cultural representation in India through a not yet fully theorized concept of the sublime. This concept, over two centuries later, may enable us to understand some of the crucial metaphysical determinants of that culture. It might also lead to a much more meaningful theory of devotional poetics. Without suggesting in any way that the sublime as the second half of the eighteenth century understood the term fully explains the special nature of Indian cultural texts, I would nevertheless argue that the definitions of concepts such as Brahman, moksha, dharma, and karma we have advanced may be grasped best through an understanding of the sublime. However, in making this theoretical intervention, I do not want to reduce Hindu culture to one hermeneutic or to one cultural paradigm (whether indigenous to the culture or alien; whether critically self-aware or Orientalist). My aim in fact is to draw upon theories of the sublime so as to make way for a more serious examination of one aspect of the literary output of this massive civilization. This literary output, as we have seen, also stresses generic fluidity over generic specificity and anticipates the proposition that theories of center, of a world locked into meaning and defined in terms of a metaphysics of presence, themselves require reexamining.

A Matter of Feeling and Emotion

Devotional or bhakti literature returns us to the crucial category of emotional response and engagement with God. In some ways devotional texts may be read in terms of Thomas Coburn's concept of dynamic retellings of scriptural texts.[97] In these retellings, as Philip Lutgendorf has pointed out, the speaking selves become "participants in the events they describe" as well as demonstrate considerable "delight in systematic physical description."[98] The discourses of bhakti then insinuate a dramatic shift in the ways in which belief itself begins to be articulated and the idea of God internalized. Not surprisingly the working definition of Hinduism we used earlier in this chapter comes straight out of bhakti discourses. Yet bhakti itself is both an ideology and a genre, both politics and aesthetics. Its dominant modes—as *nirguṇa* or *saguṇa*, as primarily monotheistic or polytheistic—have led to considerable debates about how the ideology of bhakti connects with caste and class. At the same time its generic orientation—as a form of literature marked by considerable figurative unities—opens up a whole new space for questions about how God as the sublime object of desire may be given linguistic utterance. The political dimension of bhakti is captured powerfully in David Lorenzen's account of bhakti religion in North India:

> Rarely if ever do the subaltern (Gramsci) or nonprivileged (Weber) classes of society either wholeheartedly accept the ruling ideology or knuckle under elite domination without some form of (usually covert) resistance. . . . In North India, *nirguṇ* bhakti has served as one of the more significant forms of ideological resistance of these classes.[99]

Lorenzen also examines *saguṇa* bhakti, which he links more directly with the ideology of higher-caste Hindus. For him *nirguṇa* and *saguṇa* forms of bhakti are different from each other both epistemologically and socially. There is, suggests Lorenzen, a much more active contestation on the part of *nirguṇī* poets of the "religious authority of the Vedas and their Brahmin exponents," [100] for instance. However, while the social differences between the poets of these two traditions are considerable, their epistemological differences are less dramatic than Lorenzen makes them out to be. Even the pallbearer of *saguṇa* bhakti, the great Tulsidas, was "closer to the spiritual sensibility of the *sant* poet of the *nirguṇ* 'school' than is commonly understood," writes Philip Lutgendorf.[101] Here I am in agreement with John Stratton Hawley, who gives much less weight to the differences and emphasizes the interconnections and continuities between *nirguṇa* and *saguṇa* schools of thought.[102] About these matters we'll have more to say later. For the moment if we accept bhakti as a multifaceted discourse characterized by the language of emotionalism and the enunciation of specific speaking positions (of weavers, bureaucrats, leather-workers, or cotton-carders) we could then go on to examine a range of texts to see how the Indian sublime gets expressed in them. In speaking about the literary work of art we need to keep Stephen Greenblatt's warning firmly in mind though:

> [A]rt does not simply exist in all cultures; it is made up along with other products, practices, discourses of a given culture. (In practice, "made up" means inherited, transmitted, altered, modified, reproduced far more than it means invented: as a rule there is very little invention in culture.)[103]

An important text on the subject of emotionalism and the discourses of devotion is Friedhelm Hardy's monumental study of *viraha-bhakti*.[104] However, admirable as this book is, its focus is primarily on a pragmatic, and largely non-theoretical examination of the growth of religious emotionalism with special reference to the figure of Krishna in South India. Hardy's concern is with establishing in a relatively straightforward manner the effects of emotion in the religious life of a community. Combining the strengths of a thorough Sanskritist with the skills of the student of literary criticism, Hardy underlines the continuity of a devotional tradition in Hindu religious thought. Yet even as such a continuity is demonstrated, Hardy detects a much more decisive shift from intellectualism to emotionalism in the great ninth-century compendium of Hindu myths and devotionalism, the *Bhāgavata Purāṇa*. Between the *Viṣṇu Purāṇa*—the last *purāṇa* in which intellectual bhakti is dominant—and the *Bhāgavata Purāṇa*, argues Hardy, there is no transitional or mediating text that would have prepared us for the quite revolutionary foregrounding of the religion of love found in the latter. Suddenly the discourses of emotion and grief, of passion and participation make their entry into Puranic tales of cosmogony and devotion. In the absence of a clear transitional text, the appearance of these themes can only be explained through some kind of dramatic cross-fertilization that must have occurred in the intervening period. Friedhelm Hardy isolates the songs of the Alvar mystics as exemplifying the nature of this "new religion" as it emerged in the vernaculars. The "new religion" in turn transformed the "character of intellectual bhakti" we have come to associate directly with the middle sections of the *Bhagavadgītā*.

The relationship between high Sanskrit culture and the indigenous or vernacular is then much more complex (as it has to be in matters of cultural transmission) and is not simply a matter of "regional dilutions of Sanskrit models" (44), the generally accepted Orientalist reading of the phenomenon. The interactions were clearly a two-way process since the vernaculars, finally, invaded the hallowed discourses of high Sanskrit culture. Because the phenomenon of bhakti is so intriguing and exciting, Hardy's question is worth repeating here: "*Why* has the phenomenon of emotionalism not been studied more extensively?" (46). The answers are many and varied depending very much upon the nature of our archive and our point of view. To begin with, it should be obvious that a normative Hindu ideology based on a highly intellectual conception of self and God as found in the canonical texts would have rejected emotionalism outright because it lacked mental rigor. The same ideology would have seen emotionalism as a threat that could open up levels of desire and sexuality that the classical tradition had relegated to secular texts such as the *Kāma Sūtra* and related manuals of love. Its repression, then, was a function of a "canonical imperative" and, as a consequence, the religio-emotional complex did not "penetrate Indian conceptual awareness" and, moreover, did not lead to any thorough-going reflection on it. Hardy's own theorization of *viraha-bhakti* is in many ways an attempt to spell out, to bring into the open, a history of religious emotionalism that an earlier classical Sanskrit (and later Orientalist) ideology had effectively silenced. The growth of emotionalism, especially through the writing of a counter but parallel narrative around Krishna's passion for the gopis, is then traced at length by Hardy with an exhaustive analysis of how the mysticism of the Alvars, initially fertilized by the Northern tradition, (re)invested the North Indian religious corpus with an emotional bhakti discourse. While Hardy's work cannot be faulted on grounds of scholarship, his theorization remains grounded in a literary criticism that forces us to read devotional narratives in an allegorical fashion. In this interpretation, outpourings of personal desire continue to be read as a coded language in which the speaker says one thing and means another: where there is profane love read religious love, where there is love of man read love of God, and so on. It is suggested, moreover, that this reliance on the principles of correspondence theory is, in many ways, endemic to the culture and necessary if the boundlessly frantic nature of emotions is to be kept in check, which is what Hardy himself does. The real picture is more complex since instead of opening up the canon through an economy of the emotional, the entry of the emotional into the religious domain in fact had the opposite effect. It spawned a reading practice designed to contain the new religiosity within norms of reading that the priestly caste endorsed so that the new religion of emotion would not threaten the established religion. Friedhelm Hardy's study understands this line of argument. What it doesn't understand as well are the metaphysical and aesthetic issues in the ideology of bhakti that underpinned this religion of emotionalism. To get to the heart of this ideology (about which I shall have more to say later), our first question has to do with the relationship between the subject-devotee and the object-God. Is there something in the nature of bhakti that demonstrates a hitherto hidden impulse in Indian culture generally? If we examine the literary corpus of bhakti, can we detect a much larger principle at work here? Are there in fact quite specific ontological questions at stake here? What, for instance, is the nature of the divine object in Hinduism that bhakti tries to represent? Can this object be represented anyway? Contrary to the implied argument of Hardy that the religion of emotionalism eases one into the problematic of self and God, what the real discourse of emotionalism raises is another, ontological, question about the nature of representation in Hindu culture. I would want to argue that the God of bhakti—as Brahman—ultimately defies representation even though there is a constant tendency for it to be displaced by a lesser God (Brahman in the masculine) who is then troped into avataric icons through Brahma's creator counterpart Vishnu. For the fact is that neither the devotee's relationship to God nor God himself can ever be represented. In its place what we get is an "inadequation," a mismatch, a lack of an objective correlative, and, finally, a failure to present the unpresentable in spite of the excessive symbolization. There is something deeper going on here as the genre of bhakti gets dragged into a larger, much more pervasive Hindu narrative of imaging the unimaginable. We must, therefore, move away from explanations in terms of the principle of correspondences or of allegory to the sublime for a critique of this genre and use this trope to uncover and retheorize what "two hundred years of Western Indology" (12) had not provided us with. A fundamental question we ask is: what is the Indian sublime for Indians themselves and how is the genre of bhakti linked to it? Before we can take up this challenge, we must address the issue of comparatist versus nativist theory. My point of departure is G. N. Devy's provocative book on cultural amnesia because it is an important critique of the suitability of the kind of comparative methodology I use in this book. [105]

At the risk of some oversimplification Devy may be read as a nativist scholar who wants to pursue a double agenda. The first is to strengthen the claims of vernacular literatures against the great Sanskrit and Sanskrit-derived tradition, mother tongues, in fact, against the acquired "father tongue" of Sanskrit. His second aim is to pursue the argument that texts generate their own theory and *deśī* or *bhāṣā* (vernacular) texts have their rich theories through which they should be read. From Devy's perspective, the argument I advance below would be yet another instance of the hegemony of colonial regimes of literary criticism and theory (and hence Orientalist in a new guise). What may concern him even more is the fact that though my archive is largely *bhāṣā*, I do not use *bhāṣā* theories, except in a fleeting and largely anecdotal fashion, to read *bhāṣā* literature. Why might Devy be so angry about this approach? To begin with Devy is convinced that *bhāṣā* literatures produced vibrant models of criticism that should be the starting point for any reading of those literatures.

Since texts are their own theory, we should begin by listening to the critical voices embedded in the texts themselves. But in making this argument, persuasive as it is, Devy's case is powerful not because *bhāṣā* theories would yield better results but because any deference to nativist theory is both a radical affirmation of one's own culture and a demonstration of its efficacy in a postcolonial world. The real lines of confrontation is not really between a colonial regime of reading that legitimated Sanskrit poetics and then its own (that is English literature) and vernacular theory but rather between a prescriptive, alien Orientalism and a resourceful but neglected nativism. *Bhāṣā* literatures then push the dichotomy to its limits since *bhāṣā* literatures are as native as you can get, especially if they are written in vernaculars that are in a subaltern relationship to the language of the ruling classes, be it Sanskrit, Persian, court Urdu, English, or high Hindi. I will return to Devy toward the end of this book but I invoke him here because I have to state quite explicitly that in matters of comparative theory (and not English literary criticism, which seems to be the target of Devy's own analysis) any attempt to retrieve a nativist hermeneutic on the grounds that it would somehow lead us to the truth of the texts must be highly suspect. Moreover, what theory attempts to do is not proscribe questions of value but make *bhāṣā* just as legitimate an object of knowledge as the *mārga* or canonical tradition. My aim is to explore questions for which, at least in my reading, answers have not been forthcoming, or which have been placed in the too difficult basket because these questions take us to archives whose cultural otherness make them difficult texts to handle. In an attempt to blast open the archive once again, I will have to part company with Devy on theoretical grounds but will remain with him on the issue that *bhāṣā* texts constitute a fascinating body of material in need of rigorous critique and analysis. It is for this reason that I move from a nativist hermeneutic to the comparatist by way of the aesthetics of the sublime.

The Textual Tradition

Any number of proof texts may be used to support the theoretical assumptions that underlie the foregoing account of the Indian sublime. The starting point of my textual analysis will have to be the *Bhagavadgītā* to which the next chapter will be devoted almost in its entirety. From there on my proof texts will be devotional verse from the devotional traditions of medieval India written in Sanskrit and in Old and Middle Hindi. Toward the end of this book one exemplary poet, Kabir, will be used more extensively to establish the links between the poetry of devotion and the sublime.[106] The attractiveness of the poet Kabir (over and above say Surdas or Mirabai or Namdev) lies in his very problematic status as a devotional poet. What did he really believe in? Did he try to give Brahman a material basis by linking it to questions of equity and fairness among the lower Hindu castes thereby positing, inter alia, a corporeal, particularized subject that remains detached from the Absolute? Was he in fact a *nirguṇa* (one whose devotion is directed to a quality-less image of God) or a *saguṇa* (one whose devotion is toward a personal God in an essentially dualistic framework) poet? But beyond answering these questions, the turn to Kabir allows us to address in highly complex ways the whole process by which Hinduism acquired a fully developed theistic base. As a recent convert to Islam Kabir hybridizes the local and the grand Sanskrit tradition. From the latter Kabir critically takes the ground of Hindu philosophical thinking: How can the One be represented to consciousness in language when this One is beyond any kind of "adequation?" How can one create an experience beyond the limits of language? Like others before him, it seems that Kabir too was finally confronted with the object of devotion—Brahman—as something quite beyond representation. Although Kabir stresses a *nirguṇa* or quality-less conception of God—in this respect his sublime is untouched by any form of avataric mediation—the distinction between *nirguṇa* and *saguṇa* bhakti is not particularly helpful when it comes to understanding devotionalism. The desire to unite with the First Principle, which is the cornerstone of the Indian sublime, is no different whether one approaches it through a quality-less conception of Brahman or through the mediation of Rama or Krishna. As we shall see later, in this desire for unity it is not unusual to find, especially in the domain of the literary, the subject rechannelling his/her desire by and large through the metaphorics of sexual ravishment and love-longing.[107] The feelings engendered through these metaphors are mixed, combining, as Schiller wrote about the sublime, melancholy and rapture.[108] To continue to insist upon a *nirguṇa/saguṇa* distinction beyond what is necessary for purposes of a social or literary history is not very helpful. In any religious enactment of the law of desire, the transformation of the object of desire back into some kind of an anthropomorphism (as a personalized God for instance) is fundamental to the process itself. All that happens in these substantializations is that in theory at any rate the sublime gets displaced by a lower principle that outwardly contradicts one of its own fundamental laws, ie., that the sublime object as Brahman cannot be represented to begin with.

Theories of the sublime have, historically, been readings of a particular aesthetic phenomenon through categories of the mind. To return to Kant, the sublime, after all, is possible only because reason momentarily gives full power to the imagination but imposes its law just when imagination is about to embrace the sublime in all its apocalyptic plenitude: "I am become death, the destroyer of the universe," says Krishna at the moment of his sublime expression in the *Bhagavadgītā*. This is heavy, disembodied, intellectual stuff. Against this form of disembodiment, what is most interesting about the bhakti phenomenon is the effort to bring metaphors of the body into discussions about the nature of the mind's communion with God. One of the means by which the body is involved in these religious practices is through the language of Tantra. Many commentators, both Indian and Western, have attempted to marginalize Tantric practices as something aberrant or unworthy of the great traditions of Hinduism, though it seems beyond doubt that it was through Tantra that the submerged forms of Buddhism, that strictly deconstructive philosophy of the mind, found a voice yet again on Indian soil. Tantric practices take the body very seriously, both as a site of the movement of "mystical energy," and as an equal partner of the mind. Tantric energy drew its strength from its associations with Shakti, Shiva's androgynous principle of creativity, which in itself was nothing less than an insistence on sexuality as the source of creation, and sex generally as the ground metaphor of desire. An extreme version of this is the Shakta *vāmamārga* ("the left-hand path"), which placed strong emphasis on sexual acts including the control of the flow of semen during sex. The use of Tantric terminology and structures by bhakti poets like Kabir is part of a system of signification that recognizes corporeality as the cornerstone of devotionalism. It is interesting that Hatha-yoga, Kabir's preferred version of Tantra, sees the state of *sahaja samādhi* or the subject's "spontaneous" state of union with Godhead as a function of the movement of the life-force through the various nerve-plexuses or centers of the human body. Much of the body-geography of the saint-singers or *santas* (etymologically, the present participle of the verb to be, *as*[109]) of North India, including their highly cryptic discourses and antilanguages—*sandhyā-bhāṣā* ("twilight language") and *ulṭabāṃsī* ("inverted language")—become meaningful once the body itself is seen as an integral part of the cognitive process. To borrow a phrase from Slavoj Žižek these discourses are so absurd that they materialize their own absurdity. The subversive force of Tantric sexuality is not lost on Kabir since alongside sexual desire there is also the desire to control both mental and physical processes. In this respect, the medieval devotional strategist Gorakhnath formulated the philosophy of *dvaitādvaita-vilakṣaṇa-vāda* or "duality-nonduality-nondifference-thesis" (an earlier formulation of Ronald Inden's "ontology of plurality-with-unity"), which provided Kabir with an important frame of reference with which to reread a presumed (but inherently false) distinction between dualist *saguṇa* and nondualist *nirguṇa*.

It is not uncommon to find theories of bhakti that link the religion of devotion to more general material conditions of being. It has been argued, for instance, that bhakti was primarily an anti-establishment religion that triumphed precisely because its roots were in low culture. While there may be some truth in this, as A. K. Ramanujan's admirable little book demonstrated many years ago,[110] the history of Indian religious beliefs by and large offers a rather different picture and one that suggests that both "the general interpretation of bhakti by historians of religion and anthropologists and the communal interpretation by Hindu historians have to be rejected."[111] This is van der Veer's claim but he doesn't elaborate on this. My own understanding of the bhakti phenomenon persuades me that no religious movement of such magnitude could have been successful if the priestly caste had not very quickly incorporated the new religion into its own ritual. Bhakti's symbolic incorporation in the many temples built in praise of individual Gods shows that the Brahmins may not have found it so threatening in spite of the strong anti-Brahmin tenor of much of bhakti verse, especially those designated as *nirguṇa* verse. Of course, this is not to say that Indian tradition is by its very nature assimilative, "incorporating and amalgamating any and all practices" within a linear narrative; rather the procedures of incorporation work on the basis of an ongoing and systemic tension between individual or group (here caste) self-expression and its *a priori* negation by the master narrative of the civilization.[112] In this version, incorporation presupposes, at some stage, an original clash of ideologies that is then smothered over through specific sociocultural and political instrumentalities. It is a telling testimony to the strength of Brahmanism that low-caste bhakti poets began to accept their roles in a karmically controlled world through a none too sophisticated process that M. N. Srinivas referred to as the process of Sanskritization.[113] Perhaps the most striking example of this process is to be found in the lives of the Maharashtrian Untouchable bhakti poets of the Mahar caste such as Chokamela, Karmamela, Banka, and Nirmala.[114] Chokamela, the best known of these poets, lived in the early part of the fourteenth century and like all Mahars was excluded from participating in temple worship. Chokamela was undeterred by this prohibition, and his self-proclaimed love for God led him to claim that the Divine could be approached through the religion of love. In Chokamela's poetry there is certainly acrimony toward God for his own terrible life as an Untouchable but the solution to redemption is not social change but "the merging of oneself with the Divine through bhakti."[115] In the following poem the poet resigns himself to a life of both self-denial and social exclusion but not before, it seems, he has made a decisive poetic intervention into the conventional discourses of devotionalism:

I am your Mahārs' Mahar
I am hungry
For your leftovers
I am hopeful
I am the servant of your slaves
For your leavings
I've brought my basket.[116]

This is poetry of forgiveness even as it proceeds to proclaim the subject's condition in terms of a karmic inevitability. The poet makes no request for change in his social condition, nor does he denounce the totally discriminatory Hindu world order; instead what we are presented with is the usual bhakti quietism, where the suppliant devotee brings to his Lord a humble basket in which to carry offerings already made by others. Elsewhere Chokamela connects his caste with the sins of his previous birth: "this impurity is the fruit of our past."[117] This sentiment gets a more sweeping treatment in another poem:

> The Vedas are polluted; the Śāstras are polluted; the Purāṇas are full of pollution.
> The soul is polluted; the oversoul is polluted; the body is full of pollution.
> Brahmā is polluted; Vishnu is polluted; Śaṇkar is full of pollution.
> Birth is polluted; death is polluted.
> Chokhā says: there's pollution at the beginning and at the end.[118]

In Chokhamela's son Karmamela we get a greater sense of defiance and, it seems, a less positive reading of the eschatological possibilities of the Brahmanical worldview:

> You made us impure
> I don't know why Lord
> We've eaten leftovers all our life
> Doesn't that trouble you
> Our house is stocked with rice and yogurt
> How do you refuse it
> Choka's Karma Mela asks
> Why did you give me birth.[119]

The positions of Chokamela and his son Karmamela demonstrate that a radical resocialization or even a proto-Sanskritization of the self was not an alternative, even though the poets themselves were keenly conscious of their contradictory status as at once devotees of God and social rejects. Although radically questioned, *varṇa* or caste remains a social absolute that cannot be transcended. Not surprisingly the symbolic structure that all bhakti poets work through presupposes an understanding of the ineffable mystery of Brahman. In this reading the "I" (in whatever social or caste form) can find its ground of being, its "I-ness," only by trying to achieve the impossible condition of Brahman. The deflection of an urgent need to resocialize in the case of Untouchable bhakti poets is met with a prior discourse that on the one hand gives a language of religious empowerment ("Sanskritization") to the dispossessed and on the other leaves them where they are. Yet even this is, in a way, a radical achievement because the appropriation of a subject position itself would not have been possible if bhakti were not a religion of emotionalism that had effectively rewritten the old economic relationship between Bhagavan (literally "patron" or "master") and bhakta (as owner and producer) into Bhagavan and bhakta as Brahman and "suppliant devotee."[120] Against the incorporation of the lower castes as speakers on behalf of Hinduism through a religion of emotionalism, the point needs to be made that bhakti has not been read by the Indian Untouchable as a precursor moment in their own struggle toward political legitimation. Indeed, the absence of any agonistic or *virodha* poetics in bhakti has led to the disavowal of bhakti as a precursor moment in contemporary Dalit Sahitya (Untouchable writing) itself. As Gokhale-Turner has observed, "[Since] for the bhakti tradition no social solution to Untouchability is possible . . . the very question [of Dalit empowerment] is irrelevant." Consequently, Dalit writers have not turned to bhakti as a radical instance of social mobilization. The opposite is in fact the case. Except for occasional references to Chokamela and Karmamela ("The blood of Chokha Mela/Runs through my veins," writes Dalit poet Harish Bansode[121]) in their literature, contemporary Dalit intellectuals, by and large, have repudiated bhakti and have instead returned either to the teachings of the Buddha or to Marxism for epistemologies of social change.

Although many bhakti poets were from the lower castes—tailors, carpenters, potters, gardeners, shopkeepers, barbers, and even Mahars[122]—their reaction against casteism was nevertheless, as R. V. Oturkar has pointed out, primarily conceptual in character and "severely confined to the field of religious thinking."[123] Bhakti poets were, therefore, not great social reformers even though they often spoke extensively about questions of equity. For the fact remains that social change is a matter of power and power—both intellectual and political—lay in the hands of the upper castes. Given the fact that bhakti cannot be seen as an action-oriented social movement (for reasons we have outlined), its radical fervor has to be located at the level of the kinds of discursive choices these poets made and especially in their radical use of the vernacular for self-expression. Bhakti is then the great moment in *deśī* or *bhāṣā* writing when the Sanskrit *mārga* tradition is seriously contested. At the philosophical level what is at stake is the capacity of the disempowered to enter into the age-old debate about self and Brahman through "nativist" theories and practices that included working through a personal God, the language of emotionalism, and local Tantric practices. Both Eknath (1523–99), a Brahmin, and Chokamela and Kabir, who were lower caste, could therefore entertain the possibility of embracing their personal Gods. Yet it is precisely the not so complete disavowal of the intellect and the deference to practices that presuppose sophisticated cognitive judgments that makes bhakti poetry itself so very exciting. The complex ways in which Indian devotional texts then reflect the larger problematic of self and God within an aesthetics of the sublime will be explored at length in this book. But our immediate task is to examine *the* canonical text on the subject in the context of the paradigm of the renouncer and the man-in-the-world. This we do in the next chapter.

CHAPTER TWO

Two Truths Are Told

Prologues to the Swelling Act

In matters of devotion, and in much else besides, the Hindu orthodoxy valorized the renouncer's view of the world. Retreat from the world was valued (outwardly at any rate) because it signified the power of abstinence and other-worldliness in one's search for the religion of interiority. It was argued that real devotion was possible only through the symbolic adoption of the renouncer's discourse. Such was the force of the renouncer-ideal in orthodox Hinduism that Louis Dumont used it to identify the "secret of Hinduism":

> [T]he secret of Hinduism may be found in the dialogue between the renouncer and the man-in-the-world. . . . There are two kinds of men in Hindu India, those that live in the world and those that have renounced it.[1]

The binary is perhaps far too simplistic because no culture can cope with two such hostile groups. Even so, the dialogue between the renouncer and the man-in-the-world (the secret after all may be found in dialogue, says Dumont) surely has quite subversive possibilities. The dichotomy that both Dumont and, as we shall note later, Heesterman observed derive in part from sets of abstract cultural oppositions documented in early Sanskrit texts that classified dharma as *pravṛttidharma* (the dharma of the real, of lived experience) and *nivṛttidharma* (the dharma of the nonreal that transcended spatial or temporal limits). The dramatic manner in which the texts offer these distinctions seems to suggest that in classical Hindu culture these two types of dharmas (or "arche-dharmas") were meant to subsume all branches of social activity: in theory one either followed the dharma of the man-in-the-world (*pravṛtti-dharma*) or the dharma of the renouncer (*nivṛttidharma*). When we turn to Monier-Williams for a definition of these two terms, we get a clearer picture of the uses of these words in everyday social discourses. Thus *pravṛtti* is defined as "moving onwards, advance, progress . . . coming forth, appearance, manifestation . . . activity, exertion, efficacy . . . active life (as opposed to *ni-vṛtti*), etc."[2] and *nivṛtti* as "returning, return . . . ceasing, cessation . . . leaving off, abstaining or desisting from (ablative) . . . ceasing from worldly acts, inactivity, rest repose (as opposed to *pra-vṛtti*), etc."[3] Through the Latin cognate *vertere* "to turn" we may legitimately conclude that the words are etymologically related to "extrovert" (literally, "turning outwards") and "introvert" (literally, "turning inwards") and were not meant to be just highly specialized terms limited to philosophical discourses. In fact one of their best-known uses is to be found in the epic tradition:

> Nārāyaṇa has said there is a norm which is characterized by *pravṛtti* and on it are based the entire three-worlds, moving and non-moving. The norm characterized by *nivṛtti*, is the unmanifest, eternal norm.
>
> Prajāpati has said there is a norm characterized by *pravṛtti*. *Pravṛtti* is repeated returning (to samsara), whereas *nivṛtti* is the highest refuge. The sage who is intent upon true knowledge and always perceives pleasantness and unpleasantness [as being the same] is completely occupied with *nivṛtti*. He goes to the highest refuge.[4]

If the three worlds are based on the principle of *pravṛtti* it would follow that the spatiotemporal order (expressed as *triloka* and *kalpa*) cannot exist outside of a dharma of action or work. In Narayana's classification, *nivṛtti* is presented as a *svadharma* (a self-dharma) necessary for personal enlightenment. The state of *nivṛtti* is seen as a precondition for union with the "eternal Brahman" while *pravṛtti* is part of the process of creation. But no social system could have survived if these principles were actually put into practice. The Brahmins, for instance, endorsed *nivṛtti* as the goal of life but depended on the ruling class, the Kshatriyas, for patronage. At the same time the Kshatriyas, the rulers for whom living-in-the-world was absolutely crucial, symbolically adopted the norm of *nivṛtti* because renunciation had such power in culture and had been, in theory at least, so systematically valorized by the Brahmins. Thus the intermediate category of *vānaprastha*, the third, forest stage in the ideal development of the Hindu subject, was often adopted by the Kshatriya to symbolically endorse the power of renunciation as it represented a "compromise between 'life-in-the-world' and the solitary existence of an ascetic."[5] In the ambiguous setting of the forest the *pravṛtti* of the *gṛhastha* (the second, householder, phase) combined with the *nivṛtti* of the *brahmacarya* (the first phase) and the *saṃnyāsin* (the fourth phase). Rama, the prince of the dynasty of Raghu, accepts banishment (that is, embraces *nivṛtti*) but continues to offer sacrifice, is not free from the imperatives of *kāma*, desire, and stresses the importance of *pravṛtti-dharma*. What the actual evidence contradicts is the presumed universality of a theory that divides Hindu society so neatly into two mutually exclusive orders. And, indeed, the ambiguous appropriation of *nivṛtti* and *pravṛtti* by the various castes toward their own ideological ends is surely indicative of the highly fluid manner in which the categories functioned in reality. Not surprisingly, the literature shows many instances of orthodox Brahmanism denigrating renunciation even as the Kshatriyas symbolically embraced it. In other words, the apparent conflation of Brahmin-ascetic with *nivṛtti* (the precise history of this conflation is not too clear) hides a much more complicated process at work in Hindu culture where, one thinks, abstractions were constantly linked to contingent historical or social needs. Madeleine Biardeau, in fact, goes to the extent of saying quite conclusively that in practice the Brahmins remained distrustful of *nivṛtti* and made no secret of their antagonism toward it.[6] It is thus not surprising that the orthodoxy could find little difficulty, finally, in accepting in general terms bhakti's "reconciliation" of the ideal of *saṃnyāsa* and secular life.

It should be clear from what we have said that no system of classification can be discussed in isolation from the social structures that produce the system. The model of the renouncer and the man-in-the-world, therefore, must be connected to two broad sections of Indian society: the privileged twice-born castes and the nonprivileged. The ruling class whose dharma was most clearly defined, the Kshatriyas, aligned themselves with the other twice-born caste, the Brahmins. What this alliance demonstrates is that the neat opposition between the renouncer and the man-in-the-world was in reality no more than an abstraction, a framework that allowed for much more complex social alignments because in terms of their normative social affiliations Brahmins and Kshatriyas should have held divergent views. Technically, *nivṛtti* (the presumed Brahmin-ideal) was defined as a suprasocial "system" that constructed the renouncer as "an antisocial entity" who lived outside of society and yet was parasitic on it for sustenance. In its extreme form renunciation was linked to ascetic power that, through *tapas* or severe practice of self-denial, could rival the strength of Gods. The number of stories about Gods being weary of the disruptive power of capricious renouncers with immense power is very vast indeed. The "disruptive" power of the renouncer remains one of the targets of the Krishna of the *Bhagavadgītā* too who gives sacrifice (action or work) and renunciation the same goal, both of which emanate from Krishna himself. Yet it is clear that Krishna's own solution is to unite *nivṛtti* and *pravṛtti* through the principle of action in inaction, the condition of the *karmaphalatyāga* Yogin who acts without regard to consequences. In such a redefinition of action, the presumed primacy of *nivṛttidharma* is undercut by a redefinition of the Hindu agent who acts without reference to worldly consequences. If we push these concepts even further to the Brahmin authors themselves (the composers of texts such as the *Bhagavadgītā*) we become even more aware of the extent to which Dumont's observation about the *dialogue* between the renouncer and the man-in-the-world had been an ongoing characteristic of Indian culture generally. To mediate social reality and power (or ideology) brahminical culture invested its grand narratives with the competing claims of the renouncer and the man-in-the-world and then attempted to mediate between them. The grand narratives, however, made little distinction between the ideology of Gods and that of humans. Indeed the narratives demand that we must also consider Gods and humans as if they were part of a reciprocal system. It is appropriate, then, to shift gear at this point and consider how Gods fit into this picture.

Behind the claims of the renouncer lie a narrative of intense competition between gods (*deva*s) and demons (*asura*s) in which the gods, and occasionally demigods and mortals too, opt for *tapas* (austere ascetic practice, self-denial) to strengthen their power. *Tapas*, meditation, and renunciation, therefore, occupy positions in the same continuum and as such have been in the habit of displacing each other so that the *tapasvin* (the Yogin who undertakes *tapas*), in some contexts, is identical with the *saṃnyāsin*, the renouncer. But the power that comes through *tapoyajñā* (*Bhagavadgītā* 4.28) as distinct from *saṃnyāsa* has consequences that invariably involve the major Hindu Gods. Thus Ravana, the demonic antihero of the *Rāmāyaṇa*, threatens to destroy the cosmic order soon after obtaining immortality from Brahma after years of intense *tapas*.[7] Vishnu must therefore reincarnate himself to destroy the power of this demon. The use of *tapas* is thus a matter of choice for Ravana (who knows the godlike strength of the *tapasvin*) as his grand aim is to subvert the *nivṛtti/pravṛtti* divide. The case of Ravaṇa also underlines the fact that the dialogue between the renouncer and the man-in-the-world took place between humans, between humans and gods, and between demons and gods. The insight of Dumont (that in Hindu India one is either a renouncer or a man-of-the-world) can thus be projected onto a whole range of Hindu "essences" that implicate both men and gods. We may use the following chart to make the connections more explicit:

A *Deva* (god)	B *Varṇa* (caste)	C *Functions* (social ends)	D *Yoga* (discipline)	E *Metatexts*	F *Acceptance/ Denial*
Brahma	Brahmin	priesthood	*jñāna*	dharma	*pravṛtti*
Vishnu	Kshatriya	kingship	karma	*artha*	*pravṛtti*
Shiva	Vaishya/ Shudra	fertility	bhakti	*kāma*	*nivṛtti*

The trifunctional scheme operating under A, B, C, D, and E, gets transformed into a bifunctional scheme in F. The schema is clearly a bit skewed since, in this highly simplified outline, the chart identifies[8] Shiva with the lower castes when in fact this was not necessarily the case. But insofar as Dionysian Shiva may be opposed to a fundamentally Apollonian Brahma/Vishnu, the functional identity of Shiva with Vaishya/Shudra has some merit. The discipline of bhakti in this scheme gets narrowly linked to Shiva on the one hand and to *nivṛtti* on the other, which can only be partly true. The point of this highly "normative" chart ("normative" in the sense of being "orthodox") is that the nexus between gods and castes is purely schematic or heuristic (perhaps even a necessary starting point) that cannot adequately reflect the complex ways in which *nivṛtti* and *pravṛtti* functioned in society. Indian religious traditions are so complex and open-ended that the distinctive roles of gods eventually collapse and the primacy given to a particular god is often a matter of historical contingencies. The nature of the belief of a particular Hindu community and the positions given to various gods in temples play a crucial role in the ascendancy of a given god. The meteoric rise of the cult of Sai Baba in the Indian diaspora is a case in point. Thus a thorough Vaishnavite and Brahmin such as Tulsidas has no difficulty in making Shiva the "oral amanuensis" of the tale of Rama in his Avadhi *Ramayaṇa* (the *Rāmacaritamānasa*, composed around 1574–80). Shiva's role here is that of the supreme bhakta paying dutiful obeisance to a more powerful God.

The portrayal of Shiva as alternatively man-in-the-world and ascetic symbolizes the pervasiveness of an unresolved tendency in Hindu thought.[9] To a lesser extent, the same ambivalence may be detected in Vishnu, who seems to repose in a state of asceticism as Narayana asleep on his lotus bed and as man-in-the-world in his avataric forms, where he must restore back to order a universe from the brink of collapse. On the other hand, instances of Brahma's asceticism are rare, although not unusual. After all it is Prajapati (a precursor of Brahma) whom the rishi Narayana quotes in the *Mahābhārata* passage cited above to make a defense of *nivṛtti*. Yet Brahma's very ambiguity on this matter and his connection with the Brahmins in the world of mortals explains the paradoxical acceptance of symbolic (not necessarily real) renunciation on the part of Brahmins. Their insistence on outer ritual as somehow affirming inner substance (the *Laws of Manu* 4.7; 6.1ff.; etc.) is indicative of the highly flexible usage of the principle of renunciation by them.[10] Hence J. C. Heesterman concludes:

> As a specialist of religious merit he (the Brahmin) can be called a priest. But in this sense he can only be a priest in virtue of renunciation. Thus the preeminence of the Brahmin is not based on his priesthood but on his being the exponent of the values of renunciation.[11]

The Brahmin's great skill has always been his capacity to market himself so that while sacrifice and ritual (acts that he performs to survive) certainly link him to *pravṛtti*, he must also present himself as the unqualified symbol of the renouncer. This he does by constant acts of purification and by refusing to come into contact with anything that may pollute his self-imposed sense of purity.

It is because of this ambivalence on the part of Brahmins (and it is a necessary ambivalence because *pravṛtti* is essential to keep the social order intact) that the "pure" ascetics of the Buddhists, Jains, and Ajivikas could be seen as unwanted, quotidian aberrations. In spite of the evidence of actual social realities, *nivṛtti* and *pravṛtti* surface as a pervasive binary through which other classificatory systems are defined. Thus in the Araṇyaka Parva [The Forest Book] of the *Mahābhārata* the hunter's reply to a Brahmin when asked to define the properties of *sattva, rajas* and *tamas* takes the following form:

> The *tamas* among them is characterized by ignorance, the *rajas* by motivation, while the *sattva* is declared to be the highest of them because of its great illuminating power. Governed by *tamas* is one who is largely ignorant, stupid, habitually drowsy, witless, ill-looking, darkling, resentful and lazy. Governed by *rajas* is one of ready speech [*pravṛttavākya*] and good advice, friendly, argumentative, eager to learn, arrogant, and proud, O brahmin seer. Governed by *sattva* is one who is illumined, steady, aloof, unprotesting, free from anger, wise and self-controlled. Enlightenment, the mark of *sattva*, is troubled by the ways of the world [*lokavṛtta*]; when one has learned that which is to be learned, he loathes the way of the world. . . . Thereupon all the pairs of opposites are mutually appeased, and he does not exert himself at all in any cause.[12]

In this essentialist and brahminical worldview (which also produced a huge dispossessed class who were barely defined as human) the reified notions of *rajas* and *sattva* correspond to the culture's definitions of *nivṛtti* and *pravṛtti* (which are also, we must repeat, reified categories). But the difficulty of transforming *nivṛtti* into a social fact is equally evident here since it is hard to see how far the ideal of *sattva* could have been endorsed in practice. There is also an overvaluation of asceticism (*nivṛtti*), an aestheticization of it in fact, going on here that has little to do with how the Brahmins really felt toward renunciation. In the hunter's definition above, *sattva* is virtually identical with *nivṛtti* and the characteristics of *rajas* match the presumed qualities of a Brahmin. On this basis it could be argued that the assignation of *rajas* to the Brahmins places them within *pravṛtti*, but the fact that *sattva* is also their natural condition places them within *nivṛtti*. The ontological identification of Brahmins with

Brahma also supports the theory of connecting the Brahmins with *pravṛtti*. In this scenario *nivṛtti*, self-denial or a means to moksha, was hence theoretically an aberration and antisocial. To the Brahmins it was always a matter of how to convert what was clearly socially unacceptable into the raison d'être of Hindu life. In theory the Brahmins then overvalued *nivṛtti* but in practice made sure that rituals were performed, the political system maintained and the seemingly irreconcilable principles of the renouncer and the man-in-the-world contained within the concept of individual agents as selves bound to the four stages of life. The symbolic rather than the real enactment of these four stages has always been the decisive characteristic of this culture. It is perhaps only in the Buddhist concept of *duḥkha* ("suffering") and in the lives of the Buddhist monks that we find the logical connection between *nivṛtti* and the renunciation of a world where suffering is seen as the condition of samsara itself. The Brahmins knew this only too well but shirked from endorsing it because of its clearly antisocial consequences. As in many other instances, Buddhism simply made explicit, in a manner that only radical breakaway groups can do, a feature that had always been at the heart of Brahmanism: that is, the logic of *nivṛtti* must lead to a reading of a world that is impossible to live in. While the categories of *nivṛtti* and *pravṛtti* may be thoroughly essentialist and of little value to an understanding of the real conditions of life in Indian culture, the dialogue that the two categories ensured is much more important. Yet Dumont is not content with the dialogue itself and pushes the relationship between selfhood and the world to a transsocial level:

> I regard it as fundamental and would therefore posit firmly, if at the risk of crudity, that on the level of life in the world the individual *is* not.[13]

There is no "risk of crudity" here because the formulation is essentially cryptic and highly ambiguous. From the essential dialogue between the two irreconcilable orders of the renouncer and the man-in-the-world, Dumont moves toward a definition of the individual agent in Hindu culture. The "individual"—as a subject that can be defined in terms of absolute otherness—is not a "social being." Since the "individual *is* not" societal but "essential," he/she is the being who has achieved the identity of self and Brahman. In this definition we return to the sublime definition of the ascetic (the *nivṛtti*-ideal) who has achieved the identity of the self and the ground of Being (Atman and Brahman) and, therefore, claims to have arrived at the real (*sat*) as opposed to the unreal (*asat*) self. In terms of this Dumontian ideal of the individual (which is highly canonical and abstract), the intervention of bhakti could be seen as that moment when an emotional semantics blasts open the austere intellectualism of the canon and advances ways in which, to rephrase Dumont, "on the level of life in the world, the individual *is*." The emphasis on the individual's *iṣṭadevatā*, his personal God, was certainly one of the decisive moves in the direction of establishing selfhood without first renouncing the world as it is.

The theoretical incorporation of the renouncer into society at large or at least society's toleration of him/her constitutes one of the major social shifts that is reflected in the ideology of bhakti, as we shall see in the next chapter. I use "is reflected in" and not "occurred with" to suggest that bhakti (in all its heterogeneity) gave a specific semantics to discourses that had been taking shape alongside the views of the orthodoxy. Nevertheless, we would not want to valorize bhakti through a misplaced identification of it with conflict resolution—that in fact bhakti resolved a fundamental division between those who lived in this world and those who renounced it. The renouncer's position in a society as deeply decentered as the Hindu is highly ambiguous and not at all easy to explain through the presumed polarity of *nivṛtti* and *pravṛtti*. It is true, as we have argued at some length, that *nivṛtti* privileged renunciation, and Brahmins, in theory at any rate, presented it as the highest vocation in life. Against this theoretical prioritization, however, we need to point out that if every one renounced, the social order itself would have collapsed, and this certainly would not have been in the interests of the very patrons, the ruling princely castes, who supported the Brahmins in the first place. The projection of the renouncer as the ideal by the Brahmins was part of a larger ideology aimed at legitimating the self-interest of Brahmins in a highly complex, intricate but astute manner.

The acceptance and coexistence of the "renouncer" within society is thus part of a complex Hindu worldview that gradually attached the self to a number of religious/philosophical practices. As we shall see later, one such practice was Tantrism, a largely quasi-speculative, quasi-ascetic yogic method that made the geography of the human body itself the focal point of liberation. In this practice the body (always "ungendered") is not an impediment to release; rather the Yogi appropriates the characteristics of the renouncer even as he is a man-in-the-world. In one way, the transition to renunciation is also reversed: instead of the man-in-the-world rejecting the worldly for the otherworldly we find an instance of the renouncer actually embracing material conditions such as the essential rites of the *pañcatattva* (eating, drinking, copulation, etc.) through which he finds his mental discipline.[14] Since some versions of *nirguṇa* bhakti especially embraced Tantric symbolism with enthusiasm, its role in connecting the individual to the corporeal should not be underestimated.

The power of the renouncer, nevertheless, remains terrifying. From Bhishma to Gandhi Indians have demonstrated what vows of renunciation—whether symbolic or real—can do to human history. But the ideology of the renouncer is terrifying in another way because in some sense it undercuts the foundations upon which a civic society is based. If the renouncer is awe-inspiring, he is also a sign of the threat to the social order; if he is the agency of perfect bliss, he is also the instrument of inaction. But acts are essential, as the Brahmins and society at large recognized, and they must be given philosophical endorsement. Nevertheless, to endorse acts is to refute principles of otherworldliness so closely identified with the priestly caste. Conversely to abstain from acts would make living impossible. Either way we have a situation where the texts (composed by the Brahmins) said one thing and social practice something completely different. It is a contradiction the Brahmins were well aware of and so they opted for ambiguity rather than clarity. They endorsed renunciation but maintained the importance of acts. As van Buitenen has pointed out, "Neither the religious enthusiasts nor the unsocialized ascetics could offer stability to an expanding society that was badly in need of an ordered world and society."[15] So the obligatory rituals performed around Brahma's sacrificial fire were defined as acts that even the renouncer must perform, without in any way compromising his right to renunciation. Furthermore, there is no guarantee that the renouncer, who claims to curb the faculties of action, will not act since, in this reappraisal, acts can be both physical as well as mental. This is the central message of the *Bhagavadgītā* as well, which situates itself in the midst of these contradictory positions but tries to resolve them by asking what may be called a quasi-transcendental, and seemingly circular, question: If this is the world of experience, the world of the real, how do we then explain the conditions under which this world gets constructed?

The conceptual framework of the renouncer and the man-in-the-world controls much of what has been written about devotion in Hindu culture. To underline this point further I want to examine the *Bhagavadgītā* as the key canonical text of the Indian sublime. More immediately, my aim here is to show how the power of the renouncer is transformed into a form of pure action so that in the real world it is no longer a question of polarizing the renouncer and the man-in-the-world but of integrating the two through a complex theory of human agency. In this accommodation or quasi-synthesis bhakti has to be read as both ideology and practice. The reference to practice is important because people's actual practices may not reflect any given dominant ideology as such. Moreover no ideology in itself is ever totally homogeneous at any given time as it always carries a number of internal contradictions. Bhakti in the *Bhagavadgītā*, for instance, is of a decidedly different order from its later avatars. In the *Bhagavadgītā* bhakti is still very much a reworking of the Mimansa doctrine of ritualist acts in the critical context of the beliefs of the Vedantins, the Buddhists and the Sankhyan dualists.[16] These ritualist acts were gradually linked to self-control or Yoga, and although sacrifice also implied obeisance to a higher principle these acts were not to be confused with bhakti. In Krishna's reformulation of ritual as bhakti within the larger philosophy of disinterested action, yogic control and metaphysical connections between action and agents remain paramount. Who acts, why and how? How can the self also become part of the transcendent self of Krishna? Bhakti in the *Bhagavadgītā* answers these questions or at least it attempts to do so. But the answers are neither straightforward nor self-evidently true. There is, moreover, no unproblematic, linear history of bhakti that we can narrate, and certainly not one that would give priority to a given text. Here is R. S. McGregor's interpretation:

> In the famous section of the *Mahābhārata* called *Bhagavadgītā* "Song of Bhagavat," the mood of religious devotion or bhakti for this composite God, who is here called Krishna, finds its first clear expression. The *Gītā* plays a vital part in the development of theistic Hinduism, which, as far as texts are concerned, finds its beginnings here. It strongly stresses the importance of bhakti, while endeavouring at the same time to make some accommodation or synthesis between its *Bhāgavata* theism and the Upanishads' monist teaching of the transcendent *brahman*.[17]

This is a very clear-headed summary of the pivotal position of the *Bhagavadgītā* in the development of the religion of devotionalism. However, McGregor's own argument may be faulted precisely on the grounds of its clarity and its enthusiasm for the *Bhagavadgītā* as the text that laid the groundwork for "theistic Hinduism" by which McGregor obviously means the religion of bhakti. What McGregor clearly overlooks is the highly problematic nature of a text that gives clear expression to bhakti without a rigorous semantics of emotionalism. On the contrary, the manner in which acts become bhakti and "instil" into (a pre-existent) intellectual Hinduism the religion of love is part of an extremely complex history that requires us to seriously reexamine the whole question of the transmission of bhakti from the canonical Sanskrit texts to the vernacular.

The Moment of the Bhagavadgītā

To speak of the "moment" of a canonical Hindu religious text is fraught with difficulties. The most urgent of these difficulties is linked, in ways that are never straightforward, to the magic and mystery of the idea of Hindu *śruti* texts (notably the Vedas and the Upanishads), which are deemed not to have been written down. The argument here is that the "incantatory" or mystical force of religious utterance, of the sound, when represented (such as through writing) undermines its value as absolute truth. Since writing mediates between the word and the receiver and contaminates the unpresentability of the "sound," *śruti* texts declare themselves to be wholly unmediated phenomena. They are thus spoken of as "heard" texts against *smṛti* or "remembered" texts of the larger epic tradition. In the Upanishads these heard texts are largely framed in a monistic discourse where the final union of self in Brahman through some form of absolute identity is the norm. This is true, however, only to a point since in the heterogeneous and at times unwieldy Upanishads, a different, quasi-subversive tendency toward dualism also rears its head. In the *Śvetāśvatara Upaniṣad* (6.21–23) and in a variant reading of the *Kaṭha Upaniṣad* (2.20), for instance, there persist an underlying, though somewhat ephemeral, notice of devotion and love toward a personal God.[18] The *Bhagavadgītā* itself occupies an odd position in the tradition of *śruti* texts because its frame is essentially *smṛti* or the "remembered" textual tradition exemplified in the epics. At some point—-the exact moment is unclear— it gets incorporated into the Vedantic canon as another high point of unmediated *śruti* composition since it is now argued that in this text too the words of God are self-evidently presented before our eyes.

The tradition of *śruti* notwithstanding, textual criticism (which respects the informants' version of textual composition and transmission) is able to date the *Bhagavadgītā* with some accuracy. We know that it began to reach its "final" form after the fourth or third century B.C.E. and we know too that, as the "Book of the *Bhagavadgītā*," it constitutes chapters 14 to 41 of the sixth book (the Bhīṣma Parva or the Book of Bhīṣma) of the vast Sanskrit epic the *Mahābhārata* (in the Poona critical edition).[19] This massive epic is itself a city text, not a country text. It is about the establishment of urban communities, about court intrigue and about the politics of a protean nation-state. It is also largely about games that boys play and so even its religious message, as found in its philosophical fragments including the *Bhagavadgītā*, is really presented as a boys' guide to illumination. The "Book of the *Bhagavadgītā*" is ten chapters longer than the eighteen-chapter *Bhagavadgītā* that has come down to us. Clearly the eighteen chapters were taken out at some stage as constituting the essential *Bhagavadgītā* with chapters 14 to 22 and chapter 41, the final chapter, excised as not being necessary to the argument. The *Bhagavadgītā* as defined by tradition has a total of 700 verses divided into eighteen chapters. The number of verses per chapter range from 20 in chapter 12 to 78 in chapter 18. There is an extra verse—at the beginning of chapter 13—that tradition does not include in its count leaving the text with precisely 700 verses (and not 701 if the extra verse were included). Yet it is worth our while to examine how the *Bhagavadgītā*, as defined by the *Mahābhārata* itself, gets under way. We may then wish to begin not at chapter 23 but at chapter 14 of the "Book of the *Bhagavadgītā* " (that is not at the beginning of the *Bhagavadgītā* as transmitted to us but as it exists in the critical edition of the *Mahābhārata*) to get a sense of both the context and the crucial themes of the text.

After ten days of battle Sanjaya, the narrator at this point in the epic, returns to Dhritarashtra with his report. We read that Sanjaya tells the blind king that "Bhishma, peerless among the Bharatas, lay dead": *ācaṣṭa nihataṃ bhīṣmam bharatānām amadhyamam*. He has been killed by Shikhandin: *nihataḥ . . . bhīsmaḥ śikhaṇḍina*. This comes as a shock to Dhritarashtra, who spends much time in extensively speaking about the seeming (and hitherto accepted) immortality of venerable Bhishma.

Sanjaya begins his discourse by speaking about his own mystical insight. Through the power of Yoga and divine insight (given to him by Parashara who was none other than Dhritarashtra's natural father Krishna Dvaipayana Vyasa) he is able to narrate the events. He also has the gift of being immune in battle, so that he can wander without fear for his safety. The presentation of events in battle which according to the "Book of the *Bhagavadgītā* " is yet to begin (after chapter 41 in fact) raises very interesting narratological issues about the design of the epic and *Bhagavadgītā*'s place in it. We can summarize a number of them here. First, the text recounts events that are already known, events that are always "twice-told tales."[20] Second, breaks in linear narrative is part of the Indian tradition of constantly recounting events even as the narrative moves forward. Every narrative moment in the *Mahābhārata* in this reading is simultaneously synchronic and diachronic. Third, the poets would want to situate the encounter between Arjuna and Krishna in the context of a battle that has already begun since these events were destined to happen long ago. Finally, the death of Bhishma establishes a fundamental theme at the very beginning: If Bhishma is dead, can dharma survive? It is this last point that I believe is crucial here because Dhritarashtra says (15.43): "When I hear that Shamtanava [Bhishma] has been slain, he who knew the use of every weapon, a man of self-control, serenity, and spirit [virtues that Krishna would approve of], I know the rest of my army is lost. Lawlessness, I now know, has prevailed over Law (*dharmād adharmo balavān saṃprāpta iti me matiḥ*)."[21]

When we encounter Yudhishthira in chapter 21 (two chapters before the *Bhagavadgītā* proper begins), it is Arjuna who assures him that "where law goes there goes victory (*yato dharmas tato jayaḥ*)" but also adds, since dharma is also a synonym here for Yudhishthira himself, "where Krishna goes there goes victory (*yataḥ kṛṣṇas tato jayaḥ*)." The emphasis is again on dharma but through a poetically parallel construction the equation is made between dharma and Krishna: that Krishna is in fact the higher dharma. It is clear from this that dharma and its loss is the point of reference in the *Bhagavadgītā* when Krishna begins to explain the necessity of action to Arjuna. It is a point to which the "Book of the *Bhagavadgītā* " returns in the final chapter. As we have already recounted in the previous chapter, before the battle starts Yudhishthira goes to his gurus to ask their permission to fight. First of all it is the resolute, incomparable, peerless renouncer Bhishma who is addressed: "I seek permission from you who are inviolate to me, so that I may fight you, Father. Give your consent and wish me well." Bhishma feels constrained by his role (he knows he is on the wrong side but dharma requires fortitude and loyalty), he feels like a eunuch ("*klībavad*" is a word that Krishna will use for Arjuna, too, at *Bhagavadgītā* 2.3) and adds "If you had not come to me like this on the field of battle, I would have sworn an oath to your total defeat." He warns Yudhishthira, however, that the hour of his death had not yet come. Next Yudhishthira approaches the greatest of all archers, his teacher Drona. Drona repeats

Bhishma's words but on the question of how he could be killed he says those memorable words that every reader of the *Mahābhārata* remembers so well:

> śastraṃ cāhaṃ raṇe jāhyaṃ śrutvā sumahad apriyam
> śraddheyavākyāt puruṣād etat satyaṃ bravīmi te (41.61)
>
> And I swear to you, I shall put down my weapons only when I have heard most grievous tidings from a man whose word I trust.

We know that Drona will lay down his arms when Yudhishthira falsely confirms that Drona's son Ashvatthaman is dead when he knew that his brother Bhima had only killed an elephant (also called *aśvatthaman*). In his reply Drona also brings the earlier equation of dharma and Krishna together when Drona tells him, repeating those very words: "Where the Law is there is Krishna, and where Krishna is lies victory: *yato dharmas tataḥ kṛṣṇo yataḥ kṛṣṇas tato jayaḥ*" (41.55).

In the end dharma itself becomes topsy-turvy, and the *Mahābhārata* proves that Arjuna's anxieties about the propriety of violence were correct. Dharma is the fundamental law of the Hindu that is threatened and it is around this grand metanarrative that the *Bhagavadgītā* positions its case about the nature of action in life. Dharma is a pregiven; it is ubiquitous in Hindu culture. When God comes as man, he doesn't come to establish the Law (as in Christianity) but to become part of it. So when Krishna came he was not a lawgiver, for dharma was already given. This point is made in van Buitenen's brilliant exposition:

> [H]e was also not a God of Justice—or, for that matter, necessarily even a just God—for divine justice was already taken care of by the *dharma* which through *karman* ruled on the rewards of the good and the punishment of the wicked. . . . He was eternal and self-sufficient, and in his self-sufficiency knew the bliss of wanting nothing.[22]

The message about Hindu dharma in Hindu history will be given to Arjuna the left-handed archer (*savyasācin* is translated by others as "ambidextrous"), not to Yudhishthira the upholder of dharma, the dharma-raja. Dharma as the theme of the message will be presented as a dialogue between two people, Krishna and Arjuna, whose bonds are very close, perhaps even dangerously close.[23] Although self-contained, this dialogue will be constrained by its epic frame of narrative. And this is no infant epic, such is its immensity that generic boundaries cannot be readily imposed on it. Indeed it makes an extraordinary claim about itself:

> dharme ca arthe ca kāme ca mokṣe ca bharata ṛṣabha
> yad iha asti tad anyatra yad na iha asti na tat kvacit (1. 56.34)
>
> Giant among Bharatas whatever is here on Law, on commerce, on sex, on liberation is found elsewhere, but what is not here is nowhere else.

The *Bhagavadgītā* is an integral portion of an epic narrative in which acts must always override detachment and where the encyclopaedic claims of the epic will demand that it take on a vast number of targets. At the narrower level it is the function and place of action within dharma that Krishna will attempt to resolve through the logic of acts without consequences. The epic writers, however, cannot let the *Bhagavadgītā* dictate their terms of reference and soon after Krishna's final words to Arjuna the text unproblematically connects the idea of victory in this world to Krishna himself through Drona's words already quoted above: *yato dharmas tataḥ kṛṣṇo yataḥ kṛṣṇas tato jayaḥ* ("Where the Law is there is Krishna and where Krishna is there is victory"). The *Bhagavadgītā* makes sense not in spite of the *Mahābhārata* but because of it. And since it is part of this sprawling epic, the *Bhagavadgītā* does not stand as one independent moment in the text. It is framed by at least two other related discourses. The first is Bhishma's death-bed colloquy on the principles of moksha-dharma (the dharma of liberation), the second is the "Anugītā" section at the end of the epic battle when Arjuna asks Krishna to repeat the message of the *Bhagavadgītā.*[24] Krishna does not oblige this time around—he says his memory is faulty—but I think it is because the unfolding of the battle and the various strands around it have placed dharma itself under such a huge strain that in the end the world itself becomes decidedly meaningless. In place of certainty and will, there is only chaos and paradox.

One of the crucial ambiguities of the *Bhagavadgītā* arises precisely out of this rather new, and as yet not fully theorized, devotionalism framed by an epic that pushes the concept of order and civic behavior to its limits. In the *Bhagavadgītā* the problematic of the representation of God must take on almost every conceivable philosophical debate about the nature of being and the nature of God. To do this the *Bhagavadgītā* must establish a new type of reader-as-participant. This reader is an "infra reader" who participates in Arjuna's own dilemma, grappling as Arjuna himself does with a radical moment in time when "newness enters the world."[25] In the process of bracketing the infra reader with Arjuna the text offers us a questioning, somewhat skeptical, subject who is afflicted by the radical nature of the knowledge before him, especially since to him Krishna's words rock the very foundations of a social system he had taken for granted: Arjuna's initial defense is that war would lead to miscegenation and caste conflict. Furthermore, the knowledge-giver makes claims about his own being in a manner unheard of in the epic itself, and which, at times, baffles the immediate recipient of that knowledge, Arjuna. As Arvind Sharma has observed: "When Arjuna argued against fighting on ethical grounds, Krishna countered on metaphysical grounds."[26]

In this early formulation of bhakti ideology (which reaches its "mature" and for us a more readily recognizable form in the Puranic texts), the text proposes to examine the devotee-God relationship as a problematic rather than as an uncritical devotional speech-act situation. At one level this problematic relates to the "doubt" of the believer in the initial phase of the meditative/bhakti act. The *Bhagavadgītā* therefore has to defer to its epic frame to begin with before dropping it more or less completely as the heroic quest, for Arjuna at any rate, becomes an inner quest for spiritual awareness. In the event what was, in the context of the epic, a momentary pause, a monologue on duty, becomes a meditation on the age-old question of the nature of dharma and of the relationship between action and renunciation. The sheer depth of this meditation, its philosophical sweep and rhetorical finesse, its capacity to rebut all possible alternative positions in the culture led many scholars to look upon it as a text "composed" (by many redactors) around a whole series of interpolations or *kṣepaka* that has changed its original "kernel" beyond recognition. To some scholars (who read the *Bhagavadgītā* as "novel and exotic"[27]) the logic of an "Ur-text" has therefore become irresistible and they have suggested that the various layers, superimpositions, or accretions in the *Bhagavadgītā* can be explained once this true or real "Ur-text" is recovered. German scholars, notably Oldenberg, Garbe and Otto, and scholars of their persuasion, argued that the *Bhagavadgītā* was an independent text that, like the moon, was pulled into the orbit of the monstrous and encyclopaedic text called the *Mahābhārata*.[28] Few modern scholars would, however, go so far as to say that the text is really an "Ur-text" plus its accretions where the "Ur" is its primal meaning and the accretions its secondary or subsidiary meaning. As Ronald Inden has said the *Bhagavadgītā* is not simply a compendium of diverse views but a confirmation of a very Indian "ontology of plurality-with-unity."[29] It is the latter sort of argument that the tradition itself endorses, and with which recent scholars like van Buitenen agree: the *Bhagavadgītā* grows out of the *Mahābhārata* as a central part of it. The *Mahābhārata*, after all, is in the habit of incorporating fragments from all texts—this is its design (which also explains why we know the entire story of the *Mahābhārata* within a few pages of the first volume). And which explains why at the beginning of the "Book of the *Bhagavadgītā*," as we have seen, Sanjaya announces to Dhritarashtra that Bhishma is dead. The choice of this dialogue as the "moment" when Krishna makes himself known as God has to be located in the value placed on the ritual of battle as the site where the crucial categories of dharma and karma, and by extension moksha, are severely tested. How does one survive the end of time and the end of the world? What do these categories mean when faced with limit situations? The ritual of battle in the *Mahābhārata* is decisive for Hindu definitions of dharma and karma,

Law and Action. The battle provides Krishna with a context in which to rethink these concepts so that they don't become otiose, or worn out. The text then tells us that at any given time these fundamental principles must be rethought and it is for great commentators to make this explicit.

Whatever the state of the "composite" authorship of the *Bhagavadgītā*, the fact remains that the work had to "evolve" quite naturally out of the epic. This "evolution" meant that certain epic assumptions about the hero—those of honour, chivalry and duty for instance—could not be completely overlooked. If these assumptions may be classified as belonging to a text's formal features, there are others that belong to a text's language and discourse. The latter features direct our attention to the complex ways in which the laws of oral composition (for these laws are central to the *Mahābhārata* itself) dictate not only the "what" of a text but the "how" of it as well. The question of the "how" may be examined with reference to research already done on the nature of oral poetry. It seems highly unlikely that once a "respectable" text was established, say in the second or first century B.C.E., the *Bhagavadgītā* underwent any further significant changes. If this moment of the establishment of the canonical text can be read as the moment also of the written text, research in the nature of oral poetry, especially that undertaken by Parry and Lord, tells us that the text so constructed would have now parted company with the earlier oral tradition. Presenting itself as a new written text and not as a transitional text combining features of both oral and written techniques, it would now be part of a "written technique . . . not compatible with the oral technique, [as] the two could not possibly combine, to form another, a third, a 'transitional' technique."[30] The technology of writing now constructs a "new chirographically styled noetic world"[31] that releases poets from the domination of "theme" and "formula" as they stitch together a narrative not bound to the demands of the live oral audience, although it must be said that the written text would continue to be read out aloud to groups of people. At the level of the "writerly" too the "original" written text (composed perhaps during an uneventful oral recitation) cannot completely erase the palimpsestic oral composition upon which it is "overwritten." The real difference between the oral and the written, however, lies in the ways in which in the latter variant readings (extrapolations, additions as well as interpretation) are done in much more complex and historically accountable ways.

To proceed with our argument, then, we would now claim with some certainty that the contradictions and inconsistencies that scholars have discovered in the *Bhagavadgītā* are as much a consequence of its form as of any confusion on the part of its authors/redactors/amanuenses. And since the "roots of oral traditional narrative are not artistic but religious in the broadest sense,"[32] it would follow that shifts in the religious episteme of the "nation" would make their way into an oral composition. One such shift was the ideology of bhakti, which made its entry in a slightly dramatic manner in the *Bhagavadgītā*. The word "dramatic," however, must be used with caution. While it is true that the *Bhagavadgītā* clearly intervenes into the hitherto excessive intellectualism of the Vedic tradition through structures of devotionalism based on a God-devotee system, the intervention does not radically alter the real relation between self and God. Nor does bhakti totally displace the other methods of devotion (notably those of karma and knowledge). Indeed a dispassionate reader may argue that the *Bhagavadgītā* emphasizes all three Yogas equally: *jñāna*, karma, and bhakti all have a role to play in Krishna's world. Two of the most influential commentators on the *Bhagavadgītā*, Shankara (eight–ninth century) and Ramanuja (eleventh century), are symptomatic of the attempts by thinkers to skew the *Bhagavadgītā* toward a specific Yoga. In the case of Shankara it was *jñāna*, in the case of Ramanuja bhakti. But the skewing of the text toward a specific Yoga may also reflect the ascendancy of a given Yoga at the time. Writing around the middle of the eleventh century Ramanuja probably had a much more sophisticated bhakti discourse at his disposal than Shankara who preceded him by some three centuries.

In this new narrative of devotionalism the renouncer–God relationship (the ideal of Hinduism) is now recast as a man-in-the-world–God structure in which the warrior (Arjuna) who wishes to renounce is persuaded that the old renouncer–God prioritization is no longer the desired norm. Instead social beings must renegotiate spiritual life through a radical reexamination of the meaning of action itself, which is possible only after the self can embrace the will of God. Thus Krishna speaks of participation in him as a prerequisite to this new knowledge through devotion (*Bhagavadgītā* 9.34):

> Your mind, your devotion on me; your sacrifice for me;
> to me your reverence: having thus integrated yourself,
> intent on me, come.

The integration referred to here is made explicit in an earlier chapter in which the state of equanimity is defined, using Buddhist terminology, as *brahma-nirvāṇa* or *brahma-sthiti*, the fixed, still state of Brahman. Clearly this particular state can be presented only as an ideal since Brahman is "pure negativity," the sign of the sublime in its most sophisticated form. Its negativity—the state of nirvana as an absence, a void like the sublime—is no hindrance to the self's final awareness of Krishna who presents himself as the highest God who can be reached only after the nirvanic condition has been experienced. The claim, however, should not be read in terms of pure causality as though the stages themselves were readily identifiable—first the state of Brahman, then the ultimate condition of Krishna. What is more likely is that the use of the idea of a personal God, as a higher state of "Brahman," was meant to neutralize the claims made by the Buddhists. In the *Bhagavadgītā* Krishna seems to be "containing" Buddhism within Brahmanism by using its discourses while at the same time claiming that the idea of an all-powerful personal God remains important. The Buddhist state of nirvanahood is therefore linked to the Hindu Brahman but not as the final goal of life. Beyond *brahma-sthiti* is Krishna himself. But the hidden Buddhist text also makes clear that the *Bhagavadgītā*, as the text of the Brahmins, cannot present itself as a totally radical devotional text (which it is not even though many commentators, struck by its quasi-Christian ethos, would like to see it as such). R. C. Zaehner, for instance, certainly sees the subject's relationship with the condition of Brahman and his devotion to Krishna as demonstrating at long last the entry of a powerfully theistic conception of God into a largely abstract and mythic Hindu worldview.[33]

Within these frames—epic narrative on the one hand, Buddhist metaphysics on the other—the *Bhagavadgītā* offers the ideal of action within renunciation as the preferred alternative. This seemingly contradictory idea occupies central position in Krishna's insistence on the significance of a dharmic apparatus that stressed the proper duty of a particular caste. Krishna's endorsement of action does not contradict the dharma of one's caste while at the same time in insisting upon the selfless nature of action he can give the idea of devotion itself a purely "religious" context. He does this by stressing *niṣkāma-karma*, "disinterested activity," or *karma-phala-tyāga*, "renunciation of the fruit of action," the denial and abandonment of all self-interest in the "accomplishment of one's God-appointed duties."[34] Krishna refers to his own disinterested action that keeps the cosmos rolling. "There is nothing that I have to do in the three worlds; nothing that I have not obtained . . . yet do I work," he says and adds, "For if I didn't, men too would take up repose and the very order that keeps the world going would come to an end" (3.22–24). Renunciation and detachment (from the world) therefore is not the preferred option. Instead, renunciation is reread through a deeper understanding of the principles that lead to social cohesion. In this respect the emphasis on bhakti as a superior mode of Yoga is a carefully argued proposition designed to ensure that the Indian body politic itself does not relapse into lethargy or moral stupor, something that seems to have worried Hindu philosophers such as Ramanuja, and Hindu nationalists such as Nehru. In this respect the ideology of the *Bhagavadgītā* does not contradict the ideology of the *Mahābhārata* itself, which is centrally about the nature of the nation state and the conditions of its becoming.

The condition of the renouncer as a man of disinterested action is presented in a carefully structured fashion in the *Bhagavadgītā.* Given the persistence of structure in bhakti generally, the steps undertaken by the subject is predictable. When through self-control and knowledge, the devotees reach the condition of self-surrender where they demonstrate an undivided (*ananya*), unwavering (*avyabhicārinī*) love of God,[35] infra readers are persuaded that what they too have been involved in is part of a typology of progressive involvement in an Absolute Being. What the *Bhagavadgītā* is at pains to show is the fact that there is, finally, a thin membrane that separates the subject from Krishna, who in turn is inseparable from him/her. At one point Krishna lifts this to the level of an intersubjective metaphysics when he says that the subject (Arjuna or even the infra reader) grants being to the Gods which is then reciprocated in kind:

> You grant the Gods being, and the Gods will grant you being;
> In giving each other being you will reach the highest good.[36]

If we interpret the "granting of being" ritualistically, then the "highest good" referred to here may be considered as the condition of material bliss (for the subject though not for Krishna himself) as a consequence of the right kind of sacrifice. However, Krishna is at pains to distinguish between Vedic sacrifice linked to personal gain (I pour clarified butter on this fire because I desire something) and the same sacrifice done for the purity of the act itself. The message may be transposed on to matters of devotion: devotion in this argument should not be linked to consequences, to the advancement of one's own self, a point that Kapiladeva made his own in the *Bhāgavata Purāṇa*. It is within this overall scheme that Krishna emerges as a personal God. Glossing a well-known verse from the *Bhagavadgītā* (6.47) where the idea of the subject indwelling in Krishna is most readily evident, Ramanuja writes:

> "His inmost soul lost in me." By "inmost soul" is meant the mind which is the receptacle of all external and internal impressions. Such a Yogin's mind, then, from the excess of love he bears me, is lost in me because I am different in essence from all else. Out of the excess of his love for me, he cannot continue to exist without me.[37]

Ramanuja skews the text toward a primarily bhakti ideology but in doing so he hits upon a decisive orientation of the self (in the self-other relationship) found in a devotional text. Since the self exists, as R. C. Zaehner remarks, only in the "felt participation of the soul in the total being of God rather than the achievement of an individual nirvana,"[38] the devotional text, in Ramanuja's gloss, will now rewrite the economy of desire through a strategic devaluation of renunciation and a transvaluation of bhakti in the world itself.

But we have gone ahead of ourselves. What we need to do is to reprise the above argument and pursue it through a systematic analysis of this the most foundational of all texts of the Indian sublime. There is an established mode of philosophizing in classical Hinduism that begins with (a) the theory of knowledge, moves to the construction of (b) the proper world-picture with reference to all the elements of existence such as *guṇas*, incorporates (c) the spatiotemporal order of the world based on these elements, and then draws (d) inferences arising out of the world-picture such as ethics and the doctrine of deliverance. Now stages (a) and (d) are extensively argued in the *Bhagavadgītā* while

(c) surfaces more fully from chapter 13 onwards when the discourse on Sankhya gets going in earnest.

Much of what we have said follow the Hindu analytic of philosophizing mentioned above. To push our argument further, it must be stressed that the *Bhagavadgītā* shows how the austere precision of a "savior" religion is tempered by the comforts of a "tribal" religion.[39] Bhakti, the comfort of the tribal religion, now introduces (albeit in a form that would undergo serious modification) the "security" of the idea of a personal God who can be worshipped basically with a little bit of faith and belief. In its pure form the savior religion of Krishna requires the austere idea of purity of action. But the same Krishna opens a window into the world of "tribal" comforts, the world that could embrace God as a sojourner among humankind, as the figure who would attend to all our needs whenever we request him to do so. When religion becomes too austere (as in Islam or Judaism) the comforts of the tribal gets incorporated into the demands of the savior religion as prophets are adulated and shrines are built such as those of Sufi mystics in Indian Islam. Where these tribal comforts are not available martyrdom and the promise of bliss in life hereafter become substitutes for these comforts. In short the values, the metaphors, the narratives of the tribal become a necessary part of all savior religions no matter how austere their principles are to begin with.

The next question that arises out of the principles of the Hindu analytic deals with the general idea of how knowledge about the world and the world itself is produced in the first instance. I would want to think through the concept of "production" with reference to Hegel the idealist philosopher of Geist and Marx the materialist philosopher of knowledge as the product of labor. One of the finest summaries of their respective positions is given by Henri Lefebvre in his brilliant book *The Production of Space.* I would want to quote from that book at some length here.

> In Hegelianism "production" has a cardinal role: first the (absolute) Idea produces the world; next nature produces the human being; and the human being in turn, by dint of struggle and labour, produces at once history, knowledge and self-consciousness—and hence that Mind which reproduces the initial and ultimate Idea.
>
> For Marx and Engels, the concept of production never emerges from the ambiguity which makes it such a fertile idea. It has two senses, one very broad, the other restrictive and precise. In its broad sense, humans as social beings are said to produce their own life, their own consciousness, their own world. There is nothing, in history or in society, which does not have to be achieved or produced. "Nature" itself, as apprehended in social life by the sense organs, has been modified

> and therefore in a sense produced. Human beings have produced juridical, political, religious, artistic and philosophical forms. Thus production in the broad sense of the term embraces a multiplicity of works and a great diversity of forms, even forms that do not bear the stamp of the producer or of the production process (as is the case with the logical form: an abstract form which can easily be perceived as atemporal and therefore non-produced—that is, metaphysical).[40]

For Hegel then, the fact that the Mind produces the ultimate Idea (we might call it Brahman) is the foundation of knowledge. Without the ultimate Idea the process of the production of knowledge cannot begin. However, as we have seen, for Hegel it is only when we recognize our capacity to produce history that we can create the Ultimate Idea. Marx himself kept the nature of production quite abstract. It was Engels who in a letter to Bloch (21 September 1890) linked production directly to labor: "the *ultimately* determining element in history is the production and reproduction of real life."[41]

It is clear that both Hegel and Marx's readings of "production" can be applied to a text such as the *Bhagavadgītā.* Where a modified Hegelianism would begin with the production of the absolute Idea of Brahman as the starting point of knowledge and awareness, Marxist production of real life would link the *Bhagavadgītā* to the historical conditions of labor and the production of knowledge (for instance the social need to temper the austerity of a savior religion with the comforts of the tribal) and the degree to which Brahmins needed to reproduce their own ideology throughout history.

So how is the argument produced and reproduced? The crucial term that has to be critically reproduced, as we have remarked often enough, is dharma. This is the starting point of Arjuna's initial argument against fighting in the battle that is about to begin. He does not wish to kill his own family members (*svabāndhvān*) since this would be against ancient family laws (*kuladharmāḥ sanātanāḥ*). And if through war the social order is destroyed, lawlessness (adharma) will arise, women will be corrupted (*strīṣu duṣṭāsu*) leading to the unthinkable miscegenation of caste (*jāyate varṇasaṃkaraḥ*). Arjuna is "producing" a case for family law (the *kuladharma*) since he sees even salvation (those without *kuladharma* live eternally in hell) in terms of this dharma.

Krishna is clearly not very happy with this argument largely because it is, in terms of real, lived cultural norms so very powerful. Fratricidal wars have always destroyed the social and political fabric of a nation and a social order based on the severity of a caste system simply could not handle the idea of miscegenation. Krishna does not want to address these issues largely because, one suspects, he believes in them himself. Instead he mounts an attack on metaphysical grounds. He redefines the concept of action itself in terms of the idea of right or proper action against Vedic ritualism (where acts were connected to specific kinds of outcomes or promise thereof) and the beliefs of the Mimansakas (for whom it is the self that acts and therefore consequences accrue to the self). The exegetes and advocates of the act (of ritual) stress personal reward for the sacrificer from the act; rites are for personal interest (*puruṣārtha*); their discourse is flowery (*puṣpitāṃ vācaṃ*); they are ignorant (*avipaścitaḥ*); and they declare there is nothing else beyond Vedic ritual (*na anyat asti iti vādinaḥ*). The actions of the ritualists need total reformation because the act of ritual (karma) is linked to the rewards of rebirth (2.43). But Krishna accepts Vedic ritual if it is pursued correctly (2.46 and again 3.10ff.). However, if sacrifice is offered for reasons other than sacrifice, the original "spirit" is lost. This much the learned knows: *brāhmaṇasya vijānataḥ*.

For Arjuna there remains the question of what he sees is the fundamentally ethical and moral virtue of renunciation. To renounce is to not act; to not act is to save the world from pending doom. Krishna cannot let Arjuna get away with this and not simply because it is a matter of "epic necessity"—the fact that the ritual of battle must take its course. Krishna would want to persuade Arjuna that the equation of morality with the renouncer-ideal is fundamentally wrong because there can be no renunciation of acts: to renounce is to act; to not fight is to act. Rebirth cannot be stopped because one does not act. What must be defined very clearly, says Krishna, is the distinction between the corporeal and the "real": the body and the soul. The latter, it is suggested, survives the former, because as the Atman it is identical with Brahman. Moreover, the eternal Law of Dharma has to be seen apart from one's own *svadharma*, one's self-dharma, which is the prime "agency" of life in this world. These distinctions underlie the argument of the rest of the *Bhagavadgītā*. In developing them Krishna would take the unity of Atman and Brahman for granted (which in itself says something about the role of metanarratives in the civilization). On the matter of *svadharma* he is much more insistent and elaborate. Indeed he would begin by accusing Arjuna of cowardice by suggesting that he is indeed behaving not like a warrior caste but a eunuch (*klaibyam*). This is a strong term. In the context of the "Book of the *Bhagavadgītā*" we know that Bhishma is killed at the hands of the "eunuch" Shikhandin. It doesn't take long to see the effect of the description on Arjuna especially in the immediate narrative frame of the text. We remember that when Yudhishthira approaches Bhishma to seek his permission to fight him, Bhishma refers to himself as a eunuch (*klībavad*) because he is unable to take the side of those who hold the moral high ground.

So in his one-line manifesto on *svadharma*, where he targets, in particular, the Vedic ritualists and the Mimansakas Krishna says, "Your entitlement is only to the rite, not ever at all to its fruits" (2.47). The word for "entitlement" is *adhikāra*, a word that also carries the meanings of jurisdiction, authority, prerogative, office, claim, privilege and so on. In its technical Mimansaka sense *adhikāra* includes the sum total of birth, initiation, stages of life as well as specific purpose (i.e., entitlement).[42] Krishna thus keeps the Mimansakas in mind (those who stress the reaping of the rewards) when he admonishes Arjuna at the end of the verse: "Be not motivated by the fruits of acts, but also do not purposely seek to avoid acting (2.47)." Of course, to get this right one needs a disciplined mind or *buddhi*: *buddhiyukta* (2.49–51). *Kāma* or desire gets in the way of proper action and Krishna then exhorts the self to remove desire (including greed, wealth, power, fame, generally *ahaṃkāra*, or "I-ness") and through the exercise of one's *buddhi* go beyond delusion (*moha*). Through a steady mind, through tranquillity/equanimity of the self is the condition of *brahmi sthiti* (the state of Brahman) reached (*brahmanirvāṇam ṛcchati*).

But Arjuna has misunderstood and so Krishna goes over the argument yet again. What Krishna must insist upon is the primacy of action which to him is exceedingly important: *na hi kaścit . . . jātu tiṣṭhati akarmakṛt*, "no one . . . ever exists without performing action" (3.5). And he makes a simple case for the causality of action: Brahman → Vedas (Brahman originates in the Vedas through ritual action) → ritual → sacrifice → rain god → food → beings → Brahman. To emphasize the importance of unattached action (*asaktaḥ karma*) Krishna speaks of his own action: "If I should not perform action, these people would collapse (*utsīdeyur imā loke na kuryāṃ karma cedaham*) and then indeed not only would I bring confusion and miscegenation (*saṃkarasya*) but bring an end to all people" (3.23–24). This latter point is made in the context of Arjuna's refusal to fight on the grounds that if he acts he would bring about miscegenation and confusion. Here, in a pointed reference to Arjuna Krishna emphasizes that it is not by acting that these things happen but by not acting. He reverses the argument but before doing so he redefines the nature of action by ending the binary between the renouncer and the man-in-the-world. At 5.3 Krishna calls the renouncer the eternal renouncer thereby removing him from a temporal frame of reference. He is the *nitya saṃnyāsī*, who neither hates nor desires: *yo na dveṣṭi, na kāṅkṣati*. Renunciation is then removed from the action versus inaction controversy, the controversy of the renouncer and the man-in-the-world.

Because the idea of action in nonaction is confusing (even to poets) Krishna proposes to explain this at length (4.17–23). He emphasizes his own act in the cycle of reincarnation when he defines reincarnation as a considered response to the rise of adharma through nondharmic acts. He underlines his role in the creation of the four castes on the basis of the distribution of *guṇas* (which nevertheless keeps him as the eternal "doer") and he establishes the connection between Atman and Brahman so that in the act of sacrifice Brahman in fact acts through the agent, which is the Atman (4.24). All processes (ritual sacrifice, sensory responses, Vedic recitation, restraint from acting) are forms of action. And you must *know* that these are born out of action (4.32). Even if you yourself don't know those who do know, the *jñāninaḥ* or the *darśinaḥ* (4.34), will teach you knowledge (*upadekṣyanti te jñānam*). Knowledge is power says

Krishna (4.35–42) but knowledge is also a mode of action. Again there is no such thing as a nonactive form of being. Yet Arjuna, like us, fails to understand partly because Krishna constantly fine-tunes his thesis. At the end of chapter 4, for instance, when Krishna tells Arjuna to resort to Yoga what he means is the Yoga of knowledge that would enable him to see the nature of action as Krishna had so far defined it. At the same time Arjuna should not be given the impression that action is not paramount. To make action ambiguous, as Krishna seems to have done with his reference to the power of knowledge, may be counterproductive because Arjuna must not be allowed to desist from participating in the battle that is about to begin (but which has already taken place). Having established this, all that remains to be done is for Krishna to reaffirm that this knowledge leads to the condition of *brahmanirvāṇa* (5.24–26) and hence to liberation, which, of course, also means knowledge of Krishna (5.29).

The reference to the condition of *brahmanirvāṇa* takes Krishna to the argument of the Buddhists (who are one of the major targets throughout the *Bhagavadgītā*) since to them renunciation is the refusal to perform "sacred rites" (*akriyas*). To Krishna the person of discipline performs rites but abandons the intention of fruits. This person of discipline is a transcendental person, he is not bound to the laws of causality or to nature, he is not of *prakṛti* but of *puruṣa* (in Sankhyan terminology). Again the perfect Yogin is presented as someone who has achieved equanimity and for whom the final moment of nirvana is union in a personal God (*śāntiṃ nirvāṇaparamāṃ matsaṃsthām adhigacchati*) and not the condition of Buddhist extinction (6.15). This is important. But we also note at 6.16–17 allusions to an as yet undertheorized *madhyamaka* path (the middle path of the later system of Nagarjuna) as the Yogi is defined as one who eats moderately, has controlled his thoughts (18), is steady of mind (26), and meditates on Krishna (29–31). To Arjuna's practical question about those people who having arrived at understanding lose it because their mind has fallen away from Yoga, Krishna replies that these people (while certainly not reaching nirvana) are born again in the family of wise Yogins (42) and carry on from where they had left off in their previous life. Perfected they would some day reach Krishna (45). This is practical ethics underpinned by a theory of the movement of souls from one body to another. One need not achieve nirvana in this life; it is the right kind of action that is important. Clearly practical ethics here is aimed at counteracting the idea of Buddhist extinction.

The information given is powerful but not easily grasped and so Krishna must refer to himself as the sublime object: How is he to be known, how is he to be understood? He refers to his two natures in largely Sankhyan terms: an inferior nature (7.4) and a higher nature, which is the nature of his spiritual being (7.5) by which this universe is sustained. Krishna can then tell Arjuna that he has both these forms, a lower nature, which is his material being (*prakṛti*), and a supernal nature. The production of creatures (*sarvāṇi bhūtāni*) for instance is in the realm of his higher nature because he is the origin and the dissolution of the entire universe (*ahaṃ kṛtsnasya jagataḥ prabhavaḥ pralayas tathā*). Once these references are given, the chapter begins to prepare us for the sublime vision that Krishna will grant Arjuna. Krishna's supernal sense is prepared with reference to the sun, the sacred syllable Om (7.8–12), to his authorship of the Sankhyan categories of *guṇas* (although he is not bound by them) and so on. The true self can be freed from bondage only when there is self-transcendence over the world as a *guṇa*-made illusion, the world as the production of Maya. In more specific terms Krishna then spells out those who can reach him. They are: (a) those who are afflicted or those who suffer, (b) those who desire knowledge, (c) those who want to reach the highest truth, and (d) the person of wisdom. Of these four Krishna makes a clear preference for the person of wisdom (7.17) but the definition of the man of wisdom is the man of action stipulated in chapter 2. This man of wisdom is one who accepts a theistic reading of Krishna as God saying "Vasudeva (son of Vasudeva) is all (*vāsudevaḥ sarvam iti*)." This man of wisdom also does not follow other gods (7.20) as Krishna distinguishes between those who go to the gods and those who go to him (7.23: *madbhaktā yānti mām*). Krishna also insists upon his unmanifest being, which only the ignorant confuse with the manifest (7.24–25) and in doing so fail to understand how sages from time immemorial have understood his unmanifest being (7.26). The chapter ends with Krishna's extensive insistence on his unmanifest being as *adhyātman, adhibhūta, adhidaiva, adhiyajña*, and so on (7.29–30). These are difficult terms and Arjuna needs to have them clarified. He also needs greater clarity on the definition of action. The reference to action once again underlines the singular importance of the relationship between dharma and action in the *Bhagavadgītā*. This interrelationship holds the key to the text. It is overlaid, in particular, with Sankhya and Buddhist terminologies and with the idea that the condition of *brahmanirvāṇa* is the prerequisite for union with Krishna as God. In doing so Krishna uses a number of ideas that were current at the time and some that, to us, may sound self-contradictory. There is the reference to practical things such as the importance of saying the syllable "Om" at death to ensure a sure passage to God (8.13). Another common idea is that of the transmigration of souls that Krishna links to the condition of the lower Brahman (where the self is still subject to successive births) and not to his own condition (beyond that of Brahman) where there is no rebirth (8.16). Chapter 8, then, is all about the means by which one may worship and the nature of a personal God such as Krishna.[43] The chapter once again stresses the self (as Yogin) who knows and who goes beyond the fruits of action. Discipline as well as knowledge of the true state of Krishna makes union with him possible. The text has now moved dramatically toward religious and theistic ends and postulates, in a quite radical fashion, the importance of a monotheistic God. For Hinduism this is the point at which newness certainly begins to enter the world.

With the move toward a theorization of a personal God above the absolute Brahman (although there is some confusion here) the comforts of the tribal religion get under way in a much stronger fashion. The "comforting discourse" of the tribal (against the austere intellectualism of a savior religion) is emphasized through a number of "new" facts. First, people who do not follow Krishna are reborn in the cycle of death and transmigration (9.3). Second, Krishna is the source of all phenomena but is not touched by them (that is he is beyond the distinctions made in Sankhya theory). Third, although he acts, he is not bound by them. Fourth, those who see him in human form and despise him are deluded because they do not know his divine form (9.11). Fifth, reemphasizing a point he made at 7.8–11, Krishna stresses that he is "the ritual, the sacrifice . . . father, mother, the sacred syllable Om" (9.17). Sixth, those who sacrifice to other gods go to those gods (*yānti devavratā devān*) and those who sacrifice to Krishna go to him (*yānti madyājino api mām*). These are all elements that one would associate with the "comforts" of a tribal religion especially insofar as they stress sacrifice and ritual offering to Krishna. With the "tribal" comes a shift in the nature of the discourse as the emphasis moves to simple acts. Provided it is offered with devotion, a leaf, a flower, fruit or water is all that is expected of the believer (9.26). The comfort of liberation is again stressed with reference to simple acts and not to difficult philosophy. Even those who are evil (*sudurācāra*) become virtuous (9.30–31). Even those born of evil wombs—as Krishna says in a markedly sexist and caste-ridden passage: *striyo vaiśyās tathā śūdrās te 'pi yānti parāṃ gatim* (9.32)—also reach Krishna. It must be added in defence of this text at this point that all religious texts are sexist, although it must be said that the *Bhagavadgītā* as well as the *Mahābhārata* as a whole are certainly much less so than other religious texts.

Even as Krishna appropriates the discourses of a personal God, he must return, periodically, to his own self as the sublime object of devotion. Following on from 7.8–11 and 9.16–17, we can see the presentation of this sublime object under way, especially in chapters 10 and 11. In these chapters Krishna employs a number of essentially literary strategies. He speaks of his essence in terms of the first element or the foremost or primal item in any series: of Gods he is Vishnu, of the Vedas Sama, of utterances the syllable Om, of sages Kapila (the founder of Sankhya), among warriors Rama, of letters A, of compounds *dvandva*, of words that are feminine *smṛti* (memory), *medhā* (wisdom), *dhṛti* (courage), and *kṣamā* (patience, endurance), of meters *gāyatrī*, of seasons, spring, of sages Vyasa, of poets, Ushanas, and so on. Krishna ends by saying that there is nothing that can exist without existing through him, and there is no end to his divine manifestation (10.40).

We now arrive at the central moment in the theory of the Indian sublime. It occurs in chapter 11 in the form of Krishna's transfiguration as observed by Arjuna. The moment is also punctuated by Krishna's commentary on his own visual representation. The dominant metaphors that are used in this description are metaphors of light. This is not an unusual religious code since in both Mark 9.2–8 and Matthew 17.1–3 Christ's transfiguration is also narrated through the metaphors of light. In the *Bhagavadgītā* Arjuna requests to see Krishna's "godly form": *draṣṭum icchāmi te rūpam aiśvaraṃ* (11.3). The decision to show his form and to whom it should be shown has to be Krishna's own: Arjuna the privileged recipient of this sublime vision can see only after he has been given "a divine eye" (*divyaṃ cakṣuḥ*) by Krishna. When through this divine eye Arjuna is able to see phenomena quite beyond "adequation," phenomena so absolutely great, he senses that metaphors themselves are strained under the weight of superlatives, the limitless counters of the mathematical sublime: *anantam* ("endless"), *aprameyam* ("immeasurable"), *sanātana* ("primeval"), *amita* ("boundless"), *anādimadhyāntam* ("without beginning, middle or end"), and so on. Krishna's radiance blinds not only the viewer but the entire cosmos with the force of a thousand suns, an image that presages the apocalyptic vision of a nuclear holocaust.[44] His radiance is such that it burns all the universe: *svatejasā viśvam idaṃ tapantam* (11.19). Although addressed as Vishnu, the reassuring and immensely steady God (but only twice at 11.24 and 11.30), the images through which Krishna continues to be presented are meant to threaten and overpower as not only Gods but the main players of the grand epic as well are seen within Krishna's body. In spite of the excess of the visual, Arjuna still wants to know what the sublime presentation actually means, what is its epistemology, what does the symbology underline? He declares that he does not understand Krishna's working: *na hi prajānāmi tava pravṛttim* (11.31).[45] In response to Arjuna's request Krishna states what the vision actually means. The key to the answer is to be found at 11.32 where Krishna presents himself as *kāla*, which in Sanskrit means both time and death, and which, to quote Franklin Edgerton, is "a sort of cosmic Will, reminding us of Schopenhauer."[46]

> kālo 'smi lokakṣayakṛt pravṛddhaḥ
> I am become time/death destroyer of the universe.

Because I am the instrument of time, Krishna says, it doesn't matter whether you fight or not. The question of human agency therefore becomes one of working within a history that has already been written down: so the death of Bhishma is proclaimed even before the "Book of the *Bhagavadgītā*" begins. With clamorous and resounding imperatives Krishna declares: "Kill! Do not hesitate! Fight! You will conquer the enemy in battle: *tvam jahi mā vyathiṣṭhā yudhyasva jetāsi raṇe sapatnān*" (11.34).

Arjuna has been given this very privileged insight, never before seen by anyone else—*tvadanyena na dṛṣṭapūrvam* (11.47)—and not available even to gods (11.52). What is more this vision is not available through Vedic sacrifice or recitation of texts, through the giving of various gifts to God or by ritual acts or intense *tapas* (terrible austerities). And this vision as well as everything else Krishna himself "causes" since he is the origin and mover of causality, a point underlined in Sanskrit by the use of causative forms. Arjuna is the self that hears and judges, Krishna is the self that interprets, debates, and takes interjections without being ruffled by them.

"After such knowledge, what forgiveness," wrote T. S. Eliot and indeed after such knowledge what else can be said by Krishna. In a not insignificant manner one could argue that the *Bhagavadgītā* should in fact end here. Krishna grants Arjuna a rare insight, the sort of thing that happens only once in time like the time when the thief on the cross is granted salvation by Christ. Another thief misses out on this historic opportunity. Arjuna is given this extraordinary insight at such a moment in history. There is nothing more that can be said specifically on the question of action and on the concept of the writing of history. This is true though only up to a point because there is another matter that Krishna wants to take up in a much more elaborate manner. After a very brief interlude on devotion in the twelfth chapter, the *Bhagavadgītā* takes up India's dominant philosophy, Sankhya, yet again and links it to the "new" teaching of Krishna. There have been a number of significantly Sankhyan engagements in the text so far, especially in chapter 2 and at 11.38 where Arjuna had addressed Krishna in significantly Sankhyan terminology by equating him with both the "knower" and the "object of knowledge" (*vettā asi vedyaṃ ca*) but nothing serious and thorough-going had been attempted. Before we examine the rest of the *Bhagavadgītā*, this time with particular reference to Sankhya, we need to bring our commentary so far (and specifically on chapters 1 to 11) to a conclusion.

In the dialogue between Krishna and Arjuna three ideas are extensively debated. So far we have looked at two of them. The first deals with the self and its relationship to two fundamental and founding principles of Hindu culture: dharma and karma. Both of these principles are debated but both are discussed in their narrow individual as well as in their universal context, especially insofar as the ritual of battle is such a context. In this argument Krishna must first of all distinguish between phenomenal and transcendental selves. He does so by making the case that in Sankhya terminology the *puruṣa* is deluded into thinking that it acts by lodging itself in the body. This delusion leads to statements about "I acting" and so on. Much is made of this knowledge and Krishna's strategy is to make the nature of the *puruṣa* as Atman clear. Having established that the self is in fact the changeless Brahman, Krishna wants to advance an agent who acts in full awareness of the self that responds to stimulus. In other words, this agent now makes a distinction between involuntary acts (like sense perceptions, tactile responses, etc.) and those acts that demand analysis and knowledge. Here Krishna introduces the idea of action without consequences (*niṣphala karman*) as well as the idea of an underlying link between one's dharma and action. At no point, however, does Krishna praise inaction; rather he stresses that even Buddhist renunciation is a form of action.

Indeed all Yogas (of knowledge, etc.) are forms of action because only through action is the world kept in motion. Krishna himself always acts: "nevertheless I engage in action . . . if I should not perform action, these worlds would collapse" (*varta eva ca karmaṇi . . . utsīdeyur ime lokā na kuryāṃ karma cedaham*). Ethical principles, good and evil, the salvation of the soul (moksha) are all linked to acts (for Krishna not to stress acts would contradict the "occasion" of the dialogue itself, which is the battle of the *Mahābhārata*). Although many of the terms used by Krishna are part of Indian philosophy generally (as they have to be) the primacy given to action is highly original.

The second aspect that is extensively argued deals with Krishna himself. Here he is equally emphatic: there are no other Gods besides himself. He claims to be above Brahman, a Parabrahman, for whom the Buddhist nirvana is in fact nirvana in his own self. He does concede that some beings may go to other Gods and worship them (chapter 7 and 9.23) but they would be subject to rebirth. There is some ambiguity here because at 9.23 he does not repeat the limited nature of the salvation for those who worship other Gods. Although at 9.25 he does say that those who sacrifice to the other Gods go to them, it is clear that only those who sacrifice to him come to him. To go beyond the cycle of rebirth, to attain the beatitude of a savior religion he alone is to be worshipped. But he gives Arjuna the comforts of the tribal religion too. After stressing the nature of pure action, he gives the comforting language of a loving God to whom believers can come. He speaks about personal bhakti, by which I think he means the performance of rituals with one's mind set on him but not seeking any consequences.[47] This issue (of acts without consequences) remains unresolved but for Krishna the qualifications help him "reproduce" a specific and highly original redefinition of the link between karma, action, and dharma. So as God Krishna tells us that we are self-sufficient in him. We need not worship any other God. True, he says, there will be people who may tell you the correct path by dint of knowledge (but theirs must be uncompromising knowledge without any self-interest) but these people are not to be confused with him. Krishna refers to his earthly birth (as Vasudeva) once but beyond that there are no references to him of the kind we find in other parts of the *Mahābhārata*, in the Harivaṃśa addendum of the epic or in the later Puranic texts. So the point is clear, either you are with him or not with him. If you want your Hinduism to be monotheistic, austere, profoundly interrogatory and demanding, but with room for the comforts of the "tribal," than you need not go beyond the *Bhagavadgītā*. What then do we make of 4.7? This is the "*yadā yadā hi dharmasya* . . ." passage: "Whenever dharma is threatened then do I reincarnate myself," Krishna had said. By and large this has been read as Krishna endorsing earlier avatars. But must this be so, why should "*yadā yadā* . . ." be read as something that has already happened and not as an "as if" conditional: when this happens, when dharma is threatened, then will I reincarnate myself. It looks like a statement about the future, not about the past. In the other avatars how was dharma threatened?[48] Was there the same crisis of dharma? We would argue that Krishna is not alluding to prior reincarnations but explaining the present contingent moment, explaining his moment of birth as human here and now and presaging the possibility of his return should a threat to dharma of the magnitude raised by the specter of battle arise again. This is in line with the logic of the *Bhagavadgītā*, which does not speak about other avatars. Although it must be added that in the larger context of Hinduism the systemic nature of avatars is a master code that endorses the theory of rebirth.

As we have already remarked, the high point of the *Bhagavadgītā* is reached in chapter 11, at the point of religious transfiguration when Arjuna, alone in history, is given the sublime, unpresentable (in the phenomenal world) vision of God. The chapter is also rich in rasas with elements of *adbhuta* (marvellous), *bhayānaka* (fearful), *bībhatsa* (horrific), *raudra* (furious), *vīra* (heroic), plus touches of the later rasa of bhakti (devotion) being placed alongside one another. When we look back at the *Bhagavadgītā*, as I have done in my summary above, we find that Krishna has made the point clearly and concisely: there is a transcendental absolute in Hinduism (who is Krishna), *brahmanirvāṇa* is a necessary stage in one's road to an understanding of this absolute, and a distinction has to be made between the transcendental and the phenomenal. But all along the *Bhagavadgītā* has insisted upon a radical retheorizing of action and agency so that there is no such thing as nonaction: even the renouncer acts, and in this redefinition of karma is to be found the energy that keeps social practices going. There is then, in one way, a material dimension to Krishna's views that is of a piece with the philosophy of the epic itself.

I now move on to the third element in my critique of the *Bhagavadgītā*. This element, as already foreshadowed, is Sankhya. The philosophy of Sankhya occurs throughout the text, emerging very strongly in chapter 2 but surfacing in all sorts of unlikely places. At 11.38, in the midst of the sublime image of Krishna we hear Arjuna addressing Krishna as the "knower and the object of knowledge." This idea, reformulated as "the field" and "the knower of the field," is taken up again at the beginning of chapter 13, which marks the return to Sankhya terminology in a significant way in the text. From this chapter onwards the ideas of Sankhya "form the scaffolding of the doctrinal edifice"[49] in a much more systematic fashion. Whereas in chapter two the *Bhagavadgītā* had taken up some of the crucial determinants of this theory and reinflected it to show two things—that the *puruṣa* should not be confused with the elements of *buddhi* (*ahaṃkāra*, etc.) since this *puruṣa* is outside of *prakṛti* and never changes, and that action is the essence of the self—from chapter 13 onwards the discussion becomes taxonomic, somewhat more technical and classificatory in a manner not unlike Bhishma's discourse in the *mokṣadharma* section of the *Mahābhārata* (12.19ff. in the Poona critical edition).[50] Cautiously, then, we could say that in the *Bhagavadgītā* chapter 13 to 18.49 mark a Sankhya interlude. The argument has been won by chapter 12; Arjuna has no counter case to make. Why then should Krishna (or the narrator Sanjaya or the unknown amanuensis) spend so long on Sankhya philosophy, and on its technical side? I do think it has a lot to do with the enormous influence of Sankhya in Indian philosophy. The great Indian philosopher Gopinath Kaviraj, when asked by James Larson, the American scholar of Hindu philosophy, to comment on Sankhya (which he, Larson, had referred to as one of the ancient systems of Indian philosophy) corrected him: "Sankhya is not *one* of the systems of Indian philosophy. Sankhya *is* the philosophy of India."[51] Coming from someone else we may read this as the exaggeration of enthusiasm; coming from Gopinath Kaviraj, the doyen of Indian philosophers, we have to take this very seriously indeed. The *Bhagavadgītā* too takes Sankhya very seriously and although the other schools of thought—Mimansa, Nyaya-Vaisheshika, Buddhism, and so on—were not unknown to its writers, it specifically singles this philosophy out for extensive treatment. Indeed Sankhya acts as a template for our understanding of the *Bhagavadgītā*.

Sankhya, the oldest inclusive philosophy of India, is attributed to Kapila (about whom we know very little except that he may have lived in fifth century B.C.E.). It is fundamentally a dualistic doctrine of deliverance that developed out of the ideas of the Vedic and Epic periods of which the *Bhagavadgītā* itself is a part. Its inclusiveness or comprehensiveness reflects the "ancient Indian predilection for elaborate enumerations, classifications, and numerical schemes."[52] In this remarkably ambitious philosophy the world is constructed through a number of "constituents" that are classified in a "vertical" manner, from "primeval 'nature,' *prakṛti*, and its twenty-three evolutes," to the *puruṣu* and the essential self.[53] The doctrine of deliverance (in both nonreligious and religious senses of the word) permeates all (complete) Hindu theories, and Sankhya is no exception. Put in another way, the human soul had to find deliverance from the world that it inhabits out of its own volition. Once we grasp this we can see how the *Bhagavadgītā* reinflects a doctrine of deliverance which in the hands of the Buddhists had emerged as a "pure" deliverance theory that grew out of a very intense examination of the grounds of the Sankhya system and its offshoots. For the Siddhartha Shakyamuni deliverance was release from the shackles of transmigration, and freedom from the sorrows of existence. The difficult questions about the condition of the soul and its place after death were pushed aside. What the Buddha examined was the cause of our entanglement in the world of *duḥkha/dukkha* ("suffering") and its elimination. Theoretical knowledge was dispensed with because theory was replaced by direct experience through Yoga which, argued the Buddha, alone led to the destruction of desire. For Krishna to maintain that the Buddhists, therefore, were entangled in desire is a misreading of Shakyamuni's own teaching. For the Buddhists the unreal as the result of desire is a transcendental fact and the starting point of contemplation. Contrary ways of overcoming an unreal world so constructed then become essential. For Krishna, however, accepting the world as a product of desire and not of God in itself leads to serious and unacceptable propositions.

In Sankhya theory the phenomenal world is part of primeval matter to be distinguished from the soul. Change and "evolution" take place in this primeval matter, *prakṛti*, the field (*kṣetram*); the soul (Atman) is simply the knower of the field (*kṣetrajña*) and not a participant in it. The *Bhagavadgītā* accepts this proposition very much as it is with the proviso that *prakṛti* itself has its genesis in Brahma (Krishna speaks about planting the seed in the womb of Brahma). The key categories of *prakṛti* and *puruṣa*, however, remain and we need to look at them once again. Primeval or Ur-matter is *prakṛti*, permanent and ubiquitous. It is subtle and cannot be perceived. Like the Brahma of the *mokṣadharma* section of the *Mahābhārata* it is active while the soul is inactive. The origin of the world out of Brahma (the standard argument) was rejected and replaced by the origin of the world out of matter (*prakṛti*). To the first question, "How does the phenomenal world spring out of *prakṛti*?" the standard reply is "All things arise out of three Ur-elements or qualities called *guṇas*: *sattva* (goodness), *rajas* (passion), and *tamas* (darkness)." The whole evolution series (through the *guṇas*) lay in the sphere of matter (*prakṛti*); the Atman stands away and perfectly apart from it. The highest psychical organ, *buddhi* or the knowledge agent, also derives from matter or *prakṛti*. The Atman, however, believes that it suffers, erroneously, and so makes deliverance impossible. The point is that in believing that it suffers the Atman is in fact confusing itself with the ahamkaric principle or with "I-consciousness."[54] *Ahaṃkāra* appears in threefold form reflecting the *guṇas* that preponderate but is also linked to the mind or *manas*, which stands above the ten sense organs. Two immediate questions arise out of this scheme. The first: What is the cause that keeps the world in process? The standard Sankhya answer is: the interest of the Atman (*puruṣa*). Matter comes into activity to bring about the deliverance of the Atman although the Atman is not able to exert any influence on it. The second question is: How is deliverance possible? Before answering this question it is important, first of all, to understand the fateful error of the Atman. The Atman (mistakenly) confounds itself with *buddhi* (the faculty of knowledge) and refers to itself everything that belongs to *buddhi*. It regards *buddhi* as "I" and all processes in the *buddhi* as "mine." It believes that it suffers the pain that belongs only to *buddhi*. This apparent entanglement of the Atman in existence depends upon a mistake. It is necessary to eliminate this mistake by recognizing that matter is different from *puruṣa* which is neither *buddhi*, nor I or Mine. Deliverance occurs only upon this recognition. When does existence, the processes of *prakṛti* cease? Does it stop upon deliverance? The answer here is "Never." Like the potter's wheel that continues moving even after the pot has been completed, likewise the phenomenal world rolls itself out. Finally, how is knowledge of deliverance found? The simple answer here is: through logical thinking and inference.

Before we can examine Sankhya through the *Bhagavadgītā*, we need to return to causality and the idea of the reproduction of knowledge. Causality is basic to all logical thinking. We need a primary cause and then we speak about its effects. In religion God is seen as the primal cause of creation; he is also seen as the primal cause of thought, of the world of phenomenon and so on. The Buddha had located the origin of the phenomenal world in desire. Sankhya theory argued that cause and effect were inherent to *prakṛti*, like pots returning into clay, or fire to flint. Effects are already present in the cause. As we have seen, Krishna's argument is that it is karma, action or work, that sets the universe in motion. Read through Sankhya we would say that through the introduction of the idea of obligation and commitment (*adhikāra*) *prakṛti* feels obligated to work until *puruṣa* is liberated. It is this obligation, *adhikāra*, that causes world creation. Hence obligation and work are present as a double cause of world creation.

On this question of causality we get the Sankhya view in the *Bhagavadgītā*. At 5.8–9, for instance, Krishna invokes, without explicitly mentioning it, the Sankhya argument that the *puruṣa* never acts, or "causes," only *prakṛti* does. The argument here is that nature acts, not *puruṣa*, which is outside of the senses that are still located within *prakṛti*: the senses abide in the objects of senses (*indriyāṇi indriyārtheṣu vartante*). The category of *puruṣa* that Krishna has in mind is the *parampuruṣa*, the Atman that never acts because it has placed its actions in Brahman (5.10). The difficulty, however, surfaces when we look at 5.14 in its entirety: "The Lord has not created into people either authorship of acts, or the acts themselves, or the concatenation of act and fruit: that is the doing of Nature."[55] The word for "Nature" is *svabhāva* used in the technical Sankhya sense of *prakṛti*. As we have said, in Sankhya doctrine all agency, acts and their flowering (fruiting) belong to the domain of *prakṛti* and do not ultimately affect the *puruṣa* (because the self that responds to senses is not identical with the self that experiences: I taste but it is another I that reads the I that tastes). For Krishna the I that interprets and the I that experiences is Atman, and hence he sees no contradiction between Sankhya and Yoga. By Yoga Krishna, of course, means self-control (and the technology of self-control) by the agency of the self.

We need, finally, greater clarity on the part of Krishna as to who really is the agent in all this acting. In Mimansa doctrine the self is the agent, he/she does the acting and the consequences rightly accrue to him/her. Sankhya posits two categorically different orders: *puruṣa* and *prakṛti*. It is in *prakṛti* that all activity occur because in its pure state the *puruṣa* is unchanging (like the Atman). But when the *puruṣa* (mysteriously) gets involved with *prakṛti* or when the unchanging *puruṣa* finds itself in the *prakṛti*-produced body it wrongly identifies itself with the body and begins to think "I am the agent." It senses and thinks that it acts when in fact it is *prakṛti* that acts. Krishna's point is that only when through the act of *buddhi* we realize this bondage of the *puruṣa* in *prakṛti* (in the body) are we able to get out of the rut. The rest follows because this knowledge then allows us to understand the true nature of the self and its relationship to action.

Sankhya theory is more conducive to Krishna who is, after all, a transcendentalist. As we have noted in an earlier context, in chapter 13 we are introduced to two key concepts, both straight out of Sankhya philosophy: *kṣetram* (the field), which is the body, and *kṣetrajña* (the knower of the place or the field), the guide or the soul. Making himself the knower and guide of all the fields, Krishna goes on to say that knowledge is considered by him to be true knowledge: *yat tat jñānam matam mama*. The key words used in Krishna's explanation—*mahābhūtāni* (elements), *ahaṃkāra* (I-consciousness), *buddhi* (knowledge/intelligence), *avyaktam* (unmanifest), *indriyāṇi* (senses), *prakṛti*, *puruṣa*, *guṇa*—are all straight out of Sankhya philosophy. Having established the basic outline of the system in chapter 13, in subsequent chapters Krishna refines key concepts or at least takes up specific notions that may have had a more general currency in the culture of the time. Thus in chapter 14 Sankhya evolution theory is addressed especially with reference to the planting (by Krishna himself) of the seed (of "production") in the womb of Brahma. The role of the three *guṇa*s as evolutes (i.e. as "items" that transform the nonindividualized *prakṛti* into the phenomenal) is then linked to bliss, activity, and negligence. Each of these qualities of course can overpower the other and become the dominant force in any given individual. They also preordain the nature of the self in the next life. To Krishna a person must know that it is not the Atman but *guṇa*s (that are part of *prakṛti*) that act. Armed with this knowledge this person would achieve liberation because he/she understands the fixed, unchanging nature of the *puruṣa*. To Arjuna's question as to how one may know that transcendence has been achieved Krishna characteristically replies that this is achieved by persons of equanimity who through Yoga (as variously defined) understand the ultimate unity of being and Krishna's own status as the foundation of Brahman (*brahmaṇo hi pratiṣṭhā aham*). In chapter 15, then, Krishna can speak more explicitly about this third supracategory, which is the foundation of Brahman. In Sankhya there is the duality of *prakṛti* and *puruṣa* (one is transient, the other intransient): "there are two persons in the world, the transient and the intransient": *dvāv imau puruṣau loke/kṣaraś ca akṣaraḥ* (15.16). In Krishna's argument there is also a third person, the Supreme Soul, the everlasting Lord that permeates and supports the three worlds (*uttamaḥ puruṣas tu anyaḥ/paramātmā iti*). This knowledge (of the third supracategory) is again presented, as in the above chapters, in the general context of achieving eternal bliss.

Finally in chapter 16 is introduced the *daivīm* and the *āsurīm* complements (or destinies): the *daivīm* is the divine complement (linked to the virtues that Krishna has described at length, virtues of purity, fortitude, self-control, truthfulness, and so on); the *āsurīm* is the demonic complement. The divine complement Krishna tells Arjuna leads to release (*daivī saṃpad vimokṣāya*), the demonic complement to bondage (*nibandhāya āsurī*). Krishna speaks at length about the demonic complement and links that complement quite clearly to both Sankhya theory and its related expression in Buddhism. The argument is pursued at two levels: the first is clearly philosophical, the second, for lack of a better word, didactic, or moral. The first makes a distinction between a non-foundational system (such as Buddhism and early Sankhya) and a foundational one (in chapter 14 Krishna had declared himself to be the foundation of Brahman) where God is the source and origin of meaning. The second is related to a much more physical definition of desire. So what is Krishna's argument here? At the philosophical level the place to go to is 16.8. Let us consider the first of two translations of this verse:

> They [the demonic men] (*āsurāḥ janāḥ*) are without truth (*asatyam*) and unstable (*apratiṣṭhaṃ*).
> "The universe (*jagat*)," they say (*āhur*), "is without a God (*anīśvaram*)."
> It is not brought into being (*saṃbhūtaṃ*) by a succession of causes (*aparaspara*).
> How else (*kim anyat*)? It is caused (*haitukam*) by desire (*kāma*) alone. [56]

Note that *aparaspara saṃbhutaṃ* should really be translated as "brought about by mutual union of man and woman, that is by sex." This interpretation, that sexual passion was the cause of all beings, is not uncommon among certain commentators on Sankhya who want to explain how *prakṛti* gets transformed into the phenomenal world. In cultural theory (especially post-Freudian cultural theory) and in radical feminism (especially difference feminism) the patriarchal order is linked to the "production" of the social through phallic desire and power. Krishna is, of course, against this argument, but it does say something about the degree to which Buddhism and entropic philosophy generally had pursued a more materialist theory of causality. To ask the question whether the world is created out of desire (which does not require a God) can lead to a rigorous debate about the consequences of the links between *kāma* (desire/lust) and the production of the world. Before I proceed here is the second translation:

> They [the demonic people] maintain that this world has no true reality, or foundation, or God, and is not produced by the interdependence of causes. By what then? By mere desire.[57]

Here the word *satyam* is translated as reality and not truth and *pratiṣṭhaṃ* as foundation. Further *aparaspara saṃbhūtaṃ* is rendered as "the interdependence of causes."

Now what happens in the text is that the foundational argument or antifoundational argument (created by God or created by desire) is presented in ontological terms and individuals are read in terms of where they position themselves on this divide. Those who opt for the creation of the universe by God are clearly on the right side; those who opt for the creation of the world by desire are on the wrong side. However, it is one thing to say that the production of the world from *prakṛti* is a consequence of desire; it is quite another to say that we as individuals are therefore locked in the "economy" of desire. Krishna, however, must insist on the importance of the foundational argument (that is, creation by God) and connect liberation itself with whether you accept this fact or not. Those who follow the antifoundational argument (the world as a consequence of desire) would continue to speak in terms of "this I got today, that craving I still have to satisfy. This much I have as of now, but I'll get more riches . . . I am a master . . . I am rich of high family . . . I shall make donations." The enlightened ones (those who know that the elements of *buddhi* are not identical with the *puruṣa*) on the other hand being beyond desire can act through the *daivīm* (the divine) principle. Through its expression in the real world, desire is then linked to the *āsurīm* (the demonic) principle. The question at issue relates to the kind of argument we can advance to say that the shift from *prakṛti* to phenomenon is linked to God and not to desire. That the world is imperfect is no argument against desire being the imperfect nature of its cause. What one asks is why was there a need for an anti-Buddhist rhetoric in the first instance? Krishna has already made the case that desire, anger, and greed destroy the self's understanding of his/her own "real" self. But Krishna is always speaking about the transcendental self (the self that knows *puruṣa* with a capital *P*) against whom the corporeal self will always be seen as a lesser being. Even in chapter 16 the criticisms are really directed against a corporeal *puruṣa* who confuses two kinds of *puruṣa* (with and without the capital). I think Krishna wins the moral argument no doubt because the person who has transcended knows the true nature of the *puruṣa*, but in doing so releases an epistemological cat among the pigeons. The antifoundational demonic principle—the world as the creation of desire—introduces through the back door elements that lead to questions about gender, power, and sexuality in Indian culture. Although Krishna himself remains adamant about the superior value of the foundational argument, the "release" of the antifoundational (even as a means of making the foundational look more attractive) nevertheless presents us with a powerful alternative that links phenomena (and God itself) to the economy of desire. Read in this deconstructive fashion (which is also part of the brahminical commentarial tradition) the *Bhagavadgītā* shows that classical Indian culture had grasped the nettle of a desire-based origin of the world of phenomena long before the European Enlightenment began to grapple with the idea. Perhaps the growth of Buddhism is a testimony to that idea.

To dwell on the *Bhagavadgītā* at length is a demand that the definition of the Indian sublime makes on a theorist. For the *Bhagavadgītā* is *the* text that lays down the ground rules of the encounter between the subject and God as the unpresentable. By situating itself in the midst of current discussions about philosophy and truth (as well as in the midst of deconstructive philosophies such as Buddhism), the *Bhagavadgītā* sums up what may be referred to as classical or high Hindu thought. But as we contextualize the work in the grand epic and as we gradually work our way through this intricate and dense text, as we read a text "overdetermined" both by the "native" as well as orientalist commentarial traditions, we are finally confronted by the grand vision of the Krishna of chapter 11 and Krishna's response to that vision. In that moment, the Indian sublime explodes into our consciousness with images so vast, so grand (in the Kantian sense of the sublime) that, with Arjuna, we want to return to the security of the beautiful and in doing so ask Krishna to return to the form by which we know him.

In Hegel's circular argument, it is the absolute Idea that produces the world (nature) which produces human beings and human beings through labor produce history, knowledge, and self-consciousness and hence the Mind that ultimately reproduces the absolute Idea. In some senses this is very much Krishna's thesis too. The absolute Idea as Brahman produces the world, which then gets the Hegelian narrative going. Why then the terrible unease shown by Hegel on Indian matters? Part of the unease relates directly to the excessive figuration of the divine that defeats (so Hegel argued) the sublime otherness of the Absolute. And it is here that the *Bhagavadgītā* is the text with which to answer Hegel's unease. In the *Bhagavadgītā* "fantastic symbolism" is not rampant since there is always a dual narrative at work in the text. At every level the *Bhagavadgītā* emphasizes the avataric (the necessity of God to reincarnate himself if need be) even as it stresses the unpresentability of Brahman. And so in the vision granted to Arjuna (arguably the "scene" that Hegel had in mind when he composed his Hindu critique with reference to its fantastic symbolism) the excessive symbolization does not lead to any adequation between the idea and its referents. Indeed the referents simply confound Arjuna who, finally, has no means of transforming them into a totality. Arjuna remains baffled but there is a moment, the moment of the letting-go on the part of the law of reason, that allows Arjuna an insight into the sublime otherness of Krishna. What we get here is precisely the sublime narrative of success-in-failure, the logical end of desire in the apocalyptic moment and one's retreat from it, that is at the center of this the grandest of all texts of the Indian sublime. Devotional poetics is composed in the shadow of this extraordinary text.

CHAPTER THREE

Devotional Poetics

No knowledge is self-evidently present in a text; no information or message is given unambiguously. All texts (scientific documents, legal tracts, historical manuscripts, and the like) must be interpreted before their meanings can be understood or divulged. Yet of all texts it is to the literary that the term *interpretation* (or *reading*) is most often applied. This is because the literary—and especially the literary work of art—is consciously designed as a network of dense semantic configurations that requires the most systematic acts of interpretation. It is in the literary that nothing is redundant; every word, every period, even its layout, carry meaning. One emphasizes the act of interpretation because the coming into being of a literary text is the result of a dialectical process along an axis that involves both the text and the reader. This prioritization of the literary above other written texts—the legal, the scientific, or the historical (which, as we have said, too require interpretation)—is part of a process of cultural prioritization based on the assumption that the literary is the most complex of all discourses. It must be said, however, that not all literary texts are equally dense or complex, or equally open to the same norms of interpretation. A given text may yield a lot more through one kind of interpretation than another, and each interpretation has its own ground rules. Texts that explore the voices of repression, or texts that, for the first time, speak about matters that are new and different, may not be stylistically dense but may be some of the most exciting to a particular class of readers. But even as we make these qualifications (or indeed because we make these qualifications), it does not follow that every reading is as good or as valid as another; it does not follow that since, finally, the literary too is a cultural commodity, all literary texts should be "levelled out" because of a "higher" principle of cultural democratization.

There are some interpretations (of a given text or corpus) that are more valid than others, some that seek out the signals given in the text with a greater degree of sensitivity, some that are more sincere to the generic parameters within which texts have been composed and some (the intentional fallacy not withstanding) that do come closer to the spirit of the author or the specific culture at whose behest the text was "authored." In short, any reading of a text cannot be divorced from its precise literary system, from its rhetorical organization, from the formal conventions that govern its production (poesis), and from the prevailing social and historical conditions (ideology) of which it is a product. To rephrase John Guillory's definition of "canonicity," we can say that reading or the construction of meaning "is not a property of the work itself but of its transmission, its relation to other works in a collocation of works."[1]

The genre of the poetry of devotion has all the qualities of a literary text: it is written in a code that requires a community of speakers for its decoding; it conveys a message; it presupposes a reader or interpreter of that message; its meaning is socially constituted; its discourse is linked to the generic conventions of poetry; and it cannot be wrenched from its prior intertexts. As a speech-act it possesses the four crucial elements of sender, message, receiver, and a sociosemantic context. These characteristics of the speech-act model follow the principle that for real communication to take place the sender must convey to the receiver a message that the receiver does not know. In certain situations (in flattery for instance) the message may well be redundant as senders simply reinforce what receivers wish to know about themselves. Now in the case of the poetry of devotion we begin to get very close to the latter situation where the sender (the poetic self) wishes to send a message to God (the object of desire) that both God and the reader of the text already know. In this situation the sender simply wishes to ingratiate himself in the eyes of the Lord by reconfirming knowledge of which God is always the source. As for the informed reader the "communicability" of the devotional is a transcendental argument since a devotional poem cannot exist without this *a priori* presupposition. (Indeed one could argue that no literary text can exist without this transcendental principle of "communicability.") If this were not so it is unlikely that the (ideal) reader in question would be interested in a devotional poem in the first instance. It must be said, however, that like any other speech-act, the devotional poem too can be radically misread by a reader who, to use Harold Bloom's well-known phrase, may be tempted to "misprision" it. Without any knowledge of the "rules" of devotional composition and reception, this barely tamed reader can become an "intellectual entrepreneur" on an aesthetic rampage playing havoc with the text. The upshot of this proposition is that without an explicit category of the (ideal) reader of the devotional text (as one finds in George Herbert for instance), devotional texts may forego their "intrinsic" semantics and point of view. What we need to stress is that of all the genres of literature, the devotional poem is one that is most prescriptive about who its ideal reader should be. While even this genre can be read in any number of ways, as a systemic form it must still insist upon its own generic specificity insofar as its very existence as a genre apart presupposes that it should not be "misread." In reading theories of devotional verse we need to keep the concept of the reader firmly in mind. Thus in devotional verse questions about the phenomenology of reading become particularly urgent.

The first of three readers of devotional verse I would want to discuss at this point is the English man of letters and lexicographer Dr. Samuel Johnson (1709–84). Dr. Johnson held strong opinions on just about everything and when it came to devotional verse he approached it with the same opinionated attitude. There are, he said, transcendental arguments about what poetry should do and what it should represent. In terms of these arguments poetry should always delight through unusual or uncommon modes of representing the world. Its value is directly proportional to the extent to which it succeeds in communicating and "delighting." Now the difficulty with devotional verse is that it wants to give symbolic form not to objects and ideas in the phenomenal world (which can be both communicated and aesthetically transformed into the "pleasing") but to the sublime object of religious belief (which can neither be communicated nor aesthetically embellished). Since this sublime object is by definition ungraspable (or unpresentable), it cannot be aestheticized through a genre (poetry) in which the poet as believer is simply overawed by the idea of God. This is how Dr. Johnson makes his case:

> It has been the frequent lamentation of good men, that verse has been too little applied to the purposes of worship, and many attempts have been made to animate devotion by pious poetry; that they have seldom attained their end is sufficiently known, and it may not be improper to inquire why they have miscarried.
>
> Let no pious ear be offended if I advance, in opposition to many authorities, that poetical devotion cannot often please. The doctrines of religion may indeed be defended in a didactick poem, and he who has the happy power of arguing in verse, will not lose it because his subject is sacred. . . .
>
> Contemplative piety, or the intercourse between God and the human soul, cannot be poetical. Man admitted to implore the mercy of his Creator, and plead the merits of his Redeemer, is already in a higher state than poetry can confer.[2]

These are very strong words indeed. According to Dr. Johnson you can argue in verse (there is nothing wrong with using the form to make a didactic point) but heaven forbid if you want to actually write a religious poem. There can be no argument on this: since God is far too good for words, the act of using words to speak about one's special ("contemplative") relationship with God is to attempt the impossible. In a typically eighteenth-century English fashion Johnson simply tells poets to stay away from this sublime object. However, even as Johnson implicitly equates God with the sublime, there is little evidence that he had any real time for the concept of the sublime itself although Longinus's *Peri Hupsous* ("On the Sublime") had been available in Boileau's French translation for many years, and was familiar to English aestheticians from Addison to Dennis and Burke.[3] Dr. Johnson's concern remains centrally with questions of correct representationalism:

> Poetry loses its lustre and its power, because it is applied to the decoration of something more excellent than itself. All that pious verse can do is to help the memory, and delight the ear, and for these purposes it may be very useful; but it supplies nothing to the mind. The ideas of Christian Theology are too simple for eloquence, too sacred for fiction, and too majestik for ornament; to recommend them by tropes and figures, is to magnify by a concave mirror the sidereal hemisphere.[4]

It is clear that Dr. Johnson wants poetry to reflect the innermost reality of things and to present it in an essentially beautiful way. This is the role of poetry: to embellish the world so that it too can become beautiful. But even if Dr. Johnson did not care to understand the sublime as a philosophical term (references to the Franco-English Longinian tradition is absent from his dictionary published in 1755), it is clear that, for him, God is unpresentable to the imagination. One embellishes nature (a general term for everything within the grasp of our cognitive faculties) by making it more than it is; one doesn't add to something that cannot be grasped in the first instance and is perfect. So this is Dr. Johnson's advice: Do not attempt devotional verse, period. The advice is, of course, based on a very English distinction between literature and didacticism and indeed between literature and philosophy. So if poetry is beautiful (an aesthetic code) then its object, God, is sublime (a philosophical code). And since the sublime as God is not simply more "excellent" than poetry (the beautiful) but belongs to a nonpoetic field, it should be left to philosophers and theologians to argue about it. The exclusion of God from the domain of poetry underlines the dual agenda behind Dr. Johnson's rhetoric. The genre of poetry can reinforce memory (what we already know) but not create a new idea. The mind is not enriched by pious (that is devotional) verse because it has the impossible agenda of representing the unpresentable simplicity of Christian theology, something that can neither be troped nor fictionalized. According to Dr. Johnson the trouble with pious verse is that in attempting to represent the ineffable it is in danger of becoming both idolatrous and heretical. In defending the indefensible—that poetry can capture the glory of God—devotional verse just simply takes on too much, although it must be said that it is in the nature of this genre to attempt the impossible. It doesn't take too long for us to realize that a large part of Dr. Johnson's unease about the nature of devotional verse arises from what he sees is its intrinsic failure to distinguish between the reader of the text and the object of devotion in the text. The collapse of God/poet means that there is no new knowledge to impart (as epistemology) and no redefinition of the nature of God possible (as an ontological premise). What we need to do is to rethink Dr. Johnson's "common" reader so that textual meaning becomes a matter of interpretation and participation (and not a matter of "failure") within the norms of devotional verse. We must therefore construct a theoretical category called "reader" (already referred to as the ideal reader) in such a fashion that it can be applied specifically to the reader of a devotional text. We must redefine this reader as an active participant in the poetic process, someone who, like the oral poets of old, is willing to become a co-producer of the text and who knows how to read/interpret its underlying subtext. We call such an ideal reader an *infra reader* of devotional texts. This infra reader is not a real member of a community of believers; rather he/she is a "critical reading position" from which a particular kind of an intentional object—the devotional text—may be best understood. Without bracketing one's reading practice in this fashion (which, of course, also requires the imposition of certain limits to one's reading) devotional verse loses its own specific mode of being.

As part of our initial strategy of reading, let us quote a sentence out of context from a well-known work: "Actions do not stick to me." The word action, if we follow Hannah Arendt for a moment, is one of three fundamental human activities, the others being labor and work. Now in Arendt's powerful analysis action is shown to be *the* condition of humanity since it is the one condition that "engages in founding and preserving political bodies" and hence "creates the condition of remembrance, that is, history."[5] At the moment of birth it is action that creates the possibilities of a new world as we begin to move toward fulfilling our human destiny. To be born is to act. To claim that "actions do not stick to me" in terms of this reading would be absurd since actions are not only "the *conditio sine qua non*, but the *conditio per quam*"[6] of all political, and therefore human, life. A reader not familiar with action as a metaphysical category may respond to the sentence by substituting the word "actions" with "mud" so that the speaker of this utterance becomes a smooth operator on whom mud does not stick and who is "political" in a very different sense of the word. This reading does not add any further meaning to the utterance per se beyond suggesting that the speaker is simply a very slick operator. Most competent readers faced with this utterance would arrive at the same conclusion, even when they are told that the work from which this sentence comes is a well-known religious text of a particular culture. This information, however, does not destroy the reading advanced because these competent readers would argue that there are many priests for whom the statement is equally appropriate. Their actions do not stick to them either. They remain immune from responsibility because culture has defined priests as arbiters of our spiritual well-being who know what is good for us. Where ordinary humans are always subject to social criticism for their actions, priests, by and large, occupy a bracketed space because their actions are essential for our spiritual life. But imagine for a moment a situation in which the speaker is neither a politician nor a priest but God himself. And imagine also a speech act that is composed in a dead language that has acquired an extraordinary degree of mystical power in its own right. Imagine, then, the culture's own response to a Sanskrit sentence that is found in one of Hinduism's foundational religious texts, namely the *Bhagavadgītā:* "*na māṃ karmāṇi limpanti.*"[7] Placed in its proper context the statement now acquires unusual power. The context now provides a "reading-frame" for the sentence. Since the frame is a major Hindu text, concepts like "work" will have to be read in terms of their full metaphysical import. It is no longer a question of an open-ended reading or interpretation, no longer a question of total freedom to interpret or disclose one's judgement of it as though the sentence were endlessly interpretable (the definition of the literary) but one of "foreclosure." My use of the terms disclose/disclosure and foreclosure are by no means original as they were first used in this context some years back by Stanley Fish. I invoke them here because they are very useful terms with which to reenter the world of devotional verse.[8] I would want to tease my way through these terms once again to explain the special parameters of reading that surround devotional verse. Where the general community of speakers "discloses" the meaning of the sentence through a strong, open reading, the presumed religious reader (or more precisely our infra reader) of the sentence "forecloses" it. "Disclosure" implies reading the above sentence as an open-ended discourse, it implies reading it as if it were always eminently and endlessly interpretable. "Foreclosure," in this devotional economy of reception, on the other hand, stipulates that for believers there is a "correct" reading that they must first theorize so that they can understand the ideological network that governs the text in question. Disagreements with this stipulated reading, while always possible in any reading regime, must nevertheless be placed in brackets in the infra reader's reading of the text. In the sentence under discussion, the law of foreclosure (and only within this particular reception aesthetic, let me insist) excludes other meanings because it wishes to insist equally on both poetics and the cultural specificity of the text. In this semantic framework, then, Krishna's words to Arjuna are related ultimately to a theory of "action in inaction" so that the idea of renunciation or the pursuit of knowledge as an end in itself is not, finally, a statement of total inaction. Krishna's teaching at this point is simple and radical: the problem is not with action itself (implicit in Arjuna's unease about his proposed action in battle) but with how its consequences are linked to the self.

In this respect, when Krishna speaks of actions not sticking to him, he is not being a lucky politician or a Ronald Reagan but someone whose actions are pure since he has no wish to link his actions to the fulfilment of need and desire: *na me karmaphale spṛha* ("for I have no desire for the fruits of my actions"). Later in the *Bhagavadgītā* (9.9), the same idea is repeated with another verb: *na ca māṃ tāni karmāṇi nibadhnanti* ("And these acts do not bind me"). Except for the introduction of "and" (*ca*) and "these" (*tāni*), *na māṃ karmāṇi limpanti* and *na (ca) māṃ (tāni) karmāṇi nibadhnanti* are parallel constructions meant, as they do in poetry, to reinforce each other. The change in the nature of the verb from *lip* (smear, befoul, stick) to *ni* + *badh* (bind, fetter) is related to the imperative of variations on set patterns (both thematic as well as metrical) in oral poetry. At the philosophical level the variation, as we saw in the previous chapter, also underlines precisely the new relationship between agent and action that Krishna borrows from Sankhya philosophy. The text then generates sets of expectations and establishes a field of meaning potentials from which the reader selects a particular meaning that is in harmony with the claims of the text. Foreclosure becomes a necessary part of this reading process because what is required of the reader (the infra reader to be precise) is a level of restraint not available to Dr. Johnson's "common" reader, who will not be party to a text that "supplies nothing to the mind," that is, a text that constantly forecloses rather than discloses. Dr. Johnson, therefore, cannot cross his "common" reader with our "infra" reader because the didacticism of the latter conflicts with the former's desire for plenitude of meaning and freedom to construct alternative artistic worlds. The conflicting interest of these two readers is unresolvable since at issue here is the definition of the artistic object in question. To Dr. Johnson God is unpresentable to the imagination but since a theory of mimesis would claim otherwise poetry should leave the mystery of God to other discourses. This is not a directive that poetry can follow because it has never left this sublime object. In spite of the enormous impact of Dr. Johnson on the place of devotional verse in academia, it must be said that the demise of devotional verse had little to do with Dr. Johnson—in England its high point was reached in the seventeenth century anyway—and a lot more with a decisive shift from the religious to the secular and the democratic in matters of culture.

If we move away from the common reader to the infra reader, we may be able to do greater justice to the real merits of devotional verse. Since the proof of any theory of reading lies in its capacity to be universally applicable, it would be useful if we applied this theory to a Western literary text. Here are the opening lines of John Donne's *Divine Meditations*:

> As due by many titles I resigne
> My selfe to thee, O God, first I was made
> By thee, and for thee, and when I was decay'd[9]

When we read these lines as competent infra readers, the moment we encounter the words "to thee, O God" our act of reading shifts from free associations of words generated by "titles I resigne"—resignation from a post, refusal to accept a title, surrender to other forces, reconciliation of oneself to a new situation, acceptance of the inevitable or even a desire to reappropriate since "re-signe" is a homonym for "re-sign"—to the specific religious meaning of humble acquiescence to God's will. The moment this happens, the moment semantic excess (poetry says one thing and means another) is replaced by semantic parsimony or textual delimitation, we become complicit partners with the unseen author of the text and forego our right to construct meaning independently of the text's quite specific devotional directives. We could call this a form of intersubjective reading since the text is the origin as well as the limit of the hermeneutic circle. The overriding presupposition here is that the reader is familiar with the underlying codes of devotional discourse. These codes may undergo degrees of variation as is clear from the opening words of another of John Donne's *Divine Meditations* (Sonnet 10). The opening words of this sonnet—"Batter my heart"—are by any count an aggressive metaphor with a strong masochistic undercurrent. As an imperative statement it invites any number of interpretations linked to violence: rape, torture, imprisonment, isolation, and so on. But the moment the addressee is introduced in the same breath as the "three person'd God" the reader immediately forecloses his/her reading and invests the text with quite specific religious meaning. Someone unfamiliar with the conventions that govern homologous transpositions of profane discourses to the register of the sacred will misread this poem (some would say that this is not necessarily a bad thing) as an instance of a text in which two irreconcilable principles (the worldly and the spiritual) are violently put together to suggest a fundamental doubt in the mind of the poet himself. The argument is not without merit since in his earlier, secular verse Donne's subject matter had scarcely been religious. In his secular verse (for which he is best known), sex was celebrated as a form of social energy in its own right. But what happens in Donne's religious verse is that the same social energy is now deflected or rechannelled so as to underline a similar and equally intense desire for God himself on the part of the subject. To get to grips with the systemic use of these metaphors, what one needs are prior instantiations of the same kind of usage in a supporting intertext. In the *Cántico Espiritual* of the best known of all Spanish mystics, San Juan de la Cruz (1542–91), we get perhaps the definitive embodiment of the deflection of human sexuality on to the figure of God/Christ. Although the tradition itself goes further back to the *Song of Solomon* and beyond, San Juan's late-sixteenth-century composition is perhaps the most forceful articulation of this theme. Its structure in fact has so close parallels with Jayadeva's twelfth-century Sanskrit poem, the *Gītagovinda*, that one may even offer the structure as a narrative universal of devotional verse itself. The dialogue between the "bride" and the "bridegroom" with its dramatic question and answer sequence with the "creatures" (one recalls the mystical use of dialogue in Blake's *Book of Thel* as well) is framed in the discourse of the lover-beloved where the image of "battering" is strong. So the bride in San Juan de la Cruz's poem laments in the opening lines:

> Where is it that you hid,
> Beloved, and left me to lament?
> Like the stag you fled,
> having wounded me,
> calling, I came out after you, and you were gone.[10]

The strong sense of intense love and betrayal, the force of what C. S. Lewis once called the "frontal assault" metaphor, immediately recalls to the minds of common readers a highly charged, passionate encounter that has left the subject scarred for life. The loss is so intense that the subject conceptualizes sex as suffering, grief, and death ("I suffer, grieve, and die"). Of course, there is nothing against reading the poem through the semantics of repressed sexuality, and mystical texts are probably as good proof texts of such a reading as any. Nevertheless, the point I wish to make, and one that may also have a trace of political correctness about it, is that devotional poetry can be theorized only if we open ourselves to the culturally constructed and genre-specific signifieds of so many of the words in the text. The question of homology between the sacred and the profane thus becomes crucial to one's reading practice. It is the only way in which an often misunderstood but massive literary archive can be reinserted into contemporary literary poetics generally.

The persistence of some kind of homology in devotional texts was not lost on a remarkably subtle theorist of the poetry of meditation, Louis Martz, to whose extraordinary, though recently neglected, work I must now turn. Louis Martz read religious verse as a discourse whose structure followed quite specific meditative exercises. In this reading a religious poem may manifest some (or all) of the significant stages of a meditative process. In his path-breaking *The Poetry of Meditation* Louis Martz applied this theory to a number of English metaphysical poets and asked if a structural analysis may not explain a key characteristic of their verse:

> May it not be that all three poets [Southwell, Donne and Herbert] are working, to some extent, under the influence of methods of meditation that led toward the deliberate evolution of a threefold structure of composition (memory), analysis (understanding), and colloquy (affections, will)?[11]

The methods of meditation that Martz has in mind here are those prescribed, in particular, by St. Ignatius of Loyola and St. François de Sales. The general pattern of these meditative practices took the form of an introductory meditation which set the scene, followed by analysis (often through introspection), and a conclusion by way of a colloquy or dialogue with the addressee, that is, God. While the exercises themselves were terribly complex, long, and often quite convoluted, the poems of Southwell, Donne, and Herbert demonstrate a more selective use of the meditative exercises. For example, very often a poem would emphasize the later stages of an exercise with the result that the colloquy would occupy a much more central position in the poem. Much of the tone and manner of Donne's religious verse—"subtle theological analysis, punctuated with passionate questions and exclamations," as one critic put it—reflects a more elastic treatment of these meditative methods. The point is clearly evident in Donne's *Divine Meditations* [Holy Sonnet 11]:

> Wilt thou love God, as he thee! then digest,
> My Soule, this wholsome meditation,
> How God the Spirit, by Angels waited on
> In heaven, doth make his Temple in thy brest,
> The Father having begot a Sonne most blest,
> And still begetting, (for he ne'r begonne)
> Hath deign'd to chuse thee by adoption,
> Coheire to'his glory, 'and Sabbaths endlesse rest;
> And as a robb'd man, which by search doth finde
> His stolne stuffe sold, must lose or buy'it againe:
> The Sonne of glory came downe, and was slaine,
> Us whom he'had made, and Satan stolne, to unbinde.
> 'Twas much, that man was made like God before,
> But, that God should be made like man, much more.

Louis Martz sees in this sonnet a repetition of a special meditative pattern set down by St. Ignatius entitled "Contemplation for obtaining love." In this meditation the subject considers the many gifts God has given him and how willingly God wishes to become part of his life. The act of generosity from a being who desires nothing and who need not show compassion toward the sinner then leads to a meditation on how "God the Spirit . . . doth make his Temple" in the soul's "brest." This quite extraordinary and historically crucial moment that happens by God's own "adoption" (that is through God's indwelling in Christ) has to be reiterated and spelled out endlessly without simplifying the force of the paradox, which, as the concluding couplet shows, is actually the paradox of Christ's human form mirroring the primal moment of creation. Humans, after all, were created in the image of God in the first instance. The "wholsome meditation," however, is no complete duplication of a meditative exercise because the poem does not deal with the opening and concluding sections of the Ignatian meditative pattern. Instead, what we find is an exemplification of "understanding" or "analysis," the middle section of a meditative exercise, as the subject concentrates on his own inner self: "then digest,/My Soule, this wholsome meditation." In Louis Martz's reading a devotional poetics is directly linked to those mechanisms or technologies that a culture constructs for its own religious enlightenment. There is something of a mathematical procedure involved here: so many steps, on so many days, in such a manner. Thus in the Ignatian method, a meditation on Good Friday would require readings from the Bible that lead up to Christ's crucifixion. The readings would then be followed by three analytical procedures: concentration on the event, understanding of the event, and self-reflection. Now in the Donne poem under discussion the emphasis is only on the middle section, that is, on understanding or analysis. This is not uncommon in religious verse generally, though what Martz is suggesting here is that the other two stages constitute an absent structure that frames the middle portion. Since this is a sonnet, it could be argued that the generic structure of the sonnet (characterized as it is by a "turn" or *volta*) is a particularly useful vehicle for the deployment of an Ignatian meditative exercise. After all the English or Shakespearian sonnet's division into three four-line stanzas followed by a rhyming couplet is a ready-made structure into which a meditative pattern may be slotted. Conversely, the traditional division of the [Petrarchan] sonnet into an octave (first eight lines) and a sestet (the last six lines) is remarkably amenable to more extensive meditations on the moment of encounter (the image of God) followed by an analysis of the devotee's talk with God. Perhaps the confluence of the two—meditative structures superimposed upon generic conventions—explains why the sonnet lends itself so well to such an enterprise. In short, the meditative narrative that emerges in the poem could have a basis either in the underlying Ignatian meditative practice or in the generic conventions of the sonnet form. To give Martz due credit, he is certainly aware of this interconnection when he writes:

> Such a threefold structure, of course, easily accords with the traditional 4-4-6 division of the Petrarchan sonnet, and thus provides a particularly interesting illustration of the way in which poetical tradition may be fertilized and developed by the meditative tradition.[12]

In this basically protostructuralist theory (that devotional poetics is really a matter of locating underlying meditative structures endorsed by a community of believers) the emphasis is on cultural practice. It has to be emphasized, nevertheless, that no cultural practice of itself is meaningful unless our attention is drawn to it. What we get in Martz, then, is a powerful endorsement of the strengths of recusant Catholic practices in Protestant England. The picture, however, is not as clear or simple as all that because "a self-consciously Protestant concept of meditation was [also] taking shape" in England especially with

Thomas Rogers and Edward Bunny's "bowdlerized versions of some of the famous Catholic treatises."[13] These would be very valid criticisms if my aim here were to offer an exhaustive summary of the competing meditative exercises available in seventeenth-century England (Joseph Hall's Protestant meditations would become just as important as Ignatius Loyola's in this respect). What I am determined to do is to show through Martz a line of thinking that so powerfully suggests the existence of structural homologies between devotional verse and other religious practices. Whatever the value of the structuralist model—and Martz's structural connections between meditative practice and poetic composition is a decisive contribution to devotional theory—we must not forget the role of the reader whose entrepreneurial skills invariably lead to the construction of alternative (and to the believer more real) worlds. It is here that we must keep in mind the very special role of the model infra reader in any retheorization of devotional verse, even as we remember the importance of meditative practices (as structure and as performance) in the context of this verse.

Let me return to some of my introductory remarks, this time with a view to framing it further with reference to Stanley Fish's work. The following passage from *Self-Consuming Artefacts* is as good a point of entry as any:

> [T]he insight that God's word is all is *self-destructive*, since acquiring it involves abandoning the perceptual and conceptual categories within which the self moves and by means of which it separately exists.[14]

If the statement referred to another literary genre, its claims would indeed strike us as being somewhat excessive. However, in the context of devotional verse the desire to abandon one's "perceptual and conceptual categories," so as to merge one's self-knowledge and self-identity with God, is in no way unusual. The implied abandonment of one's perceptual and conceptual categories (which can never be totally abandoned to begin with) in the face of devotional poetry is part of the design of the genre itself. Implicit in this demand is a strategy that is linked to the need to differentiate devotional verse from other genres, as well as to mark out an epistemological space in which devotional speech act(s) can take place. What happens to Fish's model may be examined best if we were to return to the complete text of John Donne's *Divine Meditations* Holy Sonnet 1:

> As due by many titles I resigne
> My selfe to thee, O God, first I was made
> By thee, and for thee, and when I was decay'd
> Thy blood bought that, the which before was thine,
> I am thy sonne, made with thy selfe to shine,

Thy servant, whose paines thou hast still repaid,
Thy sheepe, thine Image, and till I betray'd
My selfe, a temple of thy Spirit divine;
Why doth the devill then usurpe in mee?
Why doth he steale, nay ravish that's thy right?
Except thou rise and for thine owne worke fight,
Oh I shall soone despaire, when I doe see
That thou lov'st mankind well, yet wilt'not chuse me,
And Satan hates mee, yet is loth to lose mee.

How does this poem become a self-consuming artefact? For one the text denies/consumes its sense of separateness (from God) as it does not offer itself as a repository of meanings independent of another authority. Since meaning, in this instance, exists only insofar as God endows a text with meaning (a "conceit" that we must accept) the text has no self-evident authority of its own. Reformulated, we can say that in devotional verse God speaks through the poetic persona, who in turn becomes a voice of anxiety. The voice and its semantic coding should not be read in isolation as the sonnet is part of a series (number 2 in the 1635 and all subsequent critical editions except Helen Gardner's). Many of the important words in this sonnet may be found elsewhere in the series and are therefore loaded with both intertextual and religiocultural associations. Thus words such as "resigne," "decay'd," "blood," "sonne," "servant," "betray'd," "temple," and "ravish" have a repertoire of meanings that go beyond the closed confines of a single sonnet. This feature is crucial to our understanding of the nature of meaning production in operation here. If devotional texts become meaningful in terms of their relationship to the "authority of God," then the idea of the self too is linked to ways in which this "authority" is defined. The concept of the self as an autonomous being will have to be destroyed: the uniqueness of the "I" (through which "I-ness" or presence is defined) is radically altered since, finally, the "I" no longer has a voice of its own. Absence of "textual" separateness is now reinforced by an equally emphatic demonstration of the absence of the "I" as ego. And this "dissolution" of the "I" takes place precisely through a radical transference: "I" becomes "thy sonne," "thy servant," "thy sheepe," "thine Image," "a temple," and so on. Finally, the usual speech-act model (sender → message → receiver) becomes redundant since the persona has no "new" message he/she can communicate. The final couplet cannot affirm "new knowledge" of any kind because the addressee (God) is perfectly aware of the nature of the subject's knowledge. A final question remains. If there is no message to communicate, why doesn't the poet simply destroy the poem upon writing it, and relapse into silence, or not write a poem at all? Perhaps the vast bulk of devotional verse is precisely of this nature, not unlike private confessions that are not meant to be offered to the world at large as intentional objects.

Why compose when nothing new can be imparted? Dr. Johnson didn't feel that devotional verse communicated anything that we didn't already know about God. It is a superfluous form because it cannot add anything more to the beauty of its sublime object. But it is precisely because the idea of the "new," the demand for originality, is so difficult to establish in this genre that the theoretical challenge of it is so exciting. For Stanley Fish the aim of the devotional poet is neither originality nor the dissolution of devotional poetry's generic frames, but to give what is known something of a semantic surcharge. For the reader, the "joy" of reading resides in the method of presentation, in the ways in which the already-known subject matter may be reformulated and the extent to which suspension of disbelief may be maintained or levels of meanings teased out without making the "message" itself superfluous (though in fact we know that the message is always redundant). In the second sonnet of Donne's *Divine Meditations* (Holy Sonnet 2) ["Oh my blacke Soule! now thou art summoned"] the sinner's need for grace, which comes ultimately from God, is "deferred" by a method of representation in which the "blacke Soule" is written in the code of a suspicious felon. As we have already noted this method (characterized by indirection, redundancy, etc.) is obviously the defining feature of poetic discourse. Here "indirection" is used to anchor the plight of the persona so as to "defer" a very simple prior knowledge about salvation in Christ. If we explore Sonnet 2 further, we discover a special instance of literary semiosis.[15] At the mimetic or referential level the text is relatively straightforward. However, at the level of "significance" (the process of semiosis that shifts meaning from the referential to the poetic) the poem signals the reader to take up the position of the infra reader. This "model" reader must now participate in the persona's religious experience. He/she activates the text and allows key words such as "herald," "pilgrim," "holy mourning blacke," to tyrannize the text in such a way that the reader is now faced with a parallel or alternative "modelling system" with its own quite specific semantics. In a text that we shall examine later—Jayadeva's *Gītagovinda*—the role of the infra reader is taken over by a participant (the *sahṛdaya*) in the poem itself. In this way the usual polysemy of the poetic text—its multiplicity of meanings—is structurally contained within a devotional regime of reading around the figure of the *sahṛdaya*.

Stanley Fish considers the self-consuming business of devotional poems as a series of "undoings" or "letting-go's" in which the perceptual frameworks in which we live and move and have our (separate) beings are undone. Thus the many pronominal and demonstrative markers of the self in Donne's poems—"I/me/Mine/My," "Thy/thou/thine/thee," "that"—lose their separate identities as the divide between individual self and God disappears in these poems. Written in the code of the maid who is ravished, Holy Sonnet 10 is an exemplary instance of a poem in which the identity of the will of the self and God's will is firmly underlined:

> Divorce mee, 'untie, or breake that knot againe,
> Take mee to you, imprison mee, for I
> Except you'enthrall mee, never shall be free,
> Nor ever chast, except you ravish mee.

Such a move leads to the surrender of initiative, will, and being and, above all, to the silencing of one's voice and the relinquishing of one's claims to authorship. Like oral texts, the devotional too becomes a product of collective composition in which author, addressee, and reader become indistinguishable. The upshot of the procedure is the undoing of the concept that the poem is a product of a mind distinct from the mind of God. Thus John Donne can write, "Your force, to breake, blowe, burn and make me new." Finally there is the undoing of the validity of discourse itself since the insight a poem yields ("Oh let that last Will stand!" in Donne's words) renders superfluous the "mode of discourse and knowing of which they themselves are examples." Not surprisingly devotional poetry aspires to the condition of silence.

I have adapted Stanley Fish's arguments, which he developed to explain George Herbert's verse, to clarify a number of theoretical positions that are implicit in this book. In a very real sense devotional texts are, as Stanley Fish suggests, "self-consuming artefacts" because in these artistic products of the mind the subject that writes ceases to have a separate existence since it is God alone who speaks through him/her. No truth that devotional verse imparts can compete with the absolute truth of God, nothing a poet can express in language can displace the authority of God as the Absolute Signified, which, of course, is another way of saying that in this sublime aesthetics God is ultimately read as a thing beyond representation. If God can't be presented to consciousness (something that worried Dr. Johnson as well), devotional verse knowingly participates in the impossible and the self-destructive but proceeds with it nonetheless because the compulsion toward religious self-expression is so very strong. But even as poetic language grapples with the mystery of the divine, its insistence on its own inadequacy as a mimetic mode becomes increasingly evident. The occluded texts of devotion are in fact the inexpressible texts of silence. In this respect the mystical tradition that underpins devotional poetics remains a powerful force. So the moment of composition is also the moment of de-composition, creativity is self-consuming, the subject faced with the sublime object of (non) representation can speak only to be overpowered by the voice of the Other.

One can, of course, reject the foregoing propositions outright. Religion, after all, may be read as a pathological instance of the secular and therefore the great discourse of the repressed. It is to overcome this alternative (and to many a highly persuasive alternative) reading that a devotional poetics requires the category of the infra reader, an artificial but necessary reading position for a devotional text. There are a number of strategies in the devotional text about which we should be cognisant. It is necessary for the subject in verse to undergo a process of continuous undermining. This "instability" on the part of the subject is paralleled by a similar instability at the level of the referents of the words in the poems themselves. Not surprisingly, interpretation often becomes quasi-allegorical because the reader is constantly reminded that the poem is other than what it seems since words are to be read neither in terms of their semantic plenitude nor in terms of their narrow dictionary meanings. At one level this is true of all verse. The difference here is that a countermimetic mode of reading acquires the status of a first principle in devotional verse. Indeed, how else are we to read something written on a subject as profoundly elusive as the sublime? Two theories—a theory of the subject and a theory of discourse—take on radically different and almost countercultural meanings here. In this argument the devotional subject is not an autonomous individual, the product of an historical process in which the subject comes into being through a high level of self-reflexivity. And discourse too is not a matter of free-floating signifiers with a galaxy of competing signifieds revolving around them. Instead semantic overcoding is replaced by semantic parsimony, an arbitrary mode of delimitation and control. Thus there is neither the powerfully free subject in total control of him/herself nor a language that plays havoc with the normal rules of semantics. Both the speaker and what he/she speaks are reduced to effects of the supreme, ineffable presence, and subject to a very particular cultural norm. In the face of the sublime the subject ceases to have a separate existence. But even as we say this it does become clear that the ultimate problematic of devotional verse, whether read through Dr. Johnson, Louis Martz, or Stanley Fish, is the awareness that God cannot be presented to consciousness. And it is here that devotional poetics intersects with what we have referred to as sublime poetics, the poetics indeed of non-representation. We return to points made in chapter 1 and move toward the corpus of poems foregrounded there. This corpus is North Indian bhakti verse, arguably the most comprehensive surviving archive of the genre of devotional verse in any language. To get our argument right and to establish the general context of the Indian sublime we begin with the semantics of this poetic archive.

The Semantics of Bhakti

As we have already noted in earlier sections of this book, the key word in Indian religious verse is *bhakti* or personal devotion to a loving God. Simple as the term looks in this definition, it is fraught with dangers. To begin with the social ideology of those who followed this path of devotion—and the followers never constituted a single homogeneous group by any count—was originally at odds with what we know were the beliefs of the Hindu orthodoxy. Where the orthodoxy maintained the undisputed continuity of its own great traditions, bhakti showed strong signs of being anti-establishment although as always in the process of vigorously resisting the establishment it too produced its own quite distinct concepts of order, design, and structure. A. K. Ramanujan's intervention—to which we return again later—is worth recalling at this point:

> Yet bhakti-communities, while proclaiming anti-structure, necessarily develop their own structures for behaviour and belief, often minimal, frequently composed of elements selected from the very structures they deny or reject.[16]

Thus a radical social ideology that affirmed worship or devotion over ritual, and individual goodness over collective dharma, in turn gets absorbed into structures that gradually drop many of the signs of bhakti's radical origins. The appropriation of bhakti toward ideological ends in some ways contrary to its original uses by the great Hindu tradition and its reappropriation by the culture's hermeneutic overlords, the Brahmins, as a central constituent of temple worship itself (the ritual of puja is rechannelled through the ideology of bhakti) meant that the radical antistructural possibilities of bhakti were neutralized and incorporated within orthodox Hinduism albeit with varying degrees of success, it must be added. In his remarkable materialist critique of Hindu culture, D. D. Kosambi, mathematician, Sanskritist, archaeologist, and historian of ancient India, came close to recognizing the complex manner in which bhakti ideology functioned when he spoke of it as one of the two "incomplete solutions" to the problem of "internal dissension" in India. Since Marxist theory is based on conflict between classes, Kosambi's argument presents bhakti as an alternative, class-based ideology that, unfortunately, failed to attract patrons. Why a ruling class would support an ideology that was not in its own self interest (until that ideology could be made into its own) in the first place seems not to have been registered by Kosambi. Referring to the later Shaivite and Vaishnavite divisions, Kosambi wrote:

> There is clearly more than theology involved. . . . The basis lay in the terms of possession and exploitation of the land, the followers of Shiva or Devi remaining for a long time the great landlords, while the small producer or landowner worshipped Vishnu; theological conflict developed only because economic conflict was a reality. Within a couple of centuries we have Vaishnava works, which put the follower of Shiva on the same level with a beast or untouchable, though there existed great Shiva temples at places like Banaras which were crowded with worshipers from all parts of the country.[17]

We go to Kosambi because he is one of those rare Indian scholars of his time bold enough to entertain the idea of a close nexus between power, privilege, and religious belief. The interrelatedness of these domains also explained, he felt, the considerable dearth of a genuine working-class literature in India because artists working in the vernacular languages found little patronage.

> The real potentialities lay in the languages of the people, but our Minnesingers found no steady patrons. Only in religious literature does a poet like Kabir survive to prove how great was the loss.

Kosambi should not have been surprised by the failure of these largely bhakti vernacular minstrels to find patrons. But some did—Tulsidas comes to mind—although patronage may indeed have stifled their original sense of protest and outrage. Yet Kosambi's history is perhaps more useful to our understanding of the politics of bhakti than other purely "literary" readings such as that proposed by Daniel Ingalls, who, responding to the Kosambi thesis, argued that theories of society should be admitted only after "one has in mind clearly what the texts mean and what their authors were seeking to achieve":

> The path to a proper understanding of Sanskrit poetry must begin with Sanskrit poetry itself, with trying to understand and if possible to reproduce its specifically poetic effects. In finding one's way one must seek guidance from those versed in the tradition, from the great critics of the ninth to the thirteenth centuries, and from those few modern Indians and fewer Europeans who can understand and interpret their works . . . the path of the critic of poetry must begin with poetry, not with theories of society.[18]

We won't begin with poetry as such but with another kind of literary evidence that connects us with questions of usage. To complete our account of the semantics of bhakti we will examine in quick succession, the philological basis of the word *bhakti*, its presence in the textual tradition, before concluding with a reading of key bhakti treatises of Shandilya and Narada. If we begin by deferring to the authority of a dictionary once again it is not because we want to endorse everything a dictionary says about language. We go to a good dictionary because it offers us a compendium of literary uses of language that, though partial and often ideologically skewed, is our only point of entry into linguistic worlds no longer available to us. Thus the extensively cited M. Monier-Williams's *Sanskrit-English Dictionary* informs us that the Sanskrit term *bhakti* and the related word *bhagavat* have a common verbal root *bhaj*.[19] It also informs us that this root belongs to the first of the ten Sanskrit verb classes and can take either of the two sets of conjugational terminations, *parasmaipada* and *ātmanepada*.[20] *Bhaj* means "to divide, distribute, allot or apportion to (dative or genitive), share with (instrumental)" and so on. In the *ātmanepada*, the middle voice, it expresses the idea of "to grant, bestow, furnish, supply . . . to obtain as one's share, receive, partake of, enjoy, possess." The idea of sharing present in the root *bhaj* persuades a major scholar of bhakti, Mariasusai Dhavamony, to write: "Since sharing and participation, when used with regard to persons, indicate a certain communion of mind and heart and attachment, *bhaj* is often used to express love."[21] Some of the expressions of love—as affection, loyalty, possession—are directly related to the basic meanings of this verbal root. Formations of phrases with the root *bhaj* certainly demonstrate this. *Patnīm bhaj* ("to take someone as wife"), for instance, carries with it the notion of "possession," while *sukham bhaj* ("to experience pleasure") connects it to desire and fulfilment. Perhaps one of the most common declensions of this word in the literature of devotion is to be found in the word *bhajan,* which means "devotional song."

The Sanskrit word for devotee or worshipper is *bhakta*, a verbal adjective (a past passive participle) of *bhaj*, that is often translated as "distributed, assigned, allotted, divided." At the end of compounds it usually implies "forming part of, belonging to" and other similar relations. In the *Mahābhārata* there are instances of its early religious meaning: "devoted to, loyal, faithful," and so forth. The related *bhakti* ("devotion") has also, historically, carried meanings such as "distribution," "partition," "separation," and even "attachment," but its most common received meaning is "devotion." As the first word in compounds, it lent itself to word formations that were to become particularly important in bhakti thought. Compounds such as *bhakti-mārga* ("the path of devotion"), *bhakti-yoga* ("the discipline of loving devotion"), and *bhakti-rasa* ("the essence of devotion," which later developed into a poetics of bhakti[22]) are just a few of the many *bhakti–* compounds. Words that begin to have a very wide semantic range—the Tamil word *aṉpu* is not unlike *bhakti* since it too opened out to include meanings such as desire, complacency, love, favor, kindness, tenderness, and so on—have a tendency to collapse secular and religious meanings.[23]

There are other synonyms of *bhakti* that must be mentioned, especially since these words are used by later medieval bhakti poets. Among the synonyms are: *prīti* ("gratification"), *sneha* ("love"), and *anurāga* ("emotional attachment"). Whenever these synonyms are used, the bhakti implied in them invariably carries the sense of "emotional and passionate desire."[24] However, as Friedhelm Hardy has shown, the shift from intellectual to emotional bhakti marks a significant epistemic shift in Hindu culture largely because it was through the discourse of emotional bhakti that many of the lesser-known meanings of the root *bhaj* began to reemerge. It was only when emotional bhakti could be legitimately used toward religious ends that an entire poetics of devotional verse became possible. In this poetics, which reached its theoretical apotheosis in the writings of the early sixteenth-century devotional theorist Rupa Gosvamin, bhakti acquired the status of an aesthetic rasa. The tendency toward an emotional or even mystical reading of the word becomes more dramatic when we recall that this deep sense of mysticism was missing from the Sanskrit contexts in which the word (and its cognates) initially existed. In the *Bhagavadgītā*, for instance, it is difficult to see how bhakti could have been anything other than an intellectual form of Yoga that emphasized another, radical, way in which the mind may be disciplined. While the presence of the basic meaning of a devotional relationship between self and God cannot be denied in any use of the word *bhakti*, Sanskrit texts like the *Bhagavadgītā* do not show many examples of the more vigorous, passionate nature of bhakti's subsequent usage. The kind of recoding of bhakti through the semantics of desire that led H. Guntert to argue that bhakti was libido raised to the higher state of *amor Dei*[25] is lacking in the canonical Sanskrit texts. The semantics of bhakti begins to take a radically different shape only when concepts such as "empathy," "encounter," and, most significantly, "participation" become part of its semantic field. It is the latter possibility that encouraged Louis Renou to define *bhakti* as "participation amoureuse," that is the "affective participation of the soul in the divine."[26] Thus the lineage of bhakti from the early canonical texts to, say, the verse of sixteenth-century poets such as Surdas and Mirabai, is not a simple, unproblematic sequence. In fact something quite significant occurred between Krishna's exhortation that the devotee is his beloved and Narada and Shandilya's catalog of the diverse kinship metaphors that one could use to speak about one's relationship with God.[27] Jeffrey R. Timm's examination of emotion in the religious experience of the philosopher-theologian Vallabha (1479–1531) has drawn our attention to the power of the affective in bhakti. As Timm demonstrates "Vallabha's devaluation of asceticism and his affirmation of emotional worship"[28] has both an aesthetic and a clearly philosophical dimension. Aesthetically "emotion" stresses *bhāva* (felt experience) over *rasa* (abstract aesthetic response) and in doing so subverts one of the crucial determinants of Indian reception theory. Philosophically, "emotion" turns the renouncer/man-in-the-world system on its head by again denying the "trans-dharmic" status granted to the renouncer. Between the Krishna of the *Bhagavadgītā* and the Krishna of Vallabha the definition of *bhakti* is certainly not identical.

Bhakti is thus not a straightforward word, either in terms of its intrinsic meaning or in terms of its use as a description for a major religious movement. Sometimes, however, its essential heterogeneity is skewed by scholars for purposes of establishing massive historical continuities. Often the motive here, it seems, is to connect devotionalism with a stronger intellectual tradition in Hinduism even when it leads to a naive historical revisionism. Munshiram Sharma is one such contemporary Indian scholar whose critical works in Hindi indicate a reading of the growth of Hindu theism (from at least the late Vedic texts onwards[29]) as an essentially linear bhakti phenomenon. Munshiram Sharma in fact argued:

> Beyond the worlds of reality, consciousness and time, there is a *tattva* ("essence") which is not bound to "causality," attributes or time. The aim of bhakti is to enable the bhakta to realise this "essence." This *tattva* is *īśvara*. How can we find *īśvara*?[30]

Historically this leads to a neat and systematic theological formulation: the quest for Godhead is coterminous with *bhakti*, a term that Sharma indeed uses as a descriptive term for Hinduism generally. Bhakti, in short, becomes a complete religion in its own right.

The insistence on theistic continuity on the part of Indian and Western scholars such as Munshiram Sharma and Dhavamony is really based on the idea of bhakti as the eternal or the *sanātana* religion. At one level there is support for this since in an early reference to "bhakti" in the *Śvetāśvatara Upaniṣad* we read: "These subjects which have been declared shine forth to the high-souled one who has the highest devotion [*para bhakti*] for God."[31] Although S. Radhakrishnan himself emphasizes that the *Śvetāśvatara Upaniṣad* is theistic in character because it stresses not so much Brahman the Absolute but *īśvara*, the personal God,[32] to argue as M. Dhavamony does ("The *Śvetāśvatara* . . . attempts a new synthesis of Vedic and Upanishadic doctrines under the aegis of a personal God . . . and crowns the ancient spiritual ways with its doctrines of grace and bhakti to Shiva"[33]) is to overlook the discontinuous and markedly heterogeneous nature of the development and growth of bhakti. Against its presumed use in the Hindu intellectual tradition (and even there it is by no means simple) the term *bhakti* had a decidedly different meaning when it referred to emotional discourses. The idea of liberation found in the Upanishadic reading of bhakti in fact underwent significant changes as its key terms (renunciation, meditation, asceticism, and so on) were subjected to vigorous interpretations. It is certainly possible to argue that the new political and religious affiliations in India at the start of the second millennium began to advance different ways in which erstwhile concepts were interpreted. And in the new political climate too, religious orders began to come under patronage (and threat) of a different kind. Timur, the Central Asian tyrant, for instance, ransacked Meerut and Hardwar in 1399 C.E. convinced that "he had come to Hindustan to wage a Holy war upon the infidels."[34] The impact of such full scale destruction of sacred Hindu sites should not be underestimated since destruction of sacred sites often meant the loss of a timeless point of reference.

It seems more likely, then, that far from being an unproblematic development of an earlier theistic impulse—the sort of linear development endorsed by someone like Munshiram Sharma or Mariasusai Dhavamony—emotional devotion as bhakti was problematically incorporated into the dominant religious ideology by the Brahmins. To them emotional bhakti had a twofold function. First, its roots in a barely articulated pre-Aryan aboriginal religiosity meant that marginal traditions could be given a place in the major tradition without offending the orthodoxy. And second, as Biardeau suggests, the orthodoxy looked within for a solution to the abolition of "kāma in the very heart of man's ordinary activity."[35] "In other words," continues Biardeau, "it would seek to imbue secular life with the sannyāsin's ideal." Since the ideal to which the culture aspired was renunciation, bhakti, a selfless devotion toward a personal God (devotion through *svadharma*) was an exemplary instance of escape from the condition of the world. Two fundamental concepts—the renouncer and the man-in-the-world—remain crucial to our understanding of bhakti as a possible solution to an irresolvable binary in Hindu culture.

The Ideology of Bhakti

In terms of the foregoing I would want to argue that the ideology of bhakti cannot be divorced from three aspects of Hinduism we have discussed thus far: (a) the sublime object of desire, (b) the nature of the Indian self, and (c) the role of *nivṛtti* and *pravṛtti* in Indian culture. Furthermore, it is important to realize that there is perhaps a less continuous line of descent from the bhakti of the *Bhagavadgītā* to the bhakti of the *Bhāgavata Purāṇa* (a crucial text behind the growth of emotional bhakti) although to be sure Kapiladeva's account of bhakti to his mother Devahuti in the *Bhāgavata Purāṇa* uses many of the ideas of the *Bhagavadgītā* including the concept of "desireless devotion" (book 3, chapter 26). In the *Bhagavadgītā*, bhakti was rendered as a yogic alternative to knowledge and action in which the intellect remained important since the four types of bhaktas that Krishna distinguishes (*ārtas, jijñāsus, arthārthī, jñāni*, the suffering self, the seekers of knowledge who have not as yet found knowledge, the seekers of wealth, and the wise[36]) expressed quite categorically their intellectual leanings. We need to acknowledge that the shift from the intellectual bhakti of the classical texts to the emotional bhakti of the later period is directly related to a number of significant historical and epistemic shifts in Indian society. For one Muslim invasions had begun to change the social map of India in a big way. Second, the growth in population and the expansion of a laboring class whose goods were needed for the urban masses meant that the feudal underpinning of Hindu social order were undergoing change. Thus there was a slightly freer market for the labor of weavers, tinkers, tailors, leather-workers, and so on. Finally, this economic mobility also meant that religion too became more mobile. Fragments of religious texts (often memorially constructed), homilies from an itinerant saint, an icon or two were sufficient for the emotional needs of people on the move. The bhakti solution to the perennial question of representing the unpresentable (Brahman) is to energize the idea of God with the language of emotion and passion and then to personalize it. The relationship between desire (for self-gratification or for union with God) gets rearticulated in terms of a personal relationship between self and God. As a participatory form of inner religiosity (after all its root *bhaj* has this meaning of sharing), bhakti therefore presented the orthodoxy with a revolutionary doctrine that transcended the limitations of caste and the dichotomy of the renouncer and the man-in-the-world. Louis Dumont had in fact argued:

> As distinct from Tantrism, here is, in my opinion, a sannyasic development, an invention of the renouncer. This religion of love supposes two perfectly individualised terms; in order to conceive of a personal Lord there must also be a believer who sees himself as an individual.[37]

Dumont overstates the case—bhakti is as much a creation of the Brahmin man-in-the-world as of his alter ego the renouncer, the *saṃnyāsī*—but his foregrounding of the self as the center of the man-God relationship is certainly true. The concept of the believer now suggests an individual who participates and not one who denies and retreats.

In medieval India—a "periodization" that is itself problematic although for our purposes it may be defined as the first half of the second millennium that was identical with Muslim hegemony in North India—bhakti takes shape in a soil that is vastly different from another Hindu age when Sanskrit was the court language and when the collective ethos of Hinduism had not been fundamentally challenged. The ideology of bhakti that emerges in this period is marked by a number of characteristics that are social and historical as well as metaphysical. The growth of vernacular languages (a direct consequence of the relatively new economic freedom of the artisan classes and the competing presence of a Muslim court language) meant that much of the spontaneity of religious expression could be captured in one's own language while Sanskrit texts themselves began to decline in importance. Toward the end of the high point of bhakti, the singularly powerful Tulsidas's version of the Valmiki *Rāmāyaṇa* (the *Rāmacaritamānasa*) displaced the Sanskrit original as the text through which the life and times of Lord Rama were disseminated in North India. The concept of the *satsang* or collective temple singing arises straight out of this shift toward vernacular devotionalism. But even vernacular devotional narratives depended upon Sanskrit models, the most important of which were the various Puranas, notably the *Bhāgavata* and *Vāmana Purāṇas*. These vast Puranas—eighteen massive compositions spanning by some accounts the period from 500 to 1200 C.E.—are a compendia of myths, instructions, religious lore, philosophy, indeed a veritable encyclopaedia of Indian intellectual thought. What the Puranas did was more than just catalog a range of myths. They were highly structured narratives that worked on a very systematic use of a "bewildering mass" (in V. Raghavan's words) of narrative combinations organized in a particular manner. Indeed, as F. E. Pargiter points out, the Puranas are a heterogeneous collection, of quite diverse writings that form

> a class of books written in Sanskrit expounding ancient Indian theogony, cosmogony, genealogies, and accounts of kings and rishis religious belief, worship, observances, and philosophy, personal, social and political ordinances, and opinions about all kinds of miscellaneous matters—the whole illustrated and enforced by tales, legends, old songs, anecdotes, and fables.[38]

In a very real sense there is nothing unusual about the design of the Puranas. Their generic flux is an extreme instance of the generic mixture one finds in all classical Indian texts whether epic, dramatic, or even, in modern times, filmic. But what is of importance to devotional theory is that the Absolute now gets rechannelled through its distinct avatars, notably as Rama and Krishna, who between them become the object of Vaishnava devotionalism. Since the *Bhāgavata Purāṇa* is essentially a Southern devotional text it carries the kinds of mystical experimentation that had been a feature of the Tamil-speaking South for some four centuries already. Its language reflects the special mixture of rapture and passion that was part of the Southern tradition. In time the Puranic texts with their undoubted contributions to "the continuity of Hinduism through the ages,"[39] began to provide the Indian with a framework in which devotional practices could be related to readily identifiable personal Gods or *iṣṭadevatās*. Moreover, the Puranas offer instantiations of the crisis of devotees as they go through various stages in search of their true God. The object of desire—union with God—thus finds a narrative structure that acts like a grid upon which the devotees' own steps toward self-enlightenment may be superimposed. Thus the "conflation" of the relatively autonomous figures of the Hindu *trimūrti*—Brahma the Creator, Vishnu the Preserver, and Shiva the Destroyer—not only leads to a confirmation of their equal status but makes way for the isolation of any one of these, notably Vishnu or Shiva, as the stand-in for the object of bhakti. In actual practice, the Puranas in all their multifaceted recensions become the immediate source texts of devotional Hinduism. Writing specifically on the *Bhāgavata Purāṇa*, J. N. Farquhar emphasized its significance as the source of a "new theory" of devotionalism: "What distinguishes it from all earlier literature is its new theory of bhakti; and therein lies its true greatness."[40]

In an exciting structuralist exploration of the *Vāmana Purāṇa* Greg Bailey has isolated a "bhakti structure" that lies behind Puranic narratives. Upon examining this structure carefully we notice that it lies behind any number of devotional texts and may be read as the structural dominant of bhakti. Following on from Greg Bailey's analysis, this structure may be represented as a series of narrative events or functions that may occur in the following systematic order:

1. Introduction
2. The state of ignorance
3. The start of spiritual realization
4. Commentary on God's grace
5. The devotee's conversion
6. The devotee's praise of the Lord
7. God's offer of boons to the devotee
8. The devotee's acceptance of boons
9. The devotee reconfirms his devotion by performing *karmayoga*[41]

If a subject is in a state of complete ignorance, like Saul (St. Paul) on the road to Damascus, then we may get the complete structure enacted in a given narrative. However, few narratives of bhakti actually demonstrate the complete pattern from *avidyā* (ignorance) to *vidyā* or *jñāna* (knowledge). In most cases, notably in the archetypal stories of Hanuman and Prahlada, the first five stages may be missing. Yet the force of the actual number of stages adopted lies precisely in the manner in which selected elements of the overall generative structure get actualized. As in Louis Martz's persuasive study, it is not so much the complete rendition of the abstract pattern that is important as the degree and extent to which the text is aware of the full pattern. This is one side of a theory of devotional poetics—that in fact the poetry of devotion is marked by significant correspondences between a systemic gridlike bhakti structure and the growth of the self toward some form of union with a personal God. The more dramatic the transformation (such as that of the non-devotee who finds bliss in devotion), the greater the impact of the poetic text upon the reader. Apart from the theoretical connections that we can legitimately make between the Puranic pattern and Propp's functions or Greimas's *actants*, it is important for us to also recognize a second side of this theory that would lead us to a consciousness about a radical ideological shift that underpins bhakti.[42] As is clear from Kapiladeva's comments on bhakti in the *Bhāgavata Purāṇa*, the intellectual and analytical positioning of the self in Krishna's dharmic exhortations are now replaced by the analogical and the anecdotal. In place of the metaphysical (as in the *Bhagavadgītā*) in the *Bhāgavata Purāṇa* there is a greater emphasis on the experiential, with appropriate digressions to the lives of bhaktas, from Harishchandra to Sati. It is as though one were moving from detached observation and judgement to involvement and enjoyment in the lives of exemplary bhaktas. Although superseded by many more recent works, J. N. Farquhar's early study captured the dramatic shift in bhakti rather well:

> Bhakti in this work [the *Bhāgavata Purāṇa*] is a surging emotion which chokes the speech, makes the tears flow and the hair thrill with pleasureable excitement, and often leads to

> hysterical laughing and weeping by turns, to sudden fainting fits and to long trances of unconsciousness.[43]

The emotions here arise out of a confusion between the subject's real experience and Farquhar's reading of them (in ways not uncommon in British readings of Hindu texts as a whole) but the point that must be made is that from around the twelfth century onwards in North India, the ideology of bhakti crosses over into the domain of emotion and feeling and begins to express itself in discourses marked by intense emotionalism.

As we have already noted, the crucial text of the ideology of bhakti—the *Bhāgavata Purāṇa*—contains a wide variety of influences, many of which came from South India. If we return to this the largest of the Puranas, we discover that it contains vast accounts of "popular" stories about Krishna, his "play" with enchanting herd girls and the stories of the child Krishna as both the butter-thief and the destroyer of demons. Book X of this Purana has a special place in bhakti verse as it is in this book that most of the popular themes associated with Krishna's life are given prominence. In particular, the ecstasy and obsessions of the cowherd girls become part of an overall cosmic "dance" on earth enacted by Krishna and his devotees. Indian writers have called this "Krishna-lila," the inexplicable sport of Krishna. In the other eleven "books" of the *Bhāgavata Purāṇa*, a host of related subjects—*jñāna* (knowledge), bhakti, and *vairāgya* (asceticism) among them—are discussed.[44] One of the curious paradoxes that the *Bhāgavata Purāṇa* successfully straddles (and one that underlies much of bhakti verse as well) is the conflict between a monistic or *nirguṇa* view of Brahman without quality or essence and a *saguṇa* view of it as multifaceted, that is, linked to the idea of avatars.[45] The *Bhāgavata Purāṇa* does not cast its vote either way as both these views—*nirguṇa* and *saguṇa*—may be found in the text. However, as a work whose "philosophic teaching stands nearer to Shankara's system than to the theistic Sankhya which dominates earlier Puranic works,"[46] the *Bhāgavata Purāṇa* is informed by a strong bias for the absolute unity of the self and Brahman. In this reading the phenomenal world is presented as the unreal work of Maya. But even as this essentially monistic view is endorsed we continue to find innumerable instances of actual physical encounters between humans and Gods in which ecstatic love supplants intellectualism. This anagogical-symbolic mode invests the text with an emotional dimension that makes the *Bhāgavata Purāṇa* such an invaluable source text for emotional bhakti. From 3.28–34 we may quote the following passage at this juncture:

> By such courses of meditation the Yogi earns love for the Reverend One and his heart melts in devotion, and his body is exhilarated by virtue of His love when he merges in the ocean of joy arising out from tears brought forth by his earnest search after the Supreme Being (Sri Hari). Thus his

> mind resembles a fishing-hook in the matter of such contemplation, whereby the mind gradually loses attachment for the object of thought [*citta-baḍiśaṃ śanakair viyuṇkte*].[47]

The translation here is literal but convoluted (or probably convoluted because it is so literal). However, the idea of meditation as intoxication through love as the "heart melts through devotion [and] one's hair stands on end, and one floats in tears of excessive delight"[48] is seen as a means of detaching oneself from sense objects. It is this excessive emotionalism, the positing ("posting") of divergent ideas and emotions in the same context, that made the *Bhāgavata Purāṇa* such an important document in the literature of Indian devotionalism. In fact, Hazariprasad Dvivedi called the *Bhāgavata Purāṇa* the text of the religion of the "common" people[49] because its definitions of key words such as *ātmā, paramātmā, īśvara, jīva,* and *jagat* were always constructed with feeling and emotion in mind.

The narrative of bhakti ideology thus gets refashioned through a discourse of emotionalism and through a metaphysics that transforms the phenomenal world into a Maya-ridden world of illusion and deceit. The view itself is not original but its discursive frames are. Shankara's intellectual position about true knowledge of Brahman being obfuscated by the web of Maya is rendered through analogies and narratives that bring metaphysics down to earth notably through a rich variety of anecdotal narratives.[50] So much so that this Purana is seen as the source text of so many of the anecdotes that have become the stock-in-trade of Hindu believers everywhere. The movement away from absorption in Brahman and dissolution in the Ultimate Reality (*sa yo ha vai tat paramam brahma veda brahmaiva bhavati*[51]) to participation and belonging to God (*yo madbhaktaḥ sa me priyaḥ*[52]) laid the foundation for a personal encounter between the devotional poet and his God.

In the new ideology of bhakti that is being forged out of a pan-Indian spirituality, the renouncer (as the bhakta) ceases to function, in theory and in practice, within the absolute binary of the renouncer and the man-in-the world. Referring to Jayadeva's *Gītagovinda*, an extraordinary aesthetic rendition of the Krishna-Radha love story, Greg Bailey observes:

> Vishnu gives liberation yet simultaneously preserves and sanctifies the worldly life for those who are his bhaktas. The bhakti tradition has always represented an ideological compromise between ascetics, those who seek liberation beyond the world of caste society, and ritualists, those who seek liberation within the confines of caste society. Bhakti sanctifies the idea of liberation within caste society.[53]

The sanctification of liberation within "caste society" implies a basic limitation of bhakti ideology itself. It is one that M. N. Srinivas tried to handle through his theory of "Sanskritization" only to acknowledge, finally, that while bhakti proclaimed a universal brotherhood and sisterhood, it never really transcended social class.[54] In fact, most bhakti poets produced a posthumous *panth* (path, sect, group) that simply reproduced a kind of "ethnic solidarity" among the caste of the founding bhakti poet. These qualifications clearly make the Dumontian construction of the mutual exclusiveness of society and the absolute order far too simplistic. Dumont had written:

> the society must submit and entirely conform to the absolute order, that consequently the temporal, and hence the human, will be subordinate, and that, while there is no room here for the individual, whoever wants to become one may leave society proper.[55]

Again Dumont connects individuality with *nivṛtti*, the rejection of society as such, because to be in society is to conform to the grand order of the Hindu world. Of course, as we have seen, the bifurcation of society itself is symbolic or "explanatory" rather than real and has very little to do with actual social practices. More importantly, in the ideology of bhakti, these exclusive principles are no longer a possibility because the self is itself an offshoot of a social order undergoing immense changes. It is not surprising, therefore, that even as bhakti made the erstwhile distinctions between the renouncer and the man-in-the-world archaic, its indebtedness to the symbolic power of the renouncer remained clear.

All texts are in varying degrees contaminated. In the case of the *Bhāgavata Purāṇa* its strong links to the Tamil Alvar mystical tradition can be explained, as we have already observed, by the simple fact that this Purana was an essentially South Indian text.[56] In the Tamil-speaking South, a poet such as Manikkavacakar, author of the *Tiruvācakam*, could write with an extraordinary sense of the mystical about the final two stages of the bhakti structure where the devotee seeks union with God:

> I do not crave for heaven itself; I do not deem it worthwhile to rule this earth . . . my only desire is: when shall I obtain your grace of love?[57]

The emphasis is on craving and desire, on emotion and passion and not on abstract reasoning as the soul is captivated by the sacred music of God. Liberation is no longer simply a matter of union with the timeless, spaceless Brahman; it becomes a union in love with a personal God. Again in lines so remarkably suggestive of the seventeenth-century English poet George Herbert we read: "Love joined me to your feet in mystic union."[58] In this way, the Tamil South was able to forge a "devotional form" that contributed to the growth of one of the most exciting devotional verses of the world—the poetry of the saint-singers of North India.[59] In a lot of North Indian *saguṇa* bhakti verse (one recalls Mirabai and Surdas in particular), there is a flood of passionate spirituality that undoubtedly reflects the poetry of the South Indian (notably Alvar) tradition. We now turn to this tradition before examining Jayadeva's *Gītagovinda* and, in conclusion, the bhakti *sūtras* of Shandilya and Narada.

The Tamil Alvars and the Vira-Shaivas

The complexity of cultural formations in India and their interactions are often overlooked in studies that deal with the general issues of devotionalism and the sublime. While the Puranas are crucial precursor texts for our understanding of the gradual refinement of devotional practice or indeed for the coming into being of devotionalism as we understand it, the Tamil Alvars and the Vira Shaivas added their own impassioned, quasi-erotic dimension to the entire problematic of self and God in the narrative of devotionalism. In this respect the Alvar Vaishnava saint-poets were among the first to understand the importance of intuition and the special nature of the love of God. The most famous of these Alvars, Nammalvar, in fact denied the validity of liberation or moksha without love of God: "Until the soul had made itself 'female,' it cannot receive the love of God," he wrote.[60] This mysticism with its "frank sexuality" and the feminization of the *bhakta-jīva* was an important step in the construction of an erotic language with which to explain the special nature of the devotee's relationship with God. In the verse of the Sufis (Rumi, for instance), the Spanish mystics (San Juan de la Cruz and Santa Teresa de Avila among them) and in the English devotional poets, we find a similar homology of the erotic and the sacred. In the end it led to the establishment of the lover-beloved as an indispensable structure in devotional poetry.

The defiance of a purely mechanistic conception of Godhead (the constant search for reintegration into the primal unity) that began with the *Bhagavadgītā*'s reformulation of the Upanishadic doctrines gets consolidated in these bhakti texts. In the teachings of the Vira-Shaivas, or the Lingayats, a twelfth-century sect found on the borders of Maratha and Karnataka country, religious devotionalism is again framed in the discourse of passion, love, and desire.[61] This sect seems to have been an organized community responsible for the construction of a number of monasteries where "ethical preachings and Yoga mysticism" were given privileged status.[62] The founders of the sect as well as Basava, its best-known exponent, were at pains to emphasize the link between the sect's practices and those of God Shiva himself.[63] The Vira-Shaivas are taught that each person can attain release in this life by practicing the prescribed meditations and by passing through the six stages or *sthalas: bhakti, maheṣa, prasāda, prāṇaliṇga, śaraṇa* and *aikya*. The *vacanas* or verses composed by these Vira-Shaiva mystics demonstrate an ardent devotion to an all-pervading God.[64] In them we find outpourings of emotion well in excess of anything we read in the North Indian tradition. However, this excess does not necessarily mean that the two main "systems" of Hinduism—the followers of Shiva and the followers of Vishnu—were in a constant state of antagonism, scoring easy points at the expense of the other. Although there are numerous instances of the Shaivite distrust of the exclusivism (*ekāntibhāva*) of the Vaishnavites, most of their prejudices such as the greater power of either God or their temporary friendly or unfriendly relationships are illustrated by "more or less casual remarks or references."[65]

In the *Siddhānta-sikhāmaṇi* of Renukacarya, a work written to amplify the nature of Shiva, we encounter the most systematic view of the sect. The conception of Brahman given here is basically Upanishadic—*sat-cid-ānanda* (being, bliss, consciousness)—without differentiation, beyond knowledge, and so forth. Shiva's qualities are described in transcendental terms with emphasis on his shakti ("cosmic power") though his dual nature as "creator" and "destroyer" is not lost sight of. The doctrine of *ṣaṭ-sthala*, which is central to Vira-Shaiva thought, stresses "the necessity on the part of every individual to look upon him and the world as being sustained in God and being completely identified with God."[66] These are S. N. Dasgupta's words who goes on to contrast *ṣaṭ-sthala* with Shankara's Vedanta. In the latter, the pupil is told by the guru that although the self does not melt into the pure consciousness of Brahman, ultimate knowledge is one of unity of self with Brahman. Dasgupta continues:

> In the Vīra-śaiva system the scheme of *ṣaṭ-sthala* is a scheme of the performance of the yogic processes. By them the vital processes as associated with the various vital forces and the nerve plexuses, are controlled, and by that very means the yogin gets a mastery over his passions and is also introduced to new and advanced stages of knowledge, until his soul becomes so united with the permanent reality, Śiva, that all appearance and duality cease both in fact and in thought. Thus a successful Vīra-śaiva saint should not only perceive his identity with Śiva, but his whole body, which was an appearance or shadow over the reality, would also cease to exist.[67]

This philosophical view sits comfortably with the *Siddha-siddhānta-paddhati* attributed to the ubiquitous Gorakhnath, the North Indian saint-poet.[68] In Gorakhnath we find a curious combination of Hath-yoga with the philosophical idea that the world and the individual have the same reality. Here a version of *bhedābheda* theory (called *dvaitādvaita-vilakṣana-vāda* or "duality-nonduality-difference-thesis") is upheld as the answer to Shankara's excessive nondualism. These hurried references to a number of philosophers is not gratuitous but meant to establish the highly complex ways in which cultural capital was disseminated and reappropriated in India. The echoes of Shankara in both the philosophy of the Vira-Shaivas and in Gorakhnath demonstrate a rather fluid religious milieu in which discrete boundaries between one sect and another or between one religious system and another were virtually nonexistent. Referring to the impact of the Vira-Shaivas on the North Indian tradition, Charlotte Vaudeville wrote:

> The deep similarity between the religious attitude of the Vira-Shaiva mystics whose teachings had already spread to Northern India in Kabir's time, and that of Kabir and the older Sant poets, is striking.[69]

We can now turn our attention to the *vacanas* or bhakti poems of these Vira-Shaivas to examine the strategies the poets employed to exemplify the six *sthalas* of the sect. The best way in which to do this is through A. K. Ramanujan's highly accessible translation and edition of a selection of their *vacanas*. In his introduction to this volume, Ramanujan points to two "traditions" that exist in any established "structure," which he designates "Little" and "Great" traditions: folk/classical, popular/learned, low/high, lay/hieratic, or peasant/aristocratic. The "Great" tradition brings together Vedic texts, Vedic ritual, a hierarchical caste system, and pan-Indian deities. The "Little" tradition is more firmly based on Puranic lore, regional sects and deities and on "minor" ritual. The two—Great and Little—collectively constitute the established, public religion of India. Against this public face of religion and culture, Ramanujan posits a "protest, personal religion" of bhakti, which while still being part of the "greater establishment" religion presents itself as an "anti- 'structure'," or to phrase it more strongly as an "ideological rejection of the idea of structure itself."[70] Having said this Ramanujan is quick to address the manner in which any "anti- structure" may be incorporated into a preexistent and sanctioned order if this is in the interests of the ruling/priestly caste. The process is made easier because "bhakti-communities, while proclaiming anti-structure, necessarily develop their own structures for behaviour and belief, often minimal, frequently composed of elements selected from the very structures they deny or reject."[71]

We know that any dominant ideology will always neutralize rebellion through its own inner dynamism. The case of bhakti makes this process abundantly clear. Although bhakti was instrumental in establishing an alternative space in the very interstices of the high/low divide of the public religion, it was very quickly reabsorbed into the dominant religious ideology so that what we get in India too is a process of ideological osmosis that leads to the reestablishment of the dominant ideology the moment it is under threat. The history of Buddhism in India and Hinduism's reaction to it bear ample testimony to this process. Hence, although bhakti as an antistructure begins by denying and defying the establishment, it soon gets reabsorbed as "the heretics are canonized; temples are erected to them, Sanskrit hagiographies are composed about them."[72] It too can become, in turn, defiantly esoteric and complex, and invite reactions similar to those it encouraged against the traditional structure.

In spite of this tendency, the initial moment of radical awareness is captured in the *vacanas,* where a new poetics of *sandhyā-bhāṣā* (*beḍagina* in Kannada) or twilight language advances the antistructural epistemology of the "new" religion with considerable force. *Sandhyā-bhāṣā* may be likened to what Michael Halliday has isolated as an alternative mode of linguistic expression or an antilanguage that is meant only for the ears of the initiate.[73] Examples of this discourse may be seen in the following two *vacana*s of Allama:[74]

> If mountains shiver in the cold
> with what
> will they wrap them?
>
> If space goes naked
> with what
> shall they clothe it?
>
> If the lord's men become worldlings
> where will I find the metaphor,
>
> O Lord of Caves.

> They don't know the day
> is the dark's face,
> and the dark the day's.
>
> A necklace of nine jewels
> lies buried, intact, in the face of the night;
> in the face of day a tree
> with leaves of nine designs.
>
> When you feed the necklace
> to the tree,
> the Breath enjoys it
> in the Lord of Caves.

The "interiorization" of experience expressed in these poems is couched in an anti-language that, at one level, challenges the critical doxa that poetry can be paraphrased in a "minimalist" fashion. Vira-Shaiva verse not so much constructs meaning as "deconstructs" it: the world represented through language cannot be grasped by the mind because the laws of linguistic association are being dispensed with. The secret of these poems exists beyond the immediate world of our sense perceptions since the words of these poems refer to an alternative—even a virtual—semantic universe. This semantic universe is the world of Tantra and Kundalini Yoga, which have their own special geography for the human body.[75] Thus the complex, inverted, metaphors of the poems link up with the movement of the Kundalini force as it progressively "arouses" the six *cakras* of the body. So far as subjects themselves are concerned, they "must constantly experience the process of homologization and convergence that is at the root of cosmic manifestation."[76] Yet there is no simple correspondence between *sandhyā-bhāṣā* and Tantrism as the isolation of Tantric metaphors in the discourses of this intentional language does not lead to the construction of an unambiguous world easily recoverable through the act of interpretation. *Sandhyā-bhāṣā* is then purposefully absurd, its constructed world so topsy-turvy that, as a devotional antilanguage, it requires complex discursive negotiations on the part of the reader. These negotiations also push the whole issue of poetic representation to the very limits of language and draw us to the impossibility of representing the sublime moment. In case we have missed the point, from the *Bhagavadgītā* to the Vira-Shaivas the sublime is being presented as an absence in the symbolic order itself. How this absence impinges on the poetics of love-longing may be best discussed through Jayadeva's magnificent love-poem, the *Gītagovinda*.

Jayadeva's Gītagovinda

An Indian Pastoral

The great text in the tradition of love (erotic and divine) and the "feminization of the self" that came in the wake of the poetry of the Tamil Alvars,[77] is Jayadeva's *Gītagovinda*. We shall read this text as an instance of the successful conflation of the sacred and the profane. Jayadeva's twelfth-century Sanskrit masterpiece is an extraordinary text, full of erotic exuberance and wonderfully creative uses of language.[78] Its preeminent place in the canon of Indian love poetry is due to its continued reading as a religio-aesthetic object even though its erotic sensuality must have made many religiously correct readers uncomfortable. It seems that Jayadeva was aware of this eventuality and inserted alternative reading possibilities in the text itself so that the transformation of the poem's strong erotic flavor, its Eros or earthly and sexual love, into what Nygren, in another context, has called Agape or "divine love," would be seen as a sign of spiritual commitment.[79] A text at once exquisite and so enchantingly daring produced its predictable effects. By the end of the fourteenth century exemplary verses from it were translated into Indian vernacular languages, its popularity underlined by an inscription from the text carved in stone in the Jaganatha Temple at Puri and dated 1499.[80] The reasons for its popularity are, however, not difficult to gauge. As a dramatic poem (often referred to as "unacted drama") it presented a literary narrative in which "the tradition of Radha as Krishna's favorite and the tradition of the *gopīs* came together to form the central heroine [theme] of the text."[81] Jayadeva's text is the seminal text when it comes to placing Radha in the story of Hindu goddesses. Later poets such as Vidyapati (1352–1448) and Chandidas (fl. 14th–15th centuries) would take up Jayadeva's version of the illicit love between Krishna and Radha. The importance of the rasa of *śṛṅgāra* (or the erotic) as the best means of expressing one's love for God would gradually become the dominant motif in other Vaishnava texts and practices, especially those subsequently associated with the charismatic figure of Chaitanya (1486–1553) in Bengal. In this "novel" expression of the love of God the distinction will be made between *kāma*, sexual desire for its own sake, and *prema*, which, though also involving sex and adulterous, is selfless and intense. The paradigmatic text of this mode of expressing bhakti is Jayadeva's richly textured paean on love, a text that captures the imagination because its Sanskrit is so totally unmannered and full of vernacular cadences and rhythms.[82]

The reception of the *Gītagovinda*, the commentaries written on it and the general incorporation of an essentially erotic text into Hindu mainstream religiosity fit into patterns we have already outlined.[83] The transformation, in other words, of the erotic into a religious metadiscourse, where the chanting of the text is equated with the worship of Vishnu himself, is suggestive of a complex but ongoing interaction between Indian religious and artistic sensibilities. However, since the theoreticians had not included a specific religious category in the original eight rasas (though Abhinavagupta's ninth rasa, *śānta* or peace, may fit the bill), religious texts were read through existing rasas because "the experience of union with *brahman*"[84] could be linked to any one of the existing rasas. The argument at this point, it seems, is one that avoided the linking of rasas with specific genres. The rasa of *śānta*, in theory, was equally available in the epics as well as in the devotional texts, provided that the reader could link elements of these genres to an appropriate emotional state. In due course, however, the sheer weight and extent of bhakti as a genre necessitated the creation of a rasa that would capture an aesthetic condition missing from the existing eight (or nine) rasas. While it is not possible to be absolutely precise about this, it may be suggested that the move toward a specific bhakti rasa began in response to literary representations of the subject's rapturous love for Krishna. And again in the context of this move we may locate the followers of the Bengali Vaishnava Sahajiya cult and Rupa Gosvamin, the author of the *Bhaktirasāmṛtasindhu*, as important figures in the construction and dissemination of this "new" rasa of bhakti.[85] However, Jayadeva himself did not have a specific bhakti rasa available to him and so he does not mention it in his poem. The idea of devotional love had to be overwritten through the discourse of *śṛṅgāra* which also meant that union with God had to be established through metaphorical tropes of sexual desire.

Indian poetics work on a complicated system of structure, "suggestion," and response. Lyrics, in this system, may occur as one-strophed songs, independent verses (*gaṭha*, *śloka*) or as a number of verses strung together to form a *khaṇḍakāvya* (a long poem) or *kāvya* (a short poem). They may be organized around a single emotion or may, indeed, be adapted to handle a longer narrative. Jayadeva's *Gītagovinda* is lyrical in the latter sense of the word. The poem is cast in the genre of the pastoral, a very simple though much neglected genre in literature. In the Indian tradition, especially, little attempt has been made to theorize this genre even though it is such a dominant form in the literature. I must therefore go to Western genre theory in search of a model of the pastoral. Here we find a remarkably user-friendly work by William Empson called *Some Versions of Pastoral* with which we can begin reading Jayadeva's marvellous poem.[86] Empson isolates two major functions of the pastoral. First, the pastoral process consists of "putting the complex into the simple," and second, the pastoral has a unifying social force as it reconciles divergent social classes and bridges differences. The principle of reslotting complex issues into a simple form is, however, not alien to the manner in which Indian literature itself operates. There is always a seeming simplicity of the literary text: to the untrained reader the Indian poet seems to be saying the obvious without paying due attention to the kinds of psychological complexities that a trained Western reader would take for granted. The reconciliation of social classes (Empson's second function) is a slightly more difficult matter to establish in Indian literature. In the West the reconciliation is often marked by the use of a parallel or subplot in which people from different social classes hold center stage. Although in the epic and in drama subplots may have this function, in Indian devotional texts we find a different kind of reconciliation of differences. In them it is the nature of participation in the text itself through chanting (*satsang*) that marks the beginnings of social solidarity. During the duration of the chanting of the *Gītagovinda* in the temple participants forego their social differences as they unite in singing the text. At the same time the text's seeming solidarity with cowherds means that the status of that humble caste undergoes a radical revaluation. This is one of the social functions of the pastoral—to give voice to the disempowered:

> Clearly it is important for a nation with a strong class-system to have an art-form that not merely evades but breaks through it, that makes the classes feel part of a larger unity or simply at home with each other.[87]

As a genre the pastoral has other functions too. One of its less obvious functions is that it always pretends that its limited semantic universe is the full and complete one. By extension the pastoral implies that this is what we should do with all art, that is, read it as a microcosm of the big picture. Other features of the pastoral that we may want to keep in mind are: an art–nature antithesis, a self-consciousness about literary continuity, a certain anecdotal predilection, an emphasis on the idyllic landscape, and finally a tendency toward a vision of the world as a game, a play or *līlā* of the Gods. In short, the pastoral's overriding concern is with harmony that sublimates desire. It is here, in the narratives of harmony and desire, that the *Gītagovinda* becomes so very important. And it will be left to the genre to rechannel or neutralize the energies of sexual passion that are suddenly unleashed in the text.

A clue to the pastoral orientation of the *Gītagovinda* is to be found in the title itself. Unlike the other song, the *Bhagavadgītā*, the song of the Lord, here we have a text that proclaims itself to be the song of "Govinda," probably a Prakrit form of *gopendra*, "chief of the cowherds." Govinda is in fact one of the many epithets of Krishna found in the text (one of at least thirteen in fact) and clearly connects the hero of the poem to his pastoral antecedents. More specifically, we come across the epithet "Govinda" in those stories that celebrate Krishna's childhood among the cowherds in the forests of Vrindavan. So unlike the *Bhagavadgītā*, the *Gītagovinda* is the love song about a pastoral swain, the flute-playing dark herdsman of a cattle-owning tribe who is both the divine lover and God incarnate. As a pastoral form, the *Gītagovinda*, therefore, becomes a crucial text for precisely the transformation of the complex into the simple—the complex divine song into a pastoral refrain—as the text attempts to mediate the gap between two seemingly irreconcilable worlds.

Our argument about the pastoral saying one thing and meaning another may be explored with reference to the manner in which the *Gītagovinda* articulates a number of oppositions: desire and its lack, the sacred and the profane, physical devotion and religious quietism, and so on. All these oppositions make their way into a poem that is structurally very straightforward. Divided into twelve cantos of between one and four poems per canto, the *Gītagovinda* follows the traditional principle of incorporating a number of signature verses (*bhaṇita*) through which the poet's own name and sometimes even point of view are made explicit. The convention of inscribing one's own name in the poetic text is designed to draw the reader's attention to the author as both creator and didact since he is the first person to be affected by the poem's "message." The convention, however, also has the effect of collapsing author and persona into one. Conflict is then not acted out or shown but simply told. Sanskrit theoreticians have called a poem of this kind a *citrakāvya*, literally a "picture poem" or an unacted anecdotal narrative. As V. Rahgavan has pointed out in his exhaustive study of Bhoja's *Śṛṅgāra Prakāśa*:

> [T]o the cultured soul of the Sahṛdaya, there is no difference between un-acted drama and poem. When a drama is not acted but yet can be relished as keenly by mere reading, it is only Kavya and it is supremely the art of the poet's genius only.[88]

The poem thus has a kind of stilled dramatic structure made up of a set of monologues spoken by Krishna, the *sakhī/sahṛdaya* (or friend) and Radha. It begins in an anecdotal fashion with a pastoral narrative that ends in a presumed sexual tryst on the banks of the Jamuna River.

> "Clouds thicken the sky.
> Tamala trees darken the forest.
> The night frightens him,
> Radha, you take him home!"
> They leave at Nanda's door,
> Passing trees in thickets on the way,
> Until secret passions of Radha and Madhava
> Triumph on the Jumna riverbank.[89]

In the original Sanskrit these lines have a tight metrical pattern designed to bring together the poetic devices of *śabda alaṃkāra* (in Sanskrit poetic theory formal patterns of rhythm and meter related to the "materiality" of the word) and *artha alaṃkāra* (the use of figurative language). The somewhat looser rendition of alliteration (*anuprāsa*) on the part of the Sanskrit theoreticians as any sequence of repetitions gives the poem an even greater sense of euphonic unity. And, of course, all the songs must be sung in a particular raga, with a specific beat or *tāla*. So the first invocatory song carries the colophon *rāga mālava, tāla rūpaka,* indicating precisely how it ought to be sung.

Linguistic tightness is supplemented by an equally tight narrative in which, within a very short space of time, we encounter shifts in point of view (from the *sahṛdaya* to the participants in the love-play for instance) as well as sudden bursts of activity in this traditional "stilled drama." Within the space of two cantos we move from love-in-union to love-in-separation. In canto I, stanza 26, for instance, we chance upon the triumph of love as the lovers lie fatigued after "tumultuous loving." Yet at the end of the second song of this canto, Radha is shown wandering alone, tormented by love, by separation, while her friend, the *sakhī*, speaks to her.

> When spring came, tender-limbed Radha wandered
> Like a flowering creeper in the forest wilderness,
> Seeking Krishna in his many haunts.

The God of love increased her ordeal,
Tormenting her with fevered thoughts,
And her friend sang to heighten the mood.

After this point, the passion of Radha seems to threaten and subvert the convention of harmony associated with the form of the pastoral. But since a disturbance has surfaced, the pastoral must contain this threat, it must neutralize it. And as the threat becomes real only insofar as we, the readers, must detect it as such, the poet neutralizes it through the identity of friend with reader (original listener). Here then is a version of our infra reader as someone actually embedded in the text itself. The friend (Bhoja's *sahṛdaya*, the kindred heart) is thus a kind of a conduit through whom the devotional poem is read and its sexual discourses "rewritten" in the code of the religious. Yet at this juncture the parallel text of love and desire is expressed in a muted fashion, and connected with the divine game of Krishna:

Friend, in spring young Hari plays
Like erotic mood incarnate.

The crucial words here are *śṛṅgāra* (the erotic rasa) and *kridati* (the ludic, the play, the divine game of Krishna, his *rasa-līlā*). These suggestive lines are meant to intensify Radha's sense of loneliness and separation. It is now Radha's turn to speak as she recalls her union throughout the second canto: "I reach the lonely forest hut where he secretly lies at night."

The third canto begins with Krishna "burning with passion of love":

Forgive me now!
I won't do this to you again!
Give me a vision, beautiful Radha!
I burn with passion of love.

Krishna too suffers from *viraha*, from separation and loss, anticipating Radha's own much more poignant sense of love as she later laments, laughs, collapses, cries, trembles, utters refrains of love-longing. She suffers and imagines herself lying on a "ritual bed of flames," alluding to the consummate figure of the burning bride, the sati, as she now seeks unity through death: *jīvanmṛta* (life-in-death) alone is *jīvanmukta* (life-in-salvation). This state of Radha is again conveyed to Krishna through the mediatory figure of the *sakhī* (friend) who, as we have seen, is our first interpreter of the text.

The dramatic oscillation between estrangement and union is a structural characteristic of the genre itself and is a form of "*différance*" that Western theory seems not to have grasped. In Derrida's well-known summary our "epoch" has been characterized by the following major "conjunctions" of difference/ "*différance*":

> the difference of forces in Nietzsche, Saussure's principle of semiological difference, differing as the possibility of [neurone] facilitation (the opening-up or clearing-out of a pathway), impression and delayed effect in Freud, difference as the irreducibility of the trace of the other as in Levinas, and the ontic-ontological difference in Heidegger.[90]

Against these conjunctures of difference, the idea of union-in-separation is aimed at cancelling out difference as oppositional (as in the citations from Nietzsche to Heidegger) in favor of a difference (as in Derrida's "*différance*") where binaries are always deferred. The endless deferral implicit in the Radha-Krishna erotics is what prevents us from a purely erotic reading, a point underlined in the penultimate verse of the final song of the *Gītagovinda*. There Jayadeva defines the poetic act as one of dispassionate writing where eroticism is seen as a purely poetic sensibility totally detached from the object of poetic representation:

> His musical skill, his meditation on Vishnu,
> His vision of reality in the erotic mood,
> His graceful play in these poems,
> All show that master-poet Jayadeva's soul
> Is in perfect tune with Krishna—
> Let blissful men of wisdom purify the world
> By singing his *Gītagovinda*.

There are two crucial bits of information that we are given here: master-poet Jayadeva has a special capacity to be in "perfect tune with Krishna" and we as readers/participants can "purify the world" by chanting this poem. To make the message an effective strategy of reading we have to interpret the text in a manner—largely allegorical—to explain how erotic meaning can be made to function as an analogue for metaphysics and religion. On this point we may very legitimately draw close parallels between the *Gītagovinda* and texts such as the *Song of Songs* and the *Cántico Espiritual* of San Juan de la Cruz where too there is a tendency to offer allegory as a super-paradigm with which to explain a narrative seemingly at odds with religion. The category of the infra reader is again useful here because this model reader, for the moment, places in abeyance matters that might lead to different readings of the text. Indeed, the nature of sexual love as a paradigm for divine love is part of a theologization of sexual love that led John Donne in Holy Sonnet 10 to cry out, "Nor ever chast, except you ravish mee."

The relationship between devotionalism and aesthetic form is part of a massive tradition whose codifiers included bhakti taxonomers such as Shandilya and Narada. The aesthetic form endorsed in their bhakti *sūtra*s was based upon a structural principle of love-in-union and love-in-separation in which key agents (referred to as the *nāyaka* and the *nāyikā*) emphasized the joys of the discourses of emotional love without actual physical consummation.[91] Apart from the *nāyaka* and the *nāyikā* as male and female participants, other issues raised in the man-woman relationship included the following: the nature of the female in question (whether *parakīyā, the* woman outside of "ordinary dharma" who enters into an "adulterous" relationship, or *svakīyā*, the "woman who does not depart from the dharma of her wifely vows"[92]) and the role of the lover's friends, her *sakhīs*.[93] Since the *parakīyā* has a lot more to lose in any sexual relationship (especially the *paroḍhā parakīyā* or the "married woman") her passion is all the more intense and focused. The infra reader, however, makes a radical semantic turn and interprets this *prema* (love) not as desire as *kāma* (sexual action) but desire as spiritual release. It is clear that the action of Radha must be read as that of the right kind of believer. An interpretative solution to this form of dual coding (sacred/profane, literal/metaphorical, earthly/heavenly, etc.) is offered by Lee Siegel:

> It is rasa theory rather than allegory (although there is an allegorical tradition in Sanskrit literature) which invests the *Gītagovinda* with its sacred dimension—the bhakta, the devotional *rasika*, tasting the flavour of the poem, experiences the great joy of love, the loving relationship with Krishna, in its various phases.[94]

Nowhere is this investment of sacred meaning more obvious than in the reading of the *Gītagovinda* by the followers of the Vaishnava Sahajiya tradition and Chaitanya. In their reading Radha's unqualified devotion to Krishna at the exclusion of all else is understood as confirming the sentiments of the ideal bhakta.[95] This essentially religious response was then transformed into a bhakti-rasa or the aesthetic relish of bhakti by codifiers such as Rupa Gosvamin who probably picked the idea up from Chaitanya himself.[96] Here, of course, bhakti becomes a category of poetic theory like the other rasas.[97] As such bhakti becomes a formal aesthetic relish or reception that a contemporary Indian critic such as Jaidev, if pushed, would probably identify with Raymond Williams's "structure of feeling."[98] Bhakti-rasa then becomes a second order of codification above and beyond the primary erotic rasa of *śṛṅgāra*. What in the latter is a celebration of the interface between the poles of *vipralambha* (separation) and *sambhoga* (union) is thus lifted to the level of a secondary modelling (or meaning-making) system that would now allow for the pairing of two distinct narratives. To do this we need a reader willing to accept that this procedure is not only possible but essential for a "proper" reading of the text.[99]

The broad outline of this argument has been adequately discussed by Siegel and Miller and may be followed up in their researches. What concerns me here, in particular, is the way in which the *rasika* combines the characteristics of both the *praśnikas* (the arbitrators) and *prekṣakas* (spectators) of the *Nāṭyaśāstra.* Among these characteristics are: piety, impartiality, nobility, equanimity, as well as the ability to weigh the merits of an argument and consider the achievements of a performer quite dispassionately.[100] The identification of the *rasika*'s responses with those of the devotee leads to the "tasting" of bhakti rasa. The *rasika*, as the devotee or reader, is like the *sakhī* in the text, the female friend of Radha who passively meditates upon the sexual act in all its purity without undergoing any desire to enact it herself. Coalescing the *rasika*, devotee, and author Jayadeva, S. B. Dasgupta speculates:

> This eternal *līlā* is the eternal truth, and, therefore, it is this eternal *līlā*—the playful love-making of Radha and Krishna, which the Vaishnava poets desired to enjoy. If we analyse the *Gīta-govinda* of Jayadeva we shall find not a single statement which shows the poet's desire to have union with Krishna as Radha had,—he only sings praises of the *līlā* of Radha and Krishna and hankers after chance just to have a peep into the divine *līlā*, and this peep into the divine *līlā* is the highest spiritual gain which these poets could think of.[101]

The world as divine play, as *kridati*, gets integrated into the play of sexual desire.[102] There are a number of things that must come together here which, of course, makes good sense if we keep the idea of the pastoral firmly in mind. Without some such generic understanding of texts that slot the complex into the simple, we will be at a loss to explain why the *Gītagovinda* is able to sustain so many layers of meaning. In short much more is at work here than just unbridled emotionalism (a crude theory of bhakti adopted by many commentators) that would explain why the "*Gīta-govinda*, the most perfect *rasa/dhvani* poem, came to be the most influential single example for the religious poetry of the medieval period."[103]

The *Gītagovinda* is a powerful poem that challenges both the definition of bhakti and our ability to read it. To emphasize its bhakti rasa does not mean that it cannot be enjoyed as a text that is driven by the erotic rasa of *śṛṅgāra.* The latter reading is the defining point of entry into the text and we cannot escape from it. For many this point of entry is sufficient for purposes of critical practice as the poem can be enjoyed in terms of its formal aesthetic design. For a devotional theory and for the special category of reader we have advanced, we need to recognize the way in which sexual desire is being deflected toward a sublime end in which the larger question of the "presentability" of God becomes the central concern. To do this we need to superimpose a parallel text upon the existing narrative so that the text says one thing and means another. This principle of "double-coding" is clearly an attempt on the part of the

Brahmins to ensure that the text's rampant sexuality (made all the more powerful through the poet's use of Apabhramsha or vernacular semantics, his use of Tantric metaphors, and so on) is rechannelled into a religious fervor so that desire for sex becomes love of God. Once we have made that connection, we then become conscious of the ways in which the two narratives of the profane and the sacred work with an older brahminical structure of meditation where union of any kind is ultimately union with Brahman or its surrogate representative in the form of a God. That the two levels can be so effectively sustained is testimony to the power of the larger generic conventions that govern the work. Here the structure of the pastoral becomes important since this genre constantly transforms the complex into the simple. One senses this in the formal design of the poem. The *Gītagovinda* is an extraordinarily accomplished piece of work. Yet its very perfection hides and disfigures real social forces at work in twelfth-century India. India is represented as a pastoral paradise when we know very well that this wasn't the case. The excessive use of figurative tropes thus overdetermines the text and glosses over ruptures in the matrix of the society that produced the text. A crucial word in the text is *mleccha* (unclean), which is used three times to designate the barbarian hordes, the dark age, and the return of Krishna as Kalki respectively. Clearly the use of *mleccha* in these instances echoes the enormous unease within Hindu society in the wake of Muslim invasions begun in earnest at the turn of the second millennium. This elaborate pastoral of a lost golden age (of Krishna and Radha cavorting in pastoral serenity) is thus an illusion that seeks to represent a world order that was really on the brink of collapse. Yet the official, devotional reading of the text offers none of these. It seeks to transform the rasa of *śṛṅgāra* into bhakti, which is then presented by the orthodoxy as the great code with which to read this text. In suggesting the elements that are silenced we have attempted to demonstrate the degree to which devotional verse also espouses specific class positions and alludes to historical events even when the allusions are not historically specified. Not surprisingly, the orthodoxy brought a very radical text into mainstream Hindu thought by emphasizing its homologous/allegorical tendencies and by connecting it with what we have referred to as bhakti ideology. It read Jayadeva as a bhakta who glorified the essential paradox of Godhead within an established structure, and whose "lonely Radha," crying "her pain aloud, in pitiful sobbing"[104] (*viracita-vividha-vilāpaṃ sā paritāpaṃ cakaroccaiḥ*) symbolized the cruel paradox of the bhakta forever yearning for fulfilment.[105] It also read some of the crucial precursor texts of bhakti—the *Bhagavadgītā*, the Puranas, the songs of the Alvars and the Vira-Shaivas—as part of an ongoing continuum of interrelated texts. But in all these texts the trace that needs to be recovered and theorized is the link between desire, its fulfilment, and its lack with the problematic of the Indian sublime. The texts examined thus far explore this problematic by transforming the abstract Brahman into a personal God, and by advancing aesthetic strategies to explain the special nature of the sėlf's relationship with God. The nirvanic sublime gets rewritten as a sublime that one can live by in the world as it is.

Prescribing the Text

As already mentioned in passing, the structure of bhakti ideology was influenced by and in turn fed into two key texts that emphasized the steps by which the self could achieve union with God. Collected under the names of Shandilya and Narada these texts called *Bhakti Sūtras* ("Treatises on Devotion") probably reached their final recension in the thirteenth century C.E.[106] The *sūtras* collected under the name of Shandilya carry a commentary by the Bengali Shvapneshvara, who deftly combines Shankara's theory of the identity of the self and Brahman with Ramanuja's insistence on the ultimate reality of the world.[107] In the *sūtras* themselves the position of the self as devotee is made explicit so that there is no ambiguity about the reading position we should adopt. The emphasis is on devotion as a superior form of cognition that does not require empirical knowledge for its validity. In these aphoristic *sūtras* the emphatic insistence on encounter and on mystical realization against knowledge mark an important shift in the definition of bhakti itself. In Shandilya's *sūtras* 57–59 we therefore read that the signs of bhakti are total absorption of individual will in the will of God and the denial of desire (*kāma*). This total absorption (*ekānta bhāva*), the endless condition of being, is the desired means of salvation. What is missing from Shandilya's system (if indeed one can distinguish between Narada and Shandilya as two distinct texts and not two commentaries on the same theme) is the place of love in devotional outpourings. It is here that the sister *sūtra* of Narada becomes important. The sentiment of love finds its most succinct formulation in Narada's *sūtra* 66:

> Having kept clear of the three modified forms of secondary devotion, one should cultivate love and love alone, which has its principle in those stages of devotion, which are known as constant service and constant wifely conduct.[108]

We may wish to recall that an infra reader would accept that the devotion of the bhakta is *ekāntin* (single-minded and without end). This reader would connect devotion with *viraha*, separation of lovers and their love-longing primarily associated with the *pastorales* of the poets of Bengal Vaishnavism. Like the Sermon on the Mount, Narada's *sūtra* at this point sanctions the humble and the meek, the *dainya priyatvāt* ("the meek, the distressed"), who are loved by God against the conceited, the proud—*abhimāni-dveṣitvāt*—whom the Lord castigates. Throughout, of course, the *sūtras*' underlying claim, which gets articulated most forcefully in *sūtra* 80, is that knowledge (of the kind traditionally revered) is at best dispensable and at worst an impediment to the devotee's search for liberation.

Both Shandilya and Narada are important "compilers" and system-builders. Narada's eighty-four aphorisms, especially, set out in summary form the salient definitions and characteristics of bhakti. These aphorisms also indicate Narada's modifications of the work of commentators other than Shandilya, notably Garga and Vyasa, the latter more likely an "author function" to whom commentaries and texts may be attributed rather than an "actual" author as such.[109] Narada's aphorisms begin with a definition of divine love as *amṛta* ("eternal nectar"), which only the *siddha* (" the perfected one") attains and in doing so brings desire to an end. By aphorism 6 Narada begins to signal the effect of this state on the body itself as the subject becomes intoxicated (*mattaḥ)* and stiff (*stabdhaḥ*). In case these bodily manifestations are read simply as another version of feelings and desires, the next *sūtra* (7) speaks of bhakti as *nirodharūpatvāt*, a form of renunciation. However, once realization (the condition of bliss through bhakti) is achieved, it does not follow that the subject's interest in bhakti wanes. One must be forever vigilant—selflessly devoted as the *Bhāgavata Purāṇa* says—or else there is the likelihood of fall from grace. Where the earlier commentators had stressed devotion through ritual and sacred dialogue or, in the case of Shandilya, through a mode of behavior that the Atman itself endorsed, Narada advances the view that bhakti is marked by two overriding characteristics: complete self-surrender to God (*vismaraṇa*) and extreme anguish (*vyākulatā*) in his absence. At this point Narada cites the love of the gopis toward Krishna as the archetypal instance of bhakti because for these gopis love for Krishna was never *jārāṇāmiva* ("like sex"). Narada, however, reads sexual love from a decidedly patriarchal point of view and makes the curious observation that in profane love a woman seeks pleasure only for herself. The simile ("like sex") works because bhakti is coded through a language of intense and even passionate love of God. It would not work if we were to read this, as our age perhaps demands that we should, from an informed feminist perspective. Although the latter discourse was certainly not available to someone like Narada (or if available had not been theorized) the emphasis on the structural dimension of bhakti means that Narada's *sūtras* were more like manuals of devotion than documents aware of sexual politics or power relations. Of course, this does not mean that we cannot read them through critiques of these kinds.

The shift from bhakti as ritual and action (as a Yoga) is underlined in *sūtra* 25 where Narada speaks of divine love as something more than karma, *jñāna*, and Yoga. The fact is that bhakti is its own fruit (*svayaṃ phalarūpatā*) for seekers of liberation and is therefore selfless. It cannot be described precisely (*anirvacanīyam*), it is self-evident (*svayam pramāṇatvāt)* but upon achieving its "fruit" one's mind is set only on God. However, it should not follow that the bhakta becomes a renouncer; on the contrary, he/she continues to live in the world but vigilantly ensures that the material benefits of living in the world do not stunt his/her commitment to God. Although Narada defers to the authority of the canonical texts—as he has to—and refers to earlier definitions of bhakti, it soon becomes clear that bhakti requires the submission of both self and textual authority (*ātma-loka-vedatvāt*) to God. The reference to submission to the Vedas (which is not unusual as these *śruti* texts have the highest canonical authority) clearly emphasizes the shift that Narada's treatise makes from the controlled, ritualistic bhakti of the earlier period to the personal, emotional bhakti of his own time. Those who are steadfast in their devotion to God (*ekāntin*) express their feelings quite unashamedly with their voice choking, tearful eyes, hair on end and so on (*kaṇṭha-avarodha-romāñca-aśrubhiḥ*). Since love of God is very much a personal matter, greater (*garīyasī*) than the eternal truth (*trisatyasya*), and not restricted by ritual or sacrifice, no one is excluded from it regardless of caste, learning, and so on (*nāsti teṣu jātividyā*). Echoing Krishna's own references to those who, through him, may achieve *brahmanirvāṇa*, Narada states that the aphorisms laid down in this treatise lead to the highest form of the religion of love.

It should be clear from the foregoing summary of Narada's position that there are some similarities between his treatise and those Counter-Reformation devotional manuals that one associates with St. Ignatius of Loyola, St. François de Sales, Luis de Granada, and Luis de la Puente.[110] Like Ignatius of Loyola, Narada too stresses degrees and forms of meditation. Toward the end of his *sūtras*, Narada refers to the various kinds of devotional practices:

> Devotion, though one in kind, still appears in eleven forms according as it takes the course of attachment to the attributes and greatness of God, attachment to His beauty, attachment to His worship, attachment to His memories, attachment to His service, attachment to His friendship, attachment to parental affection towards Him, attachment to Him (as) of a beloved wife, attachment to self-consecration, attachment to self-absorption (or Godliness), and attachment to permanent self-effacement.[111]

In the *sūtras* themselves, Narada classifies these eleven types into four broad groups, each one of which elaborates a particular kind of attachment. For instance, under one group the type of attachment defined deals with the subject's examination of the wonderful attributes of God, his beauty and so on. Under other groupings we may encounter the subject's selfless adoration of the deity or the special master-servant or lover-beloved relationship so often found in devotional verse. One of the more subtle variations of the devotee-God relationship is given the description *parama-viraha-āsakti*, or supreme attachment in separation. In this paradoxical endorsement of attachment in separation we get the strongest form of love-longing. The condition demanded of the bhakta who is capable of this version of unrequited love finds its greatest symbolic representation in the love of the gopis for Krishna. These gopis must enact, constantly, the condition of "as if separated" to express their "ever renewed" emotions toward God. The decisive shift from a bhakti that was still part of disciplined action to one that now gives the body itself the capacity to entertain an emotional relationship with God led to a reformulation of the relationship between the self and the sublime object of devotion. In the poetry of devotion we find the most satisfying as well as the most complex expression of this relationship.

With the radical insertion of body and feeling into the normative ideology of Hinduism through a religious discourse that gave pride of place to the outpouring of almost unbridled emotion, bhakti texts began to contest the primacy of the canon. But even as we recognize the radical nature of the shift, bhakti is not so much an endorsement of a new synthesis that cancels out the abstract (and largely unreal) opposition of *nivṛtti* and *pravṛtti* as a statement about a new religious order that arose out of the ashes of a society undergoing enormous changes. However, although the new order is expressed, the semantics of bhakti do not necessarily allow us to get any closer to the sublime object of devotion because this object remains beyond representation. What emerges from these bhakti discourses of emotionalism are forms of representation that examine the nature of devotional desire even further. The energy of bhakti verse arises precisely out of this tension between the sublime object and its representation in language.

Friedhelm Hardy informs us that the normative ideology of Hinduism referred to above was characterized by four features: the self-evident authority of the Vedas, the classification of society through the *varṇa* (caste) system, the upholding by the self of his/her *varṇa* dharma and the power of Vedic ritual in matters of religion.[112] But this is not to say that antinormative or what we may call countercultural tendencies were not present in the margins of culture. The treatises on sexuality, the later systematizations of Tantric practices, as well as a new definition of the aesthetic order are only a handful of movements/moments in this contestation of the normative ideology. One of the most interesting writers on Kabir, Hazariprasad Dvivedi, has pointed out that before the establishment of Muslim hegemony in North India there were groups of people who were both anti-Brahmin and against the norms of *varṇa*. One such group was known as Nath-panthi Yogis.[113] In many ways the anti-orthodox views of such groups made their way into Kabir's verse. The Julaha caste to which Kabir belonged were recent converts who had taken up Islam en masse. Conversion to Islam, however, neither gave them real political clout nor changed their social behavior in any radical fashion. But as a class of weavers and tailors that had become more mobile as a result of changes in the political map of India, they could be more flexible in matters of belief. And so as orthodox Hinduism waned, lower caste poets were able to experiment with ideas ranging from orthodox Vaishnavism to Tantrism, Sufism, Buddhism and Jainism.[114] With the exception of poets such as Jayadeva and Nanak who were, quite possibly, of a higher caste, the saint-singers of medieval India represented by Kabir belonged to Indian castes who while unlikely to advance upward socially were gradually becoming more and more economically self-sufficient. The attractiveness of Islam to the weaver caste, for instance, also led to a democratization of religious belief itself. A theory of devotional poetics thus becomes exciting precisely when we become conscious of the interrelationship between aesthetics and actual social practice in the wake of changes in the social order and in the adoption of bhakti discourses by people ranging from Brahmins to leatherworkers, cobblers, tailors, and even butchers. That the genre of devotional poetry was taken up by these people need not surprise us since in an intensely religious society for art to justify its existence it had to address the mysteries of Godhead persistently.

CHAPTER FOUR

Temples of Fire

Plurality-with-Unity

The *mlecchas* may have been represented as demonic Others in the *Gītagovinda* but the fact remains that they did become part of India.[1] Whether as mainstream Muslims, Sufi dervishes, or as the *vāmamārgī*s (followers of the countercultural left-hand Tantric path), these *mlecchas* had a significant impact on the growth of bhakti ideology and strengthened its sense of capaciousness. Ronald Inden referred to bhakti as "conscious participation" and spoke of it as one of many "religions" that constituted themselves as "fully agentive with respect to their knowledge of the world."[2] Inden's reference to the "agentive" capacity of religions (which does not mean that their metaphysics are wholly exclusive) is a much more creative reinflection of the common, but largely true, argument that Indian culture has always been open to influences and borrowing. As Edward Dimock Jr. observed thirty years ago:

> There is an eternal borrowing and reborrowing of ideas and doctrines that goes on and has always gone on among religious sects in India, until the lines of derivation become very blurred indeed.[3]

To get to grips with the ideology of bhakti and its expression in the North Indian literary tradition we need to reopen debates about the manner in which countercultural or deviant movements began to encroach upon mainstream devotionalism. Since Islam was one of the most significant of these "countercultural" phenomena, we need to explore, in particular, the impact of the Muslim *mlecchas* on the culture-scape of Hindu India.

Islam came to India with invasion and territorial annexations. While there had been some contact with Arab traders in the past, it was not until Muhammad bin Qasim's occupation of Sind in the eighth century and the success of later invaders, notably the Ghaznavids, that Islamic institutions and ideas began to gain ground in India. By 1193 Delhi was the seat of both the Muslim Ghor dynasty and of Indian Islam. The changes in the political map of India had never been as profound and the impact on the Hindu world was immense. In a country that had long since lost a centralized Hindu governmental structure (the Chola empire alone maintained some form of territorial sovereignty in the South) these invasions (and subsequent Islamic hegemony) ruptured the fabric of society at both political and religious levels. A new court language, new legal systems, new forms of land tenure combined with belief systems radically different from those of the Hindus meant that North India in particular became a site of considerable social, cultural, and racial intermixing. Religious conversions often reflect gains to be made through identification with the beliefs of the ruling classes and this in turn affect the thinking of large sections of the population. Although historical details are few, the religious history of India strongly indicates a definite move away from the austere precision of Sanskrit culture to other multifaceted, heterogeneous, and assimilative cultural forms. The shift does not signify loss or gain, nor indeed a complete breakdown of Hindu culture itself; rather it reflects new levels and kinds of syncretism that began to take root in India on an unprecedented scale. However, as Wilhelm Halbfass has indicated, a new India under strong Islamic rule in many parts had to negotiate the whims of rulers who could be uncompromisingly proselytizing and generously liberal in the space of a single lifetime.[4]

Megasthenes, the envoy of the Syrian governor Seleneus Nicator to the court of Chandragupta Maurya in present-day Patna, has left behind an account of his period in India between 302 and 291 B.C.E. While Megasthenes' account gives us some invaluable insights into Indian caste systems with a priestly caste and a renouncer caste (the latter probably Buddhists plus renouncers generally) and their primarily Apollonian and Dionysian Gods (probably Indra and Shiva whom he called Heracles and Dionysius), we don't get from Megasthenes any real sense of high Indian metaphysics. This was because his emphasis was primarily on "ethical and practical aspects of the Indian tradition."[5] Not so with Alberuni (Al-Biruni, 973–1048), a giant of a scholar by any standards. His account of India comes some 1,300 years later but is of great value to us because he was taken to India by the Turkish conqueror Mahmud of Ghazni after the fall of Alberuni home city Chwarezm in Central Asia. Although tremendously important for the history of Islamic India, Mahmud of Ghazni's military activities need not concern us here. Alberuni's account of

India at the turn of the second millennium is quite another matter. It is a remarkable document about Hindu India that requires a much longer commentary than what I offer here. What strikes us immediately is that Alberuni interpreted India in such a liberal fashion that his analysis stands in stark contrast to that of the European Orientalists who, centuries later, interpreted the same data very differently. As Edward C. Sachau, Alberuni's English translator, remarks, to Alberuni "the Hindus were excellent philosophers, good mathematicians and astronomers" (1: xvii). These characteristics are warmly, though not uncritically, addressed by Alberuni. However, in the context of this chapter—which deals with a number of heterodox ideas with reference to "*mleccha*" Islam, its Sufi offshoot, and Tantric speculative thinking—what is of real interest to us are those passages in Alberuni's reading of India that throw light on the state of philosophical thinking in India in the first half of the eleventh century. To begin with we find that right from the start Alberuni is struck by three features of Hindu India. The first is the Indian sense of "inwardness," both at the social and at the geographical level. Hindus, he remarks, see their world as being totally centred on themselves; they "believe that there is no country but theirs, no nation like theirs, no kings like theirs, no science like theirs" (1:22). Civilized societies do not exist outside their domains since the world as a geographical entity is really identical with India. The second feature is a belief in a pantheistic doctrine of the unity of God, which Alberuni equates with Sufism's Wahdat al-Wujud (about this, see below) and the Greek theory of metempsychosis or belief in the transmigration of souls. Finally, observes Alberuni, much of Hindu science is the science of numerology and astrology. These three features of Hindu society as read by Alberuni throw considerable light on matters of some importance in this chapter. Even though Alberuni writes from a distance and is concerned largely with practices in the northwestern part of India, his account is a valuable document about Hindu beliefs at precisely the time when Sufism made its inroads into India and Tantrism, a very nativist speculative mode, began to establish itself in the country. It must be said that Alberuni is very uneasy about the huge gap he sees between scholarly thinking on religion and popular belief systems. Where intellectual Hinduism constructs God as a being "unattainable to thought . . . sublime beyond all likeness" (1:27) popular Hinduism is riddled with "anthropomorphic doctrines" (1:31). At the same time it is clear to Alberuni that Sufism has many points of contact with Hinduism, so much so that Alberuni makes an explicit connection between Patanjali's Yoga and Sufi thought. On Patanjali's Yoga meditations Alberuni observes:

> As long as you point to something, you are not a *monist*; but when *the Truth* seizes upon the object of your pointing and annihilates it, then there is no longer an indicating person nor an object indicated. (1:87)

We shall return to Alberuni's reading of Hindu philosophical thought later. How seriously we can take Alberuni's descriptions of Hindu social systems requires more immediate commentary. One way of judging this is by examining Alberuni's reading of the Hindu caste system. Alberuni notes that the four established castes (Brahmins, Kshatriyas, Vaishyas, and Shudras) are divinely sanctioned since they were created out of the various parts of Brahma. Besides them are the shoemakers and weavers (like Kabir) who belong to a service class without whom urban societies would collapse. Outside these are the *antyajāti* or outcastes like the Doms and Chandalas who are also a service class but whose duties are much more menial, such as taking care of the dead, removing refuse, and so on. It is the intermediate caste between the outcastes and the established four *varṇa*s that is of interest to us. It is this class (made up of a whole range of lower-caste peoples) that, in North India, interacted with Sufism most productively. Since the people who belonged to this class were self-sufficient (as artisans in feudal societies are more likely to be), it need not surprise us that they were most willing to adapt and absorb new beliefs and religious thinking. It must be added that a service class (made up of castes that occupied a liminal position in caste stratification) by itself does not become radical thinkers. What is more likely is that weavers, shoemakers, and tailors could attach themselves to business classes and to urban communities much more easily. The role of urbanization in bhakti generally has not been examined systematically (and this is not the place to do so). Nevertheless, we may want to pose a number of questions. Who were the buyers of the finished products of artisans? What was the nature of the middlemen? And, finally, what connections may be established between a syncretist ethos and the lives of people who live in urban communities? Alberuni's work makes it clear that the class of people I have referred to here were the ones who embraced Tantrism and Kundalini Yoga most extensively.

Although Alberuni continues to write from the pious high ground of Islam, and is open to criticism precisely because of it, his descriptions of people tend to suggest that many of the practices that we attribute quite specifically to ascetics were in fact quite normal forms of Hindu behavior.[6] The unchanging nature of Hindu society may also be gauged from Alberuni's description of the four stages in the life of a Brahmin. The first part of his life extends to the twenty-fifth year. It is marked by sexual abstinence, fasting, and the worship of fire. The second period is from the age of 25 to 50 when his master allows him to marry. However, the woman he marries should not have reached puberty and he must cohabit with her only once a month. The third period of life is from 50 to 75 when again he practices abstinence. He leaves his wife and children and retreats to a life in the wilderness. The fourth period extends until his death when "he wears a red garment and holds a red stick in his hand" (2:133). Since we know that life expectancy in India was rather short, it is unlikely that, in reality, many people experienced the entire four stages of life. It also seems highly improbable that a person should marry only after he had reached twenty-five.

Alberuni's account of northwestern India is also a valuable archive that provides evidence of social practices that had already become the stock in trade of Hindu life. He also spends considerable time discussing the science of astronomy, which he finds has considerable fascination for the Hindus. He also notes that this science of astronomy could not have come into being without an intense interest in number theory. From measurements of the depths of oceans to the diameters of the seven planets, everything had been carefully computed by the Hindus. But much of this knowledge is abstract as the interest of the Hindu is in the mystical force of the numbers themselves. Having discovered zero, the Hindus used it to signify infinite time and space. Hence Alberuni's observation on Hindu astronomy: "The Hindus are very little informed regarding the fixed stars. I never came across any one of them who knew the single stars of the lunar stations from eye-sight" (2:83). They applied no theorems. However, numbers were largely systemic since each number was a factor of another. Thus the diameter or distance of one planet had a mathematical relation to another planet's diameter or distance. This is what one would call numerology rather than mathematics as a science, though this is not to say that the Hindus were not good mathematicians. The length of a year of Brahma, for instance, is 3,110,400,000,000 years or 360 *kalpas*, each one of which (a day of Brahma) is 8,640,000,000 years long. But the life of Brahman, we are told, is only 72,000 *kalpas* (1:363) while one day of Shiva, for reasons known only to the gods themselves, is presented as an incredibly lengthy 37,264,147,126,589,458,187,550,720,000,000,000,000,000,000,000,000,000,000 *kalpas* which is probably another way of saying that it is infinite. As well there are figures that show the length of the *yugas*. Our current *yuga* (*kaliyuga*) is 432,000 years long (1:373). A *manvantara* is 71 *caturyugas*, which is itself the sum of all four *yugas* (*tiṣya*, *dvāpara*, *tretā*, and *kṛta yugas*). Since fantastic numerology (or Hegel's fantastic symbolism) replaces real lived history, it is not surprising that Alberuni castigates Hindus for not paying "much attention to the historical order of things" (2:10). But what is of significance is the connection between number theory, the planets, and the human body itself. Though Alberuni does not theorize this connection, it is clear that of the seven planets, the sun, and the moon (for these were defined as planets) had the most influence on human lives. Certain positions of the sun and the moon are also universally seen as unlucky. When the sun and the moon stand together on two circles as though each were seizing the other, the Yoga (union) is called *vyātipata*. The other inauspicious union is when the sun and the moon stand together on two equal circles. This Yoga is called *vaidhṛta*. The other planets—Mercury, Mars, Venus, Jupiter, and Saturn—were somewhat less significant. Earlier I quoted Alberuni's citation of a passage from Patanjali where annihilation of the self through the extinction of opposites was presented as the desired aim of life. This view is also related to what Alberuni sees is the power of the sun/moon symbology on Hindu life. Reformulated as Tantra, the antagonistic forces of the sun and the moon are read as symbolizing all other oppositions such as male and female, day and night, the east and the northeast, the colors bronze and white, the tastes bitter and salty, the castes Kshatriya and Vaishya, and so on. The aim of Tantra is to reconcile these oppositions within the geography of the body by rechannelling the life force, the normal movement of which is through the two "oppositional" channels, the *iḍā* and the *piṅgalā*, through a mediating channel (the *suṣumṇā*).

Alberuni's work is rich in such insights. For us its enormous value lies in the fact that it provides us with confirmatory evidence of the significance of self-extinction in Hindu life and the importance of the body itself in Hindu thought by the turn of the second millennium. Much of this information itself, we are told, was recast in metrical form so that it could be memorized. Since the instruments of writing—pen and bark or leaves—lacked the durability of paper or parchment (which Indians did not possess), knowledge continued to be transmitted orally even after the technology of writing had become available. Thus even though we have a firmly entrenched, though selective, written culture, the flimsiness of the materials available ensured that orality remained the dominant mode of transmission of knowledge. Often verse was the means of expressing art as well as metaphysics.

Alberuni's account of India is a fascinating, though limited, corrective to so many myths about India at the beginning of the second millennium. It is also a valuable source text for the argument of this chapter in that it spells out in some detail the contexts in which Tantrism, Nathism, and Indian Sufism developed. All these three "isms" are important features of the writings of the medieval Indian poet Kabir, who uses them to explore the phenomenon of self and God in a progressively multireligious India. To understand Kabir and his highly contaminated discourses, we must trace the growth of the three "isms" that collectively constitute the central themes of this chapter.

As we have already suggested, whereas bhakti ideology in Puranic literature remained solidly Hindu in outlook, the picture is not quite the same in post-Puranic texts. For the fact is that post-Puranic texts grew in an environment that had come under the massive impact of Islam, an impact that had altered forever what had been a relatively closed Hindu world. Under the circumstance, attractive as it is, Henry Corbin's call for "un dialogue dans la métahistoire" cannot be discussed without reference to power and politics.[7] If it were just a matter of constructing a *philosophia perennis* life would be very easy but we cannot explain lived experience (which is always linked to material conditions) through an uncritical perennial philosophy, however attractive the idea may be.

Part of the difficulty with a metahistorical dialogue of the type suggested by Corbin is that it has a tendency to dehistoricize specific situations when in fact any dialogue needs to be examined with reference to quite specific local conditions. We need to constantly contextualize this dialogue. For instance, we can no longer totally subscribe to the kinds of readings given by J. N. Farquhar about the effects of Islam on Indian society.

> The Muhammadan conquest of North India (1193–1203) was an immeasurable disaster to Hinduism as well as to the Hindu people, and it gave Buddhism its death-wound.[8]

While there is a lot of truth in this—Hindu India was never the same after Mahmud of Ghazni's and, subsequently, Muhammad bin Sam's raids on India at the turn of the second millennium C.E.—the antagonistic placing of these two great religious systems by Farquhar denies access to, or the possibility of, the more fruitful consequences of that initial confrontation, however uneven, in terms of power relations, that confrontation might have been. And even if, at one level, Islam was an "immeasurable disaster," we need to accept that cultural commodities, including literature, would have been affected by that "disaster." There is, after all, a basic structural relationship between literary genres and history. Genres, as Georg Lukács once observed, are historically constituted and reflect shifts in history as is clear from the obvious links between bourgeois individualism and the rise of the European novel.[9] One such structural relationship may be seen in the ways in which the narrative of devotion was modified by the mystical underside of Islam, Sufism, the first of the three "isms" under discussion here.[10] The term *ṣūfi* was first applied to Muslim ascetics who dressed in coarse garments of wool (*ṣūf*). These Muslim ascetics or Sufis claimed knowledge of a Real (*al-ḥaqq*) that was generally inaccessible to orthodox Muslims. They believed that one had to "travel a path" (*salak al-tarīq*) that would make this union with the Real possible. Against the systematic theology of Islam, we find here a stress on intuition, and on the various processes (*tarīqa*) by which spiritual freedom is attained. Yet Sufis themselves defended their procedures with reference to the Islamic canon and argued that it was a "natural development within Islam."[11] This shift in focus toward the mystical (the quest for gnosis or *ma'rifa* through the experiencing of "ecstatic states") found Indian soil congenial to the propagation and reinforcement of its ideals, a tendency that, not surprisingly, often invited the wrath of the Ulama, the "custodians of the interpretation of the *Sharī'a*,"[12] who objected to what they felt was a tendency toward pantheism.

Such is the nature of cultural flux in India that the influence of Sufism on North Indian bhakti or devotional verse cannot and should not be underestimated. As Charles S. J. White has pointed out:

> Besides the indigenous influences, the development of a sensibility in this regard in the bhakti sects is probably related to

> the religious synthesis that medieval Hinduism achieved under the influence of Islam, and especially under its mystic specialists, the Sufis, whose teaching includes erotic symbolism to assist the soul in its ascent toward Allah.[13]

The unusual nature of this symbiosis (rare when one recalls Christian-Islamic antagonisms in Europe) has led to debates about the degree to which the founders of Sufism, Hasan al-Basri (642–728) and Rabi'a al-Adawiyya of Basra (717–801), as well as other early Sufis were influenced by Hindu as well as Neoplatonic thought readily available to them through Middle Eastern Christian communes. With regard to Hindu influences, scholars such as Zaehner and Guillaume especially[14] are inclined to see strong metaphysical parallels between Sufism and Hinduism with Zaehner indeed going so far as to equate *fanā'* (annihilation) and *infirād* (isolation) with the Hindu concept of oneness in Brahman and the Buddhist nirvana on the grounds that Sufism must have picked up Vedantic thought from Sindhi Brahmins. This is an old and hoary chestnut that Zaehner almost alone among serious scholars has advanced with considerable passion.[15] However, what is interesting is not the question of influence but the presence of discursive forms that could be incorporated into Sufism with ease. Thus Bayazid's (Abu Yazid al-Bistami, d. 874) claims to identity with God (*anā hūwa*, "I am he") as well as the advancement of other concepts such as *āzādi* (freedom, liberation) *al-fanā 'an al-fanā* (annihilation following on annihilation), *khud'a* (deceit, illusion?), *tawḥīd* (union) can be given Hindu semantic inflection without losing much of their original meanings. In his *Kitāb-al-Fanā*, Junayd (d. 910), who lived during a time of crisis for Sufism when heretics were being persecuted throughout the Islamic world, developed a number of these ideas and introduced an important theory about the necessity of the love of God on the part of the Sufi. It was argued that only through love can the soul reach God. The intimate relationship between the self and God is then defined as "the cessation of shyness without the loss of awe."[16] In the popular tradition love of God is always reciprocated:

> "When my servant constantly draws near to me by works of supererogation, then do I love him, and once I have started to love him, I become his eye by which he sees, his ear by which he hears, his tongue by which he speaks, and his hand by which he grasps."[17]

The ideas of Junayd, Bayazid, al-Ghazali (1058–1111), and many other Sufis who emphasized *tawḥīd* or real communication between self and God through mystical insight made their way into India. As J. Spencer Trimingham points out, the fall of Baghdad at the hands of the Mongols in 1258 pushed many Sufis trained in the traditional Islamic centers of Damascus and other parts of Iraq eastwards, especially toward the Turkish sultanate of Delhi where they found sister lodges.[18] Some years earlier (toward the end of the twelfth century) Mu'in ud-Din Hasan had settled in the city of Ajmer from where he initiated a *silsilā* (a "tradition") called the Chishtia order that quickly spread to many parts of India. Although the expansion of Sufis slowed somewhat under the fiercely fundamentalist Muhammad Ibnul Tughluq (1325–51), ruler of Delhi and overlord of a vast Indian empire, in due course Indian Sufism quickly parted company from its Middle Eastern antecedents and developed, as Trimingham suggests, "along lines of its own and its phases of growth, stagnation, and revival owed little to non-Indian influences."[19] The Indian religious environment, quite naturally, influenced Sufi thinkers:

> Many branches became very syncretistic, adopting varieties of pantheistic thought and antinomian tendencies. Many practices were taken over from the Yogis—extreme ascetic disciplines, celibacy and vegetarianism. Wanderers of the qalandari type [*qalandar*, from Persian: "a dervish type that disregards appearance and flouts public opinion"] abounded. Local customs were adopted; for example, in the thirteenth century the Chishtis paid respect to their leaders by complete prostration with forehead on the ground.[20]

The Chishti and Suhrawardi sects in India were marked by deep monistic tendencies in which, according to S. A. A. Rizvi, there were no distinctions "between lover, the beloved and love itself."[21] The sectarian heads of these movements, people like Shaikh Nizam ud-Din Auliya (d. 1325) and Shaikh Nasir ud-Din Chiragh of Delhi (d. 1356), emphasized indigenous mystical practices and encouraged cultural hybridity. The qalandars or mystic dervishes of these sects, for instance, adopted a number of Hindu ascetic modes of behavior, especially those belonging to the Nath Yogis and their adherents. Since many members of these sects were by and large recent converts to Islam they spoke North Indian vernaculars and created a specialized vocabulary for their own new brand of mysticism. Arabic terms began to be interpreted with their Hindu counterparts in mind. In their literature terms such as Rama and Raḥim, *fanā'* and moksha, *ālame be kaif* and *śūnya jagat, āwāze hamas* and *anāhada nāda, iśq* and *prema, tarīqat* and *sādhanā, rūḥ* and *ātmā* became by and large interchangeable. Contacts between the Nath Yogis and the Sufi saints were not uncommon. There were, in many cases, trials of strength and magic involved; the Yogi was seen as a magician of old, one capable of extraordinary feats.[22] It is possible that the tales of magic, mystery, and imagination that made their way into Indian literature about this time (and employed by Manjhan and Jayasi in their *mathnavī*s later) reflect the popularization of these stories.

While we should not go overboard on the question of "a massive impact of Sufism on Hindu bhakti,"[23] there are a number of key philosophical cross-currents that do deserve serious treatment. One religious idea that may have had a deep and abiding influence on bhakti ideology is the Moẓarbe mystic Ibnul 'Arabi's (d. 1240) redefinition of Wahdat al-Wujud (*waḥdat al-wujūd*). For Ibnul 'Arabi, Wahdat al-Wujud implied oneness of existence both in the realm of the self's relationship to God and in the realm of the interconnectedness of all beings. This is an attractive idea as is evident in Toshihiko Izutsu's reading of it as a mystical universal:

> For expressing the same basic concept, Chuang-tzu uses the words like *t'ien ni* "Heavenly Levelling" and *t'ien chun* "Heavenly Equalization."[24]

This equation, however, is enthusiastic but misleading largely because, for Ibnul 'Arabi, Wahdat al-Wujud also implied an unresolved ontological tension between *ḥaqq* (the Real) and *mumkinat* (possible worlds), so that while the concept endorses a pluralism of beings it does not imply the total return of multiplicity into oneness. The heretical martyr Hallaj's (d. 922) earlier reading of Wahdat al-Wujud as a form of pantheism—"the qualification of God (*kān*) of all creation"[25]—survives only in the margins of Ibnul 'Arabi's usage, but survive it does, which is why in Indian Sufism Wahdat al-Wujud found fertile points of interaction with the philosophy of the much neglected (in scholarly terms) twelfth-century philosopher and theorist of the "divine body," Gorakhnath. Gorakhnath and his followers (the Nath Yogis) had also tried to refine the doctrine of unqualified monism but in a way slightly different from Ramanuja's modified nondualism. Gorakhnath called it *dvaitādvaita-vilakṣaṇa-vāda*[26] or "duality-nonduality-difference-thesis," where *vilakṣaṇa* ("varying in character, different, manifold") was used in the specialized sense of "not admitting of exact definition." One can see the attractiveness of this essentially Hindu idea to Sufism since it allowed emotional union with God to be asserted even as difference is maintained. This then becomes the Indian Sufi version of Wahdat al-Wujud though once again little will be achieved in trying to establish which came first, Goraknath's duality in nonduality or Wahdat al-Wujud. Though A. E. Affifi remained highly critical of any religious doctrine that would confuse the monistic "there is nothing in existence except God" with the monotheistic "there exists but one God," we should still want to quote his summary of Ibnul 'Arabi's position because of its clarity:

> According to Ibnul 'Arabi there is only One Reality in existence. This Reality we view from two different angles, now calling it *Haqq* (the Real) when we regard it as the essence of all phenomena; and now *Khalq* when we regard it as the

> phenomena manifesting that Essence. *Haqq* and *Khalq*: Reality and Appearance; the One and the Many are only names for two subjective aspects of One Reality; it is a real unity but empirical diversity. This reality is God.[27]

Ibnul 'Arabi is clearly concerned with the idea of being and not with that which has being because his interest is with existences and not with existents. Thus for Ibnul 'Arabi the diversity perceived by the senses can be transcended through mystic insight, which enables one to see behind seemingly contradictory phenomena a unified Reality: unity (*jam*) is behind the diversity (*farq*) that we apparently perceive. A critic like Affifi rightly points out that a conception of Reality that denies the distinctiveness of self and other is largely pantheistic, and fundamentally "illegitimate" since, from an Islamic point of view, it confuses the monotheism of Islam with the "philosophical doctrine of the unity of being (*waḥdat al-wujūd*) or pantheism."[28] The placing of the view that "there is nothing in existence except God" against the monotheistic "there exists but one God" is seen by Affifi as a Sufi strategy to circumvent the lure of polytheism (*shirk*).[29] Not surprisingly, the texts and discourses in which these ideas found expression were not philosophical but literary. It was in Ibnul 'Arabi's work that Affifi too discovered a large number of "metaphors of the highest ambiguity" that explored the issue of the relationship between Self and Other as God.[30] The literary imagination did not find the seeming pantheism of Wahdat al-Wujud as irreconcilable as the austere monotheism of doctrinal Islam especially if it were rethought in a figurative language. Not surprisingly, the key metaphors that keep surfacing in Ibnul 'Arabi's literary works are metaphors of vessel and eternal returning.[31]

A crucial literary text in which these metaphors are given literary value is the *Ruśdnāma* of the Sufi poet Shekh Abd-ul-Quddus Gangohi (1456–1537). Whatever other value we may wish to ascribe to this syncretic text, it is demonstrably true that the *Ruśdnāma* represents a classic instance of a specifically Sufi attempt at embracing philosophical positions that were intrinsically Hindu. Of special interest to 'Abdu'l-Quddus Gangohi were the Nath systems associated with the name of Gorakhnath and the Shiva and Shakta cults.

> This mind is Shakti, this mind is Shiva,
> This mind is the *jīva* of the three worlds
> He who takes this mind and "stills" it,
> Can speak about the three worlds.[32]

The passage recurs with only minor variation in the very Hindu *Gorakhbānī*.[33] More importantly, though, textual duplication suggests strong oral affinities between the Sufis and the Nath Yogis as they pick up and repeat each others discourses. Often the concept of the merging of the self into a greater immensity is designated by the use of the phrase *saraba nirantara*, technically "all is continuous, uninterrupted." Hence:

> As water, earth and mountain intermingle
> So too does Gorakhnath.[34]

This essentially pantheistic image of the unity of existence brings together both Gorakhnath's duality-nonduality-difference-thesis and the Sufi Wahdat al-Wujud. There is, of course, a much older poetic tradition of using images of water and ocean to demonstrate the essential unity of the self and Brahman. The great eighth–ninth-century monist thinker Shankara resorted to the metaphor of the vessel afloat on water on a number of occasions. So long as the water inside the vessel is contained within the earthen walls of the vessel, the water within can be distinguished from the water without. But once the walls are broken, the water inside mingles with the water outside and there is no distinction between what was inside the vessel and what was outside. This is Shankara's metaphor of complete and unqualified monism. In Quddus, however, the walls do not break, the waters do not intermingle but a unity of being continues to be emphasized:

> Just as the vessel floats on the water,
> So the drop also stays in the Lord.
> There is no distinction [to be made] between outside and inside—
> In all pervades the one Being.[35]

One could argue, and persuasively, that the philosophical distinction is not always maintained in Quddus. In the passage cited above it is difficult to see how the Self and Other remain relatively autonomous. Quddus, it seems, is symptomatic of a form of composition in which the reader is allowed considerable latitude of interpretation. A Hindu could see it as purely Vedantic, a Muslim as distinctly Sufi. In both cases neither Hinduism nor Islam is compromised. Such paradoxes were not lost on Ibnul 'Arabi either. As Affifi points out:

> Now we are in a position to understand the apparent paradoxes in which Ibnul 'Arabi often revels—such as "the Creator is the created", "I am He and He is I", "*Haqq* is not *Khalq* and *Khalq* is not *Haqq*," and so on and so on. Explained on his relative notion of the two aspects of Reality, these paradoxes are no paradoxes at all.
>
> There is a complete reciprocity between the One and the Many as understood by Ibnul 'Arabi and a complete mutual dependence. Like two logical correlatives, neither has any meaning without the other. Allowing for some poetical ele-

> ment in his Philosophy, this reciprocity is as well expressed as it can by a mystic, in his extraordinary verses.[36]

In Affifi's argument Ibnul 'Arabi is very much a radical dualist: oneness is the sum of two and not an eternal play on itself. Here, the Nathic argument of the inadmissibility of the duality-nonduality divide strikes a chord but is not to be taken as being identical with Ibnul 'Arabi's position. Nor is the latter identical with the philosophy of Wahdat al-Wujud. If this were so, the poem of Quddus cited above would be open to a reading through this interpretation of Ibnul 'Arabi's thought. But the Indian Sufis, who, like Ibnul 'Arabi himself, were more tolerant of diverging views, were not totally hooked on this reading and allowed themselves considerable freedom. In the following poem of Quddus there are no walls that would keep the water within a vessel:

> You search, you search, O my friend,
> I, the young wife, have disappeared;
> The drop has merged into the Ocean,
> pray tell how can it be found?[37]

At this juncture two distichs from Kabir's *sākhīs* may be strategically cited to show almost identical poetic content.

> You search, you search, O my friend,
> but Kabīr has disappeared:
> The drop has merged into the Ocean
> how then could it be found?
>
> You search, you search, O my friend,
> but Kabīr has disappeared:
> The Ocean has disappeared into the drop,
> how then could it be found?[38]

It is possible to argue that for the Indian Sufis Ibnul 'Arabi's insistence on the relative "autonomies" of *Haqq* and *Khalq*, of truth/creator and the created, tends to get overlaid by a somewhat more generalized and philosophically less precise monism. Nathic and Sufi readings of self and God simply fed into each other to such an extent that their differences began to collapse irretrievably. It may be argued even further, and with some force, that neither could have come into being without the other. Again we may go to Kabir for an instantiation of precisely this kind of fusion. The poem quoted below has been read by important Indian critics such as S. S. Das, P. N. Tiwari, P. D. Barthwal, M. P. Gupta, S. Shukla, and R. Chaturvedi[39] as an exemplary instance of Kabir's use of advaitic discourses to come to grips with the sublime otherness of Brahman. But if we look at the language carefully we find that Kabir is using metaphors straight out of Ibnul 'Arabi's paradox-ridden *Fuṣūṣu'l Ḥikam*. The key terms of debate for Kabir are *khālika* (the creator) and *khalaka* (the creation) in a distinct homage to Ibnul 'Arabi. What is stated is the idea of oneness of being within a pantheistic metaphysical apparatus that is similar to advaita but not identical with it.

How can you forget
Brothers, people, all
That the creator is in the created
The created in the creator
Pervading all existence?

After all
We are slaves of that one light
Created by the creator
which informs all phenomena.
And if that is so
Aren't we all one?

Well to tell the truth,
No one knows the ways of God
Though the Satguru does know
And I, Kabir, as well
Since I have seen the One in all.[40]

Kabir's signature line is important here because the line collapses all the readers into Kabir. He seems to be saying that since I know this truth, you, the reader, the listener, should also know it. Yet Kabir is not maintaining a purely monistic line here, claiming instead the more likely Nathic duality-nonduality-difference-thesis or the philosophy of Wahdat al-Wujud. The picture is thus more complex and the language shows all the hallmarks of hybrid philosophical thinking.

The self as body and not simply as a metaphysical entity began to take a much more central place in Nathic doctrines. In the narrative of desire for union with God (the central narrative of devotional poetics) what we now begin to see in Nathism (our second "ism") is a move away from the mind to the body, and more specifically to a discourse that is built around the cartography of the body rather than the quasi-analytic categories of the mind. In what is known as Hatha-yogic philosophy the body is foregrounded as the "channel" through which supreme consciousness may be achieved. Although the contextual patina of the foregoing would take us back to Gorakhnath and his legendary yogic abilities, it is not true, and probably not useful, to trace Hatha-yoga back to him.[41] The philosophy itself seems to have had its roots in antiquity. The *Bhagavadgītā* is certainly aware of proto-Tantric thinking (at

4.29–30, for instance). As it evolved, Hatha-yoga drew upon many discourses and symbolic systems and, depending upon the interpreter or "system," came to be variously equated with Tantrism, *sahaja-sādhana*, proto-Sikhism, and other esoteric disciplines. For devotional poetics what is immediately original here is the manner in which Hatha-yoga reintroduces the kinds of spiritual grids we associate with St. Ignatius Loyola and the Counter-Reformationists in Europe. But whereas the grid and devotional manuals of Loyola, de Sales, and others emphasized pure spirituality by and large divorced from the body, the kinds of grids we encounter here bring the body directly into questions about meditation and spiritual union with God. It has been said that around the eighth century one Sarhapa, a Buddhist Siddha (perfected one), introduced the dualistic symbology of the sun and the moon, which he equated with the two primal breaths of the body: the *prāṇa vāyu* (the "vital" breath) and the *apāna vāyu* (the "anal" breath). He went on to speak of the need to obliterate this dualism by stilling the mind thereby gaining entry into a transcendental reality.[42] The symbology, however, soon went beyond simple identifications with observable bodily characteristics and developed into the rewriting of the geography of the body in the language of oppositional (*iḍā* and *piṅgalā*) and mediating (*suṣumṇā*) channels through which the drama of the vital breaths was played out. The aim of this purely "fictional" system (based on structural rather than biological principles) was to redirect the movement of the *prāṇa vāyu* from the first two channels to the *suṣumṇā*. The movement itself is primarily generated by an energy called the Kundalini shakti that activates all the *cakras* or force fields in the body until it finally pierces the *sahasrāra cakra*, the dwelling place of the primal *puruṣa* or the *paramśiva*.

In the system of Hatha-yoga (also known as Kundalini Yoga) popularized by Gorakhnath the body itself is used to theorize mystical doctrines: "I will push the Ganges of the underworld toward the *brahmarandhra*/There I will drink ambrosial juice," is a common couplet found in the sayings attributed to Gorakhnath and the Nath Siddhas.[43] Since, as we have argued, the real question at issue is one of desire (its ways of expression, its emotional content, its sublime object of union, and so on), Kundalini Yoga now connects meditation with a body that had always been an important, but silenced and marginalized, site of desire itself. When the canonical "authors" connected Yoga with knowledge or action or even devotion (*jñāna,* karma, or bhakti), what they did was use the common word *yoga* (whose primary meaning related to matters of bodily control through exercise) to signify more complex intellectual matters. But the *Maitrī Upaniṣad*, for instance, is certainly aware of the associations of Yoga with the body as it refers to a sixfold Yoga in which the mystical *oṃ* itself is to be located at the midpoint of the body. The return of Yoga to its original usage in the practices of the Nath Yogis and their diverse followers, thus marks a decisive shift in the ideology of bhakti as it returns to Yoga's original emphasis on the corporeal. But this shift in fact takes us back to Yoga's fundamental relationship not only with the body but also with human sexuality. In the revised terminology of Patanjali's Yoga the body is designated as a site of seven *cakras* through which the Kundalini power moves, exploding and energizing each nerve plexus (*cakra*) in the process. Since the Kundalini is described as a coiled serpent that lies at the base of the spine (the *mūlādhāra*) its connections with the phallus is quite obvious. But where treatises on *kāma* (such as the *Kāma Sūtra*) emphasized phallic joy, this particular yogic system sees the Kundalini as a shakti that arouses the various *cakras* as it marches toward the seventh, the *sahasrāra cakra*, where a kind of nirvanic experience finally obliterates the idea of difference itself. This radical mapping of the language of sexuality onto the devotional is quite unusual and certainly very different from the sexual symbology of Western devotional verse. But the stages are, nevertheless, all of a piece with a crucial characteristic of devotional poetics itself which is the use of structure to demonstrate the movement of the subject in its search for Godhead.[44]

The manner in which this "cosmicization" of the body takes shape falls into a predictable Indian pattern of *adhyātmika* or "mystical" reading practice where structures are understood in terms of homology or allegory. Just as the sexuality of the *Gītagovinda* is reinterpreted as divine pleasure, so too the implicit history of Indian sexuality in Nathic or Tantric systems is transmuted into an allegory of the self's progress toward inner discovery. In the corresponding devotional texts, such as those of Kabir, the Sufis, and the Nath-Yogis generally, progress is referred to as a *sādhana*, a spiritual path or way toward enlightenment. Unlike Buddhism, where nirvana is given a very precise meaning (*nibbāna*: "the utter cessation [of *dukka*] without attachment, of that very craving, its renunciation, surrender, release, lack of pleasure in it"[45]), in the philosophy of these poets, philosophers, and itinerant saint-singers, the Kundalini shakti's explosion in the *sahasrāra cakra* is not given any propositional definition. And this is so because linguistic definitions are not commensurate to an experience that can never be presented to consciousness. So the body becomes both a site of the experience as well as symbolic of the structure of that experience too.

Nevertheless attempts have been made to liken the state of bliss to a trance, a state of intoxication (the Sufi *fikr*) that leads to the condition of the Siddhas or perfected ones. While many of the terms deployed for this trance, such as *samādhi*, are straight out of intellectual Hinduism, the polyphony of voices, and their semantic overcoding, that make up the heterogeneous tradition outlined thus far also emphasize its anti-intellectual dimension: *samādhi* or union may be reached without much intellectual effort at all. If any word may be singled out that would designate the special nature of this *samādhi* it is the word *sahaja*, simple, straighforward, without complication, artless. It is a word that is often coupled with *samādhi*, hence *sahaja samādhi*. At the same time the parallel tradition of the union of Shiva and Shakti (originally Shiva and his consort Parvati) grounded as it always was in the religious symbology of the phallus, had a ready-made discourse that could be linked to Tantrism. G. W. Briggs observed this many years ago when he wrote:

> The Kundalini Yoga makes large use of the doctrine of the union of Shiva and Shakti; that is, it swings around the idealization of the experience of the ecstasy that arises in creative union.[46]

Here then in the figure of Shiva we have a God who was in many ways counter-hegemonic and whose grounding in the rich and fertile rituals of India was well established.

In the *Siddha-Siddhānta-Paddhati*, the Nath-yogi sect's most important work,[47] all bodies are revealed as "elements" held together by one Shakti, a Supreme Spiritual Power identical in its "nondifferentiated aspect" with Shiva. When the Siddha Yogi reaches *samādhi*, these elements return to their nondifferentiated origins as the state of trance is now one of absolute *ānanda* ("bliss") where the word *ānanda* probably carried its older Vedic meaning of "orgasmic rapture" alongside its more common meaning of the "experience of Brahman/Atman" fusion. In such a state the subject is an Avadhuta Yogi, having obtained such a complete mastery of the self that he is "truly worthy of being *Sad-Gurū*, because he is capable of destroying the darkness of ignorance which prevails in the minds of ordinary people and of awakening the spiritual wisdom and the spiritual power which normally lie asleep in the human consciousness."[48] This is the state of difference-in-nondifference (since the Yogi still wishes to be identified as an autonomous subject) where, seemingly, there are no distinctions between deities and the various elements (earth, fire, etc.) that constitute the world of phenomena. Though the immediate philosophical underpinning here is directly taken from Gorakhnath's *dvaitādvaita-vilakṣaṇa-vāda*, both Gorakhnath himself and the Nath Yogis borrowed indiscriminately from Buddhism and intellectual Hinduism. If we then return to the discourses of Sufism, we get a much better picture of the complex nature of religious syncretism at work in medieval India of which both Gorakhnath, the Nath Yogis and Kabir were beneficiaries. From the *Gorakhbānī*, the following *sabadi* may be cited to make this point clear:

> Well here I am
> By birth a Hindu,
> By vocation a Yogi,
> By inclination a Muslim mystic.
> Isn't it time that difference forgotten
> Priests too follow
> A path that Gods themselves have embraced?[49]

The ease with which conflicting theologies come together in the above poem is evidence enough of Hazariprasad Dvivedi's contention that even before Gorakhnath there were many Shiva, Buddhist, and Shakta traditions that were neither Hindu nor Muslim.[50] In the following saying, for instance, Nath-yogic and Sufi terminologies are simply taken for granted:

> Beyond the powers of thought
> Beyond the movement of the wind
> Where neither the sun nor the moon enters,
> There O mind take your repose,
> For so says (saint) Saraha.[51]

It is now not too difficult to see the mystical/meditative tradition to which this verse belongs. The basic symbolism of the tradition of Tantra—the sun, the moon, their confluence and extinction—plays an important role in the texture of the verse. The verse then is heavily coded with a clear directive to the would-be Siddha to still the mind so that the enlightened state of *sahaja samādhi*, the mystical trance of the way of "easy" union, may be realized. In the *Gorakṣa Śataka* the concept was formulated as follows:

> Having seen that, the supreme light unending, shining in all directions, in samādhi, the adept does not experience (any more) transient existence.[52]

In other texts collectively belonging to the Nath-panthi tradition, the state of mystical trance, the highest state in fact, is termed *unmanī* or *manonmanī* (*manaḥ unmani*). The *Haṭhayogapradīpikā*, a fifteenth-century treatise on Tantric Hatha-yoga by Chintamani, for instance, designates the "stilled" state of the mind *manonmanī: yo manaḥ susthirabhāvaḥ saivāvasthā manonmanī*.[53] In descriptive terms, the process by which the mind is "reversed" and the state of *unmana* (the final union into Shiva and Shakti) achieved, is the same as those of the Siddhas:

> The *nāda* is turned downwards
> The *bindu* or shakti upwards
> The life energy is united.
> Then in the *brahmarandhra* the nectar of life rains
> The moon and the sun are put into a state of trance.[54]

The idea of "reversal" makes its way into Kabir's verse where also it presupposes a radical reexamination of our normal mental processes. Like the process by which the spindle is brought back to the wheel to wind the twisted thread around it, the mind too should be rewound:

Follow not the guidance of the mind,
forgetting the soul's true nature:
As the thread upon the spindle
reverse and wind it back[55]

Upon reversal, then, the mind enters the state of *sahaja samādhi;* it is "stilled" and it becomes eternal. Here, in this state of equanimity, pain is transformed into pleasure, foes into friends as the practice of the silent *japa*[56] reaches out for this moment of stillness in what the Nath-panthi literature has called *surati-śabda-yoga* where *surati,* the highly technical and ultimately untranslatable first item, is defined as the way to Atma-consciousness.[57] What we get here is the desire to grasp the essence of *śabda* itself, the *sāraśabda*, the innermost "elemental" *śabda* that like a phoneme cannot be broken down or split any further. Alluding to a verse from the *Gorakhbānī*,[58] Kabir expresses it as follows:

Śabda is the lock,
Śabda is the key;
Śabda is the guru's word
That awakens the inner *śabda* (*nāda*).

When in the *śabda*, through the *śabda*
The Experience is obtained,
Then *śabda* unites with *śabda*.[59]

The verse makes good sense if we remember that the Guru's *śabda* here is the finer *śabda* that one arrives at through the cruder *śabda* of the first part of the poem. What has been designated as Kabir's *surati-śabda-yoga* is thus a structure in which Atma-consciousness, initially awakening its own shakti, leads, firstly, to a vision of the inner reality and, secondly, but more importantly, to the dissolution of the self in the totality that is the *śabda*-essence. In the *caūtīsī ramainī* of Kabir we find:

Where there is the word,
There is the letter;
Where there is the letter,
There the mind cannot be fixed.
Between the letter and the word is God.
The special devotee alone sees this.[60]

The awakening remains an "inner" movement and, as Kabir elsewhere maintains, this awakening is not dependent on either the Tantric "five postures" or the "various breaths." Its essence is a performance, a theatrical act between the inner and the outer self that consumes the devotee in the very "act of devotion":

> The fire he lights, incinerates his own self;
> When he can grasp the word and the not-word,
> Then is the fire extinguished.[61]

The *śabda*-essence, reformulated, thus becomes the sublime of the Nath Yogis. But if we were to tease further meanings out of the new semantics of *śabda*, we cannot keep away from the ultimate (absent) signified of this essence, that is God. *Śabda*-essence or *sāra-śabda* may be seen as the unpresentable name of the Lord. It is here that we face yet another instance of Indian displacement where *sāra-śabda* now becomes identical with the primeval *nāma*, the eternal name, which in turn produces its own *sādhana* in what Charlotte Vaudeville has called "Religion du Nom," or *nāma sumiran*.[62] Chronologically we don't have to move too far away from our Nathic enthusiasts to find an exceptional poet in Namdev (1270–1350),[63] whose poems on the religion of the name exemplify the complex ways in which the ideology of the oneness of being was being negotiated in the period. In Namdev, too, the "name" becomes a stand-in for the construction of the devotional text as a "self-consuming artefact." If everything finally comes from the object of desire itself, then the discourses of the desiring self have no freedom; they simply repeat the Other's mysteries and in so doing must deny the subject's own specific difference from God. Upon articulating the name of God, the self ceases to be and the poem self-destructs. Thus Namdev's verses abound with cries to the Lord in which the poet repeats "You alone know your truth" or "I am guilty Father I am guilty" and so on.[64] In the *sumiran* of the name (*nāma*) the great mantra (poem 120) is the name of Rama (*japi rãma nãma mantrāvalā*) and it is through "Rama" as the ultimate sign that the devotee's relationship with God is given mystical form. I choose one poem on the subject of the name from the corpus that, needless to say, is replete with poems on the name.

> Like a fish
> out of water
> floundering
> such is Namdev
> without the name,
> *Rām*.
> My whole body is anxious
> like a cow
> without her calf.
> The milk in her udder
> painfully churns
> melting like butter
> in hot sunshine.
> Such is poor Namdev

without the name
Rām.
As the heart of a libertine
aches
for another's wife
Namdev craves
the love of
Banvārī.[65]

There is nothing particularly radical about the language here. Indeed the metaphors are in harmony with the "confraternal" saint traditions generally. It is not that Namdev is particularly different from other saint-singers for whom the name had a special significance; rather Namdev's poems define a tradition of *nāma-sumiran* that is one of the essential elements, or root metaphors, of bhakti ideology. If we return to the poem cited, there are two competing discourses at work here. The first is the simple identity of Namdev and *Rām* (the name). The second, is a heavily cadenced metaphorical discourse that works on the basic principle of the simile or *upamā*. The centers ("vehicles") of these similes are the fish, the cow, and the libertine who desires. In the first the fish out of water breaks the Wahdat al-Wujud oneness of being and is totally helpless. In fact, the fish out of water can no longer live. The second is the symbol of fertility in India: the cow that gives milk. Before we go to the next idea, it must be said that there are two kinds of desire here. The fish out of water desires to return to the seamless oneness of the sea; while the cow desires to be suckled. The third simile takes us back to desire as sexuality, the hidden (bodily) underside of Tantra. In this case the devotee's desire is analogous to that of the Dark Lord of the *Gītagovinda* who is also an expert on illicit pleasures. This particular sexual semantics is not new to devotional poetics and may be seen as one of the discursive constants of the genre. More significantly the libertine metaphor returns us to the strength of a radical *pravṛtti* where the man-in-the-world craves for the *paroḍhā parakīyā* or the married woman. And for Namdev, the tailor, the affairs of the world need not take us away from God. Thus in poem 128 we find:

The name of Rām
is my capital, my wealth.
It is a capital
Dear to my heart.

"Capital" (or *dhana* in the original) is not an uncommon word if we were to translate it simply as "wealth." But I think the translators Callewaert and Lath have chosen a much more exciting English word here because "capital" also signifies a feature of what is clearly a highly entrepreneurial culture. In the corpus of Kabir as well, capital and desire have a special role about which we shall have more to say in the next chapter. But what of the underlying principles of *dvaitādvaita-vilakṣaṇa-vāda, sufimat, nātha sampradāya,* and so on? Here is another of Namdev's poems:

Come Keshav
    my ecstatic fakir.
Come in the guise
    of an Abdāl
        O Father.

The world
    is your crown
the seven nether-regions
    your feet.
The earth
    is your leather apron.
Such is
    your guise
        Gopāl.

The green
    of the earth
is your mace
    the whole world
your bowl.
    And you have
fifty-six million sixteen thousand
    drawstrings
in your apparel.

The body
    is the mosque
the heart
    the *maulvī*
quietly praying.
    Sometimes he has
a form, but sometimes
    none.

You roamed
    over cities
and jungles.
    No one could fathom
your secret.

Namdev's heart
is drawn to him.
Come sit near me
Lord Rām.[66]

Discourses from many phrase regimes invade Namdev's cry to God as the poet draws upon a range of cultural experiences that by then had become part of the cultural dominant of large parts of Northern India.

The sound of the flute
fills the sky
O Lord.
The silent sound
resounds.
Ignorant of his Self
the fool wanders
lost.

Moving the sun
to the moon
making firm the mind
the breath
the spinal column
effortlessly I rose
through the *suṣumṇā*
to the star cluster
thus slaying desire.

I do not sit
or move
or wander.
I never starve
I never eat.
I do not live
I never die.
I am ever joyful
neither coming
nor going.

Dwelling in the skies
I have made my home
the self-born Void.
My heart is rapt
in the music within.

Rare is the yogi
who hears it.

I gather no leaves
 for ritual offerings.
There is no god
 in the shrine.

I have found shelter with Ram,
 never to be born
 again
 says Namdev.[67]

Even a cursory reading of this poem shows a clear enactment of Hatha-yoga principles. The dominant symbols of that yogic system—the sun and the moon, the mind, the vital airs, the inner channel (*suṣumṇā nāḍī*), the orbit of the firmament (*gagana maṇḍala*)—are utilized here to foreground the spontaneity of the *sahaja* state, the effortless manner in which that mystical state may be arrived at. Not surprisingly, the poem is based on a number of correspondences. The flute, the eternal word, the musical universe, the vibrations of the heart, the eternal *dhvani* ("music"), and finally the chanting of the Name (*nāma*) (itself hidden in the poet's name [*nāmdev*]) take us to a distinctly Tantric terminology. Like Kabir, however, Namdev, too, never really believed in the *anāhada śabda* as an end in itself. To him of even greater importance, always, was the "maker" of the sound. The "sound" then is only a mediator between the self and God, a fact which possibly explains the considerable force of the codicil in both their works. In the sister poem 99 the poet speaks of loving "the sound that cannot be heard" as he once again foregrounds the body:

Controlling my breath,
 I will enter
the yogic veins.
 Moving the sun
to the moon
 I will merge
into the light supreme.

As already mentioned in the context of the poetry of the Vira-Shaivas, the concept of stilling the mind or regressing the normal flow of vital fluids such as semen often gets expressed in an upside-down language called *ulṭabāṃsī* which works on the principle of absurdist inversion.[68] As a general rule these *ulṭabāṃsī*s have the structure of proverbial expressions couched in the cryptic, slanted language of *sandhyā-bhāṣā*. Explaining how the Yogin uses this kind of language to express the paradoxical condition of the moment of the sublime, Mircea Eliade notes, "this destruction of language contributes . . . toward 'breaking' the profane universe and replacing it by a universe of convertible and integrable planes."[69] The use of low forms of the vernacular to designate the identity of Self and Other in an almost absurd antilanguage is, however, part of the ideological function of the vernacular itself. The point is splendidly made by Per Kvaerne, who says that by defining a sign by its extreme opposite "that coincidentia oppositorum is achieved which alone can express the paradoxical nature of ultimate reality."[70] However, debates and disagreements about the real meaning of *ulṭabāṃsī* and *sandhyā bhāṣā* have continued. S. K. Adkar sees in *ulṭabāṃsī* a conjunction of an "attitude of contradiction" and a heavily "symbolic style" that manage to exist in harmony with each other,[71] while P. D. Barthwal reads it as a "means of startling the hearer and render him receptive to the real and hidden meaning."[72] The aim of *ulṭabāṃsī* is to foreground a certain attitude by a total inversion of the normal syntactic and logical relationships that exist between the elements that are being compared. One recalls English Metaphysical conceit and the European tradition of the *epidemica paradoxica* generally, though with some qualification because the metaphorical connections implied in a conceit are not based on a total inversion; they are simply metaphorical analogies taken to inordinate extremes, without making the technique a parody of metaphor proper.[73] In *ulṭabāṃsī*s opposites are not so much reconciled (which is a higher and more subtle poetic process) as "asked" to do "opposing acts." They are in fact negations of a very special kind where the linguistic image activates "iconic relations of non-linguistic signs"[74] that do not make sense in the natural order of things. Namdev for instance writes: "an ant gives birth to an elephant," "the water burned itself," and "I saw a bird fly without wings."[75] In the Kabir corpus as defined by the Indian oral tradition (the corpus here comprises all the texts and their variants as transmitted) we find *ulṭabāṃsī*s such as "a dog chases the rider of an elephant," and "the jackal and the lion calculate profit and loss." In the little read bhakti poet Sundardas the same discursive moves are evident:

> The ant has devoured the elephant,
> The jackal has eaten the lion,
> Uneasy in water a fish finds happiness in fire.
> A cripple climbs a mountain,
> Death dare not see the dead!
> Says Sundar why ask me?
> I understand contradictions.[76]

*Ulṭabāṃsī*s may be a combination of ambiguity, paradox, inversion, and collocational breaks in language or simply forced analogy or semantic perversion aimed at shocking the reader. Yet whenever this particular technique is used, a final *bhaṇitā* introduces the poet himself who brings the string of contradictions down to the level of a constative statement. These images, in their extreme paradoxes, always act analogously to the mysteries of the world. To give meaning and order to these paradoxes, to arrest the natural tendencies toward chaos, the grace of God (*guru kṛpā*) is required.

A twilight language is essentially an antilanguage not unlike the argot of the underworld or of other marginalized groups of people who feel that their language should be accessible only to the initiated.[77] As Mircea Eliade remarked, "[in *sandhyā-bhāṣa*] the semantic polyvalence of words finally substitutes ambiguity for the usual system of reference inherent in every ordinary language."[78] Thus pimps and procurers, drug barons and heroin pushers, prison inmates as well as corporate chiefs use a specialized antilanguage. Their antilanguages are marked by a high level of semantic overcoding of a number of key terms. Pimps and procurers, for instance, have an incredibly large vocabulary for sex. *Sandhyā-bhāṣā*, the generic term, or *ulṭabāṃsī*, the more specific form for an "inverted" language, however, deals primarily with the essential problematic of illusion and reality. We recall at this point debates surrounding distinctions between an unreal world linked to "annihilationism" (*ucchedavāda*) and a real Atman linked to eternalism (*śāśvatavāda*). Shankara had in fact insisted that Brahman alone was real, and all else was false (*mithyā*). Bhakti ideology finds Shankara's ideas a useful source for its own definition of phenomenal reality. So much so that the absolute schism that Shankara claimed existed between the *jīva*, the soul, and Brahman because of the intercession of the unreal samsara continued to be the overall structure within which the basic metaphors of bhakti poetry itself operated. Yet where Shankara left the principle of illusion or Maya as a problematic category because, finally, he couldn't quite decide whether Maya was intrinsic to Brahman itself or a principle to which subjects attached themselves because they just happened to occupy the space of samsara, the saint-singers of Northern India interpreted Maya as desire which, unchecked (unstilled) or "undeflected," destroyed the capacity of the self to become one with Brahman. The confusion is evident in Namdev who says:

I dread
I dread your terrible
māyā.
So many has it led
astray.

Brahma is not to be seen
in *māyā*.
There is no *māyā* in
Brahma.

So says the creator himself
O Nāmdev.

Do not make me ride
two horses together
O Krishna.[79]

Namdev is in this world, and therefore part of Maya yet he wishes to be part of Brahma too. His state of mental confusion is, however, intrinsic to the philosophical narrative of Maya as Shankara presents it. Indeed Namdev's poem follows Shankara to the letter here. Shankara had distinguished between a lower and a higher Brahman. Since the higher Brahman is pure consciousness, only the attributes of the lower Brahman are those of the creator in the everyday sense of the word. The world thus created out of this lower Brahman's desire for play, *līlā*, therefore, has Maya as its condition of being. In idealist philosophy we are given a world that has a reality beyond our thought projections and cannot disappear simply because we do not wish to know about it. In Shankara's thinking the world is false not because it is constructed imaginatively but because it cannot participate in the definition of the Real. This Real is the higher Brahman that classical Hindu thought could define only negatively as "not thus, not thus." In its poetically most durable forms the Brahman-Maya impasse took the shape of a dialectic in which the poet explored the constant tension between his own position (within samsara) and his search for the *alaukika* ("the otherworldly"). The Maya end of that dialectic often took the form of a *kanak kaminī* ("the deceitful woman") or a *nartaki* ("the temple dancer") or other figures (primarily women) who contaminated the pure nature of the subject's spiritual desire. The difficulty is evident in the constant push to aestheticize this dialectic as is evident in the host of rope/snake, pot/space, water/foam, object/reflection narratives that invade the discourse of religious piety at every stage.

In Namdev's poem, the Yogin requests Krishna not to make him "ride two horses together." Yet ride he must because in the world that we inhabit this is the condition of our being. The desire to break dualities, the desire to collapse categories is strong in devotional poetics but there is an equally strong sense in which this desire is also the desire for death, for the merging of the self into the oceanic sublime. Devotional poetics in this argument meets the sublime poetics of a pleasure principle blissfully unaware of the reality principle. To say this comes pretty close to affirming the principle of dissolution itself as the aim of desire. In Namdev's invocations of Maya there is evidence of this tendency though we must be careful here since Shankara's Maya was not completely identical with Namdev's reading of the world as it is. In the verses of Kabir, Namdev, the Kashmiri mystic singer Lalla Laleshvari (who, it is said, danced naked like a dervish[80]), the Nath Yogis, and the Sufis we find a complex interlocking of ideas that endorse a more pantheistic unity of being combining the Sufi Wahdat al-Wujud with Gorakhnath's *dvaitādvaita-vilakṣaṇa-vāda.*

The inner world becomes meaningful, however, not through philosophy but through emotion, and especially through the emotion of love. When the theoreticians created the rasa of bhakti, or devotion, their prototype was the rasa of *śṛṅgāra* or of eroticism. In the erotic play of the lover and his beloved (the definitive text here is undoubtedly the *Gītagovinda*), devotional poets found a ready-made structure that they could use as the basic grid for the expression of their own relationship with God. Not surprisingly, much of the symbology was drawn from the world of the erotic as it, the devotional, in turn invaded the discourses from which it borrowed. In one of the great allegorical narratives of the time called *mathnavī* (*maṭnawī*) the language of love and the structure of the lover-beloved are raised to new heights. The *mathnavī* is a Persian romance genre of the court brought to India by Islam and popularized by the Sufis.[81] Works such as *Lailā-Majnūn*, Nizami's *Khusro-Shirīṇ* and Zami's (d. 1492) *Yusuf Zulekhā* were written around the themes of intense and passionate love relationships that normally ended with the deaths of both lovers. Majnun, the demented lover of Laila, became symbolic of the mystic's annihilation in God (*fanā*). Among other well-known *mathnavī*s are Malik Muhammad Jayasi's *Padmāvat*[82] (1540) written in Avadhi (the language of Tulsidas), Maula Daud's *Candāyan* (1380), Kutuban's *Mṛgāvati* (1504), Manjhan's *Madhumālti* (1545), Usman's *Citrāvalī* (1613), and Sheikh Nabi's *Jñānadīp* (1619). In one of the most ambitious attempts at literary-philosophical conflation, the Gujarati poet Shah 'Ali Muhammad Jiw Jan (d. 1515) used the "motif of the longing bride to symbolize the longing soul, and tried to explain the mysteries of *waḥdat al-wujūd*."[83] The sixteenth century was obviously the great period of the *mathnavī*s though the genre has survived into modern times. In 1917 Nasir could still call his novel *Premekaham*, a *mathnavī*. Perhaps the best Hindu *mathnavī* is the Rajasthani *Ḍholā Mārū Rā Dūhā*. Popular Hindi films based on these and other *mathnavī*s include *Lailā Majnūn* (1931; 1945; 1953; 1976); *Alif Lailā* (1933; 1953); *Husn Kā Cor* (1953), *Lālparī* (1954), *Abe Hayāt* (1955), *Hātim Tāī* (1956), *Shirīṇ Farhād* (1956), *Ḍholā Mārū* (1956), and *Ālhā Udal* (1962). The source texts of the *mathnavī* are not religious in the strict sense of the word, and their modern filmic transformations certainly show the extent to which they can be harnessed toward purely romantic ends. But what is striking, historically, about the *mathnavī*s is that in India this essentially Persian court narrative has been used to incorporate elements that arose out of the interaction between Hindus and Sufis. The underlying structure of these narratives is, however, the lover-beloved relationship we detected in the *Gītagovinda* of Jayadeva. But where the *Gītagovinda* was emphatic on the dual referents of the actions of the lovers (both Jayadeva and the *sahṛdaya* mediate our reading of the text), the *mathnavī*s let go of this self-conscious metacommentary and offer us texts that, at one level, are pure romances. One of the great achievements of the

Indian *mathnavī* style was the Sufi poet Malik Muhammad Jayasi's *Padmāvat,* which we shall examine in some detail as representing the entire tradition.

Padmāvat is a typical *mathnavī* yarn with two distinct sections. The first part of the narrative deals with the birth of the heroine Padumavati. She is the daughter of Gandharva, king of Singhal. A beautiful girl without peer, she is given a wonderful palace by her father to which she retreats with a coterie of friends, the closest of whom is in fact a parrot. She gets all her information about the world from this parrot, who in turn becomes privy to all her thoughts. Angered by this intimacy between the princess and the parrot, the king demands that the parrot be killed but it escapes only to be caught by a seasoned fowler who sells it to a Brahmin sage. The sage takes the parrot to the city of Chittauda, where it is bought by King Ratnasen. From the parrot the king hears of the exceptional beauty of Padumavati. Infatuated he rushes to the kingdom of Singhal and marries Padumavati. This marks the end of the first part of the *mathnavī*. The second part deals with the Muslim ruler of Delhi Allaudin Khijli's infatuation with King Ratnasen's wife. He attacks Ratnasen's city, captures, and kills him. Upon hearing this, Padumavati and Nagmati, Ratnasen's first wife, also kill themselves. When Allaudin Khijli finally enters the ravaged city, all he finds are ashes of the dead. Presented in this manner *Padmāvat* is the usual medieval love-tale of desire, lust, and death with touches of political intrigue, power, and Muslim territorialization. Yet the theistic basis of Jayasi's *Padmāvat* is undeniably a Sufi vision of God and its literary enactment is based upon the Sufi principle of writing about "the love of a man for a woman . . . insofar as it served as a model for the divine-human relationship."[84] Where the norm has been the impossible desire to transcend the body so as to expand consciousness (or grasp the sublime), here there is a regression back to the body as the site of love and desire. This in itself does not (and could not) make *Padmāvat* a religious text like the *Gītagovinda*, where the homologies are clearly marked, but it does specify a particular idiom in which the discourses of the religious may also play an important part.[85] Standard intellectual definitions of God as the one, invisible, formless, quality-less, omniscient, the First Principle behind all creation are soon overtaken by references to the principle of love that not only made the Prophet Muhammad possible but also allows us to see divine beauty in spite of Maya.[86] In Usman's *Citravalī* the same idea is made more explicit:

> From the beginning of time the Creator made love,
> For love he adorned the world;
> He saw in this his own form
> Pleased, He let it flourish.[87]

Love is, however, not something that the body shirks from or despises. In fact the body revels in love but enjoys not so much real, physical union but separation, the condition of *viraha* typified by Radha and Krishna in the *Gītagovinda*. Thus when Ratnasen hears the parrot Hiraman describe the beauty of Padumavati ("As when the sun forces the moon to disappear among clouds/So beautiful maidens hide upon seeing the splendor of Padumavati"[88]) he is struck by the condition of *viraha*, love-in-separation:

> A thousand rays diffused from her body (for so Ratnasen felt)
> A thousand lotuses bloomed wherever he looked.[89]

The relationship between love-in-union and *viraha*, love-in-separation, is one of the most important motifs in bhakti literature and possibly in Indian culture generally. As we have remarked already, this is an instance of difference ("différance") where the key items are not part of an oppositional set, nor are they governed by the logic of either/or. The *virahiṇī* as lover/devotee does not seek ecstasy in union (*prema*). Instead, she wishes to remain in an in-between condition, alternating between the psychological conditions of union and separation. The condition should not be confused with perpetual indecision nor with a refusal to accept happiness; rather the alternation insinuates an unpresentable love for a lover who will never come. When we map this condition onto the devotee-God nexus, the *samādhi* that arises is frequently the purer because of it. On the subject of *prema* and *viraha*, let us quote an Indian point of view here:

> There is an essential relationship between *prema* and *viraha*. The lover always wishes for union with his beloved. But the union is achieved only after the lover has burnt himself in the flames of separation. For union with the Lord it is, similarly, essential that the devotee forsake all the pleasures of the world and concentrate on the vision of God alone. . . . For this reason in Sufi literature *viraha* is captured with such intensity.[90]

Jayasi again writes about Ratnasen's *viraha* as a fire that consumes the entire world and penetrates all its parts: "sharper than the edge of the sword is the pain of separation."[91] The total imagery against which these lines are developed is of epic dimension. The state of Ratnasen's *viraha* occurs within the context of the almost primordial image of a "burning sea" capable of consuming both the sea and the sky (*dharatī saraga jarai tehi jhārā̃*). Against this, *viraha* is presented as a state even more intense, even more overpowering and consequently "capable" of neutralizing the ferocity of the sea that Ratnasen has to cross on his way to Singhal, Padumavati's kingdom.[92] Jayasi, of course, continues to develop the *viraha* theme extensively. In verse 254, we again encounter a reversion to Ratnasen's earlier account of the pain of separation: the beginning of love has its corresponding pain that never lessens but grows progressively more vigorous and dynamic.[93] Another character, Mahadeva, tells Ratnasen, "You have cried a lot, no more please for without suffering pain first, you cannot attain your beloved. You are now pure, your body has been purified. Now you can go on the path of love."[94] Padumavati, likewise, would want to test her lover's devotion first before giving herself up. Reflecting upon a note that Ratnasen has sent her, she wonders if Ratnasen's love has in fact developed beyond simple desire, if in fact it has *rabi hoi caḍhā akāsā*, become the "sun" and climbed to the heavens.[95]

Naturally, much of the imagery in *Padmāvat* belongs to the world of profane love. Yet, as Mircea Eliade has suggested in another context,[96] a principle of sacralization is at work here which imposes a frame, a limit, upon the situation being described so that the reader reads the text, at this point, in *alaukika* (otherworldly) terms. For it is clear enough that the hero in the work considers his journey of love as an *adhyātmikayātrā* or a religious quest in which the narrative is finally allegorical and the images symbolic.

In the quest for the sublime, the self as *sādhaka* must first overcome many vicissitudes before it can reach Brahman and ultimate knowledge (*marifat* in Sufi terminology). In Usman's *Citrāvalī* this quest is projected onto the cartography of four countries/cities/fortresses arranged in concentric circles. As the four fortresses occupy the space of the innermost circle the devotee moves from the outer to the inner as though he were experiencing the various "stages of mystical consciousness" (*nasūt, malakūt, zabarūt,* and *lāhūt*[97]). Ideally, of course, as allegorical narratives *mathnavīs* should show similar correspondences. The hero should move through these mystical stages until finally he reaches the state of absolute nondifferentiation. In Sufi literature, as in bhakti generally, this final state often takes the form of a real or imagined marriage between Self and Other/Lover. In the narrative proper, however, the structural correspondences (between the lover's quest for his beloved and the implied mystical stages in an *alaukika* experience) may be either absolutely clear-cut or so heavily transformed as to make them almost unrecognizable. In verse 119 of *Padmāvat* for instance, images such as the flames from the sun (*lahari suruja kai*), the wound of love from which the king expires (*muruchāī . . . pema ghāva . . .*), are easily identifiable signs of passion that have undergone a form of spiritual recoding. The images can, and do in this instance, acquire those very mystical elements that are essential for Indian devotional verse. In its patterned intensity—the triumphant heaping of image upon image, sensuousness compounded by lushness of phrase—the passage has the power to transcend what seems banal.

Sufi *mathnavīs* are thus heavily coded romance narratives that have dual referents. If the secular (including Indian popular cinema) found in these *mathnavīs* tales of romance and adventure, the devotional interpreted these same *mathnavīs* as genres that straddle *yoga-mārga* and *prema-mārga* (the path of discipline and the path of love).[98] Of special interest, however, remained the idea of Hindu divine love fertilized by the Sufi tradition of thinkers such as Ibnul 'Arabi. In *Fuṣūsu'l Ḥikam*, for instance, Ibnul 'Arabi had in fact written:

> Just as man was made in the image of God, likewise woman was made in the image of man. Hence man loves both God and woman. The relationship of man with woman is the same as that of nature with God. Therefore, in these terms, when one loves a woman, that love is divine.[99]

One recalls *Lailā-Majnūn*, Nizami's *Khusro-Shirīṇ*, and Mulla Daud's *Candāyan*, in all of which the lover falls in love with a married woman, yet courts her with honor and without *maithuna* (sexual union) in mind. This is precisely the kind of trajectory for *kāma* or desire that, in another context, we find in Krishna's reference to desire that does not presuppose any consequences, desire that is insistent upon its own purity of action. It is that kind of perfect desire, the object of which will forever elude the *mathnavī* hero whose state once again is that of *viraha*. *Viraha* is intense and the force of that intensity is maintained throughout these narratives.[100] The best instance of this kind of pain of separation is found in Zami's Persian *mathnavī*, *Yusuf Zulekhā* in which Zulekha falls madly in love with Yusuf and sacrifices all her worldly possessions simply on hearing his name spoken aloud until finally she marries Yusuf. When this happens a new realization dawns upon Zulekha, who tells Yusuf: "I loved you only so long as I did not know God. Now that my heart is full of heavenly love, there is room for no other (kind of love)."[101] The inescapable suggestion made here is that marriage (fulfilment) lifts the *laukika* (worldly) love onto an extraworldly (*alaukika*) love and in doing so devalues the body even as it supervalues the mystical. Quite possibly, this is one of the reasons why the *mathnavī* form often worked on themes of illicit love relationships, and on the tragic separation of the lovers.

The ability to shift semiotic coding from the profane to the sacred is not possible unless the participants understand the principles of decoding involved. Here these medieval saint singers were expert decoders because they knew when to shift gear and read texts in a nonrealist fashion. The skills of the infra reader were therefore intrinsic to the poets. To later interpreters, the ability to occupy the position of these precursor infra readers is absolutely crucial. Otherwise there is no adequate reading possible as the hermeneutic act gets distorted. However, even though the poets were expressing the inexpressible, they were no protomodernist Europeans moving toward the poetry of nonrepresentation. Though silence in the seventh *cakra* is the desired aim, and *samādhi* is the desirable condition, language does not relapse into impenetrability in spite of the occasional excesses of *sandhyā-bhāṣā*. Certainly this would not have been possible if Indian metaphysics had not taken decenteredness and deferral as legitimate positions to begin with. It is here that we return to the sublime and not the beautiful with which to explain this phenomenon. Where the beautiful encompasses an orderly universe that can be framed and contained, the sublime in its search for the ineffable takes us to that moment of irrational self-surrender when the law of reason gives way to the power of the imagination and allows it freedom of expression. The freedom given, reason reestablishes its power and control. The fascinating world of devotional verse is to be discovered in that moment of "letting-go." But we cannot simply stop there because what we have attempted to demonstrate through our reading of a select number of texts is the degree to which the quest for the sublime is so intrinsic to Hindu culture itself. It has led the culture toward levels of genre-mixing and cultural accommodation or religious syncretism quite unusual in any of the civilizations of the time. It has also led it toward a reading of the ultimate object of devotional composition, Brahman, as an image so vast that it cannot be framed at all. This is the legacy of *nirguṇa* bhakti though its *saguṇa* dimension with its devotion to a loving God (the child-God Krishna in Surdas or the adult Krishna in Jayadeva or Ram in Tulsidas) continues to grapple with precisely this problematic. The reduction of the sublime to the level of a concrete being continues to be constructed in the language of longing for union with the ineffable sign that is God. In the end it is dissolution and union (with its frightening reality deflected onto a reincarnation rhetoric) that marks the condition of the devotee in this highly complex (and yet seemingly straightforward) discourse. The Vaishnava Namdev, the Shaiva Lalla, and the nonsectarian Kabir are part of this complex writing out of the devotional moment.

The poet who becomes crucial for any adequate theorizing of Indian devotional poetics and who synthesizes many of the cross-currents we have examined thus far is Kabir. In him we see those essential qualities of *nirguṇa* bhakti that emerge in all general surveys of the subject: the emphasis on *nāma japa* ("the chanting of the Name"), the strength of meditative exercises, the rhetoric of love, the Sufi oneness of being, the stress on *sahaja sādhana* (the "easy" way of union in God), and the use of a discourse of twilight language. But it would be an oversimplification to say that Kabir therefore simply expressed what may be broadly called the fundamental principles of *nirguṇa* bhakti. Ultimately he stretched devotional verse to its limits as he absorbed the various trends and influences before him, notably Vedantic tradition, Sufism, and Tantric practices. As we have seen, these last two practices had given bhakti ideology and its semantics another frame of reference and had anticipated more radical uses of the religion of devotionalism. The (heterogeneous) corpus attributed to Kabir exemplifies many of these issues. For our argument this corpus presents an exemplary summation of the Indian sublime as the poetic imagination grapples with the ultimate question (as well as the object) of desire.

CHAPTER FIVE

Desiring Selves, Undesirable Worlds

Of all the poets who make up the North Indian saint tradition (*sant paraṃparā*) Kabir is arguably the most interesting. He may not possess the mesmeric charm of Surdas with his loving attitude toward the child-God Krishna or the feverish passions of the vibrant Mirabai with her bridal desire for the Dark Lord, or indeed the epic grandeur of Tulsidas whose magisterial work, the *Ramacaritamanāsa*, is revered as the Hindu holy book of North India, but he does possess qualities at once deeply religious and radical and dangerous. He is, arguably, *the* medieval Indian poet of commitment, the nonsectarian who touches a raw nerve in us because he draws us toward elements that the Indian social order has (conveniently) repressed. Whereas Surdas, Mirabai, and Tulsidas were poets who were always religiously correct (recall Tulsidas's uncritical devotion to the figure of Ram for instance) and wrote or sang for their Vaishnavite readers/listeners, Kabir couldn't care less about political or theological correctness provided that his position on these issues was presented in a forthright manner. Without turning Kabir into a social visionary or a theological rebel, as some have done, we would still want to maintain that in Kabir one sees the conflicting tendencies of an age and a strong sense of the need for an ongoing religious revisionism in Indian culture. He is in fact the medieval poet of cultural "hybridity" par excellence. "Hybridity" has become something of an ideal condition in recent postcolonial theory, but its use here is meant to underline not so much the attractiveness of a late modern way of looking at things as a statement about interaction, intermixing, and fusion as very normal characteristics of Indian culture. Throughout its intellectual history we find examples of not necessarily compatible ideas being yoked together, sometimes even forcibly. Out of this yoking (a metaphor about Metaphysical poetry going back to Dr. Johnson) emerged some of the best-known texts of the culture including the *Bhagavadgītā*, the Sikh *Ādi Granth*, the *mathnavīs*, and the poems of Kabir. To accept the existence of this hybrid condition of religious and cultural mixing is important because it persuades us that the call for nativist aesthetics is based on a puritanism or an ethnic absolutism that Indian culture has always looked upon with extreme suspicion. This is the point that is absent from G. N. Devy's provocative book in which he claimed that *bhāṣā* (or vernacular) literature like Kabir's should be read through indigenous or nativist literary and critical discourses. Devy quite correctly draws our attention to the ways in which classical theory (the *mārga* tradition) colluded with Indological or Orientalist practices to support a colonial cultural imperialism that prioritized *mārga* over *deśī* or *bhāṣā*. In turn, imperialism (the theory behind colonization) wrapped its own vernacular (in this case English) in a classical Graeco-Roman garb and presented it to the Indians as high culture. In Devy's argument, colonial Indians then adopted English literary criticism to read their own literature and, later, when the nationalist urge gripped them, instead of exploring their vibrant vernacular literatures, they turned to Sanskrit poetics because this is what colonial high culture had always valued. Sanskrit poetics was then transformed into a brand of English literary theory because the Indian nationalists couldn't possibly see anything of value in their own vernacular literatures because they too linked the "idea" of high culture with the establishment of the Indian nation-state.[1] The "establishment" Indian thus suffers from a massive amnesia when it comes to his or her own vernaculars of which bhakti literature is the prime literary example. Devy concludes with the following cryptic manifesto:

> Literature growing out of one type of underlying linguistic and metaphysical structure cannot be understood and studied by criticism growing out of another and alien type of underlying linguistic and metaphysical structure.[2]

In his argument, then, *bhāṣā* or *deśī* (vernacular) literature requires an indigenous vernacular theory that is neither Sanskritic nor colonial. While Devy is correct in pointing out the total inadequacy of Sri Aurobindo's literary theory because he so desperately wanted to recast Indian theory in the guise of Shelley's *A Defence of Poetry*, the alternative models that he endorses, such as the criticism of the Marathi novelist Bhalchandra Nemade (b. 1938), nevertheless operate from within Western empirical modes of literary criticism. In his admirable essay on the Marathi Varkari poets (including Namdev) Nemade is careful not to confuse discrete historical analysis with nativist tendencies toward hagiography.[3] That Nemade is so sensitive toward his Marathi bhakti poets does not mean that he is not a fine comparatist on matters of theory, as Devy himself undoubtedly is.

I made a passing reference to Devy in my opening chapter, but I have returned to him again because Kabir is someone whom Devy would want to read purely through nativist theories. I have not adopted this line of reading in this book even though I have been at pains to emphasize historical specificity as well as cross-cultural influences. I have also insisted on the hybrid formation of culture and have stressed that what is at issue in any poetics is not native exclusivism but theoretical appropriateness and utility. In matters of theory I have advanced the proposition that the Western/Eastern divide is not very helpful to begin with. What is of use in a world getting smaller by the hour is not cultural absolutism but cultural relativization (in the positive sense of the word), especially if your target culture has always been open to this kind of relativization. That the consequences of the English critical model on Indian culture was appalling says something about the paucity of theory in the (English) colonizer's own culture. I suspect that had the Germans colonized India we may have had less difficulty in reading Indian texts through a more philosophically attuned hybrid Indo-Germanic literary theory. It is for this reason that in this book I make a decisive critical intervention in the erstwhile theories of devotionalism by stipulating that in the Indian context the devotional corpus reworks the Indian sublime because Brahman, finally, is unpresentable. In making my case I have borrowed freely but critically and have embraced, as my starting point, Western theories of the sublime. In spite of Devy's claims to a major break between *mārga* and *deśī* traditions (the so-called Great and Small traditions), there are significant discursive continuities between the two. What we must do is bear witness to the breaks while at the same time avoid becoming excessively paranoid about specific periods or literary cultures. Regardless of where we stand, an epistemology of a double consciousness always stalks the positions from which we speak and operate.

In our revision of religious desire as the Indian sublime, we shall be turning to the Kabir corpus (as defined both in the critical editions as well as in Indian traditions) as the proof-text(s) of the theory and of the historical conjunctions outlined in this book so far. We are interested a lot more with the rough edges of Kabir—those edges that also signify a poet not unwilling to be contaminated by divergent philosophies, not unwilling to take on both the syncretists as well as the purists. We have noted that devotional poetry has used the two poles of the self and the absolute as a grid upon which its own narrative of religious desire and fulfilment has been superimposed. For the followers of the *nirguṇa* (or monistic) path of bhakti such as Kabir, the enactment of this path is pretty straightforward. At the same time it must be said that the *nirguṇa* path acts as a template that allows Kabir to make forays into pantheistic doctrines so that these too can be reshaped and philosophically recast in the context of a highly monistic reading of religious belief. The loose term "pantheistic" has a much more culture-specific corollary in Sanskrit as well as in the vernaculars where it is expressed by the term *saguṇa* (or belief in the "incarnatory" form of Gods). Arguably the best commentator on Kabir, Hazariprasad Dvivedi senses the tension between the *nirguṇa-saguṇa* opposition when he writes:

> Kabir's road to enlightenment was different. . . . The conventional paths were not open to him. He was a Muslim and yet not one; a Hindu and not a Hindu; a Sadhu and not a Sadhu. He was a Vaishnavaite and not a Vaishnavaite; a Yogi and not a Yogi. . . . He stood at a point of convergence, combining and expressing elements of Hinduism and Islam, *yoga mārga* and *bhakti mārga*, *nirguṇa* sentiments and *saguṇa* thought. . . . He saw the oppositions inherent in them, he saw their final and divergent paths. . . . He explored and utilized the contradictions he saw. . . . Ultimately he saw solutions to life in the belief in the inviolability of the love of God: not in the elaborate Vedas or the Qur'an, nor in the temple or the mosque . . . but only in a few words of love.[4]

Since Kabir is such a monumental figure in the tradition, more serious work has been done on him than on most other North Indian writers, ancient or modern. But much of the work is also ideologically skewed because in many instances (as in Dvivedi) he has been used to advance the ideals of secularism and religious harmony. Although Dvivedi goes on to examine the social history of the weaver caste in India to which Kabir belonged, the didactic elements in his criticism bring us back to a much more firmly entrenched Indian commentarial tradition (which may be called nativist in Devy's definition of the term) to compose histories as hagiographies.[5] If we can get beyond these passages in Dvivedi's book, we can profit immeasurably from his social criticism. It is clear that by the time of Kabir, India was no longer an unchanging, timeless Hindu India, something that it never was to begin with. The Muslims had established considerable political hegemony and had created relatively independent lifestyles for the many tailors and cobblers, blacksmiths and silversmiths, who depended on the courts for their livelihood. These lower classes were also among the first to convert en masse to Islam as did Kabir's own weaving class. The picture that emerges is one of relative mobility and freedom as the artisans and skilled laborers provided services to the growing numbers of entrepreneurs—both Hindu and Muslim—in the cities and towns that played important roles as centers of trade and industry.[6] The socioeconomic milieu can be hypostasized with reasonable certainty. What is more difficult to establish are the details of Kabir's own life. The admirable works of Westcott, Grierson,

Keay, S. S. Das, P. D. Barthwal, Mohan Singh, J. N. Farquhar, K. N. Dvivedi, M. P. Gupta, R. K. Varma, H. P. Dvivedi, Parshuram Chaturvedi, P. N. Tiwari, Linda Hess, and Charlotte Vaudeville have, however, provided us with material enough to make reasonably accurate statements about the intellectual history of Kabir's age even though his dates remain a bit murky.[7] In the light of research already undertaken we can say with some certainty that Kabir probably lived in the fifteenth century—1440–1518 are the years cited by many scholars—and he came from a weaver caste only recently converted to Islam. His preeminent place in the tradition of Hindu devotionalism is stressed in the much-quoted couplet about the origins of North Indian bhakti:

> bhakti drāviḍa upajī lāye rāmānanda
> pragaṭa karī kabīra ne sapta dīpa nau khaṇḍa[8]

> Bhakti was born in the South, was brought (North) by Ramananda and was revealed by Kabir to the seven continents and nine regions.

Tradition, however, has a weakness for dramatic conjunctions and not necessarily for truth. The bringing together of Ramananda and Kabir is meant to strengthen the age-old *gurū-śiṣya* (guru-pupil) relationship so central to the transmission of knowledge. But like Vyasa, who became the composer of any number of Puranic texts because of his association with the great epic, Ramananda too became an "author function" to whom you attached yourself if you wanted to establish an impeccable lineage. In fact as a guru-figure (or as a "guru-function") Ramananda was in great demand in the bhakti age because of his status as the founder of North Indian *nirguṇa* bhakti. Whether Kabir single handedly disseminated bhakti to all the corners of the world (as the couplet implies) is not the point at issue here. What is of interest is that the hagiographical connection with a figure as important as Ramananda establishes a lineage that forces us to take Kabir seriously as a founder of a devotional discursivity in North India. However, what the couplet does not indicate (though one cannot expect it to) is the nature of the bhakti Kabir actually revealed. And it is on this point that we should dwell for a moment because Kabir's bhakti represents the union of bhakti's emotional (populist) and intellectual dimensions. The Southern connection alluded to in the couplet (brought by Ramananda from the South) is a reference to a tradition best exemplified by the songs of the Alvars and the religiosity of the Puranic texts. The admixture and dissemination (as found in Kabir's own work) is linked to the complex mechanics of Yogism, notably the practices of the Nath Yogis and the Siddhas, as well as to the tradition of Sufism.[9] Not surprisingly, Kabir gets partisan support from the Vedantins who refer to Kabir's use of terms such as *agama, agocara,* and *agādha* to argue that Kabir is in fact defining

God as *nirguṇa* or "quality-less." Similarly the historical facts of his life—he being the son of a Muslim weaver, for instance—tend to reinforce the primarily Muslim contention that he was a Muwahhid, a believer in the unity of God, in Wahdat al-Wujud. Others would just as quickly relate the incidence of words such as *śūnya, madhi,* and *nirañjana* in his sayings to Buddhist influences.[10] Conversely, the poetic transformations of yogic exercises, especially Kundalini Yoga, it was argued, connected Kabir to the Tantric practices of the Nath Yogis. Such connections can be made *ad infinitum* and would simply strengthen Dvivedi's case that it is just so difficult to isolate a specific *paraṃparā* ("tradition") and make Kabir party to it. Not surprisingly, and given the complex social and religious conditions of the times,[11] Kabir chose an interiorized view of religion where the *sahaja* ("spontaneous") state was the ultimate aim of bhakti. Moti Singh has called Kabir's synthesis *bicitra*, unusual, even baffling.[12] Despising *bhrama* ("magic, sorcery, nonempirical deductions"), Kabir took the unusual step of accepting empirical truth—the truth based on seen knowledge[13]—*ā̃khī̃ dekhī satya*—as an essential starting point even when he knew that empirical truth must be subordinated finally to a higher reality.

The themes on which Kabir wrote are expressed in three interrelated poetic genres: *sākhis*, *pada*s, and *ramainī*s. The *sākhī*s are largely short didactic verses that are looked upon as "witnesses" since they are poems about witnessing the ultimate truth from the perspective of lived experience. Indeed, Charlotte Vaudeville waxes lyrical about this genre when she writes, "From a psychological point of view, the Kabir *sākhī*s may be considered as an expression of the moral and spiritual striving of the common man of Hindustan: to a large extent they represent the higher consciousness of the masses."[14] Unlike the *sākhī*s, the second generic form, *pada*s, are lyrical verses, loosely constructed around conventional metrical patterns and set to a musical melody or raga. A *pada* begins with a *ṭeka* (or chorus) and uses several popular meters to accommodate a number of melodic variations. The flexibility also reflects the constant need to change a line so as to add a new idea or simply to shift emphasis away from an existing one. In the fourteenth and fifteenth centuries, *pada*s were the most common structure for devotional songs (*bhajan, kīrtan*). Kabir's *pada*s, however, cover a large number of themes ranging from the satirical and didactic to the devotional. Because the *pada*s are so malleable, it is very difficult to offer a precise analysis of a typical *pada*. In the *Bījak* (the Eastern collection of Kabir's works most closely identified with the Kabir-panthis, the Kabir sect) these *pada*s are in fact called *sabad*s (*śabda*), which show yet other variants. The third major form employed by Kabir is the *ramainī*, which is used mainly for didactic verse. Like the *pada*, the *ramainī* too is a flexible form. A characteristic feature of the *pada*s and *ramainī*s (and some *sākhī*s) is the signature line or *bhaṇitā* in which the poet's own name occurs. The name may be a sign of authorship but often it is a mode of address to the self in which the poet admonishes or chastises himself for not seeing a simple truth.[15] In these deceptively simple structures Kabir enacts two major themes. The first theme deals with the self's relation to Brahman in the context of a world that philosophers had already declared to be an illusion. The second equally powerful though less common theme is the impassioned encounter of the woman-subject/self and husband-Other through the symbology of the burning bride (techincally the "burning widow"), Hinduism's bleak symbol of supreme sacrifice. We will now look at both these themes in some detail.

Desire, Deceit, and Maya

Devotional poetry is all about the relationship between Self and God. Since the power relation between the speaker and God is already known, and the semantic field of that relationship is limited or confined, devotional verse cannot really tell us anything we don't already know. This is Dr. Johnson's and T. S. Eliot's position. But whereas Dr. Johnson's concern was with the idea of originality (since nothing can compare with the grandeur of God, it follows that metaphorical language cannot add anything extra to our conception of God), T. S. Eliot worried over the limited emotional range of a genre that could never transcend its own limitations as "minor poetry."[16] The challenge of devotional poetry is then a question of how to make the known more interesting. In a tradition like the Indian where the religious has been the cultural dominant (in every sense of the word), it is hard to find any area that is not affected by religion. The location of the Indian sublime in religious discourse is thus a consequence of Indian culture's massive (and systemic) overcoding of the experiential, the artistic, and the phenomenal through religious symbology. Where else do we find the sublimity of the Himalayas linked to its status as the seat of the gods? Where the American sublime is the Niagara as a grand vision that the mind cannot easily totalize, and the European Romantic sublime nature as an overpowering force arrested by the intervention of the law of reason in the nick of time, the Indian sublime is the nirvanic vision of Brahman. This principle of the religious sublime invades architecture as well as literature. Just as temples become labyrinths with an admixture of austerity and erotic exuberance, the literary texts too refuse to be contained within the limitations of a particular genre or theme. We get capaciousness, plenitude, and heterogeneity rather than confinement, restriction, limitation, and closure. In this respect the sublime rather than the beautiful (Longinus and Edmund Burke rather than Dr. Johnson) provide us with a frame of reference with which to read Indian culture.

What I have referred to as an endemic tendency to displace meaning, a tendency toward genre-mixing and decenteredness, makes more sense through a poetics of the sublime, which, again, is our point of entry into our proof texts. Kabir stands at one end of an entire cultural history that he at times critically embraced, at other times renounced. The intellectual history we have provisionally sketched in the preceding chapters finds in Kabir a "site" where so many of its cross-currents are given poetic form. This makes our treatment of Kabir at once extremely simple and extraordinarily complex. For the fact is that for him the greatest devotional poem was one in which questions of interiority were not totally divorced from living-in-the-world, in which symbolic patterns and meditative structures current in the world around him could be given felt presence in art. It is thus not at all uncommon to come across a poem in which there is an uncanny resemblance between poetic structure and the methods of mental and physical control laid down in Kundalini Yoga. Here is one example among many:

> Call the believers
> O you Muezzin
> To such a mosque
> Where there are ten doors.
>
> Make your mind Mecca
> Your body *qiblā*
> and make your "speaking" *jīva* your ultimate Guru.
>
> There will be no peace
> Until you have destroyed
> Ignorance, superstition and the five passions.
>
> But for me, says Kabir,
> I am ecstatic
> My mind ever so gently enters the *sahaja* state.[17]

In this poem Kabir invokes the traditional Tantric equations in which the mosque and *qiblā* (the direction in which Muslims turn during prayer) are the body, Mecca is the mind, and *bolanahāru,* the "speaking" *jīva,* the ultimate Guru or Brahman. The steps of meditation are clear-cut: an opening invocatory statement, a prescription (what to do), a didactic statement, and finally the presentation of the poet's own exemplary condition because he has followed the proper meditative steps. Upon constructing these symbolic equations—as any infra reader should do—we examine the steps that the self must take in its quest for unity with the Other. Since the destruction of *tā̃masu* (*tamas,* dark energy, ignorance), *bharamu* (superstition), and *paṃcai* (the five passions) are the preconditions for a higher awareness, the underlying meditative grid of the poem enables the reader to create in his/her mind the conditions under which the destruction of these overpowering forces can take place. It is only then that the self (and the reader) can enter the *sahaja* state. This structural homology between the form of the poem and the steps by which the self realizes Godhead gets repeated in devotional poems over and over again. The same relationship between a meditative form and its poetic expression can be seen in a poem where Kabir adopts the symbology of the itinerant Sufi mystic:

> I am in all, I am no other, I am all;
> split me into parts, I am in all.
> Some call me Kabir, some Ram.
>
> Neither young nor old, I don't have
> any children[18] either.
> I don't go when told to, I don't come even
> when invited: "easily" I live in the world.
>
> For shelter I have a blanket—
> The world believes I live alone.
> The weaver has found no satisfaction in stitching;
> He has torn the ten doors and then
> stitched them up again.
>
> My acts are untouched by the three *guṇas*;
> No wonder I am known as Ram.
> I see the world, the world does not see me;
> Has Kabir in fact found something?[19]

This is forthright identificatory devotional poetry in which Kabir claims to be simultaneously himself and King Ram (*rāma rāī*). The renouncer-figure is both the master of Kundalini Yoga (having exploded the ten doors of perception and then reworked them into another tapestry) and the classic Vedantin. But he is also the perfect renouncer who Krishna-like emphasizes purity of action and defines the Atman as unborn, eternal, primeval: *na jāyate mriyate vā kadācin.*[20] What remains at the heart of Kabir's contaminated discourse (a discourse that shows borrowing from Vedanta as well as contemporary Sufism and Yogism) is the claim of a fundamental union of Atman and *paramātman* that, more often than not, expresses itself through two common metaphors. These are, first, the symbolic union of a drop of water in the immense ocean, and, second, the physical union of man and woman. The following *dohā*[21] from one of the *sākhīs* may be used to exemplify the first of these metaphorical techniques:

> You search, you search, O my friend,
> but Kabīr has disappeared:
> The drop has merged into the Ocean,
> how then could it be found?[22]

Kabir is playing an interesting game here, superimposing classical metaphors of monism (the metaphor of the vessel of water in an ocean is attributed to the monist Shankara) on the Sufi Wahdat al-Wujud, but always bringing the analogies back to his own self. In a very significant manner also, the procedure shows the ways in which emotional bhakti was attempting to come to terms with intellectual Hinduism. The centrality of this metaphor from Namdev[23] to Quddus, the author of *Ruśdnāma*, underlines the links between poetry and an endemic philosophical debate about the dissolution of the self in some greater reality or being.

All this, of course, makes immensely problematic Kabir's definition of the self. Does the poem "I am in all" signify an absolutely monist position of identity of the self in Brahman? Is the use of "Ram" meant to signify a *nirguṇa* Brahman totally divorced from avataric narrative(s)? Or is Kabir using the language of identity as a means of connecting the advaitic (nondualist) tradition with a more emotional brand of bhakti?[24] A better key to the poem is through the qalandari tradition of mystical chanting in which the Sufi dervish dances as he sings about his desire to merge with the creator. In this respect the poem is not unlike the heavily Persianized poem we discussed in chapter 4 (*pada* 185). There the poet chanted "*khālika khalaka*," the creator is in the created, implying a unity of being that also signalled some understanding of Gorakhnath's *dvaitādvaita-vilakṣaṇa-vāda*. The situation is again one of creative hybridity in which Kabir at times keeps Hindu thought apart from Islamic thinking and at other times combines them to emphasize the need to separate social processes from religion. It seems to me that Hazariprasad Dvivedi wants to have it both ways when he endorses what he thinks are Kabir's essentially advaitic leanings:

> When Kabir (in the same breath) writes about the oneness of Ram and Rahim, it doesn't follow that he is equating *advaitic* Brahman with Islamic Khuda. What Kabir does here is to state a simple fact in a straightforward manner: if you believe in one God, then it is pointless to make religious distinctions (as if there were two).[25]

But religious distinctions do remain and they are a fact of life. If we want to justify Kabir it would be better to see Kabir as the radical social conscience of the age because he would argue that distinctions are always man-made (women, of course, never figure in the debates). The trouble then is not with God but with the world itself and it is here that Kabir's definition of the self involves the use of the allegory of woman as Maya. This "figuration" of the Maya factor will now confuse the erstwhile "drop of water in the ocean metaphor" we have discussed. Maya seen through metaphors of male/female sexuality is the new element in Kabir's verse. Like much else in Kabir (as seen in the Dvivedi quotation) the reference to Maya reminds us of Shankara, but only in a very general sort of a way because a closer reading of Kabir shows significant departures from the master-thinker. There is little of the higher and lower orders of Maya in Kabir, much less a profound meditation on whether Maya is in fact an *a priori* condition of Brahman itself. These are indeed advaitic concerns that Shankara philosophized at length. For Kabir it is sufficient that Maya is concretized as an enchantress, a harlot, who creates a world that finally traps/encrypts the self.

That Maya is a crucial concept for Kabir is clear from the fact that in the *Kabīr Granthāvalī* there are seven *padas* collected specifically under the heading "Maya," and an entire *sākhī* with twenty-eight *dohās* called *māyā kau aṃga* ("On Maya").[26] I will treat the latter collection first. In this *sākhī*, Maya is presented as an enchantress or a harlot (*pāpinī̃, mohinī̃*) who weaves a web of illusion around the soul (*phaṃdha lai baiṭhī hāṭi*). Throughout the *sākhī* this image of the enchantress works with *kanaka kā̃minī̃* (gold and woman) to create a series of relationships in which the self finds itself constantly imprisoned. As Kabir sees it, the problem is often one of ego, of *mana*. Ego, of course, relates, on the perceptual level, to the entire system of "I-ness" or *ahaṃkāra* that indeed makes samsara, the world that we inhabit, possible.[27] The body is presented as a "house" of blood and semen (*raja bīraja kī koṭhalī*), with a beautiful outer form (*tāpara sājā rūpa*), sunk into the very depths of Maya (here presented in the characteristically Kabirian term as *kanaka kā̃minī̃*) in the absence of the One Name (*eke nā̃ma binu būṛhihai*). This commentary may be exemplified best through a reading of the following representative *dohās* from the *sākhī*:

> When the crane polluted the water,
> the Ocean itself was soiled:
> The other birds kept on drinking
> but the Hamsa (*haṃsa*) bird did not dip its beak.
>
> Maya called out to me (*hamasaū̃*):
> "Do not turn your back on me!
> All the others are in my power"—
> but Kabir has gone in anger![28]

The crane-Maya (*bigulī-māyā*) and the *haṃsa*-Kabir correspondence work on the usual pattern of anagogical equivalence found elsewhere in Kabir. Another distinctive set—in this instance, a traditional one that relates names of birds to that of women generally[29]—connects the *bigulī* and *haṃsa* with words for the enchantress: *mohinī̃, kā̃minī̃* and so on. The use of the *haṃsa* metaphor is useful because it is the *haṃsa* alone that refuses to drink polluted water. If we examine the *sākhī* more closely, we detect an echo of the word *haṃsa* of the first *dohā* (*dohā* 25) in the *hamasaū̃* ("to me") of the next *dohā* (*dohā* 26). In connecting the *haṃsa* with the *hamasaū̃* (that is with the poetic self) what is being suggested is that, like the *haṃsa*, the self too can detach itself from the hypnotic power of Maya.

Though Maya is mentioned in various contexts as a deceiver, as the *līlā* (sport) "of the gods," Kabir does not explicitly state that the world itself is any less real.[30] The observations of an early Indian critic of Kabir, Ramkumar Varma, may be cited to show the error of slotting Kabir's eclectic use of philosophical terms into high Hindu modes of belief.[31] In making the connection between Shankara's Maya and Kabir's, Varma points out that Shankara's Maya exists primarily as a preexistent principle of illusion but Kabir's Maya concretizes this illusion (as narrowly defined by Shankara) through identification with the *kanaka kãminī*, the *mohinī* and the harlot. This very act of identification—basically an aestheticization of Shankara's metaphysic—collapses what for Kabir is a much more slippery term. To Kabir Maya is both an established metaphysical term as well as a "substantive" with which to code certain kinds of bodies. But this mode of "passing" has its dangerous consequences since it makes the construction of a definite Kabirian metaphysic so very difficult. On the other hand it is precisely the playing with contraries—a Keatsian negative capability where oppositions are poetically maintained—that explains the immense poetic power of his writings.[32]

Whichever way we look at it, it is clear that Kabir concretizes his Maya and presents it consistently as a version of the *femme fatale*. Although this conventional representation has a much older history, it seems to have come into its own during the bhakti age. The question posed in the *sākhī* we have examined is how precisely can one overcome the Maya factor because in the absence of this overcoming there can be no understanding of the ultimate ground of our being. If we return to the *sākhī* under consideration ("On Maya"), we discover that the triumph over Maya occurs in *dohā* 5, where Maya is shown to be the slave of saints who (sexually) enjoy her first and then kick her out (*lāta caṛhi*). Maya clearly intervenes and disorientates the proper processes toward enlightenment. As the final *dohā* of this *sākhī* shows, Kabir agonizes over the "eternal wandering of the saint" because he has not been able to move away from the world of Maya and become one with Brahman. The language hints at the act of "burning" (and by extension death) which is necessary to transcend the world itself.[33] The poet speaks of making *āsā* ("desire") into fuel and burning his own *manasā* ("body") into ashes so that the otherworldly (*adhyātmika*) can be experienced. Although this *sākhī* speaks of transcendence and union in the sublime object (in spite of the power of Maya) the intervention of the body (through the *kanak kãminī*, the seductive woman) destabilizes a devotional genre that had hitherto been read as an unproblematic and predictable form. In spite of the disdain in which Maya is held (since Maya has been so radically transformed into a harlot), her presence remains alluring and linked to desire or *kāma*. In the end desire has not been totally overcome as can be seen in the following poem from a series of seven collectively entitled "Maya":

Maya I know you are a bloody thug.
The three *guṇa*s are like a noose around your neck
But you speak so seductively.

Yes I know your disguises:
Lakshmi in front of Vishnu,
Parvati before Shiva,
An idol before the priest,
Holy water in the place of pilgrimage—
Talk of the chameleon!

But more:
The suppliant disciple of the Yogi,
A queen before a king,
Someone's diamond, another's brass farthing,
A believer's devotee and the wife of the Turk.

But you can't trick the Lord's servant Kabir;
For God alone buys and sells me.[34]

After the initial *ṭeka* or chorus the poem embarks upon a series of male-female relationships in which the female element is always a symbol of Maya, the word with which the poem (in the original Old Hindi) begins. Maya does wonderful things here as she transforms herself into various kinds of desire: goddess, money, woman, queen, holy water, and so forth. In the original Old Hindi text all the relationships are represented as follows:

(a) kesava–kāvalā	⇒	Vishnu–Lakshmi (the Preserver–the consort of Vishnu)
(b) siva–bhāvanī	⇒	Shiva–Parvati (the Destroyer–the consort of Shiva)
(c) paṃḍā–mūrati	⇒	Priest–his icon
(d) tīratha–pānī	⇒	holy place of pilgrimage–holy water
(e) jogī–jogini	⇒	the Yogi–the female disciple
(f) rājā–rānī	⇒	the king–queen
(g) kāhu kai–hīrā	⇒	man–diamond
(h) kāhu kai–kauṛhī kānī	⇒	man–brass farthing
(i) bhagatā–bhagatini	⇒	devotee–female devotee
(j) turakā–turakānī	⇒	the Turk–his wife

But defend as we can the conventional apparatus of poetic equivalences through which Maya is undercut, we must, finally, face up to a dangerous mysogynism implicit in the equation of Maya with female sexuality. If we connect this usage with that of other bhakti poets, notably Tulsidas, we begin to question the hidden agenda of the usage itself. We know that since the word "Maya" is feminine in gender its representations will also have to be female. But the trouble here is that the representations of Maya will have to be overcome or neutralized. In the classic sophistry of Tulsidas, this overcoming can occur only if we put in place a more powerful female principle. That female principle is bhakti itself because the word "bhakti" too is feminine. The solution is the key to the final book of the *Rāmacaritamānasa.* Since all the other paths to salvation—*jñāna* (knowledge), *vairāgya* (asceticism), *yoga* (discipline), and *vijñāna* (science)—are masculine, these paths cannot overpower Maya (which is feminine). But because bhakti is itself feminine in gender, "she" can come to the rescue. It must be added that at a broader thematic level this is possible because Tulsidas has taken pains to establish an underlying connection between bhakti and Sita herself (7, 116).

> Maya and bhakti, listen to me,
> Are both feminine as everyone knows.
> Again Ram loves bhakti
> While poor Maya is a mere dancing girl.

There are two dangers here that concern us. The first is the classification of the feminine as either Maya or Sita, in other words as damned whore or God's policewoman. On the side of Maya is desire as lust, the body and its physical attributes; on the side of Sita is asexuality, sacrifice, and devotion, the body as pure idea. The contrast cannot be greater and the choice between the two does not allow for any kind of renegotiation of the world as it is. In Tulsidas's version, the world must be denied. In Kabir, the same tendency is present but one suspects that with him the effect of the metaphor is more important than its sexist undercurrent. Clearly these are conventional set-pieces and not too much should be made of them, but the literary evidence cannot be discounted purely on this premise. What I am suggesting is that Maya becomes a screen for the denunciation of woman's sexuality, and allows the poet to insert in the "pure" discourses of religion the censored discourse of desire. But in doing so Maya itself—as a difficult philosophical premise quite at variance with its root meaning "witchcraft"—becomes an ungraspable sign, too large to be accommodated by the mind and threatening to the civic order itself. Yet women alone are the equivalent of this sign, which of course says something generally about bhakti and the patriarchal order: men after all established the importance of bhakti in grasping the sublimity of Brahman. Antifemale as the discourse on Maya is, it nevertheless introduces into bhakti striking images of desire and the impediments to self-transcendence through meditation. Tulsidas's own text ends with bhakti being played off against sexual desire where the attraction of the *nāri*, the "desirous woman" (the *kāminī* of Kabir) is juxtaposed against the everlasting love found in Ram (7, 130):

Just as the lustful man desires a woman
And just as the usurer desires wealth
In like manner, O Ram,
Be dear to me, forever!

Maya is linked to deceit and desire. She has the capacity to castrate even though her body signifies a "lack" of power. But she damages—castrates—and deflects the real object of bhakti. This object in the Siddha and Nath Yogi traditions functions under the sign of the "Name," a word which, as we have seen with reference to the poet Namdev, is its own referent: it is a transcendental signified that doesn't need a name other than "Name" itself. This idea is most powerfully present in an incantatory poem on the "Name":

I have but one treasure and that—
is Hari's name.
I do not keep it under lock and key,
nor sell it to feed myself.

Name is my farming,
Name is my garden,
At your feet I worship.

Name is my Maya,
Name is my offering,
I know no other besides you.

Name is my kith and kin,
Name my brother,
In my hour of death
Name is my guide.

The poor discovers treasure in your Name:
For Name, says Kabir, is like "sweets to the poor."[35]

Hari's name, *hari kai nāũ*, or *rāma–nāma* ("the name of Ram"), is both the mystical utterance as well as a sign of utility since "Name" now allows for living in the world to take place even as Maya makes that living impossible. By connecting many of the devotional norms of the established treatises (such as those of Shandilya and Narada) with quite specific modes of worship ("At your feet I worship," "I know no other besides you," and "In my hour of death/ Name is my guide"), Kabir emphasizes the degree to which "Name" in itself is sufficient for devotional practice. But there is nothing unusual in Kabir's emphasis on the chanting of the name of the Lord. It is related both to the *japa* ("recitation") tradition of the Nath Yogis, where *rāma* (*rā* and *ma*), furthermore, constitutes the "perfect *japa*,"[36] and to the Sufi notion of *dhikr* ("meditation"). In bhakti the remembrance of the Name as *rāma sumiri* or *nāma smaraṇa* (no distinction is made between *rāma* and *nāma* here) is the ultimate mental prayer, bringing together in one category the *śabda*, the "word," and the *anāhata* (*anāhada*) *nāda*, the "eternal sound." This is not all. The "Name" as signifier must also be grasped and it is here that the "Knower of the Name" is on par with, and possibly even greater than, the "Name" itself:

> Who is greater, Ram or he who knows him?[37]

If M a is the impediment and "Name" the solution, it does not follow that Kabir's devotionalism is thus a close set and there is no soul-searching, no trauma left to worry about. In *pada* 22 we see a dramatic presentation of the soul's search for bhakti and union with God. The conversational tone acts out a theistic dictum concerning devotion but in the process opens up a space that has considerable scope for an alternative reading or ironic undercutting. In this respect the discourse of *ulṭabāṃsī* and *sandhyā-bhāṣā* are, for Kabir, invaluable discursive conventions through which these alternative meanings may be suggested. We will have more to say about this discursive formation later. What remains to be outlined in this part of our discussion is a question about the kind of ideal devotee that Kabir advances. The tradition, of course, had thrown up any number of ideal bhaktas from the classic Arjuna and Hanuman to the innumerable renouncers, Yogis, and Sufi mystics of later bhakti. In his own definition of the ideal bhakta Kabir combines all of them. The attempt at a composite definition of the bhakta may be seen in the following *pada*:

> Your bhakta is one among many:
> Beyond passion, anger, avarice and desire
> He understands the essence of Hari.
>
> Beyond flattery,
> Beyond condemnation,
> Beyond self-esteem,
> Renunciation,
> Seeing pure and base metals with one eye,
> He captures your essence.
>
> The three *guṇas*—
> Being, energy, darkness—
> So they say—
> Are your Maya.
> Beyond them the fourth state—
> This the bhakta seeks

And finds salvation.

Struck by affliction, by doubt—
Do not despair—
Discover Madhva—
Cast your meditations on Hari.
Beyond sorrow,
Beyond doubt,
Beyond Ego,
You've found the ultimate bhakta.[38]

The ideal bhakta transcends the samsaric web through a yogic control of all his mental and physical faculties. The state that he arrives at is the *cauthai pada*, the fourth state, the Sanskrit counterpart of which is the *nistraiguṇyāvasthā* ("the fourth state" beyond the three *guṇas*).[39] In Tantric terminology it is argued that desire hinders the quest for harmony and equipoise in a bhakta's life. The "control" that is stipulated in the poem leads ultimately to a radical bhakta-Creator (Brahma) equation. In another *sākhī*, what is only implied here, is positively affirmed:

The mind is Gorakh, it is Govind
the mind is the true Yogi.
He who succeeds in stilling the mind
becomes the Creator himself.[40]

For Kabir, then, the ideal bhakta not only finds *sahaja-samadhi*, the mystical trance of the way of "easy" union, but he also consciously reverses ("As the thread upon the spindle/reverse and wind it back") normal mental processes that in turn lead to the destruction of the "fickleness" of the mind.

As we saw in the previous chapter, the "unwinding" of the mind similarly leads to a state of stillness from which it can then prepare for self-illumination. The need for "stillness" in Kabir again demonstrates the extent to which Kabir functioned within prior traditions: Tulsidas's "Ram," for instance, is presented as possessing a similar capacity for equanimity as he is neither ecstatic over the news of his coronation, nor despondent over his pending banishment. Through this stillness one arrives at the highest state, the state of *unmani*, a term originally linked to the spiritual condition achieved by the Siddhas or the "Perfected Ones."[41]

The key to this "stilled being" in readiness for a greater vision are two intricately related processes we have already discussed in chapter 4: *śabda*-essence and *surati*. In both of these the emphasis is on mystical cognition as the way of true knowledge. These are difficult terms to translate because they belong to a "closed" semantics of Tantrism: coded, secretive, and resistant to interpretation. Indeed, terms like *unmani*, *surati*, *nirati*, *sāra-śabda*, and so on push precisely the issue of the radical incommensurability between language and experiential knowledge to the brink by insisting that the condition of "union" between Atman and Brahman defies the categories of language. We return to the definition of Brahman as "neti, neti," a definition based on deferral because Brahman is neither this nor that. The "Name" too functions in very much the same fashion as the *śabda*-essence. According to Parasnath Tiwari the medium of *sahaja-samādhi* to which Kabir has given primacy in his sayings is called *surati-śabda-yoga*, where *surati* is defined as the way to Atma-consciousness. The awkwardness of some of these concepts can be understood better if we return to the term *surati* itself. Like many other words in the Kabir canon, this word too is extremely difficult to define. Originally synonymous with *maithuna* ("sexual enjoyment") it seems to have acquired, through the normal processes of semantic transference, a radically different and mystical meaning. Probably an equivalent of *śruti*, it is closer to the meanings attributed to *śabda*.[42] Like *nivṛtti/pravṛtti*, *surati* too has its counterpart, *nirati*—a state considered to be superior to *surati*.[43] The preponderance of these terms of duality in the culture effectively suggests the need for a third term that can be used for situating "true" meaning. This third term is the un-said, unsayable *śabda* that signifies neither this nor that.

In the *Macchindra-Gorakṣa-bodha*,[44] which is cast in the form of a dialogue between Gorakhnath and Matsyendranath, *surati* is offered as the disciple (*celā*) of *sabada* (*gurū*):

> *Gorakṣa*: Who is the guru, who is the disciple?
> *Macchindra*: The *śabda* is the guru, *surati* is the disciple.

Again in other verses[45] *surati* is further identified with the *sādhaka* (the devotee) while the "involvement" of the "body" in *nirati* is explained by Gorakhnath as a means by which "the illusions of the mind" may be destroyed. Some of the contexts in which *surati* occurs in the Kabir corpus may be shown with reference to the following lines from *Kabīr-Granthāvalī (Das):*

> *pada* 46: that woman - *surati* died
> who was to be endlessly reborn.
> *pada* 47: *surati* and *smṛti*
> are both the same.

The conjunction of *surati* with *smṛti* (*sumṛti* in Kabir) would then connect *nirati* with *śruti*, the corpus of unauthored, timeless texts like the Vedas. If *śabda*-essence is like the Name itself, a medium through which intense states of consciousness may be realized, then *surati* [46] is the sublime state of the mystic as he/she hears the eternal music of the Tantric Siddhas and Nath Yogis. Only the ideal bhaktas ever reach this point of awareness. In them all externalities have been interiorized:

Equilibrium and equipoise and interiority—
These are the Yogi's qualities;
  Why then must he sleep at all?
He makes his own mind a place of repose,
  and therein he dwells.
He meditates in his mind, and sings
  to his own mind.
His coconut-bowl is his mind, he plays
  the *śṛṅgī* in his mind;
And the *anāhada* sound too
  he hears in his own mind.
Says Kabir, mortify your body
  in the five fires;
Then ask me who has triumphed over
  this samsara?[47]

The world can be transcended and Maya destroyed, such is the yogic *unmani,* the bliss of complete union in Brahman. In the poem just quoted, the sublime condition of the Yogin is presented through the figure of a desireless being for whom the object of *kāma*, desire, is now deflected on to a still point in the mind. Deceit, desire and Maya threaten the self as it searches for a higher meaning in life. But we return again to the place where we began, to the place of bliss as void, nonlanguage. Since the point of union is beyond representation Hindu metaphysics work through not so much a "realist" but a mystical signifying chain with its own very specialized vocabulary. We have referred to words and concepts such as *samādhi, unmani, surati, nirati,* and so on, all of which make sense within a particular nonrealist semantics. And the signifying chain finally makes sense because all the items, individually, and collectively, link up with Brahman, the ultimate *śabda*, the absolute signified. These terms cannot be presented to consciousness since they have value only insofar as they are signs of emptiness around which the devotional "glues" itself. The discursive field of the devotional is thus overdetermined by these symbolic systems, which belong to what we may call a secondary modelling system of devotional poetics connected to a much more pervasive cultural imperative of decenteredness and the dissolution of Self and Other in Brahman. Because of its grounding in a discourse of unpresentability devotional semantics is really a "mantric" semantics.

Divine Pleasures

Kabir's Burning Brides

The world troubles Kabir so much that ultimately for him it is the non-referential Name that holds the key to any actualization of the sublime object of Indian devotionalism. Maya—and its metaphorical referent in the deceitful woman or the harlot—is the stumbling block for spiritual realization. But the story does not end there because for every embodiment of Maya in the figure of the harlot, there is the figure of the woman as renouncer whose narrative often ends with the self on the burning pyre. The sublime figure of the burning bride, arguably Hindu culture's most cruelly powerful symbol of the ultimate sacrifice of woman to the Law of the (patriarchal) Name, acts as a counterweight to the metaphor of woman as Maya. Not surprisingly, emotional bhakti uses the trope of the burning bride at key moments in its religious discourse to underline the quite extraordinary moral and spiritual strengths of this austere figure. The symbology of the burning bride or sati is used as a "sign" of separation because the sati has indeed been separated from her husband before she places herself upon the burning pyre. She is, therefore, both an object of love and a subject that suffers in separation. The sati symbol takes us back to separation as a love-theme in Indian literature. We have seen the agony of Jayasi's hero pining away for the love of the elusive Padumavati as well as Padumavati's own sacrifice on the burning pyre after the city had been ravaged by the Muslim invaders. Where the other pervasive imagery—that of water and the ocean—had been closely aligned to the metaphysics of the unity of all phenomena, the emotional metaphor of the sati may be seen as the return of the body as a signifying system in bhakti ideology.[48] Of course, the superimposition of the lover-beloved idea on to the figure of the sati is part of the larger impetus or drive of emotional bhakti that, as has been pointed out so extensively by Friedhelm Hardy, has its antecedent in the devotionalism of the Southern Alvars and the Vira-Shaivas. Emotional bhakti thus doubly integrates religious thought: first, through its propositional structures (do this to achieve that) and second, through its emotional content.[49]

When we return to the Kabir corpus, it no longer surprises us that one of the more common structures in Kabir's devotional verse is the narrative of the burning bride as she yearns for union with her absent Lord. Alberuni had remarked upon the practice of sati, which he linked to an Indian social system in which the widow could not be married off to another relation. Since the culture had also constructed the husband as a wife's protector and lord on earth (from the woman's point of view the husband is almost an avatar), self-immolation on the burning pyre was a very public avowal of the culture's valorization of the husband. This is not to say that every woman whose husband was dead faced the burning pyre. Given the occasionally huge disparity in age between husbands and wives, this would have meant that sati would be a common feature of Indian life. Women who were too old and women whose sons could look after them did not have to go through this ritual. How often women were burned is not the point here; what needs underlining is that the symbology of sati had enormous poetic power. Thus all those poems about the absent husband/lord are predicated upon the possibility of sati if the husband never came back. If we stay with this symbology a bit longer we soon become conscious of the rasa of *karuṇa* (pity, in some cases tragedy) that the figure of the burning bride evokes. This rasa is but one half of a pair of which the other half is *śṛṅgāra* or the erotic. To get intense emotional response the idea of sexual union implicit in the rasa of *śṛṅgāra* is played off against the narrative of love-longing or *vipralambha*. Thus the body of the burning bride is represented as though she were in a state of separation from her beloved. She yearns to be united with him and defines her sorrow, her *duḥkha*, as a natural corollary of the immense love that she has for her absent husband. "The stroke of death is a lover's pinch/Which hurts, and is desir'd," says Cleopatra in another literary tradition.[50] As we saw in the *Gītagovinda*, what is poetically more powerful in the narrative of *śṛṅgāra* is the sense of estrangement. When union (*sambhoga*) finally takes place, the reader wishes to return to the intensities of Radha's *vipralambha*, to her feverish desire for union. This desire goes by the name of *viraha*, intense love-longing for which both pain and bliss are essential. In another context, Edmund Burke had remarked that the condition most conducive to pain is the source of the sublime as well. We need not accept Burke's sensationist readings of the sublime as part of our overall theory, but his reference to pain (and not pleasure) does take us to something that is quite endemic in Indian culture, namely, the culture's interest in pathos or the rasa of *karuṇa*. Both Haripala and Mammata (who summarized the aesthetics of Anandavardhana and Abhinavagupta[51]) felt that some such structure of feeling may well explain the presence of both *karuṇa* and *śṛṅgāra* in the *sthāyibhāva* (basic emotion) of love (*rati*).[52]

In what follows I would want to examine Kabir's verse with particular reference to the structures of the burning bride defined very broadly as narratives of love-in-union and love-in-separation. I will be arguing that the self is now projected on to the persona of the *virahiṇi* so as to demonstrate the especially intense state of the subject as it seeks union with God. In this respect the grand intertext of devotional poetics is Jayadeva's *Gītagovinda*, which established, for later Sanskrit and vernacular literatures, the basic rules by which the profane love of man and woman could be read through the metaphorics of divine love. The cry of Bhavabhuti's Rama upon learning about Sita's abduction (*jvalayati tanuṃ antardāhaḥ karoti na bhasmasāt*: an inner burning inflames my body, but does not reduce it to ashes[53]) expresses precisely this feeling even though the speaker is a man. Like Ratnasen and Padumavati in Jayasi's monumental *mathnavī*, both male and female are struck by *viraha*, and there seems to be no escape from this human condition for either. Let us, then, begin with a relatively straightforward poem of Kabir:

> Night has passed—may the day not pass by.
> The black bee has flown away,

It is the age of the "white duck."

The virgin soul palpitates, trembles,
I don't know what my husband will do to me!

In the raw clay pot, water does not stay.
The *haṃsa* has flown, the body fades away.

From making crows fly again, my arms are aching,
Says Kabir, my tale has come to an end.[54]

The speaker of this poem, the "virgin soul," is the *virahiṇī*, who yearns for the return of her husband. She sings a *viraha-gīt*, a song of separation, evocative of the condition of *vipralambha* and infused with the *bhāva* of *śoka* (grief). The narrative here, however, insinuates that the husband will not return, as the wife's life, recounted in pastoral terms, has in fact come to an end. But not much is explicitly stated; there is no capacious discourse of loss and love-longing, no extended lament but only subtle allusions to and suggestions of a world totally ruptured and irreparably shattered. The language of suggestiveness is seen in the way in which the very peculiar *duḥkha* or suffering of the burning bride is made possible through a number of enabling conventions that work on the symbology of birds. In this lyric the birds recalled by the *virahiṇi* are the *baga* ("white duck," "heron," "crane," "curlew"), the *haṃsa* ("swan"), and the *kauvā* ("crow"). The expression of the *virahiṇī*'s suffering in terms of bird symbolism is an established feature of Indian pastoral verse and one that, in terms of the presumed origins of the *śloka* meter, goes back to the *ādi kavi* Valmiki himself. In the well-known *krauñca-vadha* episode in the *Rāmāyaṇa* Valmiki cursed the *niṣāda* (the hunter) for killing a male *krauñca* as it passionately embraced its female companion:

mā niṣāda pratiṣṭham tvamagamaḥ śāśvatiḥ samāḥ
yat krauñcamithunād ekam avadhīḥ kāmamohitam[55]

The curse is followed by the female bird's pitiable lament, which in turn leads to the poet's own reflection on the meter he had involuntarily used to compose this maledictory verse. It is not our aim here to examine the shortcomings of the claim of the Indian critical tradition itself that the commonest Sanskrit meter, the *śloka* meter, was born out of the poet's expression of grief or *śoka*.[56] The traditional argument, reinforced by the close phonetic equivalence of the two words, is that grief (*śoka*) produced the epic meter (*śloka*). Of greater interest to us is the metaphorical connection between the symbology of birds and the nature of grief specially the *viraha-duḥkha* of the lonely bride. The migratory curlew (Anthropoides virgo) alluded to by Valmiki enters into a wide paradigmatic system where it may be substituted by the *haṃsa* (both of which have the unusual faculty of separating milk from water), the *sārasa*, and other waterbirds such as the *baga* ("duck," "heron"), and the *cakavī* (ruddy sheldrake). To this list may be added the *papīhā* (*cātaka*) and the *cakorī*.[57] The cries of the *cakavī* and the *papīhā* birds are often represented as the agony of the *virahiṇī* herself, whose own *viraha* can be of such intensity that in one of the *sākhī*s of Kabir it is likened to a *pralaya* (the apocalyptic/"oceanic" moment) capable of scorching the entire universe.[58]

The crucial point established here is that the traditional linking of the state of grief with a poetic meter (*śoka-śloka*) is part of a much larger Indian folk tradition that appears throughout Indian love poetry. It may be found in the Rajasthani *Ḍholā Mārū Rā Dūhā*, in Kabir's *padas* and *sākhī*s (two specific collections of songs on the subject of *viraha* are to be found in *Kabīr Granthāvalī*: *prema*, *padas* 5–16, and *prema-viraha*, *sākhī* 2), all of which echo the "type of folk-ballad sung in the pathetic mood."[59] Not surprisingly, the rhapsodes began to equate the speaker/subject of their songs with the birds themselves. Hence analogies began to be drawn between Sita, the constant wife, and the *krauñca* bird, between the sati and the various kinds of birds, between the *virahiṇī* and the *papīhā*, the *cakavī*, and so on. Along with this identification came a blurring of categories so that the position occupied by the *virahiṇī*/self could be substituted by any number of birds and finally by Sita herself. Yet the pastoral mode here insinuates the very opposite of repose and detachment: not harmony with nature but dissolution in *pralaya*, the oceanic sublime, as the *virahiṇī*'s cries are, finally, a wish for death. The key to this sublime is the rasa of *karuṇa* (pity), which so thoroughly dominates the poems dealing with the theme of the burning bride.

If we return to the poem under examination, we find that the key to the suffering soul, the *duḥkhiyā jīva*, is a large number of symbols associated with the Indian literary tradition of love-longing. The *virahiṇī*'s first utterance, "Night has passed—may the day . . . ," opens the way for the reading of the poem through the poetics of love-longing. In Charlotte Vaudeville's words, "the soul separated from God is compared to the young bride who, on the wedding night, has waited in vain for her husband's arrival."[60] In the *caraṇa* (half-verse) that follows, the *virahiṇī*'s cry is developed with reference to the metaphor of youth and old age where the "black bee" (black hair) signifies youth and the "white duck" (white hair) old age. The estranged "wife" by analogy proclaims that separation has aged her well beyond her years. The language of yearning is foregrounded in the first verse (the chorus), which acts like a musical overture, an initial raga that establishes the mood of the poem. In the verses that follow the special nature of the wife-soul/husband-lord relationship is developed. The sense of loneliness, of alienation, evident in the chorus, is now written in the code of the virgin soul (*bālā jīu*) on her wedding night. She shakes, trembles, palpitates, unsure of her husband's response. And yet at every point in the poem, the union is only implied: it is either placed as a retrospective reverie or deflected onto the symbology of birds. The use of the word *pīu* (beloved), which recalls the pathetic cry of the *papīhā* bird, is an instance of the latter transference.

As the poem proceeds we detect a significant metaphorical shift in the poet's use of the image of the clay pot that cannot hold water. A realist reading makes the association very clear: the image reinforces the *bālā jīu*, the virgin soul, who is also "raw," a *kāṃcai karavai*. But the realist reading tells only part of the story since read again in terms of the underlying structure of devotional verse the equation of the wife-soul with the husband-lord is really the point at which serious interpretation can begin. This equation is part of a bhakti apparatus that in the tradition of texts such as Jayadeva's *Gītagovinda* and the poems of the Maharashtrian saint-singer Namdev, transforms the cry of the *virahiṇī* into the bhakta's search for God. The intensity of the *virahiṇī*'s cry (like the experience of the sati once again) is read analogously as the purest outpouring of the devotee's feelings toward her God as she sings, "The *haṃsa* has flown, the body fades away." Another tradition—and it is unlikely that this is the folk tradition so central to Indian songs of love-longing—associates the *haṃsa* with the Supreme Being. In the Tantric tradition familiar to Kabir it symbolizes the individual *jīva*, the soul. As we have seen there is also a sophist argument that the word *haṃsa* is in fact the Apabhramsha form of *so'ham* ("That am I"), the Upanishadic *japa* or *mantra*. Whether Nath-panthi use of *haṃsa* to designate *so'ham* [61] is part of this argument remains unclear. In Kabir, however, the *haṃsa* bird characterizes the ideal bhakta who is placed in opposition to the "ignorant" crow. In this poem, then, the *haṃsa* may be read on two levels: as the husband it is part of the *laukika* (worldly) structure of the husband-wife relationship; but as a symbol that identifies the self with Brahman, it is part of the *alaukika* (otherworldly) soul-lord relationship so central to the poetics of devotion.

The *haṃsa* may well stand for union with Brahman but the *virahiṇī* herself continues to pine away since in this rather Spartan version of the pastoral there can be no resolution of her agonizing sense of separation. Indeed, this sense of separation is precisely what constitutes the strength of the *viraha*-emotion. And so the *virahiṇī*'s story can be told ("my tale has come to an end") but her sense of love-longing cannot be closed off:

> From making crows fly again, my arms are aching.
> Says Kabir, my tale has come to an end.

The mythology of women flying crows in anticipation of the homecoming of their husbands brings us back to both the overall bird symbolism and to the somewhat darker statement of loss with which the poem begins. Furthermore, in the tradition of love-in-separation, "my arms are aching" alludes to the futility of this symbolic sending of messages as the husband never comes. The transfer of the pathetic final cry that inevitably follows ("my tale has come to an end") on to the poet himself through the use of a signature line (*bhaṇitā*) again attests to the two levels on which the poem operates.

If the intensity of the "burning bride" is part of a much larger Indian folk tradition that persists to this day in popular Hindi songs such as *tum bin mohe viraha satāye* ("without you I suffer in separation of *viraha*"), its "deployment" in bhakti literature as an essential bhakti structure has another significance. For in any account of Indian devotional poetics it is this system of homologous transfer of items between different discursive registers (from birds to souls for instance) that is absolutely crucial for a fuller understanding both of *viraha* itself and of the quality of the suffering involved. The essence of bhakti (which has since become systematized into a rasa in its own right) must ultimately be discovered in the *alaukika* transfer of what was initially a mode of "erotic separation." The central space occupied by the burning bride structure in Kabir's devotional formulations must now be explored in the rest of this chapter.

The power of the burning bride metaphor lies in the barbaric grandeur of the act. It is so frightening that it is unpresentable to the imagination. For Kabir, however, there was another preexistent structure into which the burning bride could be reslotted. Through another tradition that Kabir the Muslim Julaha of Kashi (in *pada* 30 we find a reference to Kabir as "By caste a weaver but patient and resolute") had inherited, the burning bride functions within a structure that had its own stages of union with God. Basically this is the voice of the Sufi tradition, which can be heard in a number of poems entitled *prema* ("love) and *prema viraha* in *Kabīr-Granthāvalī*. Let us begin by analyzing one of these poems of love.

Hari is my husband
I am his bride,
Ram is my spouse and I
His young bride.

Elegantly adorned,
I wait for union,
But I cannot find my Lord of the world.

O how so sad—
We sleep together
But are never united.

I am so fortunate
My Lord desires me.

> As Kabir says
> I will never be re-born![62]

The shift in poetic sensibility that we detect reflects the impact of Sufi ways of thinking upon Hindu devotionalism in medieval India. It need hardly be pointed out that the Hindu inversion of the Sufi God-woman/devotee-man structure leads to the articulation of the kinds of passion that, in the Islamic tradition, would normally be associated with men. Somewhat enthusiastically, Ramkumar Varma sees this as the victory of advaita thought itself:

> The female conception of the Sufi God finally bowed before the male-God image of advaita.[63]

Varma frames his critique within a Hindu-Muslim power play that distorts the real value of his insight. What he does not pursue further is the structural grid of the poem that expresses the stages of the union of the soul with God. As a first step, the Atma (concretized as the *virahiṇī*) full of love-longing, wishes to experience the Lord. She then leaves the world and moves toward the other-worldly (the *alaukika* state). This Lord (*īśvara*) who is the source of all being she calls *satpuruṣa*, the first or "primal" Being (or the *satguru*). She stands in front of him, completely baffled by his presence. She cannot understand who or what this *paramātmā* is; she is silent, she experiences an unusual "power" but she cannot reveal it. In another moment she feels an interior awakening, and in the words of one of the *ramainī*s exclaims:

> Meditating upon the *śūnya*, the *sahaja* state,
> a light manifests itself;
> I sacrifice myself to the Being who is self-existent.[64]

In this *ramainī* a sense of absolute intoxication precedes the state of union because the sublime state of *sahaja* arrived at through a concentration upon *śūnya* (nothingness) heralds the sacrificial gesture of the young wife-soul. "I sacrifice myself" (*maī balihārī*) has the meaning of the ritualistic killing of the body as the self now prepares to merge into the state of Brahman. It is the enormity of this sacrifice that leads the subject to proclaim with such enthusiasm her own sense of oneness of being. The touch of feverish possessiveness implied here is echoed in those oft-quoted lines of Kabir:

> If Hari should die, then I shall die too
> If Hari does not die, then why should I die?[65]

The *virahiṇī* who, in the words of Ramkumar Varma again, "thinks upon the words of her lover, sings his praise, laments, consoles herself, entreats,"[66] is a bhakti archetype whose origins may be traced back to the type of devotion designated in the *Ahirvudhnya samhitā* and the Narada and Shandilya *bhakti sūtras: ānukūlyasya saṃkalpaḥ* "actions in accordance with the desires of the lord."[67] The cry of the *virahiṇī*, her *viraha*-song in fact, was to become, as in Jayasi's *Padmāvat*, a kind of cosmic force where quite explicit microcosm/ macrocosm analogies were made. The force of that analogy, with reference to Ratnasen's *viraha* is best summarized by Charlotte Vaudeville:

> *Virah* seems, therefore, in Jāyasī's thought, like a cosmic force, irresistible and all-powerful, similar to the *vajrāgni* of Tantric Yoga from which the idea of this universal deflagration seems to have been borrowed: like *vajrāgni, virah* is capable of setting fire to the universe in a single moment. Through it the *siddha* (the Perfect One) arrives at power, having captured in his own body (the microcosm) the energy of the macrocosm. It is through the force of the *virah* of Ratansen that Padmavati, even before she had seen or heard a description of the hero, falls into the agonies of absence.[68]

In a number of *sākhi*s (notably the collections numbered 2, 7, and 11 in the *Kabīr Granthāvalī: prema biraha kau aṃga* ["Love in Separation"], *piu pahicānibe kau aṃga* ["The Recognition of the Spouse"], and *patibratā kau aṃga* ["The Faithful Wife"]), however, Kabir's primary aim seems to be to express the Sufi "flood of love" that follows participation in heavenly joy. The stress in these *sākhī*s is on the union itself, eternally aflame, with continuous insights made into the *alaukika* ("the otherworldly") state. The devotee, as *virahiṇī*, is constantly in the presence of her Lord as the poet explores the complex psychology of this state.

As we have seen, cutting right across the stages of union with God is a structural paradigm (a central feature of the tradition of Indian poetics) in which love is seen in terms of "absence" and isolation. In Indian aesthetics the condition of the *virahiṇī* is expressive of the rasa of *śṛṅgāra* crossed with *karuṇa*. Whereas aspects of structure such as the stages that lead to union with Godhead may be discussed primarily in terms of narrative patterns or in terms of the relationship between various *actants*,[69] aspects of judgment (such as the infra reader's emotional engagement with the text) are a matter of reception aesthetics or rasa. Mammata, who, as already noted, simply summarized the aesthetic systems of Anandavardhana and Abhinavagupta, recapitulates eight rasas:

> śṛṅgāra hāsya karuṇa raudra vīra bhayānakaḥ
> bībhatsa adbhutasaṃjñau ceti aṣṭau nāṭya rasāḥ smṛtāḥ[70]
>
> The Erotic, the Comic, the Pathetic, the Furious, the Heroic, the Terrific, the Disgustful and the Wonderful—in dramatic art these are the eight *rasas*.

The dominant emotion that has infused the verses studied in this section so far belong to the first of these rasas, namely *śṛṅgāra* (the emotion of the erotic, also called *mādhurya*). Mammata himself suggests that the erotic is of two kinds, love in union (*sambhoga*) and love in separation (*vipralambha*):

tatra śṛṅgārasya dvau bhedau sambhogo vipralambhaś ca

In a later text Rupa Gosvamin (first half of the sixteenth century) claimed that all these eight rasas can be subsumed under the super rasa of bhakti.[71] Rupa Gosvamin could make such a sweeping claim because bhakti had become such an all-pervasive religious ideology as well as the dominant poetic genre by his time. But the chief emotional center of this "new" rasa continued to be expressed through the rasa of *śṛṅgāra*. In Rupa Gosvamin's formulation (he is not being altogether original here), *śṛṅgāra rasa* undergoes a number of variations: *preyo bhakti* (the subject as the beloved, implying some sexual gratification), *vatsala bhakti* (the subject as loyal servant), and *mādhurya bhakti* (the subject intoxicated by love). These positions, which take us back to the early *bhakti sūtras*, are obviously part of a general bhakti ideology that we outlined in chapter 3.

Of the two kinds of the erotic, the one which is most prominently discussed in Kabir is *vipralambha*, separation. The symbolism of separation makes its way into at least three sets of *sākhīs* (2, 7, and 11) and is present in a large number of the lyrical *padas*. The painful aspect of the struggle of the soul toward union with God quite possibly reflects the underlying pessimism and isolation one detects in Kabir: to experience the world one has to live in it. Charlotte Vaudeville discovers this in Kabir's attitude toward standard iconoclastic images such as that of the Rajput hero, the Sur, who fights unto death, and the sati who sings her *viraha* while being burnt to death.[72] Two examples from the *sākhīs* should suffice to make this point clear:

The Virahiṇī stands up and falls again and again,
longing for your Vision, O Ram!
If you grant her the Vision after death,
what use will it be to her?[73]

and

The wife who worships her Lord
has renounced all other desires:
She will not leave his side
nor his presence for a single moment.[74]

The *virahiṇī* remains in a constant state of tension and doubt. The poet must explore the state of this uncertainty without letting that state break down into either of the two oppositions: complete union (*sambhoga*) or complete distraction (*vipralambha*). Here, of course, the entire technique of poetic suggestiveness (*vyaṅgya*) is brought to bear on the verse so that the "significance" of the poem is implied, not overtly stated. We get this in one of the *padas* that I now wish to discuss in some detail. I give below a rather prosaic and grammatically unconnected translation that, nevertheless, has the advantage of following as closely as one can in translation the word order and line sequence of the original given in brackets.

> Beloved (*bālama*) come (*āu*) to my/mine own (*hamãrai*) house (*greha*) vocative particle (*re*); without you (*tumha bina*) afflicted/in agony (*dukhiyā*) my body is (*deha re*). Everyone (*saba koi*) says (*kahai*) I am your woman (*tumhāri nārī*) why am I (*mokaũ*) of this (*yaha*) in doubt (*andeha re*)? For unless we are joined into one (*ekameka hvai*), sleep on the same bed (*seja na sovai*), then (*taba*) fulfilment (*lagi*) what kind of (*kaisā*) love (*neha re*). Food (*anna*) I dislike (*na bhāvai*), sleep (*nīṃda*) doesn't come to me (*na āvai*), within my house (*griha*), outside (*bana*), stable/peaceful (*dharai*) my mind is not (*na dhīra re*). As the lover (*jyaũ kãmī*) desires his beloved (*kau kãmini pyārī*), as (*jyaũ*) the thirsty (*pyāse*) desires water (*kau nīra re*). Isn't there someone (*hai koi aisā*) benevolent enough (*para upagārī*) the Lord (*Hari*) to tell (*saũ kahai*) to listen (*sunāi re*)? For now (*aba tau*) afflicted/"unconscious" (*behāla*) is Kabir (*kabīra bhae hai*) without seeing the Lord (*binu dekhẽ*) he expires/languishes (*jiu jāi re*).[75]

There are two determining contexts of Kabir's verse that make their way into the poem. The first is an essentially thematic context of the desire of the self for union in God. The second is an intertextual context that triggers the figurative trope of the *virahiṇī* and her song of love-longing through which this narrative gets enacted. As the latter context dominates the surface rasa of the poem, the predominant mood is *mādhurya bhāva*, the emotional expression of "love and intoxication." To read the poem as bhakti verse the infra reader must translate a profane code into the sacred.

The poem begins with the word *bālama*, lover or beloved, and is written in a *bhāva* that evokes this special relationship between Kabir and Hari, his Lord. It should be noted that an alternative version of the text begins with the word *bālhā* ("Vallabha," which is another name for Vishnu). In the bhakti tradition of verse, *bālama* has a wide synecdochic function: on the surface level it is another word for "husband," "beloved," or *svāmi*, but on another and more significant level it has the effect of a *śabda* or "word" such as *rāma-nāma*, the name of Ram. In Hinduism *śabda* is viewed as "an authoritative verbal testimony"[76] and as self-evident truth. Within the Tantric method of meditation *(sādhana)* the *śabda* is itself "divine," equivalent or identical with Brahman, in whom the Yogi is absorbed. Kabir, of course, inherited from the Nath Yogis not only the entire symbolism of Tantra but their somewhat complicated modes of reasoning as well. *Śabda* is also related to the larger theories about the "mystical" sound popular in India. The most famous of these is *oṃ* (the *prāṇava*), the ultimate expression of the cosmic energy. The two related words that occur in Kabir alongside *śabda* are *nāda* (and its cognate *anāhata* "silent," "unstruck"), resonance or vibration, and *bindu*, the still point that occurs after the experience of *nāda* and absorbs and stabilizes all divine energy. In his *bānīs* ("sayings") Gorakhanath had identified the Satguru (the Absolute Guru) with the *śabda* and it is this reading of *sábda* as the mystical *nāma* that is present in this poem. The word *bālama* thus triggers a chain (*bālama . . . śabda . . . nāma . . .*) that ends in the object of desire, Brahman. In this respect it is a more truly "mystical" concept—and many bhakti words do possess this special dimension, which is lacking in other traditional verse. Consequently, the common homecoming notion present in the first line of the poem signifies the search for spiritual awareness through a "displaced" naming of *bālama* as *śabda*. It may be argued that the kind of experience that Kabir is speaking about here is not simply *Erfahrung*, the experience of the world bound by our own common perception of it but *Begegnung*, an encounter not bound to a rigid conceptual formula.[77]

On the larger structural level we discover that Kabir's elusive style, his *sandhyā-bhāṣā*, stresses associative relationships between words in the poem and the esoteric systematization of Tantric symbolism. In the process Kabir completely identifies the "body" with "house." What is not so evident is the implied connection between the body waiting to be aroused and the Tantric beliefs where the areas of potential cosmic energy—the *cakras*, the nerve plexuses, and so on—must be aroused by the Kundalini for the body's total mystical rejuvenation. Yet the implied mysticism, "the ebullition of feelings of attachment to God," to use S. N. Dasgupta's helpful phrase,[78] is couched in a raw, everyday image. Sometimes this sense of the concrete takes the form of *ulṭabāṃsī*, an inverted language, suffused with heavy, ironic overtones.

It is only after the first series of metaphors that the language acquires a certain degree of potency, of passion, and the *viraha* becomes sexually charged. This process is interesting and requires a fuller comment. Central to this change is the intrusion of the figure of the *kā̃mī*. However, *kā̃mī* is obviously not just any man; rather it is the vigorous, lustful man who evokes the erotic aspect of the dark God Shiva himself.[79] Not only does the pedestrian train of images receive a jolt here, but an inversion is at work as well: instead of the *virahiṇī* passively waiting, she becomes the active ravisher, the *kā̃mī*, the Kamadeva in fact of Hindu mythology who constantly desires the *kā̃mini: jyaũ kāmī kau kāmini pyārī*. The role of the *virahiṇī* is linked to that of the poet Kabir, who is himself afflicted by the condition of love-longing. The key to the poem, of course, resides in the way in which the metatext of Maya invades the *kāmī/kāmini* metaphor and plays on the nature of desire in the poem. In this devotional context or, to use Paul Ricoeur's term, in this "hymnic discourse,"[80] the song of love-longing (*viraha prema*) is an exciting and dramatically immediate mode that combines the features of the usual Indian love poetry with a threefold religious pattern that may be summarized as follows:

1. An impassioned call to God normally in the form of *bālama* ("beloved"), *dulahā* ("bridegroom"), etc.
2. A "reflective" central section where the *virahiṇī*'s inner agony is explored.
3. A final stage of "unconsciousness" (*mūrcchita)* where the *virahiṇī* languishes for love, and which is presented in the form of a signature line.

The use of the language of sexual sublimation/repression is not uncommon in the Kabir corpus as can be seen in the following examples:

(a) After so long my beloved has come
Aren't I fortunate that so easily
I have found him?

(b) Now I won't let you go, beloved Ram
However you wish it, remain mine!

(c) Ram bhakti is an unusual arrow
Only those who have been struck by it
know its pain.

(d) Without Ram my body-heat doesn't go
The fire in the water rages anew.

(e) Our estrangement has been long,
And again thoughts of you return to me.

(f) Elegantly adorned, I wait for you
But I cannot find the Lord of the world.[81]

The discourse of the burning bride then becomes a powerful tool for the expression of the especially impassioned sense of union that Kabir finds particularly exciting. But what the thematic variations of the figure of the woman/wife seeking fulfilment through love-in-estrangement emphasize over and over again is the narrative of desire and its lack, union and its absence. Between these two is situated that intensity of love which connects the rasas of *śṛṅgāra* and *karuṇa* with the renouncer who finds a karma that does not seek its own fruits (*karmaphalayoga*) but transcends them (*karmaphalatyāga*). Devotional poetics thus reaches a point of consummate metaphorical synthesis as bhakti breaks away from high metaphysics to find meaning in emotional union with a loving God. The overall "system of reference" may be explored further in another poem of Kabir:

My Lord, my husband,
Tell me when will we meet?
    O protector of saints!

Born in water and lovingly living in it,
    I cry repeatedly, "thirsty, thirsty!"
I am the *virahiṇī* standing alone on this lonely road
    Hopelessly waiting for you my Ram.

I have left my home, I have attached myself to you,
    I fall at your feet.
My body vibrates within,
    Like a fish out of water.

The day brings no hunger, the night no sleep,
    I am alienated from house and environment.
My bed is my enemy,
    I spend my nights awake.

I am your slave my beloved,
    And you my husband.
Come to me, take me,
    The Creator of all, the compassionate one.

I die a sacrificial death,
    Unless you possess me!
The servant Kabir's *viraha* has reached its peak,
    Show yourself now! [82]

What we detect immediately in this poem is a structure of three parts in which the middle element—a detailed exploration of the subject's state of mind—is given extensive treatment as the *virahiṇī*'s agony is explored at length. The subject-devotee's relationship with the Lord too is now framed in a discourse that combines desire for union with desire to serve, both of which are finally linked to the desire for a "sacrificial death." The terms used for the object of desire are again variations on the two key terms found in the earlier poem: *bālama* and *hari*. We therefore encounter a whole series of words that combine the four key roles of the Lord: as a bridegroom/husband/beloved (*dulahā, sajanā, bharatāra*), as the name (*rāma*), as the creator (*sirajana hāra, abināsī*), and as the compassionate protector (*pratipāla, dīna dayāla*). The overcoding of the Lord's name by the *virahiṇī* (without whose agony as a "burning bride" there is no real poetry here) is a characteristic of devotional verse as the subject explores her relationship with the Lord through all the variations on the kinds of bhakti that the treatises had established. In this poem we can detect at least three of these variants: bhakti of the self as bride; bhakti of the self as servant; and finally bhakti of the self as believer. The monotonous regularity with which these references proliferate bhakti discourses attests to the constant need on the part of the subject to keep her object sharply in focus so that there is no lapse in concentration. In a poetics of devotion all this makes good sense, but it must be said that in the process the Lord acquires something of a surplus value as he is excessively semanticized. To use one word for the Lord (as a starkly monotheistic religion would require) would disallow the expression of the various moods of the subject as she goes through the repertoire of bhakti roles or subject positions that she must adopt. If naming is done to the point of excess, it is still part of an entire discursive mechanism in which the subject in the world renounces her life in the presence of the Lord. In the end the subject remains thirsty as desire can never be totally fulfilled. So the *virahiṇī* cries:

> Born in water and lovingly living in it,
> I cry repeatedly, "thirsty, thirsty!"

The image of "water birth" relates back to the *ātmā-paramātmā* symbolism we have already analyzed but here we find the same metaphysics recast in the language of poetic inversion. The infra reader must therefore decipher this cryptic code, read it against the grain so to speak, so as to arrive at the special manner in which the poet handles the agony of the *virahiṇī*. One assumes that the Lord's presence cancels out all desire since there is nothing more to desire. Yet the self continues to cry for water because this is part of the narrative of the *virahiṇī*, part of a structural code that gives the reader a glimpse into the very special predicament of the bhakta as he/she yearns for fulfilment. What we sense here is the discourse of *sandhyā-bhāṣā* that "secret," "enigmatic," "hidden" antilanguage (a language of concealment) which Mircea Eliade referred to as a mode of substitution in which ambiguity replaces the referential system of "every ordinary language."[83] In the act of saying "thirsty," the *virahiṇī* is in fact carrying out an inner "dialogue" with God. It soon becomes clear that no amount of thematic exposition or interpretation can lead to an adequate disambiguation of *sandhyā-bhāsā*. Language thus colludes with the object of desire in keeping it beyond the realm of representation.

The poem under discussion is not a simple series of emblematic equations in which symbols simply stand for something else. By the middle of the second verse we begin to see a much more individuated self as the *virahiṇī* comes to grips with her inner states of being. Something of this emphasis on individual emotion is present in the image of the lady standing alone on the road, deeply in love as she exclaims:

> My body vibrates within,
> Like a fish out of water.

The image of the entire body vibrating is taken up by the simile of the fish struggling for life out of water. But oral poetry, by its very nature, is based on variations on a finite number of themes (and metaphors), something we notice in the fourth verse where the metaphor from *pada* 13 is recalled:

> The day brings no hunger, the night no sleep,
> I am alienated from house and environment.

In the reflective second part of the meditative poem, the exploration of the *virahiṇī's* agony reaches its high point of frenzied confusion and divine outpouring. The feverish love on the part of the wife-soul is similar to the love that underlies the Sufi notion of *'ishq*, "tormented love." Like the love of the heroes of the *mathnavī*s, the *virahiṇī* is obsessed by an impure love that needs figurative self-immolation. It is here that the *viraha* overlaps with the terrible cries of the sati as she burns upon the pyre. This is the real image behind the "fire of viraha" that Charlotte Vaudeville detects in the popular *viraha-gīt*s (songs of absence):

> But, here (in Kabir's verse), it is no longer distance or the husband's forgetfulness that is the real obstacle—as in the traditional *virah-gīts*—since the divine Spouse is always present within: the fault lies with the wife-soul herself, it is the impurity of her love that makes her spiritually blind. Only through enduring patiently the tormenting but purifying "fire of Virah" and ultimately giving up her life in that extinguishable fire can the wife-soul obtain union, understood as total merging into her true Husband, Rām.[84]

The state of union implied here is like the condition of *jīvanmṛta* ("life-in-death") as the *virahiṇī* cries:

I die a sacrificial death,
Unless you possess me!

This is then a form of the negative sublime as divine pleasure implies the sacrifice of the self in a paradoxical death-in-life. To triumph over a world of desire, deceit, and Maya—those elements that impress upon us a definition of the world as suffering—the devotional poet has to work through a poetic structure that parallels the narrative of the subject's mystical union with God. In terms of poetic structure, poems that revolved around the theme of the "burning bride" begin with an underlying structure of belief that often parallels the stages of mystical union with Godhead. The paradigm of the "burning bride" enabled Kabir to explore intense states of devotional consciousness by fusing, with reference to the bhakta's love of God, the language of sacred and profane love. Beneath it all, however, one detects the usual bhakti concerns—the fear of death, the denunciation of Maya, and the deployment of the discourse of slantedness. What holds the often disparate elements together is the structure of meditation itself. The results, of course, are poems of extraordinary power and religious outpourings (always tempered by a sense of urgency as if time were running out) that lead to the final glory and affirmation of bhakti. And it is precisely because Kabir assimilated a wide range of imagery, transformed into verse a phenomenal array of human experience, that his verse is of such singular importance to any retheorizing of devotional poetics. The burning-bride motif is a powerful means by which one rechannels the received tradition of the Indian sublime. The agonizing search for union with God on the part of the wife-soul, as a *virahiṇī*/sati, must have symbolized for Kabir the whole dilemma of that anxiety. And this is where the poetic *viraha* merges into the larger category of *duḥkha*, suffering, in Indian thought. The transformation and distillation of that suffering into the pathetic cries of the *virahiṇī* underlines a deeper analogical equation of the erotic and the devotional in Indian religious verse. But not content with this homology, the aestheticians formulated an even more difficult strategy in which the alternation between love-in-union and love-in-separation itself became the decisive temporal moment for the self as devotee. So the burning bride will continue to yearn for her absent love, will recall the cries of the *papīhā*, will acknowledge, implicitly, the impossibility of union, because to suffer in this state of love-longing is the purest state of them all. Jayadeva's lonely Radha, crying "her pain aloud, in pitiful sobbing" (*viracita-vividha-vilāpaṃ sā paritāpaṃ cakāroccaiḥ*) remains the preeminent symbol of the cruel paradox of the bhakta forever yearning for fulfilment in the sublime otherness of her Lord.

Conclusion

The Devotional Sublime

Here are three quotations. The first is from Arthur Schopenhauer: "I owe what is best in my development to the impression made by Kant's works, the sacred writings of the Hindus, and Plato."[1] The second is from the *Bhagavadgītā*: "I am the discourse of speakers" (10.32). The third is from Kabir: "By crushing the self and adoring Hari,/ man obtains the Vision."[2] In my concluding statement I would want to think through these quotations in ways that may allow us to bring the various strands of the book together. Schopenhauer, the first of my authors, is clearly highly comparative, going beyond Western philosophy to make explicit the relationship between the intellect (or the Will) and phenomenon. It is important to recall Schopenhauer's "allegiances"—Kant, the Hindus, Plato. Yet Schopenhauer does not then build all this into a simplistic perennial philosophy; rather he is keen to examine the relationship between the thing-in-itself and phenomenon within the broad parameters of Kant's emphatic insistence that without the intellect the two—the thing-in-itself and phenomenon—cannot be adequately theorized. The absence of Hegel from Schopenhauer's "allegiances," however, remains striking. Although Schopenhauer had dismissively addressed Hegel as that "ponderous and witless Hegel,"[3] it is difficult to see how Schopenhauer could have overlooked Hegel if indeed the exploration of the thingness of things were his interest. What connects all four (and I propose to include Hegel in Schopenhauer's list) is clearly the thing-in-itself, which remains beyond representation but is nevertheless crucial to an understanding of imagination at its limits. I have endeavored to examine the sublime as the object that resists phenomenalization and to suggest that Schopenhauer's oceanic feeling, Kant's momentary relapse of the law of reason to make way for an excess that cannot be contained, Hegel's Absolute as the unpresentable, and the Hindu negation in Brahman may be productively conceptualized through the sublime, which, after all, is, as Lyotard observed, a breach "in the examination of the aesthetic faculty of judgement." In Hindu thought this breach is most powerfully handled through the category of Maya, which, as the world of phenomenon, may be radically distinguished from the transcendent thing-in-itself (we recall that for Kant the sublime is a transcendent principle to begin with). In classical Sankhya theory (as well as in the *Bhagavadgītā*) this thing-in-itself (or the "real") is then connected to the *puruṣa*, the self beyond *prakṛti*, Maya or phenomenon, that is able to understand the nature of the real. While in his lengthy essay on Kant ("Criticism of the Kantian Philosophy") Schopenhauer does not spend too much time on the *Critique of Judgement*, Kant's observations on the sublime informs Schopenhauer's highly aestheticized reading of Will and Representation throughout. Thus Schopenhauer rightly endorses Kant's claim that "between things and us there always stands the *intellect*,"[4] by which Kant meant not simply a faculty to "which things are given from without"[5] but a faculty with a demonstrable figural (or aesthetic) capability. It is this capacity for the figural (for the metaphorical to be precise) that makes "analogy" such an important part of the intellect's role.

To Kant the "sublime" is an outrage to the imagination: "The sublime is that, the mere capacity of thinking which evidences a faculty of mind transcending every standard of sense."[6] The sublime in this formulation would overpower the self and threaten it with extinction. To overcome the threat of the sublime Kant needs the transcendental principle of reason, which "legislates for our practical vocation as autonomous supersensible beings,"[7] and keeps the apocalyptic possibilities in check while at the same time allows the intellect a moment's release to entertain the possibility of immersing itself in the sublime. While Kant had suggested a number of sublime "objects" and had referred to God as the figure that is beyond simulacra, it was Hegel who grasped the direction of Kantian thinking by doing two things: first he linked the sublime to the Absolute, and second he argued that sublime meditations were not possible for races without a historical destiny. Even as Hegel now made it possible for the sublime to become cross-cultural (Hegelian Absolute, up to a point, is identical with the Hindu Brahman), he removed the category itself from the Hindu, who he argued had no history. By ignoring Hegel, Schopenhauer did not have to address this other side of European readings of the sublime. But he also failed to push the Hegelian Absolute in the direction of the Hindu Brahman. In making a case for the Indian sublime what I have done is pose another question: "What can be said about the Indian sublime, if Brahman is rethought as the thing-in-itself, beyond presentation and yet always integral to the Hindu narrative?"

The specific case for the Indian sublime takes us to our second quotation: "I am the discourse of speakers." This statement occurs midway through Krishna's account of his own (unpresentable) self. Krishna uses a whole series of metaphors to suggest ways in which in the world of phenomena he may be grasped. The language is naturally highly figurative and the technique is one of symbolic identification of the divine self (of Krishna) with the item that stretches our imagination and our reason furthest. And so in the passages before and after the one we are considering here we find references to Krishna as the beginning and the end of "creations," as the knowledge of the Supreme Self, as the letter A of the alphabet, as infinite time, and so on. In this series we pause at "I am the discourse of speakers" and ask what is the real import of this statement. To begin with, we may want to connect this to the principle of God as the origin of language, of Logos, and read it as a statement about words and Gods being identical and the world itself being meaningful because it is endowed with the *daivīm* principle. A second look at the passage, however, takes us to devotional discourse itself, which, we now see, is underpinned precisely by Krishna's reading of language. In other words, the very concept of God as the Absolute Signified cannot be disputed in a devotional discourse: the fundamental equation of language and God, and by extension the idea of speaking through a language that exists only insofar as God wills it to be, must remain unchallenged. Clearly this version of devotional poetics in terms of the "narrative" of the Indian sublime would require the construction of a (virtual) model reader whom we have named "the infra reader," the *sahṛdaya* of the Sanskrit literary theorist Abhinavagupta, for whom aesthetic experience was not unlike an *alaukika* (otherworldly) experience where the self was forgotten.[8] In hypostasizing a devotional sublime, we need to keep in mind both the reader and the object of devotion.

Our third and final passage is from the poet with whom we end this book, Kabir. In the first line of this couplet the poet too had referred to the phenomenal world as multifarious against the oneness of Brahman. Here again the essential dualism of the world of Maya and the supersensible being is stressed. So where or how do we situate the self? Kabir responds by referring to two processes: the first is the extinction of the self; the second the adoration of Hari who is God. The first is the discourse of *nirguṇa* bhakti, where the idea of the nirvanic moment of self-extinction is strong. But it is also the moment of the denial of the ahamkaric self, the ego, that prepares the way for the special relationship with God since everything must be seen to emanate from God. The second process—the adoration (*bhajai*) of God as Hari—advances another possibility against sublime nonpresentation. This is the *saguṇa* element of excessive presentation within what Bhoja had referred to as the dominant rasa of *śṛṅgāra* (the erotic). The two—*nirguṇa* absoluteness and *saguṇa* emotionalism—are held together in the same couplet without any real sense of the tension between *nirguṇa* and *saguṇa*. So what does the subject "man" in the poetic line arrive at? It is nothing less than the "Vision" sublime (*dīdār*), the mystical *paricaya* equivalent to both theological as well as philosophical engagement with the eternal being. Although the intrusion of the *saguṇa* Hari (even if in Kabir Hari is to read as the unpresentable "Name") brings about the comfort of the tribal, it is the concept of self-extinction (*āpā meṭai*) that establishes the essence of Hinduism's engagement with Brahman: the sublime does violence to the viewer, and pushes him/her toward an experience that is too large for the mind to grasp.

Indian culture, then, is built around a sublime poetics—and the culture's dominant literary form, the devotional, as well as its dominant literary hermeneutic, rasa theory, understand this very well. But a sublime poetics would make living in the world impossible because its great ideal will be that of the renouncer. Hindu culture therefore opted for the man-in-the world alternative; it tamed the renouncer, it created many gods, it tamed Brahman, decentered its hold on thinking, and effectively said that while the sublime and union of Atman in Brahman must be its grand narrative, this was not how one survived in culture. In place of the austere intellectualism of that grand narrative, it gave the security of a thousand gods, decentered history, and allowed Hindus to be both renouncers and successful capitalists. Krishna too understood this when he discoursed on the importance of action. But even as he built a new Hindu epistemology around this fact, he maintained the essential exclusiveness of his own being as Brahman. To grasp that reading of Indian culture, this book has advanced a theory of the Indian sublime. Once we have granted this massive civilization that particular category, so much that had escaped us now make good sense. We need to concede that Hegel almost got it right. The author of this book is no Hegel but hopefully the book itself has inserted the sublime into Indian culture well enough to demonstrate its effectiveness as a means of understanding its cultural productions. To get to grips with Indian culture rethinking Brahman as the sublime is fundamental. As Krishna himself declared: "*ahaṃ kratur, ahaṃ yajñaḥ . . . mantro 'haṃ . . . ahaṃ agnir.*"

NOTES

1. The Sublime Object of Devotion

1. Paul de Man, *Aesthetic Ideology*, intr. Andrzej Warminski (Minneapolis: University of Minnesota Press, 1996), 50.

2. S. H. Butcher, *Aristotle's Theory of Poetry and Fine Art* (1894; New York: Dover, 1951), 393.

3. Ronald Inden, *Imagining India* (Oxford: Blackwell, 1992), 8.

4. Jitendra Nath Mohanty, *Reason and Tradition in Indian Thought* (Oxford: Clarendon Press, 1992), 285.

5. Ronald Inden, 23.

6. See the discussion of Orientalism[1] and Orientalism[2] below.

7. A fine example is Harish Trivedi's polemical *Colonial Transactions: English Literature in India* (Manchester, U.K.: Manchester University Press, 1995).

8. Edward W. Said, *Orientalism* (1978; Harmondsworth, U.K.: Penguin Books, 1985).

9. James Clifford, *The Predicament of Culture* (Cambridge, Mass.: Harvard University Press, 1988).

10. Kate Teltscher, *India Inscribed: European and British Writing on India 1600–1800* (Delhi: Oxford University Press, 1995).

11. Friedrich von Schlegel, *Philosophy of History*, trans. James Burton Robertson (London: George Bell, 1890), 160. Quoted by Ronald Inden, 68.

12. Thomas R. Trautmann, *Aryans and British India* (Berkeley: University of Cal-

ifornia Press, 1997), 3: "In British eyes India presented the spectacle of a dark-skinned people who were evidently civilized, and as such it constituted the central problem for Victorian anthropology, whose project it was to achieve classifications of human variety consistent with the master idea of the opposition of the dark-skinned savage and the fair-skinned civilized European. To this project India was an enigma, and the intensity of the enigma deepened in the course of the nineteenth century."

13. Ronald Inden, 89.

14. Ronald Inden, 114.

15. The phrase is Alec McHoul's. See his "The Philosophical Grounds of Pragmatics (and Vice Versa?)," *Journal of Pragmatics* 27 (1997), 1.

16. Paul de Man, 73.

17. Jean-François Lyotard, *Lessons on the Analytic of the Sublime*, trans. Elizabeth Rottenberg (Stanford, Calif.: Stanford University Press, 1994), 3.

18. Paul de Man, 73.

19. Paul de Man, 74. The sentence as a whole is modelled on a number of de Man's observations.

20. Immanuel Kant, *The Critique of Judgement*, trans. James Creed Meredith (Oxford: Clarendon Press, 1986), 97.

21. Jacques Derrida, *The Truth in Painting*, trans. Geoff Bennington and Ian McLeod (Chicago: University of Chicago Press, 1987), 122.

22. Jacques Derrida, 127.

23. Immanuel Kant, 110.

24. J-F. Lyotard, 58.

25. J-F. Lyotard, 51.

26. J-F. Lyotard, 52.

27. Paul de Man, 76.

28. J-F. Lyotard, 55.

29. Paul de Man, 85.

30. Edmund Burke, *A Philosophical Enquiry into the Origin of Our Ideas of the Sublime and Beautiful*, ed. J. T. Boulton (Notre Dame, Ind.: University of Notre Dame Press, 1968). Kant read this text in Garve's German translation (1773).

31. J-F. Lyotard, 55.

32. J-F. Lyotard, 55.

33. J-F. Lyotard, 77.

34. J-F. Lyotard, 121.

35. Jean-François Lyotard, *The Differend*, trans. Georges Van Den Abbeele (Manchester, U.K.: Manchester University Press, 1988).

36. This argument is canvassed in my *The Gothic Sublime* (Albany: State University of New York Press, 1994).

37. Wilhelm Halbfass, *India and Europe* (Albany: State University of New York Press, 1988), 98.

38. Paul de Man, 104.

39. Paul de Man, 92.

40. Hayden White, *Metahistory* (Baltimore, Md.: Johns Hopkins University Press, 1980), 81.

41. Longinus, "On the Sublime," in *Classical Literary Criticism: Aristotle, Horace, Longinus*, trans. T. S. Dorsch (Harmondsworth, U.K.: Penguin Books, 1965), 100.

42. Paul de Man, 121.

43. G. W. F. Hegel, *The Philosophy of History*, trans. J. Sibree (1899; New York: Dover, 1956), 140.

44. Hayden White, 128.

45. G. W. F. Hegel, 163.

46. Wilhelm Halbfass, 89.

47. G. W. F. Hegel, *The Philosophy of Fine Art*, trans. F. P. B. Osmaston (1920; New York: Hacker Art Books, 1975), 2:49. 4 volumes. A translation of Hegel's *Vorlesungen über die Ästhetik*. Hereafter cited in the text.

48. Paul de Man, 111.

49. Wilhelm Halbfass, 89.

50. Wilhelm Halbfass, 89.

51. Terry Eagleton, *The Ideology of the Aesthetic* (Oxford: Basil Blackwell, 1990), 72.

52. Paul de Man, 121.

53. Madeleine Biardeau, *Hinduism: The Anthropology of a Civilization*, trans. Richard Nice (Delhi: Oxford University Press, 1989).

54. The argument is based on my "David Shulman and the Laughter of South Indian Kings and Clowns," *South Asia* [new series] 10. 1 (June 1987), 83–88 and "The Centre Cannot Hold: Bailey, Indian Culture and the Sublime," *South Asia* [new series] 12.1 (June 1989), 103–14.

55. David J. Kalupahana, *Nāgārjuna: The Philosophy of the Middle Way* (Albany: State University of New York Press, 1986), 17.

56. Slavoj Žižek, *The Sublime Object of Ideology* (London: Verso, 1989), 170.

57. Madeleine Biardeau, 41.

58. Slavoj Žižek, 156.

59. Stephen Greenblatt, *Shakespearean Negotiations* (Oxford: Clarendon Press, 1990), 15.

60. See, for example, Hans Robert Jauss, *Toward an Aesthetic of Reception*, trans. Timothy Bahti, intr. Paul de Man (Brighton, U.K.: Harvester Press, 1982).

61. J. A. B. van Buitenen, trans., *Two Plays of Ancient India* (New York: Columbia University Press, 1968), 23.

62. Patrick Colm Hogan and Lalita Pandit, eds., *Literary India: Comparative Studies in Aesthetics, Colonialism, and Culture* (Albany: State University of New York Press, 1995), 12.

63. S. H. Butcher, 366.

64. E. Dimock Jr., E. Gerow, C. Naim, A. Ramanujan, G. Roadarmel, and J. van Buitenen, *The Literatures of India: An Introduction* (Chicago: University of Chicago Press, 1978), 45.

65. Barbara Stoler Miller, ed., *Theater of Memory* (New York: Columbia University Press, 1984), 60.

66. Patrick Olivelle, "Orgasmic Rapture and Divine Ecstasy: The Semantic History of *Ānanda*," *Journal of Indian Philosophy* 25.2 (April 1997), 154.

67. Friedhelm Hardy, *Viraha-Bhakti: The Early History of Kṛṣṇa Devotion in South India* (Delhi: Oxford University Press, 1983), 9.

68. For an expanded version of this argument, see my "Defining the Self in Indian Literary and Filmic Texts," in Wimal Dissanayake, ed., *Narratives of the Self* (Minneapolis: University of Minnesota Press, 1996), 117–50.

69. Aijaz Ahmad, "The Politics of Literary Postcoloniality," *Race & Class* 36.3 (1995), 15.

70. Sudhir Kakar, *The Inner World* (Delhi: Oxford University Press, 1981), 17.

71. J. A. B. van Buitenen, trans. and ed., *The Bhagavadgītā in the Mahābhārata* (Chicago: University of Chicago Press, 1981), 151.

72. Barbara Stoler Miller, trans., *The Bhagavad-Gītā* (New York: Bantam Books, 1986), 164.

73. J. A. B. van Buitenen, 27.

74. Sudhir Kakar, 40.

75. Thomas R. Trautmann, 73.

76. Sudhir Kakar, 47.

77. *Bhagavadgītā* 6.1. J. A. B. van Buitenen translation, 92–93.

78. Richard Rorty, "Habermas and Lyotard on Postmodernity," in Richard J. Bernstein, ed., *Habermas and Modernity* (Cambridge: Polity Press, 1985), 167.

79. J. A. B. van Buitenen, trans., *Two Plays of Ancient India*, 7.

80. Richard Rorty, 175.

81. Immanuel Kant, 91.

82. G. W. F. Hegel, *The Philosophy of Fine Art*, 2:6.

83. J. Moussaieff Masson, *The Oceanic Feeling* (Dordrecht, Netherlands: D. Reidel, 1980), 37.

84. Arthur Schopenhauer, *The World as Will and Representation,* trans. E. F. J. Payne (New York: Dover, 1969), 1: 419.

85. Thomas R. Trautmann, 19–27.

86. Charles Wilkins, trans., *The Bhagvat-Geeta or Dialogues of Kreeshna and Arjoon* (London: C. Nourse, 1785). Facsimile reproduction edited by George Hendrick (New York: Scholars' Facsimiles and Reprints, 1972). Hereafter cited in the text.

87. P. J. Marshall's personal communication to Thomas R. Trautmann (72n. 3) concerning a notebook of Warren Hastings in the library of the University of Minnesota (Ames MS B.114) is worth citing here:

> [Hastings] recognizes that in public he is taken to be Christian but then, he admits, in "hipocricy [*sic*]; . . . prudence or rather necessity imposed silence." But, "I am unable not unwilling to receive and understand. What my inability is founded on I cannot to a certainty determine." To me, though, it is very clear. He cannot see anything that distinguishes Christianity from other religions about which he knows. "Is the incarnation of Christ more intelligible than . . . those of Bishen?" Europeans prevail over non-Europeans not because of the superiority of Christianity but for secular reasons. "a free government, cold climate and printing and navigation." Christianity does not make people "better." "Let those who know the lower uneducated class in England . . . say how much more rarely crimes are committed in England than in India."

88. See Samuel H. Monk, *The Sublime: A Study of Critical Theories in XVIII-Century England* (Ann Arbor: University of Michigan Press, 1960), 21–28.

89. Sara Suleri, *The Rhetoric of English India* (Chicago: University of Chicago Press, 1992), chapter 2.

90. The seminal American readings of the *Bhagavadgītā* by Emerson and Thoreau show a more concerted attempt at defining sublime difference. Thoreau, for instance, wrote about a sublimity that was "so remote . . . from our conceptions" but immeasurably more significant because it has no temporal dimension. Immemorial and sublime, these are the key concepts in both Emerson and Thoreau's reading of the Wilkins's translation of the *Bhagavadgītā.* See Barbara Stoler Miller, *The Bhagavad-Gītā,* 155–61. Coleridge would make the distinctions between "fancy" and "imagination" the cornerstone of his Romantic theory. See S. T. Coleridge, *Biographia Literaria,* 2 vols., ed. J. Shawcross (Oxford: Clarendon Press, 1969).

91. Jacques Derrida, 119–35.

92. Still the best summary of the English sublime is to be found in Samuel Monk. See also Neil Hertz, "A Reading of Longinus," *Critical Inquiry* 9.3 (March 1983), 579–96.

93. Edmund Burke, 39.

94. See P. J. Marshall, ed., *The British Discovery of Hinduism in the Eighteenth Century* (Cambridge: Cambridge University Press, 1970). Hereafter cited in the text.

95. Thomas R. Trautmann, 68.

96. Thomas R. Trautmann, 69.

97. Thomas Coburn, "'Scripture' in India: Towards a Typology of the Word in Hindu Life," *Journal of the American Academy of Religion* 52 (September 1984), 435–59.

98. Philip Lutgendorf, *The Life of a Text: Performing the 'Rāmcaritamānas' of Tulsīdās* (Delhi: Oxford University Press, 1994), 311.

99. David N. Lorenzen, "The Historical Vicissitudes of Bhakti Religion," in David N. Lorenzen, ed., *Bhakti Religion in North India* (Albany: State University of New York Press, 1995), 13.

100. David N. Lorenzen, "The Lives of *Nirguṇī* Saints," in David N. Lorenzen, ed., *Bhakti Religion in North India*, 182.

101. Philip Lutgendorf, 266.

102. John Stratton Hawley, "The *Nirguṇ/Saguṇ* Distinction in Early Manuscript Anthologies of Hindu Devotion," in David N. Lorenzen, ed., *Bhakti Religion in North India*, 160–80.

103. Stephen Greenblatt, 13.

104. Friedhelm Hardy, *Viraha-Bhakti: The Early History of Kṛṣṇa Devotion in South India* (Delhi: Oxford University Press, 1983). Hereafter cited in the text.

105. G. N. Devy, *After Amnesia: Tradition and Change in Indian Literary Criticism* (Bombay: Orient Longman, 1992).

106. I am indebted to Hazariprasad Dvivedi's *Madhyakālīn dharma sādhnā* (Allahabad, India: Sāhitya Bhavan, 1970) for a number of ideas raised here. In Dvivedi's argument, the "medieval" or *madhyakālīn* period refers to the millennium 700 to 1700 C.E. According to Dvivedi, the redeeming feature of this age of "decay" (*hrās*) was, fortunately, the religion of love and devotion. Most Indian scholars accept Dvivedi's periodization and read bhakti as its great literary mode. Indian literary scholars on the whole also read this as a period of decline or decadence especially since the period was associated with Muslim hegemony over large parts of India.

107. See R. G. Bhandarkar, *Vaiṣṇavism, Śaivism and Minor Religious Systems* (Varanasi, India: Indological Book House, 1965), 143ff., and W. D. O'Flaherty, *Asceticism and Eroticism in the Mythology of Śiva* (Oxford: Oxford University Press, 1973), especially 38ff., where bhakti is considered an "irrational solution" that mediates between excessive eroticism and asceticism.

108. Friedrich von Schiller, *Naive and Sentimental Poetry* and *On the Sublime*, trans. Julius A. Elias (New York: Frederick Ungar, 1980), 198.

109. See, for instance, Charlotte Vaudeville, ed. and trans., *Kabīr Granthāvalī* (*Dohā*) (Pondicherry, India: Institut Français d'Indologie, 1957), xiv–xv.

110. A. K. Ramanujan, *Speaking of Śiva* (Harmondsworth, U.K.: Penguin Books, 1973).

111. Peter van der Veer, "The Politics of Devotion to Rāma," in David N. Lorenzen, ed., *Bhakti Religion in North India*, 300.

112. Jayant Lele, ed., *Tradition and Modernity in Bhakti Movements* (Leiden, Netherlands: E. J. Brill, 1981), 5.

113. M. N. Srinivas, *Social Change in Modern India* (Berkeley: University of California Press, 1968), 6ff.

114. According to the Maharashtrian *vārkarī sant* tradition, Chokamela's *guruparaṃparā* (guru genealogy) may be traced back to none other than the great *vārkarī* poet Namdev himself. See Acharya Vinay Mohan Sharma, *Hindī ko marāṭhī santõ kī den* (Patna, India: Bihar Raṣṭrabhāṣā Pariṣad, 1957), 108.

115. Jayashree B. Gokhale-Turner, "Bhakti or Virodha" in Jayant Lele, ed., *Tradition and Modernity in Bhakti Movements*, 31.

116. Jayashree B. Gokhale-Turner, 31.

117. Eleanor Zelliot, "Chokhāmeḷā and Ekhnāth: Two *Bhakti* Modes of Legitimacy for Modern Change" in Jayant Lele, ed., *Tradition and Modernity in Bhakti Movements*, 139.

118. Eleanor Zelliot, "Chokhāmeḷā: Piety and Protest" in David N. Lorenzen, ed., *Bhakti Religion in North India*, 216.

119 Jayashree B. Gokhale-Turner, 32.

120. Jayant Lele, 4.

121. Jayashree B. Gokhale-Turner, 33.

122. M. G. Ranade, *Rise of the Maratha Power and Other Essays* (1900; Bombay: University of Bombay, 1960), 4–5. Cited by Eleanor Zelliot, "Chokhāmeḷā and Ekhnāth," 141.

123. R. V. Oturkar, Introduction to M. G. Ranade, vi–vii. Quoted by Eleanor Zelliot, "Chokhāmeḷā and Ekhnāth," 140.

2. Two Truths Are Told

The title of the chapter echoes *Macbeth* I.iii.127: "Two truths are told,/As happy prologues to the swelling act/Of the imperial theme."

1. Louis Dumont, "World Renunciation in Indian Religions," *Contributions to Indian Sociology* IV (1960), 33.

2. M. Monier-Williams, *Sanskrit-English Dictionary* (1899; Delhi: Munshiram Manoharlal, 1976), 694.

3. M. Monier-Williams, 560. From *ni-* + *vṛt*, Ātmanepada.

4. *The Mahābhārata* (Poona Critical Edition) 12, 210, 2cd–5. Quoted by Greg Bailey, *Materials for the Study of Ancient Indian Ideologies: Pravṛtti and Nivṛtti* (Turin, Italy: Pubblicazioni di Indologica Taurinensia, 1985), 18–19. K. M. Ganguli, trans., *The Mahābhārata* (Delhi: Munshiram Manoharlal, 1970), 1, 108, appends the following valuable footnote at this point:

> The religion of *pravṛtti* consists of acts. It cannot liberate one from rebirth. The whole chain of existences, being the result of acts, rests upon the religion of *pravṛtti*.

The religion of *nivṛtti*, on the other hand, or abstention from acts, leads to Emancipation or Brahma.

5. G. M. Bailey, *The Mythology of Brahmā* (Delhi: Oxford University Press, 1983), 5–6.

6. M. Biardeau, *Hinduism: The Anthropology of a Civilization*, trans. Richard Nice (Delhi: Oxford University Press, 1989), chapter 2.

7. *Valmīkī Rāmāyaṇa* [Critical Edition], gen. eds., G. H. Bhatt and U. P. Shah (Baroda, India: Oriental Institute, 1951–1975). I.14.6–14.

8. Clearly this is only a broad classification and only the starting point of analysis. Its aim is to suggest the nature of the essentialist argument about the Hindu in whose "world of relations" . . . "individuals have no reality in thought, no Being" (L. Dumont, 42). See also A. L. Herman, *An Introduction to Indian Thought* (Englewood Cliffs, N.J.: Prentice Hall, 1976).

9. Wendy Doniger O'Flaherty, *Asceticism and Eroticism in the Mythology of Śiva* (Oxford: Oxford University Press, 1973).

10. G. Bühler, trans., *The Laws of Manu* [Sacred Books of the East Series] (1886; Delhi: Motilal Banarsidass, 1975), 129 and 198ff.

11. J. C. Heesterman, "Brahmin, Ritual and Renouncer," *Wiener Zeitschrift für die Kunde süd- und Ostasiens und Archiv für Indische Philosophie* 8 (1964), 31. In note 52 Heesterman argues that while the average Brahmin was never a "renouncer," the act of renunciation became associated with the condition of the ideal Brahmin. And as *nivṛtti* or renunciation (as even our primitive schema demonstrates) had a radical tendency to invert caste strictures, non-Brahmins saw it as a means to "out-Brahmin" (Heesterman's term) the Brahmin. Heesterman perceptively concludes: "To a great extent this may be the ideological background of 'anti-brahminical' movements, past as well as present." Kabir and the bhakti tradition is germane to our understanding of such antibrahminical movements.

12. *The Mahābhārata*, trans. J. A. B. van Buitenen (Chicago: University of Chicago Press, 1973–78), 2: 630–31. [Book III: The Book of the Forest]. See also G. M. Bailey, 31. It is not uncommon to find *rajas* and *tamas* grouped together collectively as an impediment to moksha and hence placed in opposition to *sattva*.

13. Louis Dumont, 42.

14. The symbolism of Kundalini Yoga is built on the concept of the body as corporeal. See Sir John Woodroffe, *Śakti and Śākta* (1918; Madras: Ganesh, 1975), 376ff.

15. J. A. B. van Buitenen, trans. and ed., *The Bhagavadgītā in the Mahābhārata* (Chicago: University of Chicago Press, 1981), 13.

16. Mimansa was a school largely proccupied with the study of Vedic ritual in terms of an understanding of Vedic texts as "infallible revelation." In the context of the general push toward advancing a comprehensive philosophy of knowledge, Mimansa too developed a system that emphasized the reliability of the Veda as the absolute source of our understanding of the world as well as the idea of the self as the agent responsible for action. The Vedantins followed the doctrine of the "world-soul" based on the unity of Atman and Brahman. See Erich Frauwallner, *History of Indian Philosophy*, trans. V. M. Bedekar (Delhi: Motilal Banarsidass, 1984), 1:73–74; 2:9–10. For Sankhya see below.

17. R. S. McGregor, *Nanddās: The Round Dance of Krishna and Uddhav's Message* (London: Luzac 1973), 16–11.

18. Mariasusai Dhavamony, *Love of God According to Śaiva Siddhānta* (Oxford: Clarendon Press, 1971), 64–65.

19. R. C. Zaehner, *Hinduism* (Oxford: Oxford University Press, 1975), 93, suggests the fourth or third century B.C.E. as the date when the *Bhagavadgītā* reached its present form. Other commentators place the text a century or so later.

20. Alexander Pope's [Homer] *Odyssey* XII. 537–38: "Enough: In misery, can words avail?/And what so tedious as a twice-told tale?"

21. The references here are to the van Buitenen edition. Thus "15.43" at this juncture refers to the "The Book of the *Bhagavadgītā*" in the *Mahābhārata* and not to the *Bhagavadgītā* as an autonomous text as used elsewhere in this book. I use "The Book of the *Bhagavadgītā*" and "*Bhagavadgītā*" to refer to these two separate "texts."

22. van Buitenen, 26–27.

23. In the epic as a whole (which provides the context of the dialogue) though not in the *Bhagavadgītā* itself, there is a strong homoerotic undercurrent in the Krishna-Arjuna friendship.

24. Arvind Sharma, *The Hindu Gītā* (La Salle, Ill.: Open Court, 1986), 1–11.

25. The theory of the infra reader is developed more fully in chapter 3.

26. Arvind Sharma, xxvi.

27. Eric J. Sharpe, *The Universal Gītā* (La Salle, Ill.: Open Court, 1985), 166.

28. W. D. P. Hill, *The Bhagavad Gītā* (Oxford: Oxford University Press, 1928), 14–15, states:

> There seems to be a general consensus of opinion among modern scholars that the *Bhagavadgītā*, as it now appears in the Epic, is not an original poem composed by a single hand, but an ancient work re-written and enlarged. . . . Garbe propounds a very definite theory; the Gita, he says, was originally an exponent of Sankhya-Yoga philosophy, with which the Krishna Vasudeva cult was united until the beginning of the third century B.C. . . . This primitive Gita was worked over during the second century A.D. by some Vedantin, and if the pure Gita is to be recovered, the definitely Vedantic passages are to be excised. He then proceeds to show that this can be done.

See Richard Garbe, *Die Bhagavadgītā aus dem Sanskrit übersetzt, mit einer Einleitung über ihre ursprüngliche Gestalt, ihre Lehren und ihr Alter* (Leipzig: H. Haessel Verlag, 1905).

In a paper published in the *Journal of the Royal Asiatic Society* (1905), 384–89, E. W. Hopkins criticized Garbe's theory (which has since been rejected by most scholars). In a later work Hopkins argued that the Gita was "a Krishnaite version of an older Vishnuite poem; and this in turn was first an unsectarian work, perhaps a late Upanishad" (*Religions of India* [Boston: Little, Brown, 1908], 389). J. N. Farquhar, *An Outline of the Religious Literature of India* (1920; Delhi: Motilal Banarsidass, 1967), 92, offers a slightly different interpretation: "It is much more likely that the *Gītā* is an old verse Upanishad, written rather later than the *Svetāśvatara*, and worked up into the *Gītā* in the interests of Krishnaism by a poet after the Christian era."

Most modern commentators (Hill, Edgerton, Radhakrishnan, Zaehner, Bhaktivedanta, Herman, Bolle, van Buitenen, etc.) now agree that the *Bhagavadgītā* is a pre-Christian text.

Rudolf Otto, *The Original Gītā*, trans. J. E. Turner (London: George Allen and Unwin, 1939) continues, in the tradition of his guru Garbe, to look for an underlying structure, the "Ur-text," on the basis of which all later interpolations may be constructed.

29. Ronald Inden, *Imagining India* (Oxford: Blackwell, 1992), 114.

30. Albert B. Lord, *The Singer of Tales* (Cambridge, Mass.: Harvard University Press, 1960), 129.

31. Walter J. Ong, *Orality and Literacy: The Technologizing of the World* (London: Routledge, 1982), 24.

32. A. B. Lord, 67. For further discussion of oral poetry see *New Literary History* 8.3 (Spring 1977), special issue entitled "Oral Cultures and Oral Performances."

33. The transposition of this love to the level of Godhead is nothing new. In *Ṛgveda* 8.98. 11 we read:

> You are our father, you are our mother; from you
> alone can we expect the goal of happiness.

Cf. *Ṛgveda* 4.17.17; 6.1.5 etc. For a fuller analysis of Vedic bhakti, see Munshiram Sharma, *Bhakti kā vikās* (Varanasi, India: Chaukhambā Vidyābhavan, 1979), 98–164.

34. M. Dhavamony, 78–79. Cf. *Bhagavadgītā*, 6.1; 18.2; 18.5–6.

35. M. Dhavamony, 80.

36. *Bhagavadgītā* 3.11. van Buitenen translation (modified).

37. Quoted by R. C. Zaehner, *Hindu and Muslim Mysticism* (London: Athlone Press, 1960), 195.

38. R. C. Zaehner, *The Catholic Church and World Religions* (London: Athlone Press, 1964), 37.

39. Peter Munz, "India: Homo Hierarchicus or Generalised Exchange of Souls?" *Pacific Viewpoint* 11.2 (September 1970), 197.

40. Henri Lefebvre, *The Production of Space*, trans. Donald Nicholson-Smith (Oxford: Blackwell, 1991), 68.

41. Henri Lefebvre, 69.

42. These include *nitya*, daily ritual, *agnihotra*, etc.; *naimittika*, occasional ritual at death, etc.; *kāmya*, the rites of desire, procreation, etc.

43. Even as Krishna stresses this new idea of a personal God, he continues to rely heavily on cultural discourses current at the time. Of especial note are the references to a thousand yugas as a day of Brahma, the opportune time for the departure of souls, and so on. Many of these ideas go back to the *Cāndogya* and *Bṛhadāraṇyaka Upaniṣads*.

44. J. Robert Oppenheimer quoted *Bhagavadgītā* 11.12 to describe the explosion of the first atomic bomb in the Nevada desert.

45. The word for "working" here is *pravṛtti* since Krishna is addressed as the eternal man-in-the-world and not as the renouncer.

46. Franklin Edgerton, trans., *The Bhagavad Gītā* (1944; Cambridge, Mass.: Harvard University Press, 1977), 115.

47. To many this is a difficult proposition because even when one is acting without consequences one knows that pure action is done because of the hope for liberation.

48. The avatars—fish, tortoise, boar, man-lion, dwarf, Parashurama, Rama, Krishna, Buddha, and the yet-to-come Kalki —are not specifically mentioned as in Jayadeva's *Gītagovinda*. It could also be argued that except for the Rama avatar the larger question of dharma as the eternal Hindu Law is not discussed at length in the narratives of the other avatars.

49. Erich Frauwallner, 1:79.

50. This is a section of some 200 chapters in which the philosophy of the epic is gathered under various headings. Its context is the wounded and dying Bhishma around whom gather the Pandavas and their allies. To them Bhishma imparts his system of deliverance. The highest entity is presented as the Atman or the *kṣetrajña*, the knower of the field, that lies outside earthly definitions and is not accessible to thought. Although it is imperceptible, like the dark side of the moon we cannot say that it doesn't exist. The Atman wanders so long as it is entangled in the cycle of transmigration. During this period it allows itself to be embodied within a psychical organism but which organism again enters into the Atman at the moment of deliverance. This psychical organism consists of *buddhi* (knowledge), *manas* (thinking organ), and the five senses (*indriyāṇi*). The sequence is as follows: Atman generates *buddhi*, which generates *manas*, which generates the sense organs. Besides, this Atman continues to be embodied within a psychical organism (the corporeal body) as a consequence of reincarnations on the basis of one's karma. With the Atman's entry into the body, the sense organs then experience the external world made up of three *guṇas*: *sattva* (goodness), *rajas* (passion), and *tamas* (darkness). These sense organs get to know the things of the external world and are captivated by them. The Atman too gets entangled in the world of the senses (the sense organs desire the external world) because locked into karmic consequences we cannot find deliverance. In other words, deliverance comes when the soul becomes conscious of its own nature, when it recognizes that pleasure and pain belong to earthly nature, when in fact it also realizes that it had erroneously confused the psychical realm with its own self. Then, untouched by earlier karma, the soul finds deliverance.

The answer in the *mokṣadharma* discourse is that the sense organs must be withdrawn from their contact with the *guṇas* that are the elements of the external world. Only then will the *manas*, the thinking organ, gain an insight into the quality-less Atman. When one has attained this, one gets to know Brahman. Deliverance is reached forthwith, the psychical organ dissolves, the sense organs return into the thinking organ, which returns to knowledge, which in turn dissolves into the Atman and enters Brahman. This is an all too brief summary but its salient characteristic is the understanding that the Atman is essentially Upanishadic, that is, neither being nor not-being, outside the chain of cause and effect, unmanifest, with the distinction made between the embodied Atman (elemental-Atman, *bhūtātmā*) and the highest Atman. Erich Frauwallner, 1:76–84, adapted.

51. Gerald James Larson and Ram Shankar Bhattacharya, eds., *Encyclopaedia of Indian Philosophies IV* (Delhi: Motilal Banarsidass, 1987), 4:xi. I am indebted to this volume and to Erich Frauwallner, *History of Indian Philosophy,* for my discussion of Sankhya philosophy.

52. Wilhelm Halbfass, *On Being and What There Is* (Albany: State University of New York Press, 1992), 49.

53. Wilhelm Halbfass, 48. It must be said that Sankhya entered into a close connection with Yoga from an early stage so that deliverance through knowledge could be reached in two ways: logical thought (what Krishna would refer to as *jñānayoga*) and meditation. Thus was formed a classical Yoga system that reconciled Sankhya theory with actual Yoga practice (the latter came to be associated with the name Patanjali). There was also a third alternative, the Tantric way, that remains little developed until much later. The *Bhagavadgītā*, though, is aware of this school too.

54. This "I-consciousness" is the source also of a double creation: it is the source of the thinking organ (the *manas*) and of the ten sense organs (*indriyāṇi*) made up of the five senses of knowledge (ear, skin, eyes, tongue, nose) plus the five organs of action (speech, hands, feet, anus, penis/womb). In another move *prakṛti* as a female principle (matter as Ur-mother) was placed in a dualistic scheme of female-male dichotomy where *prakṛti* is female and the *puruṣa* male. This reinforced the age-old principle that the knowing principle is male whereas the creative (corporeal) principle is female.

55. Here and elsewhere I have used the J. A. B. van Buitenen translation. In places, however, I have silently modified his translation.

56. *The Bhagavad Gītā*, trans. Winthrop Sargeant (Albany: State University of New York Press, 1984).

57. J. A. B. van Buitenen translation.

3. Devotional Poetics

1. John Guillory, *Cultural Capital* (Chicago: University of Chicago Press, 1993), 55.

2. Samuel Johnson, "The Life of Waller," in *Johnson: Prose and Poetry*, ed. Mona Wilson (London: Rupert Hart-Davis, 1969), 848.

3. See Samuel H. Monk, *The Sublime* (Ann Arbor: University of Michigan Press, 1960).

4. Samuel Johnson, 849.

5. Hannah Arendt, *The Human Condition* (Chicago: University of Chicago Press, 1974), 9.

6. Hannah Arendt, 7.

7. *The Bhagavadgītā* 4.14.

8. Stanley Fish, *Self-Consuming Artefacts* (Berkeley: University of California Press, 1974).

9. *The Divine Poems of John Donne*, ed. Helen Gardner (Oxford: Clarendon Press, 1969), Holy Sonnet 1. All quotations from John Donne are taken from this edition.

10. Colin P. Thompson, *The Poet and the Mystic: A Study of the Cántico Espiritual of San Juan de la Cruz* (Oxford: Oxford University Press, 1977), 173.

11. Louis L. Martz, *The Poetry of Meditation* (New Haven, Conn.: Yale University Press, 1976), 43.

12. Louis Martz, 49.

13. Barbara Kiefer Lewalski, *Protestant Poetics and the Seventeenth-Century Religious Lyric* (Princeton, N.J.: Princeton University Press, 1979), 148. For a discussion of the impact of Protestant meditative practices on John Donne, see Barbara Kiefer Lewalski, *Donne's* "Anniversaries" *and the Poetry of Praise* (Princeton, N.J.: Princeton University Press, 1973).

14. Stanley Fish, 156–57.

15. The analysis that follows draws upon Michael Riffaterre, *Semiotics of Poetry* (London: Methuen, 1978).

16. A. K. Ramanujan, *Speaking of Śiva* (Harmondsworth, U.K.: Penguin, 1973), 35.

17. *The Subhāṣitaratnakoṣa compiled by Vidyākara*, eds. D. D. Kosambi and V. V. Gokhale (Cambridge, Mass.: Harvard University Press, 1957), 53.

18. Daniel H. H. Ingalls, *Sanskrit Poetry from Vidyākara's "Treasury"* (Cambridge, Mass.: Harvard University Press, 1972), 47.

19. M. Monier-Williams, *Sanskrit-English Dictionary* (1899; Delhi: Munshiram Manoharlal, 1976), 743–44. See also T. Burrow, *The Sanskrit Language* (London: Faber & Faber, 1977), 78.

20. Monier-Williams, 743. The Vedic use of the root *bhaj* is discussed in A. M. Esnoul, "Le courant affectif à l'intérieur du Brahmanisme ancien," *Bulletin de l'École Française d'Extrême-Orient*, 48 (1956), 141–207.

21. Mariasusai Dhavamony, *Love of God According to Śaiva Siddhānta* (Oxford: Clarendon Press, 1971), 13: In certain inscriptions the word *bhakti* is used to convey the sense of loyalty between king and soldier.

22. This is especially true of the developments in later Vaishnava bhakti verse, and especially after Rupa Gosvamin's systematic exposition on the subject. S. K. De in *Early History of the Vaiṣṇava Faith and Movement in Bengal* (Calcutta: Firma K.L. Mukhopadhyay, 1961), 166, observes:

> In Rupa Gosvamin's two systematic Sanskrit works . . . the *Bhakti-rasāmṛta-sindhu* and its supplement the *Ujjvala-nīlamaṇi*, the religious sentiment of Bhakti has been approximated to the supreme relish of literary enjoyment, known as Rasa, of orthodox Sanskrit Poetics.

23. M. Dhavamony, 14ff. In Kalidasa, in Bhasha, and in the *Pañcatantram* there are examples of the use of *bhakti* to express love between parents and children. "What is the use of a son, if he is neither wise nor devoted" we find in the *Pañcatantram: ko 'rthah*

putreṇa jātena yo na vidvān na bhaktimān? In Kalidasa there are references to *bhakti* as a word that denotes sexual love. "May you find a husband with undivided love; in such a manner did Bhava address her": *ananya-bhājaṃ patim āpnuhīti/ sā tathyam evābhihitā bhavena* (*Kumārasambhava*, canto iii, 63). The notion of respect toward masters and gurus may also be found in the literature. Vishnusharma in the first fable of the *Pañcatantram* speaks of the prince who must take as servants only those people who are wise, of good family, brave, capable, and devoted: *evam jñātvā narendreṇa bhṛtyāḥ kāryā vicakṣaṇāḥ/ kulīnāḥ śauryasaṃyuktāḥ śaktā bhaktāḥ kramāgatāḥ*. In Dandin's *Daśakumāracarita* a courtesan's devotion toward a hermit is expressed through the word *bhakti*: *ṛṣim alaghubhaktir dautodgamanīyavāsinī*.

24. M. Dhavamony, 20. In Jayaratha's *Haracaritacintāmaṇi*, canto xxvii, 64 we find, for instance, *parasparam ati-prītau*, "to each other very dear (*prīti*)." *Anurāga* and *sneha* are found in both Kalidasa (*Meghadūta*, 12) and Bhatti (*Rāvaṇavadha*, canto xix, 28b). Sometimes the word *śraddhā* (trust, confidence, faith, belief, etc.) is used interchangeably with *bhakti*, both of which are then connected, in translation, with the very Christian idea of faith. See K. L. Seshagiri Rao, *The Concept of Śraddhā* (Delhi: Motilal Banarsidass, 1974). Rao establishes twenty-one occurrences of the term *śraddhā* in the *Bhagavadgītā* alone.

25. M. Dhavamony, 21. For a fuller discussion of this view, see Jan Gonda, *Aspects of Early Viṣṇuism* (Delhi: Motilal Banarsidass, 1969), 158.

26. Louis Renou, *Religions of Ancient India* (London: Athlone Press, 1953), 72.

27. In the *Bhagavadgītā* 11.44 we do see Arjuna using "kinship metaphors" to speak of the subject's special devotion to God: "As father (*piteva*) to son (*putrasya*), as friend (*sakheva*) to friend (*sakhyuḥ*), as lover (*priyaḥ*) to beloved (*priyāya*)."

28. Jeffrey R. Timm, "The Celebration of Emotion: Vallabha's Ontology of Affective Experience," *Philosophy East & West* 41.1 (January 1991), 61.

29. I follow Patrick Olivelle's periodization of Early Vedic (principally the *Ṛg Veda* and the *Atharva Veda*), Middle Vedic (the Brahmanas), Late Vedic (the Āranyakas and the Upanishads), and Post-Vedic (principally Buddhist and epic literature) here. See Patrick Olivelle, "Orgasmic Rapture and Divine Ecstasy: The Semantic History of Ānanda," *Journal of Indian Philosophy* 25.2 (April 1997), 153.

30. Munshiram Sharma, *Bhakti kā vikās* (Varanasi, India: Chaukhambā Vidyābhavan, 1979), 69.

31. S. Radhakrishnan, ed. and trans., *The Principal Upaniṣads* (London: George Allen and Unwin, 1978), *Śvetāśvatara Upaniṣad*, 6.23.

32. S. Radhakrishnan, 707.

33. M. Dhavamony, 61.

34. Stanley Lane-Poole, *Medieval India under Mohammedan Rule* (A.D. *712–1764*) (1903; rpt. New York: Haskell House, 1970), 159.

35. Madeleine Biardeau, *Hinduism: The Anthropology of a Civilization*, trans. Richard Nice (Delhi: Oxford University Press, 1989), 88.

36. *The Bhagavadgītā* 7.16.

37. Louis Dumont, "World Renunciation in Indian Religions," *Contributions to Indian Sociology* 4 (1960), 57.

38. F. E. Pargiter, "Purāṇas," in the *Encyclopaedia of Religion and Ethics* (Edinburgh: T. & T. Clark, 1952), 10:447. The Sanskrit word *purāṇa* means "ancient" and the titles of these texts suggest that they are "timeless." Indeed, Hindu critical orthodoxy believes that they are as old as the Vedas. V. N. Shukla in *Hindī kṛṣṇa bhakti kāvyą par śrīmadbhāgvat kā prabhāv* (Aligarh, India: Bhārat Prakāśan Mandir, 1966), 4ff., suggests, with perhaps more enthusiasm than historical accuracy, that the word does not simply mean "ancient"; it transforms the old into the "eternal present."

39. Ludo Rocher, *The Purāṇas* (Wiesbaden, Germany: Otto Harrassowitz, 1986), (vol. II, facs. 3 of *A History of Indian Literature*, ed. Jan Gonda), 12.

40. J. N. Farquhar, *An Outline of the Religious Literature of India* (1920; Delhi: Motilal Banarsidass, 1967), 229. All scholars agree that the *Bhāgavata Purāṇa* is the latest of the eighteen Puranas. Hindus on the whole tend to give it a much older date, some assigning it to Vyasa, the putative author of the *Mahābhārata*. There is a strong tendency among some scholars (Farquhar, 231ff.) to attribute the work to Vopadeva (c. 1250–1300). While Colebrooke, Burnouf, and Wilson accept this attribution, it is difficult to reconcile this with the fact that the great "dualist" Madhva spoke of the work some fifty years before the birth of Vopadeva. The latter did write a number of valuable commentaries on the *Bhāgavata Purāṇa* and this may have led to some people attributing the text to him. Moreover, Alberuni mentions the *Bhāgavata Purāṇa* among the other Puranas. (See Ludo Rocher, 31.) It is highly unlikely that its early recensions were composed much later than 900 C.E. V. N. Shukla, however (15ff.), is inclined to place it closer to 600 C.E. than most other modern scholars.

41. The sequence is taken from G. M. Bailey, "For a New Study of the Vāmana Purāṇa," *Indo-Iranian Journal* 29 (1986), 11.

42. See Vladimir Propp, *Morphology of the Folktale*, trans. Laurence Scott (Austin: University of Texas Press, 1986) and A. J. Greimas, *Semantique structurale* (Paris: Larousse, 1966).

43. J. N. Farquhar, 230.

44. *Śrīmadbhāgavatamahāpurāṇa*, Book I: the nature of the narrative, how the tale was told to Vyasa who still felt somewhat "dissatisfied" even after completing the *Mahābhārata*; names of the traditional sutas, tellers of tales, such as Narada, Shringi rishi, etc. mentioned; Book II (10 sections): Sukhadeva tells the story to Parikshit and mentions in particular the roads to *mukti* or moksha, the avatars of Vishnu, etc.; Book III (33 sections): mainly the teaching of Maitreya to Vidura who has just left the battle in the *Mahābhārata*, the creation of the world, etc.; Book IV (31 sections): the teaching of Maitreya continues, including many popular tales (King Vena, Prithu, etc.) and the importance of bhakti stressed; Book V (26 sections): tales of kings continued and notes on various cosmological ideas; Book VI (19 sections): way out of *narak* (hell); tales of Ajamil and Dakshya; Book VII (15 sections): interspersed among sections on the various dharmas is the tale of Prahalada and Hiranyakashipu, one of the most popular in Puranic lore and one that follows closely the steps of meditation identified above as bhakti ideology; Book VIII (24 sections): mainly on the minor avatars—*Vāmanāvatāra*, *Matsyāvatāra*—but includes the important tale of the churning of the ocean (*samudraman-*

than); Book IX (24 sections): an important book in which many key stories are found, among them the tale of Rama, Harishchandra, Parashurama, etc.; Book X (90 sections: 49 in the first half and 41 in the second): the incarnation of Vishnu as Krishna, his "complete" story, and by far the most important section of the *Bhāgavata Purāṇa* for students of bhakti; Book XI (31 sections): an important theoretical book with notes on the various Yogas: *jñāna*, karma, bhakti, as well as comments on Maya and Brahman. This book is slightly unusual with the normal accounts of Puranic legends playing a minor role. Book XII (13 sections) uses the future tense to suggest the nature of the coming age.

45. Adalbert Gail, *Bhakti im Bhāgavatapurāṇa*, Münchener Indologische Studien, vol. VI (Wiesbaden, Germany: Otto Harrassowitz, 1969), 22ff.

46. J. N. Farquhar, 231.

47. *The Śrīmad-Bhāgavatam*, trans. J. M. Sanyal (Delhi: Munshiram Manoharlal, 1973), 1:260. A variant translation of the passage is cited in S. N. Dasgupta, *A History of Indian Philosophy* (1922; Delhi: Motilal Banarsidass, 1975), 4:28–29.

G. V. Tagare, trans. *The Bhāgavata-Purāṇa*, vol. 7 of J. L. Shastri, ed., *Ancient Indian Mythology* (Delhi: Motilal Banarsidass, 1976), 389 glosses *citta-baḍiśam śanakair viyuṅkte* with reference to the following commentators:

(a) Shridhara Svami (*Bhāvāratha dīpīka* [*advaita*]): "The angle in the form of *citta* which hooks up the Lord who is difficult to capture."

(b) Vira-raghava (*Bhāgavata candrikā* [*viśiṣṭādvaita*]): "He should gradually disengage his mind from the person of the Lord which is to be meditated. He should then meditate on his *pratyāgātma* (Soul)."

(c) Vijayadhvaja (*Padaratnāvalī* [*dvaita* "dualistic"]): "The sage who directs the hook of his heart to the Lord—the object of contemplation disengages it (and enters *samādhi* without any purposeful efforts)."

(d) Shukadeva (*Siddhānta-pradīpa*, after Nimbarka): "The heart of the Yogin is hard like a hook. Its touch is troublesome to the Lord. When this hook is removed (disengaged), God confers experience of *Pratyāgātma* and Moksha on the Yogin but not the experience of the Supreme Soul."

48. S. N. Dasgupta, 4:28.

49. Quoted by Maya Agraval, *Kabīr-vāṇī-sudhā* (Delhi: Kalā Mandir, 1978), 52.

50. For valuable summaries of Shankara's *advaita*, see *The Vedānta Sūtras of Bādarāyaṇa with a Commentary by Śaṅkara*, trans. George Thibaut (1890 and 1896; rpt. New York: Dover, 1962), 2 vols; S. N. Dasgupta, 1:406ff., 2:1–226; and Swami Gambhirananda, trans., *Brahma-Sūtra Bhāṣya of Śrī-Śaṅkaracārya* (Calcutta: Advaita Ashrama, 1972), especially T. M. P. Mahadevan's foreword.

51. *Muṇḍaka Upaniṣad* 3.2.9: "Absolute knowledge of Brahman is to become Brahman."

52. *Bhagavadgītā* 12.16: "My devotee is dear to me."

53. Greg Bailey, "Secular and Religious in Indian Literature: A Comparison of Writings on the Theme of Love in the *Gītagovinda* and the *Caurapañcāśika*," *South Asia* [new series] 4.1 (June 1981), 6.

54. M. N. Srinivas, *Religion and Society Among the Coorgs* (Oxford: Oxford University Press, 1952).

55. Louis Dumont, 62. Earlier in his essay (42n 15) Dumont, using a slightly Hegelian conceptual formula, draws a useful distinction between these two types of "individuality." What is found here is the "particular" (*Besonderheit*), not the "individual" (i.e., the particular in which the individual is reflected, that is, *Einzelnheit*). In Indian society, then, the individual who reflects or combines within himself the "tensions" or issues of the society at large is nonexistent. To Dumont bhakti had thus to resolve a much more antagonistic opposition between total societal values on the one hand and a complete negation of them on the other.

56. R. S. McGregor, *Nanddās: The Round Dance of Krishna and Uddhav's Message* (London: Luzac, 1973), 13. Charlotte Vaudeville discusses the impassioned love-symbolism in the religious literature of the Tamil saint-poets in "Evolution of Love-Symbolism in Bhāgavatism," *Journal of the American Oriental Society* 82 (1962), 31–40.

57. M. Dhavamony, 170.

58. M. Dhavamony, 171. The following are examples from Dhavamony's translation (158ff.):

(a) If you leave, I perish
None but you upholds your devotee;
Source of my life,
. . . .
Indwelling in me.

(b) Give me grace that ceaseless love for you may abide in the inmost of my heart, melting [in love] my very soul.

(c) You see that I cling to none but you . . . if you who made me your own deny your grace, to whom shall I complain? To whom shall I tell my sorrow? . . . bid me come to you.

(d) You desire me and rule me by your grace . . . I desire nothing else but intense love for you.

(e) If at all I desire a gift from you, it is your love.

For George Herbert's poems, see F. E. Hutchinson, ed., *The Works of George Herbert* (1941; Oxford: Clarendon Press, 1972).

59. R. C. Zaehner, *Hinduism* (Oxford: Oxford University Press, 1975), especially chapter 6. Zaehner sees a strong sexual impulse (or sublimation of that impulse) in bhakti verse. He considers Tamil verse to be of this sort. For a useful collection of devotional verse, see John Stratton Hawley and Mark Juergensmeyer, eds. and trans., *Songs of the Saints of India* (New York: Oxford University Press, 1988). For excellent critical studies, see also W. H. McLeod, *Gurū Nānak and the Sikh Religion* (1968; Delhi: Oxford University Press, 1976), 151ff., and Parshuram Chaturvedi, ed., *Hindī sāhitya kā bṛhat itihās* (Varanasi, India: Nāgrīpracāriṇī Sabhā, 1962), 4:95ff.

60. R. C. Zaehner, 128.

61. J. N. Farquhar, 259. R. G. Bhandarkar, *Vaiṣṇavism, Śaivism and Minor Reli-*

gious Systems (1913; rpt. Varanasi: Indological Book House, 1965), 134, argues that it came into existence a century earlier.

62. J. Gonda, *Viṣṇuism and Śivaism: A Comparison* (London: Athlone Press, 1970), 65.

63. J. N. Farquhar, 260: "[Ekorāma, Paṇḍitārādhya, Revaṇa, Marula and Viśvārādhya, the five ascetics who found the sect] are held to have sprung from the five heads of Śiva, incarnate age after age."

64. A. K. Ramanujan, *Speaking of Śiva* (Harmondsworth, U.K.: Penguin, 1973). All the poetic examples and translations are taken from this work. Ramanujan defines *vacana* as follows (37): "The Sanskrit religious texts are described as *śruti* and *smṛti. Smṛti* is what is remembered, what is memorable; *śruti*, what is heard, what is received. Virashaiva saints called their compositions, *vacana*, or 'what is said.' *Vacana*, as an active mode, stands in opposition to both *śruti* and *smṛti*: not what is heard, but what is said; not remembered or received, but uttered here and now. To the saints, religion is not a spectator sport, a reception, a consumption; it is an experience of Now, a way of being. This distinction is expressed in the language of the vacanas, the forms the vacanas take."

65. J. Gonda, 98–99.

66. S. N. Dasgupta, 5:49. *Ṣaṭ-sthala*—*ṣaṣ* "six" + *sthala* "chapter, section . . . ground . . . place, sport" (M. Monier-Williams, 1108 and 1261–62). S. N. Dasgupta (56) suggests that Allama taught the Vira-Shaiva doctrine of *ṣaṭ-sthala*. The encounters of Allama and one Goraksha, another Shaivite, is given some prominence but it seems unlikely that this Goraksha was the same as Gorakhnath. Elsewhere (46), S. N. Dasgupta maintains that the kernel of Vira-Shaiva thought goes back to the Upanishads, traces of which surface in the works of Kalidasa.

67. S. N. Dasgupta, 5:57.

68. A. K. Banerjea, *Philosophy of Gorakhnath* (Gorakhpur, India: Mahant Dig Vijai Nath Trust, 1961?).

69. Charlotte Vaudeville, *Kabīr I* (Oxford: Clarendon Press, 1974), 108. Vaudeville continues, "If this has not been noticed by writers on Indian religion it is due to the unchallenged notion according to which Kabir, as a devotee of 'Ram,' must have been a 'Vaishnava Bhakta.'"

70. A. K. Ramanujan, 35. Ramanujan borrows this structuralist methodology from Victor Turner, *The Ritual Process: Structure and Anti-Structure* (Chicago: Aldine, 1969).

71. A. K. Ramanujan, 35.

72. A. K. Ramanujan, 36.

73. M. A. K. Halliday, *Language as Social Semiotic* (London: Edward Arnold, 1979), chapter 9.

74. A. K. Ramanujan, 151 and 153.

75. Mircea Eliade, *Yoga: Immortality and Freedom*, trans. Willard R. Trask (Princeton, N.J.: Princeton University Press, 1969), 251.

76. Mircea Eliade, 251. See also Mircea Eliade, 249–54 for a valuable note on

sandhyā-bhāṣā. "Tantric texts are often composed in an 'intentional language' (*sandhyā-bhāṣā*), a secret, dark, ambiguous language in which a state of consciousness is expressed by an erotic term and the vocabulary of mythology or cosmology is charged with Hathayogic or sexual meanings." According to Eliade, Eugene Burnouf translated the term as "enigmatic language" and Max Müller called it "hidden language." Eliade, however, follows Vidhushekar Shastri, who showed that the term is based on a shortened form of the word *sandhāya,* which Shastri translates as "aiming at," "having in view," "intending," and so on ("Sandhābhāṣā," *Indian Historical Quarterly* 4.2 [1928], 287–96). V. Shastri suggests that copyists must have confused *sandhāya* (notice long second *a*) with *sandhyā* ("twilight"). The latter is also the definition of Haraprasad Shastri (*Bauddha Gān O Dohā,* Calcutta, 1916), who explains (Mircea Eliade, 410–11), "All the works of the Sahajayāna are written in the *Sandhyā-bhāṣā* . . . of light and darkness . . . partly light, partly darkness; some parts can be understood while others cannot. In other words in these discourses on dharma, which are of a high order, there are references also to different meanings." (On the Sahajiya, see S. B. Dasgupta, *Obscure Religious Cults* [Calcutta: Firma K.L.M. Private Limited, 1976] and Edward C. Dimock Jr., *The Place of the Hidden Moon* [Chicago: University of Chicago Press, 1966]). Prabodh Chandra Bagchi, "The Sandhābhāṣā and Sandhāvacana," *Indian Historical Quarterly* 6.2 (1930), 389–96, disputes once again H. Shastri's conclusions and opts for "intentional speech." I have translated *sandhyā-bhāṣā* as "twilight language" while keeping the phenomenological meaning of "intentional" whenever I use it to refer to its construction of a specific kind of (aesthetic) object.

77. Malik Muhammad, *Alvār bhaktõ kā tāmil-prabandhan aur hindī kṛṣṇa-kāvya* (Agra, India: Vinod Pustak Mandir, 1964).

78. Barbara Stoler Miller, ed. and trans., *Love Song of the Dark Lord: Jayadeva's "Gītagovinda"* (New York: Columbia University Press, 1977). I have used this critical edition throughout.

79. Anders Nygren, *Agape and Eros: A Study of the Christian Idea of Love* (London: Society for Promoting Christian Knowledge, 1937).

80. B. S. Miller, 6.

81. David Kingsley, *Hindu Goddesses* (Berkeley: University of California Press, 1988), 85.

82. It must be said that Jayadeva's Sanskrit has much of the sound and feel of Prakrit or the vernacular.

83. See B. S. Miller, 183–89, for selected commentaries on the *Gītagovinda*.

84. Greg Bailey, "Secular and Religious in Indian Literature," 3.

85. See Rūpa Gosvāmi, *Bhaktirasāmṛtasindhu,* ed. Acharya Viveshvar, intr. Vijayendra Snatak (Delhi: Delhi Viśvavidyālaya, 1963).

86. William Empson, *Some Versions of Pastoral* (1935; Harmondsworth, U.K.: Penguin Books, 1966).

87. William Empson, 181.

88. *Bhoja's Śṛṅgāra Prakāśa,* ed. V. Raghavan (Madras: Theosophical Society, 1978), 80.

89. B. S. Miller, 69.

90. Jacques Derrida, *Speech and Phenomena and Other Essays on Husserl's Theory of Signs*, trans. David B. Allison (Evanston, Ill.: Northwestern University Press, 1973), 130.

91. Lee Siegel, *Sacred and Profane Dimensions of Love in Indian Traditions as Exemplified in The "Gītagovinda" of Jayadeva* (Delhi: Oxford University Press, 1978), 90ff. Siegel discusses the various types of *nāyaka* ("lover," "hero"). He also demonstrates that the *Gītagovinda* expresses all the four subtypes of the *nāyaka: dhṛṣṭa* ("faithless"), *śaṭha* ("deceitful"), *dakṣiṇa* ("clever"), and *anukūla* ("faithful").

92. These are Rupa Gosvamin's definitions as quoted in Edward C. Dimock Jr., 17. Dimock adds "viraha [separation of lovers and the longing involved in it] is more intense in a relationship with a *parakīyā* woman than a *svakīyā* woman." Further categories of the *parakīyā* and *svakīyā* types may be found in Edward C. Dimock Jr., 200–221.

93. B. S. Miller, 50: "The perspective of the friend is later codified into the elaborate aesthetic theory of *sakhībhāva* in Bengal Vaishnavism." See also S. B. Dasgupta, 125–26.

94. Lee Siegel, 184.

95. See Lee Siegel, 26ff. et passim, and A. K. Majumdar, *Caitanya: His Life and Doctrine* (Bombay: Bharatiya Vidya Bhavan, 1969). S. K. De in *Early History of the Vaiṣṇava Faith and Movement in Bengal* (Calcutta: Firma K.L.M., 1961), 9, states:

> A Caịtanyaite Vaishnava would regard the *Gīta-govinda* not merely as a poetical composition of great beauty, but also as a great religious work, and would feign explain it in terms of his Bhakti Rasa-shastra.

As the text was written at least some three hundred years before Chaitanya, S. K. De doubts if Jayadeva wrote it "expressly for the illustration of any particular dogma or doctrine." Nevertheless, he concedes (10): "there can be no doubt that the *Gīta-govinda*, with its mystical emotions, was claimed by Caitanyaism as one of the sources of its religious inspirations."

96. It is important to note that Rupa Gosvamin used the *Gītagovinda* to illustrate the broad principles of Vaishnava devotional aesthetics.

97. Lee Siegel, 46ff.; Edward C. Dimock Jr., 21ff.; S. K. De, chapter 4; Kenneth E. Bryant, *Poems to the Child-God* (Berkeley: University of California Press, 1978), 96–97, et passim. The relationship between "basic emotion" (*sthāyi-bhāva*) and "aesthetic experience" (*rasa*) is summarized by Lee Siegel, 47:

Basia Emotion (*sthāyi-bhāva*)		Aesthetic Experience (*rasa*)	
love	(*rati*)	erotic	(*śṛṅgāra*)
humor	(*hāsa*)	comic	(*hāsya*)
grief	(*śoka*)	tragic	(*karuṇa*)
anger	(*krodha*)	furious	(*raudra*)
energy	(*utsaha*)	heroic	(*vīra*)
fear	(*bhaya*)	fearful	(*bhayānaka*)
disgust	(*jugupsā*)	horrific	(*bībhatsa*)
astonishment	(*vismaya*)	marvellous	(*adbhuta*)

98. Jaidev, *The Culture of Pastiche* (Shimla, India: Indian Institute of Advanced Study, 1993), 9.

99. The *śṛṅgāra* rasa is the aesthetic experience which corresponds to the basic emotion, *rati*. The latter word refers to love in its more mundane (i.e., passionate, sexual, or amorous) sense. See *Nāṭya Śāstra* (English trans.) (Delhi: Satguru Publications, 1985?), vi, 39–83; and Rupa Gosvamin, *Bhaktirasāmṛtasindhu*, I, iii.61. For a detailed analysis of *rati*, see Lee Siegel, 58–61.

100. *Nāṭya Śāstra*, xxvii, 49–57.

101. S. B. Dasgupta, 125–26.

102. For an interesting application of "play" (*kridati*), see also John Huizinga, *Homo Ludens: A Study of the Play Element in Culture* (Boston: Beacon Press, 1955).

103. Edward C. Dimock Jr., et al., *The Literatures of India* (Chicago: University of Chicago Press, 1978), 141.

104. B. S. Miller, *Gītagovinda*, VII.2.

105. For accounts of verses written in a similar style see Barbara Stoler Miller, ed. and trans., *Phantasies of a Love-Thief: The Caurapañcāśikā attributed to Bilhana* (New York: Columbia University Press, 1971) and Barbara Stoler Miller, ed. and trans., *Bhartrihari: Poems* (New York: Columbia University Press, 1967).

106. *The Bhakti Sūtras of Nārada*, trans. Nandlal Sinha (1911; rpt. New York: AMS Press, 1974); *Aphorisms on the Gospel of Divine Love or Nārada Bhakti Sūtras*, trans. Swami Tyāgīśānanda (Madras: Sri Ramakrishna Math, n.d.); *Śāṇḍilya Bhakti-sūtra with Bhakticandrikā by Nārāyaṇa Tīrtha*, ed. Baladeva Upadhayaya (Varanasi, India: Varanaseya Sanskrit Viśvavidyālaya, 1967); *Śāṇḍilya-sūtram*, with the commentary of Shvapneshvara, trans. Nandlal Sinha (Allahabad, India: The Panini Office, 1918).

107. J. Estlin Carpenter *Theism in Medieval India* (1921; New Delhi: Oriental Books Reprint Corporation, 1977), 419.

108. Nandlal Sinha translation. Swami Tyāgīśānanda's commentary (18) reads:

> Love and love alone such as that of a devoted servant or a wife, which transcends the three forms mentioned in Sutra 56, should be practised.

109. Michel Foucault, "What Is an Author?" in Josué V. Harari, ed., *Textual Strategies* (London: Methuen, 1980), 141–60.

110. See Pierre Pourrat, *Christian Spirituality*, trans. W. H. Mitchell and S. P. Jacques (London: Burns, Oates and Washbourne, 1922–27), 4 vols.

111. Nandlal Sinha translation, *sūtra* 82.

112. Friedhelm Hardy, *Viraha-Bhakti* (Delhi: Oxford University Press, 1983), 15.

113. Hazariprasad Dvivedi, *Kabīr* (Delhi: Rājkamal Prakāśan, 1976), 21.

114. See Hazariprasad Dvivedi, 235 (poem 2) where Kabir asks, *santana jāta na pūcho nirguṇiyā*, "It is pointless to ask a *santa* what caste he belongs to." While the poem is not found in the critical edition of Parasnath Tiwari (*Kabīr-Granthāvalī* [Prayag, India: Hindī Pariṣad, 1961]), it is nevertheless true to the ethos of the Kabir corpus gen-

erally. For an English translation of this poem, see Rabindranath Tagore, trans., *One Hundred Poems of Kabīr* (1915; London: Macmillan, 1973), 21–22.

4. Temples of Fire

1. On *mlecchas* Alberuni remarks, "They call them (foreigners) *mleccha, i.e.*, impure, and forbid having any connection with them . . . because thereby, they think, they would be polluted." See *Alberuni's India*, ed. and trans. Edward C. Sachau (1888; New Delhi: S. Chand & Co., 1964), 1:19–20. And again in 2:137 we read: "All other men except the Caṇḍāla, as far as they are not Hindus, are called *mleccha, i.e.*, unclean, all those who kill men and slaughter animals and eat the flesh of cows." Hereafter cited in the text.

2. Ronald Inden, *Imagining India* (Oxford: Blackwell, 1992), 114.

3. Edward C. Dimock Jr., *The Place of the Hidden Moon* (Chicago: University of Chicago Press, 1966), 20.

4. Wilhelm Halbfass, *India and Europe* (Albany: State University of New York Press, 1988), 31.

5. Wilhelm Halbfass, 15.

6. Alberuni may not have totally understood the symbolic nature of many Hindu practices but his observation that Hindus generally did not cut their hair, they chewed arecanuts with betel leaves and chalk and did not eat meat (1:180–81) confirm a number of things that are alluded to in the texts. There are also a lot of ethnographic material, and some explanatory material, that is of interest to us. Alberuni observes the five vegetables forbidden to Brahmins: onions, garlic, a kind of gourd, the root of a carrotlike plant (*mūlī*), and a water cress called *nali*. The prohibition against the killing of cows is linked to supply and demand. A man may keep four wives and a widow has the choice of staying alive or burning herself. Since widows are so badly treated, self-immolation upon the death of her husband is not uncommon. However, women of advanced years and women with children (but only if they are sons) are exempt from this. The attitude of Hindus toward courtesans is much more lenient (2:135ff.).

7. Quoted by Toshihiko Izutsu in *A Comparative Study of the Key Philosophical Concepts in Sufism and Taoism* (Tokyo: The Keiko Institute of Cultural and Linguistic Studies, 1967), 2:191.

8. J. N. Farquhar, *An Outline of the Religious Literature of India* (Delhi: Motilal Banarsidass, 1967), 220.

9. Georg Lukács, *The Theory of the Novel*, trans. Anna Bostock (London: Merlin Press, 1971).

10. I have drawn upon the following sources: R. A. Nicholson, *Studies in Islamic Mysticism* (Cambridge: Cambridge University Press, 1921); S. A. A. Rizvi, *A History of Sufism in India*, vol. 1 (Delhi: Munshiram Manoharlal, 1978); J. S. Trimingham, *The Sufi Orders of Islam* (Oxford: Oxford University Press, 1971); R. C. Zaehner, *Hindu and Muslim Mysticism* (London: The Athlone Press, 1960); Louis Massignon, *La Passion de Husayn Ibn Mansūr Hallāj*, 4 vols. (Paris: Gallimard, 1975); Henry Corbin, *Creative*

Imagination in the Ṣūfism of Ibn 'Arabī, trans. Ralph Manheim (London: Routledge and Kegan Paul, 1969); A. E. Affifi, *The Mystical Philosophy of Muhyid Din Ibnul 'Arabī* (Cambridge: Cambridge University Press, 1939); S. H. Nasr, *Ideals and Realities of Islam* (London: George Allen and Unwin, 1966); T. Izutsu. Other studies consulted include Tor Andrae, *Mohammed the Man and His Faith* (New York: Barnes and Noble, 1935); Alfred Guillaume, *Islam* (Harmondsworth, U.K.: Penguin, 1977); E. G. Browne, *A Literary History of Persia,* vol. 1 (Cambridge: Cambridge University Press, 1964); A. J. Arberry, *Sufism: An Account of the Mystics of Islam* (London: Unwin, 1979); A. Schimmel, *Mystical Dimensions of Islam,* (Chapel Hill: University of North Carolina Press, 1975); Margaret Smith, *The Sufi Path of Love: An Anthology of Islam* (London, 1954); F. Schoun, *Dimensions of Islam,* trans. P. Townsend (London, 1969); S. H. Nasr, "The Interior Life in Islam," *Religious Traditions* 1.2 (October 1978), 48–55; Margaret Smith, *Rābi'a the Mystic* (Cambridge: Cambridge University Press, 1925); Margaret Smith, *Al-Ghazālī the Mystic* (London: Luzac, 1944); Mir Valiuddin, *The Quranic Sufism* (Delhi: Motilal Banarsidass, n.d.); T. Burchardt, *The Art of Islam,* trans. P. Hobson (London, 1976).

11. S. A. A. Rizvi, "Sufis and Nātha Yogis in Medieval Northern India (XII to XVI Centuries)," *The Journal of the Oriental Society of Australia* 7.1–2 (December 1970), 119–33.

12. S. A. A. Rizvi, *Muslim Revivalist Movements in Northern India in the Sixteenth and Seventeenth Centuries* (Agra, India: Agra University Press, 1965), 11.

13. Charles S. J. White, *The Caurāsī Pad of Śrī Hit Harivaṃś* (Honolulu: University of Hawaii Press, 1977), x.

14. Alfred Guillaume, 154: "To the question whether personality survives in the ultimate union with God the majority of Sufis would say that it does not." S. A. A. Rizvi (*A History of Sufism in India,* 1:322–23) cites R. A. Nicholson's rebuttal of the fashionable equation of *nirvāṇa* and the Sufi *fanā'* and *baqā',* but argues that the rebuttal fails to recognize the more positive nature of *nirvāṇa* itself. While not making the same kinds of claims that Zaehner does, Rizvi, nevertheless, implies that the term "*nirvāṇa*" connotes an equivalent experience ("The state of *arhantship* in which *nirvāṇa* has been achieved . . . ," etc.).

15. R. C. Zaehner, 119: "[Abu Yazid] . . . injected into the body of Sufism a dose of Indian Vedanta that was soon to transform the whole movement."

16. Quoted by R. C. Zaehner, 146.

17. R. C. Zaehner, 148. See also S. A. A. Rizvi and S. Zaidi, eds. and trans., *Alakhbānī* (Aligarh, India: Bhārat Prakāśan Mandir, 1971), 21–22, where the quote is related to the presumed words of Angel Gabriel to Muhammad. Referring to Bayazid's use of these words, Rizvi and Zaidi (22) write, "While these words were uttered by Bayazid, the real speaker was in fact God."

18. J. Spencer Trimingham, 21 et passim.

19. J. Spencer Trimingham, 32.

20. J. Spencer Trimingham, 98.

21. S. A. A. Rizvi, *Muslim Revivalist Movements,* 15.

22. S. A. A. Rizvi, "Sufis and Nātha Yogis in Medieval Northern India," 124ff.

23. Charlotte Vaudeville, Review of Muhammad Hedayetullah, *Kabīr: The Apostle of Hindu-Muslim Unity* [Delhi: Motilal Banarsidass, 1977], *Journal of the Royal Asiatic Society of Great Britain and Ireland* 1 (1980), 103–4.

24. Toshihiko Izutsu, 1:194–95.

25. Louis Massignon, 3:82–83.

26. A. K. Banerjea, *Philosophy of Gorakhnath* (Gorakhpur, India: Mahant Dig Vijai Nath Trust, 1961?), 55. *Dvaita-advaita-vilakṣaṇa-vāda* means literally "duality-nonduality-difference-proposition." However, *vilakṣaṇa* has to be read in its rather specialized sense of "not admitting of exact definition," which clearly makes more sense. Hence we may define it more appropriately as a thesis or proposition where the duality-nonduality debate is not the key to truth. This fits in rather well with the pronouncements of Gorakhnath and his disciples. A. K. Banerjea writes (41): "Gorakhnath and his school do not seem to be infatuated with any of such categories of intellectual understanding, as *Sat* or *Asat*, *Pūrṇa* or *Śūnya*, Duality or Non-duality . . . with regard to the Absolute Truth, since in their view the Absolute truth is beyond the scope of such categories and directly realisable in absolute transcendent experience." A. K. Banerjea adds (24–25): "The ultimate basis of his philosophy was his supra-mental and supra-intellectual experience in the *samādhi*-state of his consciousness."

27. A. E. Affifi, 10. Cf. Plotinus, *Enneads*, III. 9.3. Affifi glosses (11) "Plotinus's One is everywhere as a cause: Ibnul 'Arabi's One is everywhere as an essence."

28. A. E. Affifi, 55.

29. A. E. Affifi, 55–56. Cf. Zaehner, 174ff., 180ff., et passim. R. C. Zaehner claims (174):

> The introduction of Neo-Platonic ideas into Ṣūfism from philosophy was, of course, made much of by Ibn al-'Arabī who systematized them into something very like Śaṅkara's version of the Vedānta.

Against R. C. Zaehner, cf. A. E. Affifi, 59:

> It is obvious that Ibnul 'Arabi's pantheistic doctrine is a natural outcome of typically Islamic thought with very little Hellenistic and particularly Neoplatonic element in it. It is an adaptation of the Ash'arites' theory of an external world as being essentially one substance with an infinity of attributes of changeable states.

30. A. E. Affifi, 15.

31. A. E. Affifi, 16–17.

32. S. A. A. Rizvi and S. Zaidi, Text, 66.

33. P. D. Barthwal, *Gorakhbānī* (Prayag, India: Hindī Sāhitya Sammelan, 1960), *sabadi* 50, 18. Hereafter referred to as *GB*.

34. S. A. A. Rizvi and S. Zaidi, Text, 31.

35. S. A. A. Rizvi and S. Zaidi, Text, 13.

36. A. E. Affifi, 12–13.

37. S. A. A. Rizvi and S. Zaidi, Text, 34.

38. Parasnath Tiwari, ed., *Kabīr-Granthāvalī* (Prayag, India: Hindī Pariṣad, 1961), *sākhī*, 8.6–7 (hereafter referred to as *KG*); Charlotte Vaudeville, *Kabir I* (Oxford: Clarendon Press, 1974), 196. *KG* constitutes the critical edition of the Kabir corpus used in this book. I have used Vaudeville's translation here.

39. Parasnath Tiwari, *Kabīr-vāṇī-sudhā* (Allahabad, India: Rākā Prakāśan, 1976) (hereafter referred to as *KVS*) maintains a heavy Vedantic (within Shankara's system) reading of Kabir throughout. This is followed by S. Shukla and R. Chaturvedi, eds., *Kabīr Granthāvalī* (Lucknow, India: Prakāśan Kendra. n.d.).

40. *KG, pada* 185. S. S. Das, ed., *Kabīr-Granthāvalī* (1928; Varanasi, India: Nāgrīpracāriṇī Sabhā, 1975) gives a slightly different version (*pada* 51).

M. P. Gupta, ed., *Kabīr-Granthāvalī* (Allahabad, India: Lokbhāratī Prakāśan, 1969), *pada* 51, 176 indicates that some manuscripts offer a somewhat expanded version of the poem. In the example he cites, the poem is almost twice as long. The concept of the Sikh *hukam* ("order") occurs in this version.

41. Hazariprasad Dvivedi, *Nāth-sampradāya* (Allahabad, India: Lokbhāratī Prakāśan, 1981), 123. Some fantastic claims made by the followers of the sect especially with reference to the power and influence of the Yogis on Sufis are recorded in S. A. A. Rizvi and S. Zaidi, 52ff.

42. *Sarhapā Dohākoṣa*, ed. Rahul Samkrityayana (Patna, India: Bihār Rāṣṭra Bhāsā Pariṣad, 1957), 27 and *dohā* 35.

43. *GB, sabadi* 2. The *brahmarandhra* is another name of the *sahasrāra cakra*, where the Kundalini ends its journey having blasted its way through the six *cakras*. In the space of the *brahmarandhra* the final goal of Tantric *sādhana* is realized.

44. M. Eliade, *Yoga: Immortality and Freedom*, trans. Willard R. Trask (Princeton, N.J.: Princeton University Press, 1969), 241ff., situates these *cakras* as follows:

1. *Mūlādhāra*, at the base of the spinal column (*mūla* = root).
2. *Svādhisṭhāna*, at the base of the male genital organ (sacral plexus).
3. *Maṇipūra*, at the lumbar region, around the navel.
4. *Anāhata*, near the region of the heart (the *anāhata śabda* is the mystical sound heard by Yogis and found in Kabir).
5. *Viśuddha*, in the region of the throat.
6. *Ājñā*, situated between the eyebrows.
7. *Sahasrāra*, at the top of the skull.

See also *KVS*, 89ff.

The three *nāḍīs, iḍā, piṅgalā, and suṣumṇā* meet in the *ājñā-cakra*, the meeting place is itself called Triveni (or "Trikuti") upon analogy with Prayaga, the meeting place of the three sacred rivers Ganga, Yamuna, and Sarasvati. In the *Gorakṣa śataka*, "(the) One Hundred (verses) by the knowledge of which is surely brought about the highest state," verse 50, the concept is offered as follows:

> Through the *suṣumṇā* (she), aroused through union with fire, goes upwards, like a serpent, auspicious, gleaming like a filament of a lotus.

G. W. Briggs, *Gorakhnāth and the Kānphaṭa Yogīs* (1938; Delhi: Motilal Banarsidass, 1973), 284–304.

45. Peter Harvey, *An Introduction to Buddhism* (Cambridge: Cambridge University Press, 1990), 60–61. *Nibbāna* (*nirvāṇa*) is the third holy truth of the Buddha's first sermon. Peter Harvey (61) points out that *nibbāna* literally means "extinction" and is "the word used for the 'extinction' of a fire."

46. G. W. Briggs, 322. In the transcendent state of *samādhi* "the objective world of plurality and the experiencing ego are both completely merged in one Absolute Consciousness (or Super-Consciousness) which is the Absolute Truth or Reality or both" (A. K. Banerjea, 17).

47. A. K. Banerjea, 29ff.

48. A. K. Banerjea, 32. Cf. Hazariprasad Dvivedi, *Kabīr* (Delhi: Rājkamal Prakāśan, 1976), 37–44, for a fuller definition.

49. *GB, sabadi* 14.

50. Hazariprasad Dvivedi, *Nāth siddhõ kī bānīyā̃* (Kashi, India: Nāgrīpracāriṇī Sabhā, 1957), 9ff., et passim.

51. Hazariprasad Dvivedi, *Nāth siddhõ kī bānīyā̃*, introduction, 6. The nature of the "experience" (*paramanubhava*) suggested here is made more explicit in *GB, sabadi* 110:

> In the state of primal experience there is neither *nirati* nor *surati*;
> Neither renunciation nor worldliness,
> No old age, sickness nor death,
> No sound, not even *oṃ*.
> For, says, Gorakha, here you find
> *dvaitādvaita-vilakṣana-vāda*.

52. *Gorakṣa śataka*, 21; quoted in G. W. Briggs, 289.

53. *Haṭhayogapradīpikā* 2.42. I owe this reference to Dr. Parasnath Tiwari (personal correspondence). For a brief account of this text see G. W. Briggs, 253–54.

54. *GB, sabadi* 55. Translated by Dr Parasnath Tiwari (personal correspondence). The term *mana-unmana* is defined further in Parshuram Chaturvedi, *Kabīr sāhitya kī parakh* (Allahabad, India: Bhāratī Bhaṇḍār, 1972), 229–32, and in Charlotte Vaudeville, *Kabīr Granthāvalī (Dohā)* (Pondicherry, India: Institut Français d'Indologie, 1957), xvi–xvii.

55. *KG, sākhī* 29.23; Charlotte Vaudeville translation, *Kabīr I*, 295.

56. The silent *japa* or *ajapajāpa*. In its interiorized, meditative form it relates to the chanting of the Name and ultimately to Ram himself.

57. *Śabda*, "sound," "an authoritative verbal testimony," self-evident (*pramāṇika*). Related to *mantra, yantra, bīja* or *akṣara, nāda, anāhata, bindu*, and to *haṃsa, japa, oṃ*, etc.

Throughout Kabir both *surati* and *śabda* are, ultimately, mystical terms, working as either enabling conventions in verse (points of common reference that signify mystical paradox) or *constructs*, composite categories (organizing principles), that do not have any equivalent synonym in the natural world. W. H. McLeod in "Sikhism," 294–302, in A. L. Basham, ed., *A Cultural History of India* (Oxford: Clarendon Press, 1975), adds: "and there can be no doubt that in Kabir it was the mystical strain that predominated."

58. *GB, sabadi* 21. Cf. Madan Sahab, *Śabda vilās* (Varanasi, India: Acārya Gaddi, Baraiya, 1963), 152, where the following account of *śabda* is found:

> śabda akaṇḍa aura saba khaṇḍa
> sāra śabda garajai brahmaṇḍa
> The *śabda* alone is total, all else fragmentary,
> The *śabda*-essence thunders the *brahmarandhra*.

Note that the *sára śabda* ("*śabda*-essence") is employed here.

59. *GB, sabadi* 21.

60. *KG, caũtīsī ramainī*, 3.

61. *Sadgurū kabīr saheb kā sākhī granth* (Baroda, India: Siyābāgh, 1950), verse 14.12.8. Dr. Parasnath Tiwari's reference (personal correspondence).

62. Charlotte Vaudeville, *L'Invocation le Haripāṭh de Dñyāndev* (Paris: École Française d'Extrême-Orient, 1969), 21 and 57 for comparison with Kabir.

63. The controversy surrounding Namdev's dates is documented in Bhagirath Mishra and Rajnarayan Maurya, eds., *Sant nāmdev kī hindī padāvalī* (Poona, India: Poona Viśvavidyālaya, 1964), 9–40, and in Winand M. Callwaert and Mukund Lath, *The Hindī Padāvalī of Nāmdev* (Delhi: Motilal Banarsidass, 1989), 1–54. (This latter text is hereafter referred to as *Nāmdev*.) While Mishra and Maurya do not offer any dates of their own, it is clear from their analysis of the various theories advanced about Namdev's dates that they favor the traditional dates, 1270–1350.

64. *Nāmdev, padas* 14, 15; 150–52.

65. *Nāmdev, pada* 59; 176–77.

66. *Nāmdev, pada* 94; 199–200. Namdev uses a host of names for God. Among these are: *keśav, nārāyaṇ, rām, narharī, harī, viṭṭhal, gusāī, kṛṣṇa, gopāl, govind, banvārī, sāhab, sadgurū,* and *alakh*.

67. *Nāmdev, pada* 65; 182–83. Cf. also *pada* 99.

68. Mircea Eliade, 318, states that the followers of Gorakhnath employed a Tantric technique called *ulṭā sādhana* or *ujāna sādhana*, which was a process of "regression" or "going against the current" in which the Yogi attempted a complete reversal of all natural processes. See Linda Hess and Shukdev Singh, *The Bījak of Kabīr* (San Francisco: North Point Press, 1983), appendix A, for a lucid discussion of this phenomenon.

69. Mircea Eliade, 250.

70. Per Kvaerne, *An Anthology of Buddhist Tantric Songs* (Oslo: Norwegian Research Council, 1977), 60. Quoted by Linda Hess and Shukdev Singh, 138.

71. S. K. Adkar, *Hindī nirguṇ-kāvya kā prārambh aur nāmdev kī hindī kavitā* (Allahabad, India: Racnā Prakāśan, 1972), 142. See also P. D. Barthwal, *Traditions of Indian Mysticism: The Nirguna School of Hindi Poetry* (Delhi: Heritage Publishers, 1978), 301.

72. P. D. Barthwal, *Traditions of Indian Mysticism*, 301.

73. See Rosemary Colie, *Epidemica Paradoxica: The Renaissance Tradition of Paradox* (Princeton, N.J.: Princeton University Press, 1966).

74. Horst Ruthrof, "Negation: From Frege to Freud and Beyond," *Philosophy Today* 39.3–4 (Fall 1995), 220.

75. *Nāmdev, pada* 101.

76. P. D. Barthwal, *Traditions of Indian Mysticism,* 246. I have modified the translation. P. D. Barthwal adds, "[Sundardas was] the only educated person among perhaps, the whole lot of Nirguṇīs" (222).

77. See M. A. K. Halliday, *Language as Social Semiotic* (London: Edward Arnold, 1979), chapter 9.

78. Mircea Eliade, 250.

79. *Nāmdev, pada,* 39; 166.

80. *Lallā-Vakyānī or the Wise Sayings of Lāl Ded: A Mystic Poetess of Ancient Kashmir*, ed. and trans., with notes and vocabulary, George Grierson and Lionel D. Barnett (London: The Royal Asiatic Society, 1920).

81. This account of the history of Sufi literature is based on S. M. Pandey, *Madhyayugīn premākhyan* (Allahabad, India: Mitra Prakāśan, n.d.) and Annemarie Schimmel, *Classical Urdu Literature from the Beginning to Iqbāl*, vol. 8, fasc. 3 of *A History of Indian Literature*, ed. J. Gonda (Wiesbaden, Germany: Otto Harrassowitz, 1975).

82. *Padmāvat* was written in 947 Hijri (1540) in Avadhi, an Eastern dialectal variety of Khaṛhī Bolī. Jayasi employed the Persian Nasta'liq characters and "spelt each word rigorously as it was then pronounced." See Lakshmi Dhar, *Padumāvati: A Linguistic Study of the 16th Century Hindi (Avadhi)* (London: Luzac, 1949), ix.

83. Annemarie Schimmel, 134.

84. Charles S. J. White, "Sufism in Medieval Hindi Literature," *History of Religions* 5 (Summer 1965), 118.

85. Malik Muhammad Jayasi, *Padmāvat*, ed. Mataprasad Gupta (Allahabad, India: Bhāratī Bhaṇḍār, 1973), *chand* 7. Hereafter cited as *Padmāvat.* See also *The Padumāwati of Malik Muhammad Jaīsī,* ed. and trans. G. A. Grierson and Mahamahopadhyaya Sudharkara Dvivedi (Calcutta: The Asiatic Society of Bengal, 1896–1911) VI fasciculi. Edition to *chand* 286 only as publication was suspended upon the death of Dvivedi. The entire poem has 653 stanzas in all. I have used this edition for purposes of cross-checking the text.

86. Charles S. J. White, 119. Cf. Manjhan, *Madhumālti*, ed. Mataprasad Gupta (Allahabad, India: Mitra Prakāśan, 1961), *chand* 108, where Kumar Manohar undergoes a series of quite extraordinary emotional states that parallel the state of divine infatuation upon listening to the words of Madhumalti.

87. Charles S. J. White, 123.

88. *Padmāvat, chand* 95.

89. *Padmāvat, chand* 96.

90. Pandey, *Madhyayugīn premākhyan,* 125.

91. *Padmāvat, chand* 153.

92. "From the religious point of view," writes Charles S. J. White (121), "the experience of *viraha* corresponds to the disciplined purgation of the senses of the yogi or the follower of a religious ideal for whom the sensory world with all its temptations must be overcome before enlightenment can be achieved."

93. *Padmāvat, chand* 254.

94. *Padmāvat, chand* 214.

95. *Padmāvat, chand* 231.

96. Mircea Eliade, *The Sacred and the Profane*, trans. Willard R. Trask (New York: Harcourt, Brace and World, 1957), 11ff.

97. The essential correspondence between the cities and the states of mystical ascent that the hero undergoes in *Citrāvalī* may be presented as follows:

- Bhognagar → *nasūt*, state of ignorance and worldly pleasures.
- Gorakhpur → *malakūt*, heaven of the angels, "devaloka."
- Nehanagar → *zabarūt*, yogic discipline, abandonment of all impediments, total absorption in God.
- Rupanagar → *lāhūt* or *haqikat*, the final stage, oneness in the Absolute. The result of *bekhudī* or *ātmavismṛti* in the *sādhaka*.

98. Other points of interest are: the use of *advaita vedānta* by Jayasi especially his preference for *tat tvam asi* over *aham brahman asmi* (see stanza 216); the relationship between the guru and his disciple and, possibly, a thorough knowledge of Wahdat al-Wujud.

99. Quoted by S. M. Pandey, *Madhyayugīn premākhyan*, 19 and *Padmāvat*, Mataprasad Gupta's introduction, 58–59.

100. Charlotte Vaudeville, "La conception de l'amour divin chez Muhammad Jāyasī: *Virah* et *'ishq*," *Journal Asiatique* (1962), 351–67.

101. *Padmāvat*, Mataprasad Gupta's introduction, 62.

5. Desiring Selves, Undesirable Worlds

1. See, for instance, J. C. Ghosh's essay "Vernacular Literatures" in G. T. Garratt, ed., *The Legacy of India* (1937; Oxford: Clarendon Press, 1962), 369–93. At one point Ghosh (378) writes, "They [the vernacular literatures] never acquired the adult and civilized consciousness of Sanskrit, its high culture and intellectuality."

2. G. N. Devy, *After Amnesia: Tradition and Change in Indian Literary Criticism* (Bombay: Orient Longman, 1992), 124.

3. Bhalchandra Nemade, "The Revolt of the Underprivileged," in Jayant Lele, ed., *Tradition and Modernity in Bhakti Movements* (Leiden, Netherlands: E. J. Brill, 1981), 113–23.

4. Hazariprasad Dvivedi, *Kabīr* (Delhi: Rājkamal Prakāśan, 1976), 189. Hereafter *Kabīr (Dvivedi)*.

5. It must be added that important critics and scholars like Hazariprasad Dvivedi used "nativist" critical theory quite self-consciously as a means of political empowerment at the height of Indian nationalist struggles.

6. Eugenia Vanina, "The *Ardhakathanaka* by Banarsi Das: A Socio-cultural Study," *Journal of the Royal Asiatic Society* [third series] 5.2 (July 1995), 211–24.

7. G. H. Wescott, *Kabīr and the Kabīr Panth* (rpt. Calcutta: Susil Gupta, 1953); G. Grierson, *Modern Vernacular Literature of Hindustan* (Calcutta: Royal Asiatic Society, 1889); F. E. Keay, *Kabīr and His Followers* (Calcutta: Association Press, 1931); S. S. Das, ed., *Kabīr-Granthāvalī* (1928; Varanasi, India: Nāgrīpracāriṇī Sabhā, 1975) [Hereafter *KG (Das)*]; P. D. Barthwal, *Traditions of Indian Mysticism: The Nirguna School of Hindi Poetry* (Delhi: Heritage, 1978) [Hereafter *TIM*]; Mohan Singh, *Kabir: His Biography* (Lahore: Atma Ram and Sons, 1934); J. N. Farquhar, *An Outline of the Religious Literature of India* (1920; Delhi: Motilal Banarsidass, 1967); Kedarnath Dvivedi, *Kabīr aur kabīr-panth* (Prayag, India: Hindī Sāhitya Sammelan, 1965); M. P. Gupta, ed., *Kabīr-Granthāvalī* (Allahabad, India: Lokbhāratī Prakaśan, 1969) [Hereafter *KG (Gupta)*]; R. K. Varma, *Sant Kabīr* (1947; Allahabad: Sāhitya Bhavan, 1966); Parshuram Chaturvedi, *Kabīr sāhitya kī parakh* (Allahabad, India: Bhāratī Bhaṇḍār, 1972) [Hereafter *KSP*]; Parshuram Chaturvedi, *Uttarī bhārat kī sant-paramparā* (Allahabad, India: Bhāratī Bhaṇḍār, 1972); Charlotte Vaudeville, *Kabīr Granthāvalī (Dohā)* (Pondicherry, India: Institut Français d'Indologie, 1957); Charlotte Vaudeville, *Kabīr I* (Oxford: Clarendon Press, 1974) [Hereafter *Kabīr I*]; Linda Hess and Shukdev Singh, ed. and trans., *The Bījak of Kabīr* (San Francisco: North Point Press, 1983); Charlotte Vaudeville, *Kabīr-Vāṇī: Western Recension* (Pondicherry, India: Institut Français d'Indologie, 1982).

8. Parasnath Tiwari, *Kabīr-vāṇī-sudhā* (Allahabad, India: Rākā Prakāśan, 1976), 78. [Hereafter *KVS*].

9. Hazariprasad Dvivedi, *Nāth sampradāya* (Allahabad, India: Lokbhārati Prakāśan, 1981). See chapter 4 above.

10. For an examination of Buddhist influence on Kabir, see Omprakash, "Kabīr aur baudhmat," in Vijayendra Snatak, ed., *Kabīr* (Delhi: Rādhākṛṣṇa Prakāśan, 1970), 223–30. See also Omprakash, *Madhyayugīn kāvya vivecnātmak evam samikṣātmak nibandh* (Delhi: Arya Book Depot, 1973), especially 44–53.

11. *KSP*, 113–14: "Kabir's age was marked by the existence of an unusually complex state of social and religious affairs in Northern India. Theoretically, Hinduism, Islam, Buddhism, Jainism, Nath Yogi traditions, Shaktism, etc., were the dominant 'religions.' In actual fact, minor religious systems were on the ascendant with sham, hypocrisy, doubt and stupefaction quite prevalent. . . . Inevitably, therefore, Kabir opted for *sahaja-sādhnā* (the 'spontaneous' way) as the *mārga* ('path') to happiness."

12. Moti Singh, "Kabīr kī bhakti, āsthā aur sādhnā," in Vijayendra Snatak, 137.

13. Vijayendra Snatak, 142.

14. *Kabīr I*, 53.

15. See *Kabīr I*, 49ff. and Charlotte Vaudeville, *Étude sur les sources et la composi-*

tion du Rāmayāṇa de Tulsī-dās, Hindi trans. J. K. Balbir (Pondicherry, India: Institut Français d'Indologie, 1959), ix ff.; and S. M. Pandey, "Mirabai and her contributions to the Bhakti Movement," *History of Religions* 5.1 (1965) 54–73.

16. T. S. Eliot, "What Is Minor Poetry?" in T. S. Eliot, *On Poetry and Poets* (London: Faber and Faber, 1969), 39–52.

17. Parasnath Tiwari, ed., *Kabīr-Granthāvalī* (Prayag, India: Hindī Pariṣad, 1961), *pada* 129. Hereafter *KG.*

18. S. Shukla and R. Chaturvedi, eds., *Kabīr Granthāvalī* (Lucknow, India: Prakāśan Kendra, n.d.), gloss *cilakāī pīra,* "pain." This is followed by Laxman Prasad Mishra in his Italian translation *Mistici Indiani Medievali* (Turin, Italy: Unione Tipografico-editrice, 1971), 350, verse 50. *KG (Gupta),* 176, however, glosses *cilakai pira* "child." Ramchandra Varma in his dictionary, *Mānak hindī koś* (Allahabad, India: Sāhitya Bhavan, 1962), 2:254, has the following entry: *cilkā = navjāt śiṣu* ("a newly born child").

19. *KG, pada* 53.

20. *Bhagavadgītā* 2.20.

21. *KG, sākhī* 8.6; *Kabīr I,* 196.

22. Cf. *pada* 194, 2:

> The jar in the water, inside outside water;
> The jar breaks, the water mingles within and without.
> What means this truth, can you tell me scholar?

For an examination of these metaphors in the context of the Nath Yogis generally, see chapter 4.

This metaphor occurs quite commonly in Kabir and in *sant* literature generally. For further analogies see *KG, sākhī* 8. 6–7. Interestingly enough the *Alakhbānī* (or *Ruśdnāma*) of Shekh Abd-ul-Quddus Gangohi (1456–1537), a text that, as we have seen in chapter 4, manifests distinctive Nath Yogi and Sufi convergences, uses the same set of symbols quite profusely. One of Quddus's *caupads* reads (Text, 13):

> As the jar lies still in the water
> So the phenomenal world exists in God.
> Distinctions of outer and inner are meaningless
> As multiplicity merges into the One.

See chapter 4 above for a fuller examination of Quddus's text.

23. See Bhagirath Mishra and Rajnarayan Maurya, eds., *Sant nāmdev kī hindī padāvalī* (Poona, India: Poona Viśvavidyālaya, 1964), *pada* 150, 3:

> As the wave, froth and bubble mingle in the endless sea,
> So the various forms of the world merge into him (from whom they emanate).

24. Mansur al-Hallaj's claim, Anā'l-ḥaqq—"I am the Truth" or even "I am God"—was clearly unacceptable even to the Sufis. See R. C. Zaehner, *Hindu and Muslim Mysticism* (New York: Schocken Books, 1969), 14.

25. *Kabīr (Dvivedi),* 136–37.

26. *KG, padas* 159–65; *sākhī* 31. The word *sākhī* is used here to denote all the 28 *dohās*.

27. See George Thibaut's invaluable introduction to his edition (and translation) of *The Vedānta Sūtras of Bādarāyaṇa with the Commentary by Śaṅkara* (1890/1896; New York: Dover Publications, 1962), 2 vols.

28. *KG, sākhī* 31. 25, 26; *Kabīr I*, 304.

29. In the Vedic tradition *haṃsa* symbolizes the Supreme Being. As a meditative word or *japa, haṃ-sa[ḥ]* can be reversed to *so'ham* ("I am He"), thereby making it into a mystical word. See *Kabīr I*, 129n 3.

30. The transience of saṁsara is more emphatically offered in verses written in the style of Kabir, and attributed to Kabir by the Kabir-panthis. One of the more common of these poems is the following taken from a popular "bazaar" edition of Kabir:

> Why live, this country is foreign to me.
> This world is a crumpled sheet of paper, raindrops and it's gone.
> This world is an unkempt garden in the throes of inescapable death.
> This world is dry faggot and thorns, ready to flare up any moment.
> Says Kabir, listen fellow men, the name of the Lord is the only repose.

31. Ramkumar Varma, *Kabīr kā rahasyavād* (1929; Allahabad, India: Sāhitya Bhavan, 1972), 72.

32. John Keats in a letter to George and Thomas Keats, 21 December 1817, wrote: "I mean *Negative Capability*, that is, when man is capable of being in uncertainties, mysteries, doubts, without any irritable reaching after fact and reason." Hyder Edward Rollins, ed., *Letters of John Keats*, 2 vols. (Cambridge, Mass.: Harvard University Press, 1958). A word of caution: behind this formulation lies an essentially romantic theory of poetics with a strong Truth-Imagination-Poetry "trinity." As such no outright transference should be attempted to explain Kabir's own poetry. The comparison is a purely formal one to demonstrate underlying structural similarities and not to affirm a Romantic reading of verse. Many Indian critics, especially those writing in English, have suffered from a kind of retrospective reading of Indian texts through English romanticism, and in the process have even suggested that Indian poetics is itself essentially "romantic." The latter problem emerges in an otherwise excellent study of Sanskrit poetics: S. K. De, *Sanskrit Poetics as a Study of Aesthetic* (Berkeley and Los Angeles: University of California Press, 1963), with notes by Edwin Gerow.

33. *KG, sākhī* 31. 28:

> I'll turn desire into fuel,
> I'll burn this body into ashes:
> In this way alone will the Yogi's wanderings come to an end—
> And I shall be born again without a name.

34. *KG, pada* 163.

35. *KG, pada* 22. *Padas* 20–26 are collected under *nāū mahimā* ("the greatness of the name") in *KG*.

36. *Kabīr I*, 140ff.

37. *KG, pada* 27, 2.

38. *KG, pada* 32.

39. *KG, pada* 31, *ṭeka.*

Cf. Krishna's words to Arjuna in the *Bhagavadgītā* 2.45:

> The Vedas are confined by the three *guṇas*
> Transcend them, Arjuna.

In *padas* 195 and 199 this *cauthai pada* ("the fourth state", *nistraiguṇyāvasthā*) is called *hari pada* which Tiwari (*KVS*, 257) glosses as "beyond the third state," "*sahaja* state" or *bhakti bhāva.*

40. *KG, sākhī* 29.6.

41. See Parasnath Tiwari, "Kabir's Devotionalism," trans. Vijay Mishra in *Bhakti Studies*, eds. G. M. Bailey and I. Kesarcodi-Watson (New Delhi: Sterling, 1992), 159–81.

42. *TIM*, 147ff. 294–95.

43. *KSP*, 191–93.

44. P. D. Barthwal, *Gorakh-bānī* (Prayag, India: Hindī Sāhitya Sammelan, 1960), 186–202. Hereafter *GB*.

45. *GB*, verses 107–8; 199–200.

46. Note that in *KG, pada* 47, *surati* is read as *śruti* or "unauthored texts." Cf. *KG (Gupta)*, 171–74.

47. *KG (Das), pada* 206.

48. See, for instance, *KG, pada* 54, 1:

> O Ram, if you push me away from you
> who else is my savior?
> You exist in all as one,
> why do you (then) beguile me?

The *KG* ends with a *dohā* (*sākhī* 34.3) in which the union in Ram/Rama is again presented within a sexual structure:

> "Easily, easily," indeed, they all vanished:
> sons, riches, wife, sensual desires . . .
> So now in intimate union
> is the servant Kabīr with Rām.
>
> (*Kabīr I*, 310)

49. See Ronald W. Hepburn, "Poetry and Religious Belief," in Stephen E. Toulmin, Ronald W. Hepburn, and Alasdair MacIntyre, *Metaphysical Beliefs* (London: SCM Press, 1970), 75–156.

50. William Shakespeare, *Anṭony and Cleopatra*, V.ii.294–95.

51. *The "Dhvanyāloka" of Ānandavardhana with the "Locana" of Abhinavagupta*, ed. and trans. Daniel H. H. Ingalls, Jeffrey Moussaieff Masson, and M. V. Patwardhan (Cambridge, Mass.: Harvard University Press, 1990).

52. *Mammaṭācarya Kāvyaprakāśa*, ed. Acarya Viveshvar (Varanasi, India: Jñāna-

maṇḍal Limited, 1960). See also S. K. De, *History of Sanskrit Poetics* (Calcutta: Firma KLM, 1976).

53. Bhavabhuti, *Uttararāmacarita* 3. 31.

54. *KG, pada* 70.

55. *Vālmīki Rāmāyaṇa* (Baroda Critical Edition), ed. G. H. Bhatt et al. (Baroda: Oriental Institute, 1951–1975), I.2.14: "Because you killed one of the pair of *krauñcas* during the height of their love-play, Nishada you shall not live long."

56. *The Rāmāyaṇa of Vālmīki, Vol. I: Bālakaṇḍa*, eds. and trans. Robert P. Goldman and Sally J. Sutherland (Princeton, N.J.: Princeton University Press, 1984), I.2.17: "Fixed in metrical quarters, each with a like number of syllables, and fit for the accompaniment of stringed and percussion instruments, the utterance that I produced in this access of *śoka*, grief, shall be called *śloka*, poetry, and nothing else."

57. References to a number of these birds may be found in Kabir's *sākhīs* on *prema viraha* (*sākhī* series 2 in *KG*). The pathetic cries of the water birds *kumjā (krauñca) (dohā* 2) and *cakavī* (female of *cakavā) (dohā* 4), the call of the *papīhā (cātaka*, the "rainbird") (*dohā* 48) reinforce the longings of the *virahiṇī* who exclaims (*dohā* 40):

> Crush the *virahiṇī* to paste
> or show yourself to her!
> This eternal scorching
> I find unacceptable.

The loving embrace of Shakuntala and Dushyanta is interrupted by a voice that proclaims, "O female–cakava, bid farewell to your mate; the night is at hand" (Kalidasa, *Śakuntalā*, III).

58. *KG, sākhī* 2.53.

59. Charlotte Vaudeville, "Rāmāyaṇa Studies I: The *Krauñca-vadha* episode in the Vālmīki *Rāmāyaṇa*," *Journal of the American Oriental Society* 83 (1963), 334.

60. Charlotte Vaudeville, *Au cabaret de l'amour: Par Kabīr* (Paris: Gallimard, 1959), 219.

61. See Julius Evola, *Le Yoga tantrique* (Paris?: Fayard, 1971), 258–69, and Heinrich Zimmer, *Myths and Symbols in Indian Art and Civilization* (Washington, D.C.: Pantheon Books, 1946), 49–50.

62. *KG, pada* 11.

63. Ramkumar Varma, 50.

64. Shukdev Singh, ed., *Kabīr-Bījak* (Allahabad, India: Nīlābh Prakāśan, 1972), *ramainī* 6.82.

65. *KG, pada* 106.

66. Ramkumar Varma, 49.

67. *KVS*, 87.

68. Charlotte Vaudeville, "La conception de l'amour divin chez Muhammad Jāyasī: *Virah* et *'ishq*," *Journal Asiatique* (1962), 362.

69. The French structuralist A. J. Greimas has written about the six formal classes of *actants*, defined by their narrative functions: Subject, Object, Sender, Receiver, Opponent, Helper. My point here is that devotional verse always has an implied *actant* in the form of God who can occupy any or all these functions at any given time. In these devotional poems of love-longing the status of the self/bhakta is constantly modified by his/her shifting position vis-à-vis the Object (i.e. God), such that as an *actant* he/she oscillates between the oppositions that govern Greimas's classification. See A. J. Greimas, *Sémantique structurale* (Paris: Larousse, 1966).

70. Mammata, *Kāvyaprakāśa*, 4:29–44. The division into eight rasas goes back to the great treatise on drama, the *Naṭyaśāstra*, with which all histories of Indian poetics begin. See also *The Rāmāyaṇa of Vālmīki* I.4.8: "The two disciples (Kusha and Lava) sang the poem, which is replete with all the poetic sentiments: the humorous, the erotic, the piteous, the wrathful, the heroic, the terrifying, the loathsome, and the rest."

71. Rupa Gosvamin, *Bhaktirasāmṛtasindhu*, ed. Acarya Viveshvar, with an introduction by Vijayendra Snatak (Delhi: Delhi Viśvavidyālaya, 1963). Gosvami's text abounds with numerological equations based on a factor of four. Thus there are four regions, four oceans, four "waves" or sections to the book, and so on. The number of rasas is twice the number of regions, that is eight, plus bhakti, which brings the total number of rasas to nine.

72. *Kabīr I*, 146.

73. *Kabīr I, sākhī* 2.9

74. *Kabīr I, sākhī* 11.14

75. *KG, pada* 13. The overall design of the poem resembles the *harigītika* (lit., "song of the Lord") form in Indian poetics. Two recensions (MSS collections *Dā* and *Nā*) call it a *rāga kedārau* ("kedara" = a field full of water); a third *Śabe* calls it a *biraha-prema* ("a song of love-longing"). See Vijay Mishra, "Two Truths are Told: Tagore's Kabīr," *South Asia* [new series] 1.2 (September 1978), 80–90 (reprinted in Karine Schomer and W. H. Mcleod, eds., *The Sants* [Berkeley, Calif.: Berkeley Religious Studies Series, 1987], 167–80) for a discussion of this poem with reference to the problems of literary translation.

76. *Kabīr I*, 128.

77. See Martin Buber, *I and Thou*, trans. Walter Kaufmann (Edinburgh: T. and T. Clark, 1970).

78. S. N. Dasputa, *Hindu Mysticism* (1927; New York: Frederick Ungar, 1977), 123. Dasgupta's division of mysticism into five basic types (sacrificial, Upanishadic, Yogic, Buddhist, and bhakti) is followed by R. C. Zaehner, *Hindu and Muslim Mysticism* (London: Athlone Press, 1960).

79. W. D. O'Flaherty, *Asceticism and Eroticism in the Mythology of Śiva* (Oxford: Oxford University Press, 1973).

80. Paul Ricoeur, "Toward a Hermeneutic of the Idea of Revelation," *Harvard Theological Review* 70.1–2 (January–April 1977), 1–37.

81. All these examples have been taken from the collection of *padas* entitled *prema* (*KG, padas* 5–19).

82. *KG, pada* 15.

83. Mircea Eliade, *Yoga: Immortality and Freedom* (Princeton, N.J.: Princeton University Press, 1969), 250.

84. *Kabīr I*, 147.

Conclusion

1. Arthur Schopenhauer, *The World as Will and Representation*, trans. E. F. J. Payne (New York: Dover, 1969), 1:417.

2. *Kabīr Granthāvalī*, ed. Parasnath Tiwari (Prayag, India: Hindī Pariṣad, 1961), *sākhī* 1.28. Charlotte Vaudeville translation (*Kabīr I*, Oxford: Clarendon Press, 1974, 158).

3. Arthur Schopenhauer, 1:419.

4. Arthur Schopenhauer, 1:417.

5. Arthur Schopenhauer, 1:532.

6. Immanuel Kant, *The Critique of Judgement*, trans. James Creed Meredith (Oxford: Clarendon Press, 1986), 98.

7. Paul Crowther, *The Kantian Sublime* (Oxford: Clarendon Press, 1989), 41.

8. David L. Haberman, *Acting as a Way to Salvation* (New York: Oxford University Press, 1988), 20–21.

SELECT BIBLIOGRAPHY

Primary Texts

Alakhbānī [Shekh Abd-ul-Quddus Gangohi's *Ruśdnāma*]. Ed. S. A. A. Rizvi and S. Zaidi. Aligarh, India: Bhārat Prakāśan Mandir, 1971.

Bhagavad-gītā. Ed. and trans. R. C. Zaehner. Oxford: Oxford University Press, 1975.

The Bhagavadgītā in the Mahābhārata. Ed. and trans. J. A. B. van Buitenen. Chicago: University of Chicago Press, 1981.

Śrīmadbhāgavatamahāpurāṇam. Ed. Lal Muni. Gorakhpur, India: Gita Press, 1942. 2 vols.

Śrīmad Bhāgavata Mahāpurāṇa. Ed. and trans. C. L. Goswami and M. A. Shastri. Gorakhpur, India: Gita Press, 1971.

Bhavabhuti Uttararāmacarita. Ed. P. V. Kane. Trans. C. N. Joshi. Delhi: Motilal Banarsidass, 1971.

The "Dhvanyāloka" of Ānandavardhana with the "Locana" of Abhinavagupta. Ed. and trans. Daniel H. H. Ingalls, Jeffrey Moussaieff Masson, and M. V. Patwardhan. Cambridge, Mass.: Harvard University Press, 1990.

The Divine Poems of John Donne. Ed. Helen Gardner. Oxford: Clarendon Press, 1969.

Gorakhbānī. Ed. P. D. Barthwal. Prayag, India: Hindī Sāhitya Sammelan, 1960.

Śrī Guru Granth Sahib Jī. Amritsar, India: Bhai Jvahar Singh Kripal Singh & Co., n.d. In Devanagari script.

The Works of George Herbert. Ed. F. E. Hutchinson. 1941; Oxford: Clarendon Press, 1972.

Love Song of the Dark Lord: Jayadeva's "Gītagovinda." Ed. and trans. Barbara Stoler Miller. New York: Columbia University Press, 1977.

Kabīr-Bījak. Ed. Shukdev Singh. Allahabad, India: Nīlābh Prakāśan, 1972.

Kabīr-Granthāvalī. Ed. Parasnath Tiwari. Prayag, India: Hindī Pariṣad, 1961.

Kabīr-Granthāvalī. Ed S. S. Das. 1928; Varanasi, India: Nāgrīpracāriṇī Sabhā, 1975.

Kabīr-Granthāvalī. Ed. M. P. Gupta. Allahabad, India: Lokbhāratī Prakāśan, 1969.

Sant Kabīr. Ed. R. K. Varma. 1947; Allahabad, India: Sāhitya Bhavan, 1966.

Kabīr-Vāṇī. Ed. Charlotte Vaudeville. Pondicherry, India: Institut Français d'Indologie, 1982.

Madhumālti [of Mañjhan]. Ed. Mataprasad Gupta, Allahabad, India: Mitra Prakāśan, 1961.

Mahābhārata [Book VI: Bhiṣmaparvan]. Ed. S. K. Belvakar and P. L. Vaidya. Poona, India: Bhandarkar Institute, 1947. [Poona Critical Edition of the *Mahābhārata* (1944–59)].

The Mahābhārata [Books 1–5]. Trans. J. A. B. van Buitenen. Chicago: University of Chicago Press, 1973–78.

Mammaṭācarya Kāvyaprakāśa. Ed. Acharya Viveshvar. Varanasi, India: Jñānamaṇḍal Limited, 1960.

Mīrāṃbāī kī padāvalī. Ed. Parshuram Chaturvedi. Prayag, India: Hindī Sāhitya Sammelan, 1976.

Sant nāmdev kī hindī padāvalī. Ed. Bhagirath Mishra and Rajnarayan Maurya. Poona, India: Poona Viśvavidyālaya, 1964.

The Hindī Padāvalī of Nāmdev. Ed. and trans. Winand M. Callewaert and Mukund Lath. Delhi: Motilal Banarsidass, 1989.

The Bhakti Sūtras of Nārada. Ed. and trans. Nandlal Sinha. 1911; rpt. New York: AMS Press, 1974.

Aphorisms on the Gospel of Divine Love or Nārada Bhakti Sūtras. Ed. and trans. Swāmī Tyāgīśānanda. Madras, India: Śrī Ramakrishna Math, n.d.

Padmāvat [of Malik Muhammad Jāyasī]. Ed. Mataprasad Gupta. Allahabad, India: Bhāratī Bhaṇḍar, 1973.

Rāmacaritamānasa [of Tulsīdās]. Ed. S. N. Chaube. Kashi: Nāgrīpracāriṇī Sabhā, 1948.

Rāmānuja's Gītabhāṣya with the Tatparyancandrikā of Venkatanātha. Ed. V. G. Apte. Bombay: Ānandāśrama Press, 1923. Ānandāśrama Sanskrit Series, vol. 92.

Rūpa Gosvāmin, *Bhaktirasāmṛtasindhu*. Ed. Acharya Viveshvar with an introduction by Vijayendra Snatak. Delhi: Delhi Viśvavidyālaya, 1963.

Śāṇḍilya Bhakti-Sūtra with Bhakticandrikā by Nārāyaṇa Tīrtha. Ed. Baladeva Upadhyaya. Varanasi, India: Varanaseya Sanskrit Viśvavidyālaya, 1967.

Śāṇḍilya-sūtram with the commentary of Shvapneshvara. Ed. and trans. Nandlal Sinha. Allahabad, India: The Panini Office, 1918.

Śaṅkara Gītābhāṣya. Ed. V. G. Apte. 3rd ed. Bombay: Ānandāśrama Press, 1936. Ānandāśrama Sanskrit Series, vol. 34.

Sūrsāgar. Ed. Nanddulare Vajpeyi. Varanasi, India: Nāgrīpracāriṇī Sabhā, 1972/1976. 2 vols.

Vālmīki Rāmāyaṇa [Book I: Bālakaṇḍa]. Eds. G. H. Bhatt and U. P. Shah. Baroda, India: Oriental Institute, 1951. [Baroda Critical Edition of the *Rāmāyaṇa* (1951–1975)].

The Rāmāyaṇa of Vālmīki [Volume I: Bālakaṇḍa]. Intr. and trans. Robert P. Goldman. Annotation by Robert P. Goldman and Sally J. Sutherland. Princeton, N.J.: Princeton University Press, 1984.

Secondary Texts

Abrams, M. H., ed. *Literature and Belief.* New York: Columbia University Press, 1958.

Adkar, S. K. *Hindī nirguṇ-kāvya kā prārambh aur nāmdev kī hindī kavitā*. Allahabad, India: Racnā Prakāśan, 1972.

Affifi, A. E. *The Mystical Philosophy of Muhyid Din Ibnul 'Arabī*. Cambridge: Cambridge University Press, 1939.

Agraval, Maya. *Kabīr-vāṇī-sudhā*. Delhi: Kalā Mandir, 1978.

Ahmad, Aijaz. "The Politics of Literary Postcoloniality." *Race & Class* 36.3 (1995), 1–20.

Alberuni's India. Trans. and ed. Edward C. Sachau. 1888; New Delhi: S. Chand, 1964.

Allchin, F. R., trans. *Tulsīdās Kavitāvalī*. London: George Allen and Unwin, 1964.

———. "The Place of Tulsī Dās in North Indian Devotional Tradition." *The Journal of the Royal Asiatic Society of Great Britan and Ireland* (1966), 123–40.

———. "The Reconciliation of *Jñāna*, and *Bhakti* in *Rāmacaritamānasa*" *Religious Studies* 12 (March 1976), 81–91.

Allison, W. L. *The Sadhs*. Calcutta: Y.M.C.A., 1935.

Althusser, Louis. *Essays on Ideology*. London: Verso, 1984.

Andrae, Tor. *Mohammed the Man and His Faith*. New York: Barnes and Noble, 1935.

Arberry, A. J., trans. *Muslim Saints and Mystics* [Episode from the Tadhkirat al-Auliya' by Farid al-Din Attar]. London: Routledge and Kegan Paul, 1966.

———, trans. *Mystical Poems of Rumi*. Chicago: University of Chicago Press, 1968.

———, trans. *A Sufi Martyr: The Apologia of 'Ain al-Qudāt al-Hamadhānī*. London: George Allen & Unwin, 1969.

———. *Sufism: An Account of the Mystics of Islam*. 1950; London: Unwin, 1979.

Archer, W. G. *The Loves of Krishna: In Indian Painting and Poetry*. London: George Allen and Unwin, 1957.

Arendt, Hannah. *The Human Condition*. Chicago: University of Chicago Press, 1974).

Bagchi, P. C. "The Sandhābhāṣā and Sandhāvacana." *Indian Historical Quarterly* 6.2 (1930), 389–96.

———. *Dohākoṣa*. Calcutta: Calcutta Sanskrit Series, 1938.

Bailey, G. M. "Notes on the Worship of Brahma in Ancient India." *Annali dell'Institute Orientale di Napoli* 39 [n.s. 29] (1979), 149–70.

———. "Secular and Religious in Indian Literature: A Comparison of Writings on the Theme of Love in the *Gītagovinda* and the *Caurapañcāśika*." *South Asia* [new series] 4.1 (June 1981), 1–14.

———. *The Mythology of Brahmā*. Delhi: Oxford University Press, 1983.

———. *Materials for the Study of Ancient Indian Ideologies: Pravṛtti and Nivṛtti*. Turin, Italy: Pubblicazioni di Indologica Taurinensia, 1985.

———. "For a New Study of the Vāmana Purāṇa." *Indo-Iranian Journal* 29 (1986), 1–16.

———. "The Semantics of Bhakti in the Vāmāṇa Purāṇa." *Rivista degli Studi Orientali*, vol. 62, Fasc. 1–4. Roma: Bardi Editore, 1989, 25–57.

Bailey, G. M., and I. Kesarcodi-Watson, eds. *Bhakti Studies*. New Delhi: Sterling, 1992.

Bakhtin, Mikhail. *The Dialogic Imagination*. Translated by Caryl Emerson and Michael Holquist. Austin: University of Texas Press, 1981.

Banerjea, A. K. *Philosophy of Gorakhnath with Goraksha-Vacana-Sangraha*. Gorakhpur, India: Mahant Dig Vijai Nath Trust, 1961?).

Barthwal, P. D. *Hindī kāvya mẽ nirguṇ sampradāya*. Lucknow, India: Avadh, 1950.

———. *Gorakh-bānī*. Prayag, India: Hindi Sāhitya Sammelan, 1960.

———. *Traditions of Indian Mysticism: The Nirguna School of Hindi Poetry*. Delhi: Heritage, 1978.

Barz, Richard. *The Bhakti Sect of Vallabhācārya*. Faridabad, India: Thomson Press, 1976. Australian National University Faculty of Asian Studies Oriental Monograph Series, no. 18.

Basham, A. L. *The Wonder That Was India*. London: Sidgwick and Jackson, 1967.

———. ed. *A Cultural History of India*. Oxford: Clarendon Press, 1975.

Beame, Wendel Charles. *Myth, Cult and Symbols in Śākta Hinduism*. Leiden, Netherlands: E. J. Brill, 1977.

Beardsley, Monroe C. "The Metaphorical Twist." *Philosophy and Phenomenological Research* 22 (1962), 293–307.

Bernstein, Richard J., ed. *Habermas and Modernity*. Cambridge: Polity Press, 1985.

Bhagade, Pandit Raghunath Madhava. *Jñāneśvari*. Prayag, India: Indian Press, 1955.

Bhandarkar, R. G. *Vaiṣṇavism, Śaivism and Minor Religious Systems*. 1913; Varanasi, India: Indological Book House, 1965.

Bharati, Agehananda. *The Tantric Tradition*. Garden City, N.Y.: Anchor Books, 1970.

Bhattacharya, Deben. *Love Songs of Chandidas*. London: George Allen and Unwin, 1967.

Biardeau, Madeleine. *Hinduism: The Anthropology of a Civilization.* Translated by Richard Nice. Delhi: Oxford University Press, 1989.

Bolle, Kees, trans. *The Bhagavadgītā.* Berkeley: University of California Press, 1979.

Briggs, G. W. *Gorakhnāth and the Kānphaṭa Yogīs.* 1938; Delhi: Motilal Banarsidass, 1973.

Brockington, J. L. "Religious Attitudes in Vālmīki's *Rāmāyaṇa.*" *The Journal of the Royal Asiatic Society of Great Britain and Ireland* (1976), 108–29.

———. *Righteous Rāma: The Evolution of an Epic.* Delhi: Oxford University Press, 1984.

Brown, John P. *The Darvishes or Oriental Spiritualism.* 1868; London: Frank Cass, 1968.

Bryant, Kenneth, E. *Poems to the Child-God.* Berkeley: University of California Press, 1978.

Buber, Martin. *I and Thou.* Translated by Walter Kaufmann. Edinburgh: T. and T. Clark, 1970.

Buckley, Vincent. *Poetry and the Sacred.* London: Chatto and Windus, 1968.

Bühler, G., trans. *The Laws of Manu.* Sacred Books of the East Series. 1886; Delhi: Motilal Banarsidass, 1975.

Bulke, Father Kamil. *Rāmkathā.* Prayag Viśvavidyālaya, Prayag, India: Hindī Pariṣad, 1950.

Burke, Edmund. *A Philosophical Enquiry into the Origin of Our Ideas of the Sublime and Beautiful.* Edited by J. T. Boulton. Notre Dame, Ind.: University of Notre Dame Press, 1968.

Burrow, T. *The Sanskrit Language.* London: Faber & Faber, 1977.

Butcher, S. H. *Aristotle's Theory of Poetry and Fine Art.* 1894; New York: Dover, 1951.

Callewaert, Winand M. *The Sarvāṅgi of the Dādūpanthī Rajab.* Louvain: Katholicke Universiteit, 1978. Orientalia Lovaniensia Analecta 4.

Carman, John Braisted. *The Theology of Rāmānuja: An Essay in Interpretation.* New Haven, Conn.: Yale University Press, 1974.

Carpenter, J. Estlin. *Theism in Medieval India.* 1921; Delhi: Oriental Books Reprint, 1977.

Caton, Steven C. *"Peaks of Yemen I Summon": Poetry as Cultural Practice in a North Yemeni Tribe.* Berkeley: University of California Press, 1990.

Chari, Krishna V. "Decorum as a Critical Concept in Indian and Western Poetics." *Journal of Aesthetics and Art Criticism* 26 (1967–68), 53–63.

———. "The Nature of Poetic Truth: Some Indian Views." *The British Journal of Aesthetics* 19.3 (Summer 1979), 213–23.

Chaturvedi, Parshuram, ed. *Hindī sāhitya kā bṛhat itihās: Bhaktikāl* [*Nirguṇ bhakti*]. Varanasi, India: Nāgrīpracāriṇī Sabhā, 1962. Vol. 4.

———. *Sūfi-kāvya saṃgrah.* Prayag, India: Hindī Sāhitya Sammelan, 1965.

———. *Uttarī bhārat kī sant-paramparā.* Allahabad, India : Bhāratī Bhaṇḍār, 1972.

———. *Kabīr sāhitya kī parakh.* Allahabad, India: Bhāratī Bhaṇḍār, 1972.

Chaturvedi, Parshuram and Mahendra. *Kabīr koś*. Allahabad, India: Smṛti Prakāśan, 1973.

Christie, E. "Indian Philosophers on Poetic Imagination (*Pratibhā*)." *Journal of Indian Philosophy* 7 (June 1979), 153–207.

Clifford, James. *The Predicament of Culture*. Cambridge, Mass.: Harvard University Press, 1988.

Coburn, Thomas B. "The Study of Purāṇas and the Study of Religion." *Religious Studies* 16.3 (September 1980), 341–52.

———. "'Scripture' in India: Towards a Typology of the Word in Hindu Life." *Journal of the American Academy of Religion* 52 (September 1984), 435–59.

Coleridge, Samuel Taylor. *Biographia Literaria*. Ed. J. Shawcross. 1907; Oxford: Clarendon Press, 1969.

Colie, Rosemary. *Epidemica Paradoxica: The Renaissance Tradition of Paradox*. Princeton, N.J.: Princeton University Press, 1966.

Collins, Joseph Burns. *Christian Mysticism in the Elizabethan Age*. Baltimore, Md.: Johns Hopkins University Press, 1940.

Comans, Michael. "The Question of the Importance of Samādhi in Modern and Classical Advaita Vedānta." *Philosophy East & West* 43.1 (January 1993), 19–38.

Corbin, Henry. *Creative Imagination in the Ṣūfism of Ibn 'Arabī*. Translated by Ralph Manheim. London: Routledge and Kegan Paul, 1969.

Crowther, Paul. *The Kantian Sublime: From Morality to Art*. Oxford: Clarendon Press, 1989.

Danielou, Alain. *Hindu Polytheism*. New York: Bollingen Foundation, 1964.

Dasgupta, S. B. *An Introduction to Tantric Buddhism*. Calcutta: University of Calcutta, 1974.

———. *Obscure Religious Cults*. Calcutta: Firma K. L. M., 1976.

Dasgupta, S. N. *A History of Indian Philosophy*. 1922; Delhi: Motilal Banarsidass, 1975. 5 vols.

———. *Hindu Mysticism*. 1927; New York: Frederick Ungar, 1977.

de Bolla, Peter. *The Discourse of the Sublime: History, Aesthetics and the Subject*. Oxford: Basil Blackwell, 1989.

de Man, Paul. *Blindness and Insight. Essays in the Rhetoric of Contemporary Criticism*. London: Methuen, 1983.

——— *Aesthetic Ideology*. Introduction by Andrzej Warminski. Minneapolis: University of Minnesota Press, 1996.

de Sales, St. Francis. *Introduction to the Devout Life*. Translated by John K. Ryan. New York: Image Books, 1972.

De, Sushil Kumar. *Early History of the Vaiṣṇava Faith and Movement in Bengal*. Calcutta: Firma K. L. M., 1961.

———. *Sanskrit Poetics as a Study of Aesthetic.* With notes by Edwin Gerow. Berkeley and Los Angeles: University of California Press, 1963.

———. *History of Sanskrit Poetics.* Calcutta: Firma K. L. M., 1976.

———. *Some Problems of Sanskrit Poetics.* Calcutta: Firma K. L. M., 1981.

Derrida, Jacques. *Speech and Phenomena and Other Essays on Husserl's Theory of Signs.* Translated by David B. Allison. Evanston, Ill.: Northwestern University Press, 1973.

———. *Margins of Philosophy.* Translated by Alan Bass. Chicago: University of Chicago Press, 1982.

———. *The Truth in Painting.* Translated by Geoff Bennington and Ian McLeod. Chicago: University of Chicago Press, 1987.

Devasenapathi, V. A. *Śaiva Siddhānta—As Expounded in the Śivajñānasiddhiyar and Its Six Commentaries.* Madras, India: University of Madras, 1966.

Devy, G. N. *After Amnesia: Tradition and Change in Indian Literary Criticism.* Bombay: Orient Longman, 1992.

Dhar, Lakshmi. *Padumāvati: A Linguistic Study of the 16th Century Hindi (Avadhi).* London: Luzac, 1949.

Dhavamony, Mariasusai. *Love of God According to Śaiva Siddhānta.* Oxford: Clarendon Press, 1971.

Dimmitt, Cornelia, and J. A. B. van Buitenen, eds. & trans. *Classical Hindu Mythology: A Reader in the Sanskrit Purāṇas.* Philadelphia: Temple University Press, 1978.

Dimock, Edward C. Jr. *The Place of the Hidden Moon.* Chicago: University of Chicago Press, 1966.

Dimock, Edward C. Jr., E. Gerow, C. Naim, A. Ramanujan, G. Roadarmel, and J. A. B. van Buitenen. *The Literatures of India.* Chicago: University of Chicago Press, 1978.

Dissanayake, Wimal, ed. *Narratives of the Self: Self-Making in China, India, and Japan.* Minneapolis: University of Minnesota Press, 1996.

Doniger, Wendy. "Rationalizing the Irrational Other: 'Orientalism' and the *Laws of Manu.*" *New Literary History* 23.1 (Winter 1992), 25–43.

Dorsch, T. S., ed. and trans. *Classical Literary Criticism: Aristotle, Horace, Longinus.* Harmondsworth, U.K.: Penguin Books, 1965.

Dumezil, George. *The Destiny of a King.* Translated by Alf Hiltebeitel. Chicago: University of Chicago Press, 1973.

Dumont, Louis. "World Renunciation in Indian Religions." *Contributions to Indian Sociology* 4 (1960), 33–62.

Durkheim, Émile. *The Elementary Forms of the Religious Life.* 1915; London: George Allen & Unwin, 1976.

Dvivedi, Hazariprasad. *Nāth siddhõ kī bāniyā̃.* Kashi, India: Nāgrīpracāriṇī Sabhā, 1957.

———. *Madhyakālīn dharma sādhnā.* Allahabad, India: Sāhitya Bhavan, 1970.

———. *Kabīr*. Delhi: Rājkamal Prakāśan, 1976.

———. *Nāth sampradāya*. Allahabad, India: Lokbhārati Prakāśan, 1981.

Dvivedi, Kedarnath. *Kabīr aur kabīr-panth*. Prayag, India: Hindī Sāhitya Sammelan, 1965.

Dvivedi, R. C. *Principles of Literary Criticism in Sanskrit*. Delhi: Motilal Banarsidass, 1969.

———, trans. *The Poetic Light: The Kāvyaprakāśa of Mammaṭa*. Delhi: Motilal Banarsidass, 1977.

Dwyer, William. *Kabīr kī bhakti bhāvnā*. Delhi: Macmillan, 1976.

Eagleton, T. *The Ideology of the Aesthetic*. Oxford: Basil Blackwell, 1990.

Edgerton, Franklin, trans. *The Bhagavad Gītā*. 1944; Cambridge, Mass.: Harvard University Press, 1977.

Eliade, Mircea. *The Myth of the Eternal Return*. New York: Pantheon Books, 1954. Bollingen Series 46.

———. *The Sacred and the Profane*. Translated by Willard R. Trask. New York: Harcourt, Brace and World, 1957.

———. *Patterns in Comparative Religion*. Cleveland, Ohio: Meridian Books, 1963.

———. *Patañjali and Yoga*. New York: Funk and Wagnalls, 1969.

———. *Yoga: Immortality and Freedom*. Translated by Willard R. Trask. Princeton, N.J.: Princeton University Press, 1969.

Eliot, T. S. *On Poetry and Poets*. London: Faber and Faber, 1969.

Empson, William. *Seven Types of Ambiguity*. 1930; London: Chatto & Windus, 1970.

———. *Some Versions of Pastoral*. 1935; Harmondsworth, U.K.: Penguin Books, 1966.

Esnoul, A. M. "Le courant affectif à l'intérieur du Brahmanisme ancien." *Bulletin de l'École Française d'Extrême-Orient* 48 (1956), 141–207.

Evola, Julius. *Le Yoga tantrique: Sa metaphysique, ses pratiques*. n.p.: Fayard, 1971.

Farquhar, J. N. *An Outline of the Religious Literature of India*. 1920; Delhi: Motilal Banarsidass, 1967.

Fish, Stanley. *Self-Consuming Artefacts*. Berkeley: University of California Press, 1974.

Fletcher, Angus. *Allegory: The Theory of a Symbolic Mode*. Ithaca, N.Y.: Cornell University Press, 1970.

Foss, Martin. *Symbol and Metaphor in Human Experience*. Princeton, N.J.: Princeton University Press, 1949.

Foucault, Michel. *The Order of Things: An Archaeology of the Social Sciences*. 1970; London: Tavistock, 1980.

———. "What is an Author?" In Harari, Josué V., ed., *Textual Strategies*. London: Methuen, 1980.

Frauwallner, Erich. *History of Indian Philosophy*. Translated by V. M. Bedekar. Delhi: Motilal Banarsidass, 1984. 2 vols.

Freud, Sigmund. "Beyond the Pleasure Principle." In *The Pelican Freud Library*, vol. 11. Harmondsworth, U.K.: Penguin Books, 1984, 271–338.

Frye, Northrop. *Anatomy of Criticism*. 1957; Princeton, N.J.: Princeton University Press, 1971.

Gail, Adalbert. *Bhakti im Bhāgavatapurāṇa*. Wiesbaden, Germany: Otto Harrassowitz, 1969. Münchener Indologische Studien, vol. 6.

Gambhirananda, Swami. *Brahma-Sūtra Bhaṣya of Śrī Śaṅkaracārya*. Calcutta: Advaita Ashrama, 1972.

Ganguli, K. M., trans. *The Mahābhārata*. Delhi: Munshiram Manoharlal, 1970. 12 vols.

Garbe, Richard. *Die Bhagavadgītā aus dem Sanskrit üpersetzt, mit einer Einleitung über ihre ursprüngliche Gestalt, ihre Lehren und ihr Alter*. Leipzig, Germany: H. Haessel, 1905.

Gardner, Helen. *Religion and Literature*. London: Faber and Faber, 1971.

Garratt, G. T., ed. *The Legacy of India*. 1937; Oxford: Clarendon Press, 1962.

Gerow, Edwin. *A Glossary of Indian Figures of Speech*. The Hague, Netherlands: Mouton, 1971.

———. *Indian Poetics*. Vol. 5, fasc. 3 of Jan Gonda, ed. *A History of Indian Literature*. Wiesbaden, Germany: Otto Harrassowitz, 1977.

———. "Language and Symbol in Indian Semiotics." *Philosophy East & West* 34.3 (July 1984), 245–60.

Gonda, Jan. *Remarks on Similes in Sanskrit Literature*. Leiden, Netherlands: E. J. Brill, 1949.

———. *Die Religionen Indiens*. Utrecht, Netherlands: Oosthoek, 1950.

———. *Aspects of Early Viṣṇuism*. 1954; Delhi: Motilal Banarsidass, 1969.

———. *Viṣṇuism and Śivaism: A Comparison*. London: Athlone Press, 1970.

———. *Medieval Religious Literature in Sanskrit*. Vol. 2, fasc. 1 of Jan Gonda, ed., *A History of Indian Literature*. Wiesbaden, Germany: Otto Hasrrassowitz, 1977.

Gosvami, Lalita Charan. *Śrī hit harivaṃś gosvāmī: Sampradāya aur sāhitya*. Vrindavan, India: Venu Prakāśan, 1957.

Grant, Patrick. *The Transformation of Sin: Studies in Donne, Herbert, Vaughan and Traherne*. Montreal: McGill-Queens University Press, 1974.

Greenblatt, Stephen. *Shakespearean Negotiations*. Oxford: Clarendon Press, 1990.

Greimas, A. J. *Sémantique structurale*. Paris: Larousse, 1966.

———. *Du Sens*. Paris: Seuil, 1970.

Grierson, G. A. "The Medieval Vernacular Literature of Hindustan with Special Reference to Tul'sī Dās." *7th International Congress of Orientalists*, 1896. Vienna, 1899, 157–214.

———. *Modern Vernacular Literature of Hindustan*. Calcutta: Royal Asiatic Society, 1889.

———. "Gleanings from the Bhakta-mālā." *Journal of the Royal Asiatic Society of Great Britain and Ireland* 1909: 607–44; 1910: 87–109; 1910: 269–306.

———. "Bhakti-mārga." In James Hastings, ed. *Encyclopaedia of Religion and Ethics.* Edinburgh: T. and T. Clark, 1940. 2:539–51.

Grierson, George, and Lionel D. Barnett, ed. and trans. *Lallā-Vakyāni or the Wise Sayings of Lāl Ded, A Mystic Poetess of Ancient Kashmir.* London: Royal Asiatic Society, 1920.

Grierson, G. A., and Mahamahopadhyaya Sudhakara Dvivedi. *The Padumāwati of Malik Muhammad Jaīsī.* Calcutta: Asiatic Society of Bengal, 1896–1911. 6 fasciculi.

Guillaume, Alfred. *Islam.* Harmondsworth, U.K.: Penguin Books, 1977.

Guillory, John. *Cultural Capital: The Problem of Literary Canon Formation.* Chicago: University of Chicago Press, 1993.

Haberman, David L. *Acting as a Way to Salvation: A Study of Rāgānugā Bhakti Sādhana.* New York: Oxford University Press, 1988.

Habermas, Jürgen. *The Philosophical Discourse of Modernity.* Translated by Frederick Lawrence. Cambridge: Polity Press, 1987.

Halbfass, Wilhelm. *India and Europe.* Albany: State University of New York Press, 1988.

———. *On Being and What There Is.* Albany: State University of New York Press, 1992.

Halewood, William H. *The Poetry of Grace.* New Haven, Conn.: Yale University Press, 1970.

Halliday, M. A. K. *Language as Social Semiotic.* London: Edward Arnold, 1979.

Handu, Jiyalal. *Káśmīrī aur hindī sūfī kāvya kā tulnātmak adhyayan.* Delhi: Bhārtiya Granth Niketan, 1973.

Hara, Minoru. "A Note on Two Sanskrit Religious Terms: Bhakti and Śraddhā." *Indo-Iranian Journal* 7 (1964), 124–45.

Hardy, Barbara. *The Advantage of Lyric: Essays on Feeling in Poetry.* London: Athlone Press, 1977.

Hardy, Friedhelm. *Viraha-Bhakti: The Early History of Kṛṣṇa Devotion in South India.* Delhi: Oxford University Press, 1983.

Harvey, Peter. *An Introduction to Buddhism.* Cambridge: Cambridge University Press, 1990.

Hawley, John Stratton. "Author and Authority in the *Bhakti* Poetry of North India." *The Journal of Asian Studies* 47.2 (May 1988), 269–90.

Hawley, John Stratton, and Mark Juergensmeyer, eds. and trans. *Songs of the Saints of India.* New York: Oxford University Press, 1988.

Hedayetullah, Muhammed. *Kabīr: The Apostle of Hindu-Muslim Unity.* Delhi: Motilal Banarsidass, 1977.

Heesterman, J. C. "Brahmin, Ritual and Renouncer." *Wiener Zeitschrift für die Kunde süd- und Ostasiens und Archiv für Indische Philosophie* 8 (1964), 1–31.

Hegel, G. W. F. *The Philosophy of History*. Translated by J. Sibree. 1899; New York: Dover, 1956.

———. *On Art, Religion and Philosophy*. Edited by J. Glenn Gray. New York: Harper Torchbooks, 1970.

———. *The Philosophy of Fine Art*. Translated by F. P. B. Osmaston. 1920; New York: Hacker Art Books, 1975. 4 vols.

———. *Phenomenology of Spirit*. Translated by J. N. Findlay. Oxford: Oxford University Press, 1977.

———. *On the Episode of the Mahābhārata known by the name Bhagavad-Gītā by Wilhelm von Humboldt*. Translated by Herbert Herring. New Delhi: Indian Council of Philosophical Research, 1995.

Herman, A. L., ed. and trans. *The Bhagavad Gītā*. Springfield, Ill.: Charles C. Thomas, 1973.

———. *An Introduction to Indian Thought*. Englewood Cliffs, N.J.: Prentice-Hall, 1976.

Hernadi, Paul. *Beyond Genre: New Directions in Literary Classification*. Ithaca, N.Y.: Cornell University Press, 1972.

Hertz, Neil. "A Reading of Longinus." *Critical Inquiry* 9.3 (March 1983), 579–96.

Hess, Linda, and Shukdev Singh, eds. and trans. *The Bījak of Kabīr*. San Francisco: North Point Press, 1983.

Hesse, Hermann. *Siddhartha*. Translated by Hilder Rosner. London: Picador, 1973.

Hill, W. D. P. *The Bhagavad Gītā*. Oxford: Oxford University Press, 1928.

Hiltebeitel, A. *The Ritual of Battle: Krishna in the Mahābhārata*. Ithaca, N.Y.: Cornell University Press, 1976.

Hogan, Patrick Colm, and Lalita Pandit, eds. *Literary India: Comparative Studies in Aesthetics, Colonialism, and Culture*. Albany: State University of New York Press, 1995.

Hooper, T. S. M. *Hymns of the Alvars*. Calcutta: Association Press, 1929.

Hopkins, E. Washburn. *Religions of India*. Boston: Little, Brown, 1908. Reprinted New Delhi: Munshiram Manoharlal, 1970.

———. *Epic Mythology*. Varanasi, India: Indological Book House, 1968.

Huizinga John. *Homo Ludens: A Study of the Play Element in Culture*. Boston: Beacon Press, 1955.

Hume, R. E. *The Thirteen Principal Upanishads*. Oxford: Oxford University Press, 1971.

Inden, Ronald. *Imagining India*. Oxford: Blackwell, 1992.

Ingalls, Daniel, H. H. "Words for Beauty in Classical Sanskrit Poetry." In Ernest Bender, ed., *Indological Studies in Honor of W. Norman Brown*. New Haven, Conn.: American Oriental Society, 1962.

———. *Sanskrit Poetry from Vidyākara's "Treasury."* Cambridge, Mass.: Harvard University Press, 1972.

Ingarden, Roman. *The Cognition of the Literary Work of Art*. Translated by Ruth Ann Crowley and Kenneth R. Olson. Evanston, Ill.: Northwestern University Press, 1973.

———. *The Literary Work of Art*. Translated by George A. Grabowicz. Evanston, Ill.: Northwestern University Press, 1973.

Izutsu, Toshihiko. *A Comparative Study of the Key Philosophical Concepts in Sufism and Taoism*. Tokyo: Keiko Institute of Cultural and Linguistic Studies, 1967. 2 vols.

Jacob, Colonel J. A. *A Concordance to the Principal Upanishads and the Bhagavadgītā*. 1891; Delhi: Motilal Banarsidass, 1963.

Jaidev. *The Culture of Pastiche*. Shimla, India: Indian Institute of Advanced Study, 1993.

Jauss, Hans Robert. *Toward an Aesthetic of Reception*. Translated by Timothy Bahti. Introduction by Paul de Man. Brighton, U.K.: Harvester Press, 1982.

Jaysawal, Matabadal. *Kabīr kī bhāṣā*. Allahabad, India: Kailash Brothers, 1965.

Jha, Kalanath. *Figurative Poetry in Sanskrit Literature*. Delhi: Motilal Banarsidass, 1975.

Johnson, Samuel. *Johnson: Prose and Poetry*. Edited by Mona Wilson. London: Rupert Hart-Davis, 1969.

Johnston, E. M. *Early Sāṃkhya*. 1937; Delhi: Motilal Banarsidass, 1974.

Jung, C. G. *Psychology and Religion: West and East*. Translated by R. F. C. Hull. London: Routledge and Kegan Paul, 1969.

Kailasapathy, K. *Tamil Heroic Poetry*. Oxford: Oxford University Press, 1968.

Kakar, Sudhir. *The Inner World*. Delhi: Oxford University Press, 1981.

Kalupahana, David J. *Nāgārjuna: The Philosophy of the Middle Way*. Albany: State University of New York Press, 1986.

Kant, Immanuel. *Observations on the Feeling of the Beautiful and Sublime*. Translated by John T. Goldthwait. Berkeley: University of California Press, 1973.

———. *The Critique of Judgement*. Translated by James Creed Meredith. Oxford: Clarendon Press, 1986.

Keay, F. E. *Hindi Literature*. Calcutta: Association Press, 1920.

———. *Kabir and His Followers*. Calcutta: Association Press, 1931.

Kellog, Rev. Samuel Henry. *A Grammar of the Hindi Language; In which are treated the High Hindi, Braj and the Eastern Hindi of the Ramayan of Tulsidas*. 1875; London: Routledge & Kegan Paul, 1938.

Kellogg, Robert. "Oral Narrative, Written Books." *Genre* 10 (Winter 1977), 655–65.

Kingsley, David. *Hindu Goddesses*. Berkeley: University of California Press, 1988.

Kishor, Asha. *Jāyasī koś*. Delhi: Macmillan India, 1976.

Kosambi, D.D. and V. V. Gokhale, eds. *The Subhāṣitaratnakoṣa compiled by Vidyākara*. Cambridge, Mass.: Harvard University Press, 1957.

Krishnamoorthy, K., ed. *Ānandavardhana's Dhvanyāloka*. Dharwar, India: Karnatak University, 1974.

Kvaerne, Per. *An Anthology of Buddhist Tantric Songs*. Oslo: Norwegian Research Council, 1977.

Lacan, Jacques. *Écrits: A Selection*. Translated by Alan Sheridan. London: Tavistock, 1980.

Lane-Poole, Stanley. *Medieval India under Mohammedan Rule (A.D. 712–1764)*. 1903; New York: Haskell House, 1970.

Larson, Gerald James, and Ram Shankar Bhattacharya, eds. *Encyclopaedia of Indian Philosophy IV*. Delhi: Motilal Banarsidass, 1987.

Laurence, Bruce B. *Notes from a Distant Flute: Sufi Literature in Pre-Mughal India*. Tehran, Iran: Imperial Academy of Philosophy, 1978.

Lefebvre, Henri. *The Production of Space*. Translated by Donald Nicholson-Smith. Oxford: Blackwell, 1991.

Lele, Jayant, ed. *Tradition and Modernity in Bhakti Movements*. Leiden, Netherlands: E. J. Brill, 1981.

Lewalski, Barbara Kiefer. *Donne's* "Anniversaries" *and the Poetry of Praise*. Princeton, N.J.: Princeton University Press, 1973.

———. *Protestant Poetics and the Seventeenth Century Religious Lyric*. Princeton, N.J.: Princeton University Press, 1979.

Lewis, C. S. *The Literary Impact of the Authorised Version*. London: Athlone Press, 1950.

Lings, Martin. *What is Sufism*? Berkeley: University of California Press, 1975.

Lipner, Julius. *The Face of Truth*. Albany: State University of New York Press, 1986.

Lord, Albert B. *The Singer of Tales*. Cambridge, Mass.: Harvard University Press, 1960.

Lorenzen, David N., ed. *Bhakti Religion in North India*. Albany: State University of New York Press, 1995.

Lukács, Georg. *The Theory of the Novel*. Translated by Anna Bostock. London: Merlin Press 1971.

Lutgendorf, Philip. *The Life of a Text: Performing the "Rāmcaritamanas" of Tulsīdās*. Delhi: Oxford University Press, 1994.

Lyotard, Jean-François. *The Postmodern Condition: A Report on Knowledge*. Translated by Geoff Bennington and Brian Massumi. Foreword by Fredric Jameson. Manchester, U.K.: Manchester University Press, 1986.

———. *The Differend: Phrases in Dispute*. Translated by Georges Van Den Abbeele. Manchester, U.K.: Manchester University Press, 1988.

———. *Lessons on the Analytic of the Sublime*. Translated by Elizabeth Rottenberg. Stanford, Calif.: Stanford University Press, 1994.

Macauliffe, M. A. *The Sikh Religion*. 1909; Delhi: S. Chand, 1978. 6 vols.

Macdonell, A. A. *A History of Sanskrit Literature*. 1899; Delhi: Motilal Banarsidass, 1976.

Machwe, Prabhakar. *Hindī aur marāṭhī kā nirguṇ sant kāvya*. Varanasi, India: Chaukhambā Vidyābhavan, 1962.

Macquarrie, J. M. *An Existentialist Theology*. Harmondsworth, U.K.: Penguin Books, 1973.

Madhav, Vindu. *Kabīr granthāvalī kī bhāṣā*. Delhi: Jñāna Bhāratī Prakāśan, 1972.

Magliola, Robert R. *Phenomenology and Literature: An Introduction*. West Lafayette, Ind.: Purdue University Press, 1977.

———. *Derrida on the Mend*. West Lafayette, Ind.: Purdue University Press, 1984.

Mahendra. *Kabīr kī bhāṣā*. Delhi: Śabdkar, 1969.

Mahesh, Maheshwari Sinha. *The Historical Development of Medieval Hindi Prosody: Ramananda–Kesava, 1400–1600 A.D.* Bhagalpur, India: Bhagalpur University, 1964.

Majumdar, A. K. *Caitanya: His Life and Doctrine: A Study in Vaiṣṇavism*. Bombay: Bharatiya Vidya Bhavan, 1969.

Majumdar, R. C., H.C. Raychaudhuri, and K. Datta, *An Advanced History of India*. London: Macmillan, 1967.

Malkovsky, Bradley. "The Personhood of Śaṁkara's *Para Brahman*." *The Journal of Religion* 77.4 (October 1997), 541–62.

Marshall, P. J., ed. *The British Discovery of Hinduism in the Eighteenth Century*. Cambridge: Cambridge University Press, 1970.

Martin, C. N. *Religious Belief*. New York: Cornell University Press, 1959.

Martz, Louis. *The Poetry of Meditation*. 1954; New Haven, Conn: Yale University Press, 1976.

———. *The Poem of the Mind*. New York: Oxford University Press, 1966.

Mascaró, Juan, trans. *The Bhagavad Gītā*. Harmondsworth, U.K.: Penguin Books, 1962.

Massignon, Louis. *La Passion de Husayn Ibn Mansūr Hallāj*. 1914, 1922; Paris: Gallimard, 1975. 4 Vols.

Masson, J. Moussaieff. *The Oceanic Feeling*. Dordrecht, Netherlands: D. Reidel, 1980.

McGregor, R. S., ed. & trans. *Nanddās: The Round Dance of Krishna and Uddhav's Message*. London: Luzac, 1973.

McHoul, Alec. "The Philosophical Grounds of Pragmatics (and Vice Versa?)." *Journal of Pragmatics* 27 (1997), 1–15.

McLeod, W. H. "The Influence of Islam upon the Thought of Gurū Nānak." *History of Religions* 7.4 (1968) 302–16.

———. [Review of] "Charlotte Vaudeville, *Kabīr* Volume 1." *South Asia* 5 (December 1975), 100–104.

———. *Gurū Nānak and The Sikh Religion*. 1968; Delhi: Oxford University Press, 1976.

Miller, Barbara Stoler, ed., *Bhartrihari: Poems*. New York: Columbia University Press, 1967.

———, ed. *Phantasies of a Love-Thief: The Caurapañcāśika attributed to Bilhana*. New York: Columbia University Press, 1971.

———, ed. *Theater of Memory*. New York: Columbia University Press, 1984.

———, ed. and trans. *The Bhagavad-Gītā*. New York: Bantam Books, 1986.

Mishra, Laxman Prasad, trans. *Mistici Indiani Medievali*. Turin, Italy: Unione Tipografico - editrice, 1971.

Mishra, Vijay. "Two Truths are Told: Tagore's Kabīr." *South Asia* [new series] 1.2 (September 1978), 80–90. Reprinted in Karine Schomer and W. H. McLeod, eds. *The Sants* [Berkeley Religious Studies Series]. Delhi: Motilal Banarsidass, 1987, 167–80.

———. "The Dialectic of Māyā and Principles of Narrative Structure in Indian Literature." *ACLALS Bulletin* [fifth series] 2 (January 1979), 47–60.

———. "Another Stubborn Structure: The Gītā as a Literary Text." *Journal of Studies in the Bhagavad-Gita* 2 (1982), 89–105.

———. "Ṣūfīs, Nāth-Yogīs and Indian Literary Texts." *Religious Tradition* 6.1 (1985), 42–65.

———. "The Burning Bride: Suffering in Union." In Kapil N. Tiwari, ed., *Suffering: Indian Perspectives*. Delhi: Motilal Banarsidass, 1986, 237–61.

———. "David Shulman and the Laughter of South Indian Kings and Clowns." *South Asia* [new series] 10.1 (June 1987), 83–88.

———. "The Centre Cannot Hold: Bailey, Indian Culture and the Sublime." *South Asia* [new series], 12.1 (June 1989), 103–14.

———. "Kabīr and the Bhakti Tradition." In G. M. Bailey and I. Kesarcodi-Watson, eds., *Bhakti Studies*. Delhi: Sterling Press, 1992, 182–235.

———. *The Gothic Sublime*. Albany: State University of New York Press, 1994.

Mohanty, Jitendra Nath. *Reason and Tradition in Indian Thought*. Oxford: Clarendon Press, 1992.

Monier-Williams, M. *Religious Thought in India: Vedism, Brahmanism and Hinduism*. London: John Murray, 1883.

———. *Buddhism*. 1889; Varanasi, India: The Chowkhamba Sanskrit Series Office, 1964.

———. *Sanskrit-English Dictionary*. 1899; Delhi: Munshiram Manoharlal, 1976.

Monk, Samuel H. *The Sublime: A Study of Critical Theories in XVIII-Century England*. 1935; Ann Arbor: University of Michigan Press, 1960.

Muhammad, Malik. *Alvār bhaktõ kā tāmil-prabandham aur hindī kṛṣṇa-kāvya*. Agra, India: Vinod Pustak Mandir, 1964.

Mukherjee, Sujit. "Towards a Literary History of India" *New Literary History* 8.2 (Winter 1977), 225–34.

Muni, Swami Shri Brahmalina. *Hindi Patañjalayogadarshana of Maharshi Patañjali* [with the commentary of Vyasa and a Hindi gloss]. Varanasi, India: Chowkhamba Sanskrit Series Office, 1970.

Munz, Peter. "India: Homo Hierarchicus or Generalised Exchange of Souls?" *Pacific Viewpoint* 11.2 (September 1970), 188–99.

———. "From Max Weber to Joachim of Floris: The Philosophy of Religious History." *The Journal of Religious History* 2.2 (December 1980), 167–200.

Murthy, H. V. Sreenivasa. *Vaiṣṇavism of Saṃkaradeva and Rāmānuja: A Comparative Study*. Delhi: Motilal Banarsidass, 1973.

Nasr, S. H. *Ideals and Realities of Islam*. London: George Allen and Unwin, 1966.

———. "The Interior Life in Islam." *Religious Traditions* 1.2 (October 1978), 48–55.

Nāṭya Śāstra. English trans. Delhi: Satguru Publications, 1985?

Nemade, Bhalchandra. "The Revolt of the Underprivileged." In Jayant Lele, ed., *Tradition and Modernity in Bhakti Movements*, 113–23.

New Literary History 8.3 (Spring 1977). Special Issue: "Oral Cultures and Oral Performances."

Nicholson, R. A., *Studies in Islamic Mysticism*. Cambridge: Cambridge University Press, 1921.

Nilsson, Usha S. *Mira Bai*. New Delhi: Sahitya Akademi, 1969.

Nygren, Anders. *Agape and Eros: A Study of the Christian Idea of Love*. Translated by A. G. Herbert. London: Society for Promoting Christian Knowledge, 1937.

O'Flaherty, Wendy Doniger. *Asceticism and Eroticism in the Mythology of Śiva*. Oxford: Oxford University Press, 1973.

———. *The Origins of Evil in Hindu Mythology*. Berkeley: University of California Press, 1976.

Olivelle, Patrick, "The Integration of Renunciation by Orthodox Hinduism." *Journal of the Oriental Institute* 28.1 (September 1978), 27–36.

———. "Orgasmic Rapture and Divine Ecstasy: The Semantic History of Ānanda." *Journal of Indian Philosophy* 25.2 (April 1997), 153–80.

Omprakash. *Madhyayugīn kāvya vivecnātmak evam samikṣātmak nibandh*. Delhi: Arya Book Depot, 1973.

Ong, Walter. *Orality and Literacy: The Technologizing of the World*. London: Routledge, 1982.

Otto, Rudolf. *The Original Gītā*. Translated by J. E. Turner. London: George Allen and Unwin, 1939.

———. *Mysticism East and West*. 1932; New York: Macmillan, 1970.

Pai, D. A. *Monograph on the Religious Sects in India among the Hindus*. Bombay: The Times Press, 1928.

Pandey, S. M. "Mīrābāī and Her Contributions to the Bhakti Movement." *History of Religions* 5 (1965), 54–73.

———. *Madhyayugin premākhyan*. Allahabad, India: Mitra Prakāśan, n.d.

Pandey, S. M., and N. H. Zide, trans. *The Poems of Sūrdas*. Chicago: University of Chicago Press, 1963.

Pandey, Vageesh Datt. *Mānas sandarbh koṣ*. Kanpur, India: Grantham, 1973.

Pargiter, F. E. *Ancient Indian Historical Tradition*. London: Oxford University Press, 1922.

———. "Purāṇas." In *Encyclopaedia of Religion and Ethics*. Edinburgh: T. and T. Clark, 1952. Vol. 10.

Parimoo, B. N. *The Ascent of Self*. Delhi: Motilal Banarsidass, 1978.

Peers, Allison E., ed. *The Book of the Lover and the Beloved* (translated from the Catalan of Ramón Lull). London: Society for Promoting Christian Knowledge, 1923.

———, ed. and trans. *The Complete Works of St. Teresa of Jesus*. London: Sheed and Ward, 1946. 3 vols.

Plott, John C., *A Philosophy of Devotion: A Comparative Study of Bhakti and Prapatti in Viśiṣṭādvaita and St. Bonaventura and Gabriel Marcel*. Delhi: Motilal Banarsidass, 1974.

Poddar, Hanumanprasad. *The Divine Name and Its Practice*. Gorakhpur, India: Gita Press, n.d.

Ponniah, V. *The Śaiva Siddhānta Theory of Knowledge*. Annamalainagar, India: Annamalai University, 1962.

Potter, Karl H., general ed. *Encyclopaedia of Indian Philosophies*. Delhi: Motilal Banarsidass, 1977–1987. 4 vols.

Pourrat, Pierre. *Christian Spirituality*. Translated by W. H. Mitchell and S. P. Jacques. London: Burns, Oates and Washbourne, 1922–27. 4 vols.

Pradhan, V. G., trans. and H. M. Lambert, ed. *Jñāneshvari [Bhāvārthadīpikā]*. London: George Allen and Unwin, 1967. 2 vols.

Propp, Vladimir. *Morphology of the Folktale*. Translated by Laurence Scott. Austin: University of Texas Press, 1986.

Radhakrishnan, S., trans. *The Bhagavadgītā*. London: George Allen and Unwin, 1963.

———, ed. and trans. *The Principal Upaniṣads*. 1953; London: George Allen and Unwin 1978.

Raghava, Rangeya. *Gorakhnāth aur unkā yug*. Delhi: Atma Ram and Sons, 1963.

Raghavan, V. *The Great Integrators: The Saint Singers of India*. Delhi: Government of India, 1966.

———. *The Number of Rasa-s*. Madras: Adyar Library & Research Centre, 1975.

———. *Bhoja's Śṛṅgāra Prakāśa*. Madras: Theosophical Society, 1978.

Raghavan V. and Nagendra, eds. *An Introduction to Indian Poetics*. Bombay: Macmillan, 1970.

Raina, Krishna. *Hindi nirguṇ sant-kāvya: Darśan aur bhakti*. Delhi: Śārdā Prakāśan, 1977.

Ramanujan, A. K. *Speaking of Śiva*. Harmondsworth, U.K.: Penguin Books, 1973.

Ranade, M. G. *Rise of the Maratha Power and Other Essays*. 1900; Bombay: University of Bombay, 1960.

Rao, Seshagiri K. L. *The Concept of Śraddhā*. Delhi: Motilal Banarsidass, 1974.

Raychaudhuri, Hemchandra. *Materials for the Study of the Early History of the Vaishnava Sect*. Calcutta: University of Calcutta, 1936.

Reichenbach, Bruce R. "The Law of Karma and the Principle of Causation." *Philosophy East & West* 38.4 (October 1988), 399–410.

Renou, Louis. *Religions of Ancient India*. London: Athlone Press, 1953.

Renou, L., and J. Filliozat. *L'Inde classique*. Paris: Payot, 1947. 2 vols.

Richards, I. A. *The Philosophy of Rhetoric*. 1936; New York: Oxford University Press, 1965.

Rickaby, Joseph, trans. *The Spiritual Exercises of St. Ignatius Loyola*. London: Burns and Oates, 1915.

Ricoeur, Paul. "Metaphor and the Main Problem of Hermeneutics." *New Literary History* 6 (1974), 94–110.

———. "Toward a Hermeneutic of the Idea of Revelation." *Harvard Theological Review* 70.1–2 (January-April, 1977), 1–37.

Riffaterre, Michael. *Semiotics of Poetry*. London: Methuen, 1978.

Rizvi, S. A. A., *Muslim Revivalist Movements in Northern India in the Sixteenth and Seventeenth Centuries*. Agra, India: Agra University Press, 1965.

———. "Sufis and Nātha Yogis in Medieval Northern India (XII to XVI Centuries)." *The Journal of the Oriental Society of Australia* 7.1–2 (December 1970), 119–33.

———. *A History of Sufism in India*. Delhi: Munshiram Manoharlal, 1978. Vol. 1.

Rocher, Ludo. *The Purāṇas*. Vol. 2, fasc. 3 of Jan Gonda, ed., *A History of Indian Literature*. Wiesbaden, Germany: Otto Harrassowitz, 1986.

Rollins, Hyder Edward, ed. *Letters of John Keats*. Cambridge, Mass.: Harvard University Press, 1958. 2 vols.

Rorty, Richard. "Habermas and Lyotard on Postmodernity." In Richard J. Bernstein, ed. *Habermas and Modernity*. Cambridge: Polity Press, 1985.

Ruegg, David Seyfort. *The Literature of the Madhyamaka School of Philosophy in India*. Vol. 7 of Jan Gonda, ed., *A History of Indian Literature*. Wiesbaden, Germany: Otto Harrassowitz, 1981.

Russell, Bertrand. *Mysticism and Logic*. London: George Allen and Unwin, 1918.

Ruthrof, Horst. "Negation: From Frege to Freud and Beyond." *Philosophy Today* 39.3–4 (Fall 1995), 219–44.

Said, Edward W. *Orientalism*. 1978; Harmondsworth, U.K.: Penguin Books, 1985.

Samkrityayana, Rahul, ed. *Sarhapā Dohakoṣ*. Patna, India: Bihār Rāṣṭrabhāṣā Pariṣad, 1957.

Sandahl-Forgue, Stella. *Le Gītagovinda: Tradition et innovation dans le kāvya*. Stockholm: Almqvist & Wiksell, 1977.

Sankovitch, Tilde. "Etienne Jodelle and the Mystic-Erotic Experience." *Bibliothèque d'Humanisme et Renaissance, Travaux et Documents* 40.2 (1978), 249–61.

Santayana, George. *Interpretations of Poetry and Religion.* New York: Charles Scribner's Sons, 1900.

Sanyal, J. M., trans. *The Śrīmad-Bhāgavatam of Krishna Dwarpāyāna Vyāsa.* New Delhi: Munshiram Manoharlal, 1973. 2 vols.

Sargeant, Winthrop, trans. *The Bhagavad Gītā.* Albany: State University of New York Press, 1984.

Schiller, Friedrich von. *Naive & Sentimental Poetry* and *On the Sublime.* Translated by Julius A. Elias. New York: Frederick Ungar, 1980.

Schimmel, Annemarie, *Classical Urdu Literature from the Beginning to Iqbal.* Vol. 8, fasc. 3 of Jan Gonda, ed., *A History of Indian Literature.* Wiesbaden, Germany: Otto Harrassowitz, 1975.

———. *Mystical Dimensions of Islam.* Chapel Hill: University of North Carolina Press, 1975.

Schlegel, Friedrich von. *Philosophy of History.* Translated by James Burton Robertson. London: George Bell, 1890.

Schomer, Karine and W. H. McLeod, eds., *The Sants: Studies in a Devotional Tradition of India.* Berkeley Religious Studies Series. Delhi: Motilal Banarsidass, 1987.

Schopenhauer, Arthur. *The World as Will and Representation.* Translated by E. F. J. Payne. New York: Dover, 1969. 2 vols.

Sen, Kshitimohan. *Medieval Mysticism of India.* Delhi: Oriental Books Reprint, 1974.

Shah, Ahmad, trans. *The Bījak of Kabīr.* 1917; Delhi: Asian Publications Services, 1979.

Sharma, Arvind. *The Hindu Gītā.* La Salle, Ill: Open Court, 1986.

Sharma, Mukunda Madhava. *The Dhvani Theory in Sanskrit Poetics.* Varanasi, India: Chowkhamba Sanskrit Series Office, 1968.

Sharma, Munshiram. *Bhakti kā vikās.* 1956; Varanasi, India: Chaukhambā Vidyābhavan, 1979.

Sharma, Suman, *Madhyakālīn bhakti-āndolan kā samājik vivecan.* Varanasi, India: Viśvavidyālaya Prakāśan, 1974.

Sharma, Vinay Mohan. *Hindī ko marāṭhī santō kī den.* Patna, India: Bihar Rāṣtrabhāṣā Pariṣad, 1957.

Sharpe, Eric J. *The Universal Gītā.* La Salle, Ill: Open Court, 1985.

Shastri Deodatt. *Tantra siddhānt aur sādhnā.* Allahabad, India: Smṛti Prakāśan, 1976.

Shastri, Vidhushekar. "Sandhābhāṣā." *Indian Historical Quarterly* 4.2 (1928), 287–96.

Sheridan, Daniel P. "The Religious Structure of the *Bhāgavata Purāṇa.*" Unpublished Ph.D. dissertation, Fordham University, 1976.

Shivapadasundaram, S. *The Śaiva School of Hinduism.* London: George Allen and Unwin, 1934.

Shrivastava, Badrinarayan. *Rāmānanda-sampradāya tathā hindī-sāhitya par uskā prabhāv.* Prayag, India: Hindī Pariṣad, 1957.

Shukla, Ramchandra. *Hindī sāhitya kā itihās*. Kashi, India: Nāgrīpracāriṇī Sabha, 1972.

Shukla, S., and R. Chaturvedi, eds. *Kabīr-Granthāvalī*. Lucknow: Prakāśan Kendra, n.d.

Shukla, V. N. *Hindī kṛṣṇa bhakti kāvya par śrīmadbhāgvat kā prabhāv*. Aligarh, India: Bhārat Prakāśan Mandir, 1966.

Shulman, David. "Divine order and Divine Evil in the Tamil Tale of Rāma." *The Journal of Asian Studies* 38.4 (August 1979), 651–69.

———. *The "King" and the "Clown" in South Indian Myth and Poetry*. Princeton, N.J.: Princeton University Press, 1985.

Siegel, Lee. *Sacred and Profane Dimensions of Love in Indian Traditions as Exemplified in the "Gītagovinda" of Jayadeva*. Delhi: Oxford University Press, 1978.

Simpson, Evelyn M., ed. *John Donne: Essays in Divinity*. Oxford: Clarendon Press, 1967.

Singer, Milton, ed. *Krishna: Myths, Rites and Attitudes*. Chicago: University of Chicago Press, 1971.

Singh Mohan. *Kabir: His Biography*. Lahore: Atma Ram and Sons, 1934.

Smith, Bardwell L., ed. *Hinduism: New Essays in the History of Religions*. Leiden, Netherlands: E.J. Brill, 1976.

Smith, Margaret. *Rābi'a the Mystic*. Cambridge: Cambridge University Press, 1925.

———. *Al-Ghazālī the Mystic*. London: Luzac, 1944.

———. *Readings from the Mystics of Islam*. London: Luzac, 1972.

Snatak, Vijayendra. *Rādhāvallabh sampradāya: Siddhānt aur sāhitya*. Delhi: National, 1968.

———, ed. *Kabīr*. Delhi: Rādhākṛṣṇa Prakāśan, 1970.

Srinivas, M. N. *Religion and Society Amond the Coorgs*. Oxford: Oxford University Press, 1952.

———. *Social Change in Modern India*. Berkeley: University of California Press, 1968.

Staal, J. F. *Advaita and Neoplatonism*. Madras: University of Madras, 1961.

———. *Exploring Mysticism*. Berkeley: University of California Press, 1975.

Steiner, George. *After Babel: Aspects of Language and Translation*. Oxford: Oxford University Press, 1976.

Steiner, Rudolf. *The Occult Significance of the Bhagavad Gītā*. New York: Anthroposophic Press, 1968.

Stoddart, William. *Sufism: The Mystical Doctrines and Methods of Islam*. Wellingborough, U.K.: Thorsons Publishers, 1976.

Suleri, Sara. *The Rhetoric of English India*. Chicago: University of Chicago Press, 1992.

Sullivan, Bruce M. *Kṛṣṇa Dvaipāyāna Vyāsa and the Mahābhārata*. Leiden, Netherlands: E. J. Brill, 1990.

Tagare, Ganesh Vasudeo, trans. *The Bhāgavata-Purāṇa*. Volume 7 of J. L. Shastri, ed., *Ancient Indian Mythology*. Delhi: Motilal Banarsidass, 1976.

Tagore, Rabindranath, trans. *One Hundred Poems of Kabīr*. 1915; London: Macmillan, 1973.

Tamil-English Dictionary. Compiled by V. Vishvanath-Pillai. Madras: Adyar Library, 1972.

Telang, Kashinath Trimbak, trans. *The Bhagavadgītā with the Sanatsujāta and the Anugītā*. Sacred Books of the East. 1882; Delhi: Motilal Banarsidass, 1975.

Teltscher, Kate. *India Inscribed: European and British Writing on India 1600–1800*. Delhi: Oxford University Press, 1995.

Temple, Richard Carnac. *The World of Lallā the Prophetess* [Being the sayings of Lāl Ded or Lāl Diddi of Kashmir known also as Lāleshwarī, Lallā Yogishwarī and Laslishrī, c. 1300–1400 A.D.]. Cambridge: The University Press, 1924.

Tessitori, L. P. "Yogīs (Kānphaṭa)." In *Encyclopaedia of Religion and Ethics*. Edinburgh: T. and T. Clark, 1921. 12:833–35.

Thibaut, George, trans. *The Vedānta Sūtras of Bādarāyaṇa with a Commentary by Śaṅkara*. Sacred Books of the East. 1890 and 1896; New York: Dover, 1962. 2 vols.

Thompson, Colin P. *The Poet and the Mystic: A Study of the Cántico Espiritual of San Juan de la Cruz*. Oxford: Oxford University Press, 1977.

Timm, Jeffrey, R. "The Celebration of Emotion: Vallabha's Ontology of Affective Experience." *Philosophy East & West* 41.1 (January 1991), 59–75.

Tiwari, Bholanath. *Tulsī-śabdsāgar*. Allahabad, India: Hindustani Academy, 1958?

Tiwari, Kapil, N., ed. *Suffering: Indian Perspectives*. Delhi: Motilal Banarsidass, 1986.

Tiwari, Parasnath. *Kabīr-vāṇī-sudhā*. Allahabad, India: Rākā Prakāśan, 1976.

———. "Kabir's Devotionalism." Translated by Vijay Mishra. In G. M. Bailey and I. Kesarcodi-Watson, eds., *Bhakti Studies*. Delhi: Sterling Publishers, 1992, 159–81.

Toulmin, Stephen E., Ronald W. Hepburn, and Alasdair MacIntyre. *Metaphysical Beliefs*. London: SCM Press, 1970.

Tracy, David. "Metaphor and Religion: The Test Case of Christian Texts." *Critical Inquiry* 5.1 (Autumn 1978), 91–106.

Trautmann, Thomas R. *Aryans and British India*. Berkeley: University of California Press, 1997.

Trigunayata, Govind. *Hindī kī nirguṇ kāvyadhārā aur uskī dārśnik pṛṣṭhbhūmi*. Kanpur, India: Sāhitya Niketan, 1951.

Trimingham, J. S. *The Sufi Orders of Islam*. Oxford: Oxford University Press, 1971.

Trivedi, Harish. *Colonial Transactions: English Literature in India*. Manchester, U.K.: Manchester University Press, 1995.

Trump, E., trans. *The Ādi Granth*. 1877; Delhi: Munishiram Manoharlal, 1970.

Turner, Victor. *The Ritual Process: Structure and Anti-Structure*. Chicago: Aldine, 1969.

Tuve, R. *Allegorical Imagery*. Princeton, N.J.: Princeton University Press, 1966.

Underhill, Evelyn. *Mysticism*. New York: E. P. Dutton, 1911.

———. *Worship.* New York: Harper and Brothers, 1937.

Upadhyaya, Vishvambhar Nath. *Sant-vaiṣṇav kāvya par tāntrik prabhāv.* Agra, India: Vinod Pustak Mandir, 1962.

Valiuddin, Mir. *The Quranic Sufism.* Delhi: Motilal Banarsidass, n.d.

van Buitenen, J. A. B. *Rāmānuja on the Bhagavadgītā: A condensed Rendering of His Gītābhāṣyā with Copious Notes and an Introduction.* 's- Gravenhage, Netherlands: N.V. De Ned. Boek- en Steendrukkerij v/h H.L. Smuts, 1953.

———. "Studies in Sāṃkhya, 1, 2 and 3." *Journal of the American Oriental Society* 76 (1956), 153–57; 77 (1957), 15–27; 77 (1957), 88–107.

———, trans. *Two Plays of Ancient India.* New York: Columbia University Press, 1968.

Vanina, Eugenia. "The *Ardhakathanaka* by Banarsi Das: A Socio-cultural Study." *Journal of the Royal Society* [third series] 5.2 (July 1995), 211–24.

Varma, Ramchandra. *Mānak hindī koś.* Allahabad, India: Sāhitya Bhavan, 1962.

Varma, Ramkumar. *Kabīr kā rahasyavād.* 1929; Allahabad, India: Sāhitya Bhavan, 1972.

Vaudeville, Charlotte, ed. and trans. *Kabīr Granthāvalī (Dohā).* Pondicherry, India: Institut Français d'Indologie, 1957.

———. *Étude sur les sources et la composition du Rāmāyaṇa de Tulsī-dās.* Hindi translation by J. K. Balbir. Pondicherry, India: Institut Français d'Indologie, 1959–1965. 2 vols.

———, ed. and trans. *Au cabaret de l'amour: Par Kabīr.* Paris: Gallimard, 1959.

———. "La conception de l'amour divin chez Muhammad Jāyasī: *Virah* et '*ishq*.'" *Journal Asiatique* (1962), 351–67.

———. "Evolution of Love-Symbolism in Bhagvatism." *Journal of the American Oriental Society* 82 (1962), 31–40.

———. "Rāmāyaṇa Studies I: The *Krauñca-vadha* Episode in the Vālmiki *Rāmāyaṇa*." *Journal of the American Oriental Society* 83.3 (September 1963), 327–35.

———. "Kabīr and Interior Religion." *History of Religions* 3 (1964), 191–201.

———, ed. and trans. *L'Invocation le Haripāṭh de Dñyāndev.* Paris: École Française d'Extrême-Orient, 1969.

———, trans. *Pastorales: Par Sour-Dās.* Paris: Gallimard, 1971.

———. *Kabīr I.* Oxford: Clarendon Press, 1974.

———. [Review of] Muhammad Hedayetullah, *Kabīr: The Apostle of Hindu-Muslim Unity. Journal of the Royal Asiatic Society of Great Britain and Ireland* 1 (1980), 103–4.

———. "The Govardhan Myth in Northern India." *Indo-Iranian Journal* 22.1 (January 1980), 1–45.

———. *Bārahmāsa in Indian Literatures.* Delhi: Motilal Banarsidass, 1986.

Warnke, Frank J. *Versions of Baroque*. New Haven, Conn.: Yale University Press, 1972.

Welsh, Andrew. *Roots of the Lyric. Primitive Poetry and Modern Poetics*. Princeton, N.J.: Princeton University Press, 1968.

Westcott, G. H. *Kabīr and the Kabīr Panth*. 1907; Calcutta: Susil Gupta, 1953.

White, Charles, S.J. "Bhakti as a Religious Structure in the Context of Medieval Hinduism in the Hindi-Speaking Area of North India." Unpublished Ph.D. dissertation, University of Chicago, 1964.

———. "Sufism in Medieval Hindi Literature." *History of Religions* 5 (Summer 1965), 114–32.

———. "Structure and the History of Religions: Some Bhakti Examples." *History of Religions* 8.1 (August 1968), 77–94.

———. *The Caurāsī Pad of Śrī Hit Harivaṃś*. Honolulu: University of Hawaii Press, 1977.

White, Hayden. *Metahistory: The Historical Imagination in Nineteenth-Century Europe*. Baltimore, Md.: Johns Hopkins University Press, 1980.

Wilkins, Charles. *The Bhagvat-Geeta or Dialogues of Kreeshna and Arjoon*. London: C. Nourse, 1785. Facsimile reproduction edited by George Hendrick. New York: Scholars' Facsimiles and Reprints, 1972.

Wilson, H. H. *Religious Sects of the Hindus*. 1861; Calcutta: Susil Gupta, 1958.

———. *The Vishnu Purāṇa: A System of Hindu Mythology and Tradition*. Calcutta: Punthi Pustak, 1961.

Woodhouse, A. S. P. *The Poet and His Faith*. Chicago: University of Chicago Press, 1965.

Woods, James Haughton. *The Yoga-System of Patañjali*. Delhi: Motilal Banarsidass, 1966.

Woolf, Rosemary. *The English Religious Lyric in the Middle Ages*. Oxford: Clarendon Press, 1968.

Woodroffe, Sir John ("Arthur Avalon"). *Śakti and Śākta*. 1918; Madras: Ganesh, 1975.

———. *The World as Power*. Madras: Ganesh, 1957.

Worringer, Wilhelm. *Abstraction and Empathy*. Translated by Michael Bullock. London: Routledge & Kegan Paul, 1953.

Zaehner, R. C. *The Catholic Church and World Religions*. London: Athlone Press, 1964.

———. *Hindu and Muslim Mysticism*. London: Athlone Press, 1960; New York: Schocken Books, 1969.

———. *Concordant Discord: The Interdependence of Faiths*. Oxford: Oxford University Press, 1970.

———. *Evolution in Religion, A Study of Śri Aurobindo and Pierre Teilhard de Chardin*. Oxford: Oxford University Press, 1971.

———. *Hinduism*. 1962; Oxford: Oxford University Press, 1975.

Zbavitel, Dušan. *Bengali Literature.* Vol. 9, fasc. 3 of Jan Gonda, ed., *A History of Indian Literature.* Wiesbaden, Germany: Otto Harrassowitz, 1976.

Zimmer, Heinrich. *Myths and Symbols in Indian Art and Civilization.* Washington, D.C.: Pantheon Books, 1946. Bollingen Series 6.

———. *Philosophies of India.* Princeton, N.J.: Princeton University Press, 1974. Bollingen Series 26.

Žižek, Slavoj. *The Sublime Object of Ideology.* London: Verso, 1989.

Zvelebil, Kamil. *The Poets of the Powers.* London: Rider and Company, 1973.

———. *The Smile of Murugan in Tamil Literature of South India.* Leiden, Netherlands: E. J. Brill, 1973.

———. *Tamil Literature.* Vol. 10, fasc. 1 of Jan Gonda, ed., *A History of Indian Literature.* Wiesbaden, Germany: Otto Harrassowitz, 1974.

INDEX